OXFORD MODERN LANGUAGES AND LITERATURE MONOGRAPHS

Editorial Committee

C. H. GRIFFIN   A. KAHN

K. M. KOHL   M. L. MCLAUGHLIN

I. W. F. MACLEAN   R. A. G. PEARSON

M. SHERINGHAM

On a Knife-Edge

The Poetry of João Cabral de Melo Neto

SARA BRANDELLERO

OXFORD
UNIVERSITY PRESS

OXFORD
UNIVERSITY PRESS

Great Clarendon Street, Oxford OX2 6DP

Oxford University Press is a department of the University of Oxford.
It furthers the University's objective of excellence in research, scholarship,
and education by publishing worldwide in

Oxford New York

Auckland Cape Town Dar es Salaam Hong Kong Karachi
Kuala Lumpur Madrid Melbourne Mexico City Nairobi
New Delhi Shanghai Taipei Toronto

With offices in

Argentina Austria Brazil Chile Czech Republic France Greece
Guatemala Hungary Italy Japan Poland Portugal Singapore
South Korea Switzerland Thailand Turkey Ukraine Vietnam

Oxford is a registered trade mark of Oxford University Press
in the UK and in certain other countries

Published in the United States
by Oxford University Press Inc., New York

© Sara Brandellero 2011

The moral rights of the author have been asserted
Database right Oxford University Press (maker)

First published 2011

All rights reserved. No part of this publication may be reproduced,
stored in a retrieval system, or transmitted, in any form or by any means,
without the prior permission in writing of Oxford University Press,
or as expressly permitted by law, or under terms agreed with the appropriate
reprographics rights organization. Enquiries concerning reproduction
outside the scope of the above should be sent to the Rights Department,
Oxford University Press, at the address above

You must not circulate this book in any other binding or cover
and you must impose the same condition on any acquirer

British Library Cataloguing in Publication Data

Data available

Library of Congress Cataloging in Publication Data

Data available

Typeset by SPI Publisher Services, Pondicherry, India
Printed in Great Britain
on acid-free paper by
MPG Books Group, Bodmin and King's Lynn

ISBN 978–0–19–958952–4

1 3 5 7 9 10 8 6 4 2

To the memory of my grandparents,
and for Zé and Alice

Preface

João Cabral de Melo Neto (1920–1999) is widely regarded as one of Brazil's foremost writers on the twentieth century and a unique voice in Brazilian modernism. He is recognized at home and abroad as a poet of a rare aesthetic vision, coupled with an unfailing social and political commitment towards the suffering of the poor and disenfranchised. In *On a Knife-Edge: The Poetry of João Cabral de Melo Neto*, which is the first book-length study on the author published in English, I consider traditionally overlooked aspects of his writing, such as his tantalizing exploration of ambiguity, and seek to provide an overview of his later, lesser-known works, thereby proposing fresh perspectives on his output. Mindful of the social, cultural, and political contexts in which Cabral was operating, I draw on postcolonial and feminist critical frameworks and also consider the intertextual literary and cultural dialogues that Cabral's writings elicit, with voices from Brazil and beyond. *On a Knife-Edge: The Poetry of João Cabral de Melo Neto* provides a detailed appraisal of Cabral's works from *A escola das facas* (1980), moving on to *Auto do frade* (1984), *Agrestes* (1985), *Crime na Calle Relator* (1987), *Andando Sevilha*, and *Sevilha andando* (1990). Aimed primarily at students and scholars of Portuguese and Brazilian studies, this book also extends into the broader fields of postcolonial and gender studies as well as comparative literature. Bearing in mind the book's English-speaking readership, for ease of reference translations of all material quoted are provided.

Sara Brandellero

Acknowledgements

This book stems from my doctoral research on João Cabral de Melo Neto, carried out at the Queen's College, Oxford. I am indebted to many people who, in different ways, contributed to its completion. First, I wish to express my special thanks to Cláudia Pazos Alonso, for her generous supervision of my research, for her guidance and her illuminating criticism of the various drafts of the original doctoral thesis. I am also grateful to Thomas Earle, for his unfailing support as co-supervisor during the early stages of my work, and to Stephen Parkinson, who examined parts of my doctoral thesis over the course of the various milestones of the D.Phil journey. Still in Oxford, my thanks go to Ian Michael, Eric Southworth, and John Rutherford. A special thank you goes to Robin Fiddian, who acted as Internal Examiner of my D.Phil thesis, for his meticulous reading and feedback, and to Leslie Bethell and all research fellows and staff associated with the Centre for Brazilian Studies and the Brazilian Studies Programme.

I am also indebted to many scholars and researchers from around the UK and further afield. Among them, my very special thanks go to John Gledson, who acted as External Examiner of my DPhil thesis. His study of Cabral's early work was an inspiration to me and his detailed comments at examination and his subsequent guidance in the revision of the manuscript were invaluable. I should also like to remember Alexandre Pinheiro Torres, who first introduced me to Cabral's work during my undergraduate years at Cardiff University. I am most grateful to the University of Leeds for its support, and to my friends and colleagues at the School of Modern Languages and Cultures at Leeds, who have been an important source of motivation and encouragement in the final stages of preparation of this book. I must also thank Marta de Senna, Marta Peixoto, Antonio Carlos Secchin, David Brookshaw, Eucanãa Ferraz, João Almino, Ana Maria Lisboa de Mello, Curt Meyer-Clason, Arnaldo Saraiva, Carlos Mendes de Sousa, Madalena Gonçalves, Elide Oliver, Francisco Bandeira de Mello, Lucila Nogueira, Bebeto Abrantes, Felipe Fortuna, Flora Süssekind, and researchers and staff at the Casa de Rui Barbosa, in Rio de Janeiro. I am particularly grateful to Inez Cabral, for allowing me to gain a privileged insight into her father's world.

I cannot forget the help of staff at the Taylorian Institution Library and of the Modern Languages Faculty offices in Oxford. In addition, I should like to thank the Queen's College, for awarding me a travel grant for research in Brazil, and the Faculty of Medieval and Modern Languages at Oxford for the Honorarium awarded to assist in the revision stage of the manuscript. Special thanks go to the anonymous readers commissioned by Oxford University Press, for their feedback and criticism of the various drafts of this book, and to editors and staff at Oxford University Press for their unfailing guidance and support. I particularly wish to acknowledge my gratitude to Jacqueline Baker and Ariane Petit.

An earlier version of parts of Chapter 3 appeared in my article 'In-Between Wor(l)ds: The Image of the "entre-lugar" in João Cabral de Melo Neto's *Agrestes*', *Portuguese Studies*, 18 (2002), 215–29. Sections of Chapters 3 and 5 originally appeared in '(Dis)covering the Other: Images of Women in João Cabral de Melo Neto', *Bulletin of Hispanic Studies*, University of Liverpool, 81 (2004), 247–58, while an earlier version of sections of Chapter 4 appeared in Portuguese in my article 'A revisão da história oficial em *Crime na Calle Relator*, de João Cabral de Melo Neto', *Revista USP*, 67 (set./out./2005), 317–20. I thank the Modern Humanities Research Association, Liverpool University Press, and Revista USP for granting permission to reproduce the original articles. All reasonable effort has been made to contact the holders of copyright in materials reproduced in this book. Any omissions will be rectified in future printings if notice is given to the publisher.

Last but not least, I wish to thank my friends and family in different parts of the world, and especially Zé and Alice, for their sense of humour and for their patience over these last years.

Contents

Preface vi
Note to the reader x

Introduction 1
1. Life on a knife-edge: *A escola das facas* 22
2. Speaking from the margins: the haunting voices of *Auto do frade* 49
3. In-between wor(l)ds: the image of the 'entre-lugar' in *Agrestes* 79
4. Victims or villains? Open verdicts in *Crime na Calle Relator* 124
5. 'Tu eras de mentira e ambígua': images of women and the city in *Sevilha andando* and *Andando Sevilha* 159
    Conclusion 197

Bibliography 203
Index 219

Note to the reader

Unless otherwise stated, translations of all foreign quotations have been provided by the author. English translations of poetry have been kept as literal as possible. The main edition of Cabral's work used is the *Obra completa*, published by Nova Aguilar in 1994, which was edited by the poet's wife, Marly de Oliveira, with the author's assistance. This is the most complete compilation of Cabral's writing, since it also includes his very earliest poems, *Primeiros poemas*, written between 1937 and 1940 but published only in 1990. Reference is made to other editions whenever discrepancies are identified which have some bearing on the interpretation of these works.

Introduction

João Cabral de Melo Neto (1920–99) is widely regarded as Brazil's foremost poet of the second half of the twentieth century, a figure hugely influential on generations of writers both at home and further afield in the Lusophone world. Credited with having revolutionized Brazilian modernist poetry, he ranks among the iconic figures of twentieth-century Brazilian literature, alongside his two contemporaries and great renovators of language and style, João Guimarães Rosa (1908–67) and Clarice Lispector (1920–77).

A member of the Brazilian Academy of Letters from 1969, his standing within Brazilian literature was recognized in the form of numerous national prizes, including the prestigious Jabuti Prize, in 1967 and 1993, as well as international awards. In 1990, he received the Camões Prize for Literature, the most important literary award in the Portuguese language. This was followed, in 1992, by the Neustadt International Prize for Literature and the Queen Sofia Prize for Ibero-American Literature, in 1994. He was also nominated repeatedly for the Nobel Prize for Literature.

Reflecting his reputation outside Brazil, selections of his work have been translated into a number of languages, including German, Spanish, and Italian. English-speaking readers have access to translated selections of his poems, such as by American poet Elizabeth Bishop, who lived in Brazil for many years and who edited, with Emanuel Brasil, *An Anthology of Twentieth-Century Brazilian Poetry*.[1]

---

[1] *An Anthology of Twentieth-Century Brazilian Poetry*, ed. Elizabeth Bishop and Emanuel Brasil (Middletown, CT: Wesleyan University Press, 1972). Other translations available in English include: *Two Parliaments and Poems*, trans. Richard Spock, in *Brazilian Painting and Poetry* (Rio de Janeiro: Spala, 1979); *A Knife all Blade: Or Usefulness of Fixed Ideas*, trans. Kerry Shawn Keys (Pennsylvania: Pine Press, 1980); *Selected Poetry, 1937–1990*, ed. Djelal Kadir and trans. Elizabeth Bishop and others (Hanover, NY: Wesleyan Press, 1994); *Death and Life of Severino*, trans. John Milton (São Paulo: Pleiade, 2003); *Education by Stone: Selected Poems*, trans. Richard Zenith (New York: Archipelago Books, 2005).

Cabral's life began in Recife, capital of the Brazilian north-eastern state of Pernambuco, on 9 January 1920, the incipit of what was to be a peripatetic life spent mostly outside Brazil, within the ranks of its diplomatic service.[2] His death, in 1999, marked the end of a long literary career, which would see him become the foremost poet of his generation and a key figure in the later modernist movement.

Cabral was born into a wealthy landowning family and spent his early years on the family's sugar cane plantations on the outskirts of Recife, subsequently moving to the city to attend school. He did not have fond memories of his school days, and a number of caustic poems record the misery of his time at the city's catholic Colégio Marista. It was not there that his love for literature blossomed: he recalled hating the poetry he was introduced to at school, which consisted of anthologies of verse comprising the sentimental, rhetorical, and stylistically conservative poetry of Parnassian poets such as Olavo Bilac (1865–1918).

The Parnassians' fascination with French and classical literary and cultural models went hand in hand with their elitist and reactionary social outlook; they were deeply suspicious of the social changes that modernization was about to bring and which would provide the modernists of the 1920s with the material for inspiration for their cultural revolution.

The desire to forge an authentic Brazilian tradition independent of European models lay at the heart of the revolution in Brazilian culture that would be brought about by a group of young intellectuals from São Paulo, spearheaded by the writers Oswald de Andrade (1890–1954) and Mário de Andrade (1893–1945) in the 1920s. Though indebted to the nationalist ideals of the Romantic period, they rejected the idealized conceptualizations of Brazilian national identity as embodied in the romanticized figure of the Brazilian Indian that one finds in the novels of José de Alencar (1829–77) and instead sought radical solutions for the expression of modernity, and its contradictions, grafted onto the experience of the Brazilian nation. Thus, their spirit of defiance against aesthetic conservatism also entailed a nationalist project, as they strove to redefine conceptualizations of Brazilian culture both in theoretical and aesthetic terms.

---

[2] To date, José Castello's *João Cabral de Melo Neto: o homem sem alma* (Rio de Janeiro: Rocco, 1996) remains the most comprehensive biographical overview of the poet.

Introduction 3

The iconoclastic drive of the early modernists, influenced by the European avant-garde, crystallized in the now iconic moment of the Week of Modern Art, showcasing the latest trends in literature and the arts, and organized by Oswald and Mário in 1922 at São Paulo's Municipal Theatre to coincide with the centenary of Brazil's independence from Portugal. Key texts emerged from this initial gathering of minds. The drive for cultural emancipation in the face of a history of colonial and postcolonial dependency is encapsulated in Oswald's collection *Pau-Brasil* [Brazil-wood] (first published in 1925). Here, Oswald's theory of a 'poetry for export' (Brazil-wood having been Brazil's earliest primary material sought for exportation) materialized in a series of humorous poems, often parodying iconic colonial texts, seeking to debunk Brazil's history of cultural dependency. Oswald's later *Manifesto antropófago* (1928) found in the figure of the Cannibal Indian a central metaphor for the development of his new cultural theory, with the practice of anthropophagy (traditionally demonized in colonial texts) serving as a useful metaphor for the understanding of Brazilian culture not as a passive recipient of Western cultural models, but as a dynamic process of incorporation of the foreign 'other' and its transformation into a new revitalized form.

Along with these conceptualizations of Brazilian culture, the search for not only a modern but also a truly national voice lay at the heart of the modernist project in Brazil. As Mike Gonzalez and David Treece noted, the central image of Mário de Andrade's 1924 poem 'O poeta come amendoim', part of the collection *Clã do Jaboti* (1927), encapsulates such a quest for authenticity, drawn from prosaic everyday Brazilian existence: 'Brasil...Mastigado na gostosura quente do amendoim...' [Brazil...Chewed in the warm deliciousness of the peanut...].[3]

It would be Cabral's exposure to the work of the modernist poets, and in particular that of Manuel Bandeira (1886–1968), their experimentation with free verse, the quest for an authentic Brazilian voice and engagement with everyday life, that would inspire him to write. For now, football was a much more alluring proposition for the young Cabral (he won the junior championship for Santa Cruz Futebol Club in 1935), but his passion for literature grew after he left school, at sixteen.

---

[3] Mike Gonzalez and David Treece, *The Gathering of Voices: The Twentieth-Century Poetry of Latin America* (London: Verso, 1992), pp. 73–4. The quotation and its translation are taken from this edition.

As he was turning his hand to a series of rather uninspiring office jobs, in 1938 he began frequenting the literary circle which gathered at the Café Lafayette, attended, among others, by the modernist painter Vicente do Rego Monteiro (1899–1975). He was soon mixing with the intelligentsia of Recife, not to speak of his close association with two of the major Brazilian literary figures of the time, fellow north-easterners, both of whom were his cousins: the eminent sociologist Gilberto Freyre (1900–87), and, most importantly, Manuel Bandeira himself, whose poetics of everyday life provided a literary model with which Cabral could finally identify.

During a trip with his family to Rio de Janeiro, Cabral's acquaintance with the modernists' literary circle expanded further when he met Murilo Mendes (1901–75), who in turn introduced him to Carlos Drummond de Andrade (1902–87). Both these highly influential poets from the state of Minas Gerais, alongside other writers and intellectuals, used to meet at the surgery of the doctor-cum-poet Jorge de Lima (1895–1953).

Cabral's involvement with the literary world strengthened and, back in Recife, he contributed to the city's first Poetry Conference (1941), which he helped organize and at which he presented the paper entitled 'Considerações sobre o poeta dormindo'. It was here too that Cabral published his first collections of poems, *Pedra do sono* (1942), a limited edition, which he self-financed and in which his fascination with the state of semi-consciousness was explored.

The poet's move to Rio in that same year marked a more or less definitive departure from the north-east of Brazil, where he would return only for brief visits. Cabral repeatedly claimed that he never liked Rio, but the city was to become his home for the next five years and it was here that he published his prose poem about unrequited love, *Os três mal-amados* (1943), and his collection *O engenheiro*, in 1945.

This collection is generally considered to be the work in which Cabral's lucid construction, keen eye for the concrete world, unsentimental style, and attraction for what is considered 'unpoetic', while still conveying profound human concerns, took shape in earnest. His aesthetic ideal is aptly summarized in the following lines from the collection's 'Pequena ode mineral':

> Procura a ordem
> que vês na pedra:
> nada se gasta

mas permanece.
[...]
pesado sólido
que ao fluido vence,
que sempre ao fundo
das coisas desce. (pp. 83–4)

[Seek the order | that you see in the stone: |nothing is worn | but remains. [...] | heavy solid | which conquers what is fluid, |which always to the bottom | of things descends.]

The year 1945 also saw Cabral join Brazil's diplomatic service, a career move which would impact considerably on his future literary output and redefine it for ever. In February the following year, he married Stella Maria Barbosa de Oliveira, with whom he would have five children and who would be his companion for the next four decades. Having entered the diplomatic service, Cabral spent most of the rest of his life abroad, from his first posting to Barcelona, in 1947, moving then to London, and subsequently to posts in Spain, France, Switzerland, Paraguay, Senegal, Ecuador, Honduras, and Portugal, some forty years later.

After taking up his first appointment abroad, as Brazilian Vice-Consul in Barcelona, Cabral published *Psicologia da composição com a Fábula de Anfion e Antiode* (1947), which he produced himself on his manual printer, under the label 'O Livro Inconsútil' [The Seamless Book]. There would soon be a departure from the strong meta-textual focus he adopted in this work, as his writing took a dramatic turn in favour of uncompromising social engagement, in a poetic repositioning that would guide the rest of his career.

Despite his privileged background, his striding over different cultures—from the rural world of the north-eastern interior to the urban networks of Recife and beyond—revealed his unambiguous allegiance to the cause of the oppressed and marginal communities, be they the black population of Brazil, the indigenous people of the Andes, or the gypsies of Seville, all of whom found their way into his writing. The plight of the poor and the disenfranchised was always located within a historical context, and, particularly in relation to his native land, we can identify in his writing a postcolonial critique, broadly defined by Robert Young as 'the product of resistance to colonialism and imperialism'.[4] This stemmed from his consciousness as a writer

---

[4] *Postcolonialism. An Historical Introduction* (Oxford: Blackwells, 2001), p. 15.

from Pernambuco, a former colonial outpost and, to this day, one of the poorest regions of the developing world. His criticism of the historical subordination of his native land to the southern regions of Brazil extended to forms of political, economic, and cultural domination beyond the boundaries of his country.

If the places and people he encountered in his life provided a fertile source of material for his writing, so did his encounter with foreign literatures. His poetry is rich in intertextual references to works from different periods and cultures, from medieval Spanish ballads, to modern American poetry, to Léopold Senghor's (1906–2001) postcolonial poetry. As a cultural ambassador for his country, he published on his manual printer works by Brazilian poets such as Bandeira, but he also promoted foreign literature, printing works by, among others, the Catalan poet Joan Brossa (1919–98) and translating writers such as the North American Amy Lowell (1874–1925) and William Carlos Williams (1883–1963), and Spanish playwrights Calderón de la Barca (1600–81) and Federico García Lorca (1898–1936).

Of the influences received from his travels abroad none was more defining than his encounter with Spain and its culture, since he found in the landscapes and cultural manifestations of the Spanish people tantalizing counterpoints as well as reminders of his native land. From then on, Spain and Pernambuco would become constant themes throughout his life, and his 1956 collection *Paisagens com figuras* exemplifies his ability to draw on these cultural and geographic landscapes through breathtakingly imaginative connections.

His first move abroad to Spain, therefore, helped him revisit the landscapes and human reality that he had left behind in his native north-east, which would become recurring *topoi* in his work. His fierce patriotism towards the north-east and, more specifically, the state of Pernambuco would emerge clearly from his poetry, reflecting feelings he was never reluctant to speak about, such as openly declaring his aversion to any kind of music except flamenco and, curiously enough, Pernambuco's national anthem.

Some of his best-known works centred on north-east Brazil were written during and shortly after his early years in Spain. *O cão sem plumas* (1950) and *O rio* (1954) stem from his poetic awakening to the poverty and social injustice suffered by many north-easterners. The turning point which led to the writing of *O cão sem plumas* occurred during his posting in Barcelona, when Cabral stumbled upon some statistics which prompted a radical redefinition of his writing, as he recalled in an interview with the critic Antonio Carlos Secchin:

> The book resulted from the shock I experienced when I came across statistics published in *O observador econômico e financeiro*. From these, I learnt that life expectancy in Recife was of 28 years, while in India it was 29. I had never imagined that could be the case. When there is a catastrophe in India, Brazilian upper-class ladies rally round with their knitting needles, although in fact poverty in Recife is greater.[5]

Key to both the outstandingly creative and socially engaged poetic pieces that are *O cão sem plumas* and *O rio* is the image of the Capibaribe river, which flows from the arid interior to Recife. The landscapes that Cabral knew in his youth now became a source of inspiration: the arid interior, known as *sertão*, the semi-arid *agreste*, the fertile coastal strip taken up almost entirely by sugar cane plantations, known as *zona da mata*. Be it in the harsh landscapes of the interior, plagued by periodic droughts, in the sugar cane plantations, or in the fast industrializing cities along the coast, his attention would inevitably be drawn to the plight of the poor and the marginalized. Dispelling the myth that an inclement climate lay at the root of the north-east's poverty, Cabral pinpointed Brazil's iniquitous feudal system of land ownership, which persists to this day, as a key factor of the north-east's poverty.

Cabral was reluctant to be explicit about his political allegiances. However, his left-wing political inclination and his sympathetic tendencies towards the Brazilian Communist Party (suspicion of which resulted in his being temporarily removed from the Diplomatic Service from 1952 to 1954) are manifest in his most famous work, *Morte e vida severina* (1956), a one-act play which picks up the social thread developed earlier.[6] Subtitled an 'auto de natal pernambucano'

---

[5] 'Esse livro nasceu do choque emocional que experimentei diante de uma estatística publicada em *O observador econômico e financeiro*. Nela, soube que a expectativa de vida no Recife era de 28 anos, enquanto na Índia era de 29. Nunca tinha suposto algo parecido. Quando ocorre uma catástrofe na Índia, as senhoras brasileiras fazem tricô para socorrè-la, ao passo que a miséria do Recife é maior.' 'Entrevista de João Cabral de Melo Neto', in Antonio C. Secchin, *João Cabral: a poesia do menos* (São Paulo: Duas Cidades, 1985), pp. 299–307 (p. 302).

[6] There is little evidence to suggest that Cabral was ever actively politically involved in the Brazilian Communist Party, whose tumultuous history since its foundation in 1922 saw it go through periods of illegality. Nevertheless, his support for communist ideology in his early years is well documented. In a letter to Carlos Drummond de Andrade, written in Barcelona in 1948, he spoke of his plans to write a long poem which would outline the reasons for his support of communism: see Flora Süssekind, *Cabral,*

[a Pernambucan nativity play], the work draws on the traditional ballad form of the popular north-eastern poetry known as *literatura de cordel* and the Luso-Brazilian tradition of one-act morality plays, or *autos*, to re-enact the nativity story through the experience of the protagonist, the peasant farmer Severino, epitome of the disenfranchised majority, in his desperate attempt to escape the hunger and violence on the land. His arrival in Recife coincides with the birth of a new baby, also Severino, born among the slums on the mudflats of the Capibaribe river as it flows through the city. As Gonzalez and Treece (p. 255) note, Severino's journey is one through both time and space—from the semi-feudal social and economic relations in the interior, to the capitalist conditions in the industrialized city—and the irony with which the traditional nativity story is treated suggests that neither spatial nor temporal journeys have resulted in improved social conditions for the majority of the people.[7]

Cabral's protest against Brazil's history of social neglect was superbly set to music by the internationally acclaimed Brazilian composer and songwriter Chico Buarque (b. 1944) for the play's award-winning staging in 1966 by TUCA, the São Paulo Catholic University Theatre Company. The award increased Cabral's popularity at home and projected him on to the international stage that same year, when he was honoured with the Prize for Best Living Writer at the Theatre Festival in Nancy.

The play's success at home and abroad translated into TV and film adaptations, as well as editions in a number of languages. Its presence in syllabuses of Brazilian studies courses the world over is practically undisputed, reflecting a public recognition rarely seen in Brazil's literary history.

Despite the work's public and critical acclaim, Cabral was always sceptical about its value, stating that it was not as well constructed as some of his other works. He claimed to have written it for the poor peasants who enjoyed Brazil's *literatura de cordel*. More successful, in his eyes, was his 1966 collection *A educação pela pedra*, which won the 1967 Jabuti Prize, awarded by the Brazilian Book Chamber. He wrote this

---

Bandeira, Drummond. Alguma correspondência (Rio de Janeiro: Fundação Casa de Rui Barbosa; Ministério da Cultura, 1996), p. 228. Cabral was summoned back to Brazil to respond to accusations of subversion in 1952. He was readmitted to the Diplomatic Service in 1954, after the case against him was closed, and worked for its Cultural Department in Brazil until 1956, when he returned to Spain for a second time.

[7] Gonzalez and Treece's chapter 'The Architects of Construction: Poetry and the Politics of Development in Post-War Brazil' (pp. 227–66) provides an excellent overview of Cabral's early work and an analysis of *Morte e vida severina* within its socio-political context.

collection over the course of 1962–5, years that he spent in diplomatic service in Seville and then as Delegate to the United Nations, in Geneva. It was this collection that helped establish his reputation as a cerebral poet of clarity and precision, which he himself endorsed on a number of occasions and which has become something of a truism within the field of *estudos cabralinos*.

He would go on to publish a number of successful collections up to the end of his career. *Museu de tudo* (1975), an eclectic collection of poems written between 1966 and 1974, was followed by *A escola das facas* (1980) and a new one-act play, *Auto do frade* (1984), both of which foreground north-eastern themes of a historical nature. Cabral's later years took him to new postings in Latin America as well as West Africa, and these new landscapes gained prominence in his subsequent collection, *Agrestes* (1985). The collection of narrative poems that followed, *Crime na Calle Relator* (1987), was written for the most part during Cabral's years in Portugal and coincided with two important moments in his personal life: the loss of his first wife, Stella, to cancer, in 1986, and his marriage to fellow poet Marly de Oliveira (1935–2007) later that same year. After the devastating loss of Stella, the happiness of his second marriage seemed to give renewed energy to his writing, inflecting the making of his last collections, *Sevilha andando* and *Andando Sevilha* published in 1990, and which by their very titles bear witness to the significance of his foreign travels for his poetry.

He retired that same year from diplomatic service, having reached the rank of ambassador, and moved back to Brazil, settling in Rio de Janeiro, which was to be his home for the rest of his life. It was in 1990 too that he was to become the second recipient of the recently instituted Camões Prize. Other national and international awards followed, reflecting Cabral's standing within Brazil's twentieth-century literature.

Having suffered from ill-health and progressive loss of sight, devastating for the avowedly voracious reader that he was, Cabral died on 9 October 1999, aged seventy-nine, in the knowledge that his poetry, and especially his earlier works, had earned national as well as international recognition.

It is my focus here to concentrate on his later and less studied works, and specifically from *A escola das facas* onwards, which I believe deserve a greater critical scrutiny than they have so far received. Though the critical and popular acclaim of earlier works such as *Morte e vida severina* remained unmatched, his later works were overall well received, but

Cabral himself was keen to discredit them for not reflecting the kind of lucidity in composition which he felt had crystallized in his collection of 1966, *A educação pela pedra*. His interview with fellow writer Rubem Braga (1913–90), published in November 1975, in the month following the publication of *Museu de tudo*, the collection subsequent to *A educação pela pedra*, saw Cabral express his anxieties in relation to his writing, revealing, it would seem, a moment of personal crisis and preoccupation as far as the reception of his new collection was concerned: 'What I wrote and may write after *A educação pela pedra* is something that lacks the conscience, or lucidity, of my earlier writings. I would like to be judged by what I wrote up to the age of 45. I would like to be considered a posthumous author.'[8]

The poet's own view of his later works may explain the scarce critical attention that they have received. As Secchin has remarked, the supposed 'second phase' of Cabral's writing career has been unjustly neglected.[9] Indeed, I would contend that to distinguish between two distinct phases in Cabral's career amounts to a misapprehension and that ambiguity, often through an exploration of borderline imagery, in-between spaces, both physical and metaphorical, employed as a means of articulating personal, social, and political concerns, was pivotal to Cabral's work throughout.

As a point of departure, I reject the distinction between the Cabral of earlier and that of later works. That said, it is possible to identify a more relaxed authorial stance after *A educação pela pedra*, demonstrated, for example, by the fact that *Museu de tudo* contrasts with the preceding collection in its lack of a single unifying principle be it in theme or structure, as the title itself suggests.[10]

---

[8] 'O que escrevi e talvez escreverei depois de *A educação pela pedra* é coisa que escrevi sem a mesma consciência, ou lucidez, do que escrevia antes. Gostaria de ser julgado pelo que escrevi até os 45 anos. Gostaria de ser considerado um autor póstumo.' Marta de Senna, *João Cabral: tempo e memória* (Rio de Janeiro: Antares, 1980), p. 186. In his interview with Humberto Werneck, 'Sou um poeta à margem', *IstoÉ*, 20 November 1985, pp. 84–6, (p. 86), Cabral stated that he felt his best works were those written in his early forties: *Quaderna* (1960), *Dois parlamentos* (1960), *Serial* (1961) and *A educação pela pedra*.

[9] Cover of Ivo Barbieri's *Geometria da composição. Morte e vida da palavra severina* (Rio de Janeiro: Sette Letras, 1997).

[10] Carlos Felipe Moisés noted this lack of unifying principle in 'João Cabral de Melo Neto', in *Poesia e realidade. Ensaios acerca da poesia brasileira e portuguesa* (São Paulo: Cultrix, 1977), pp. 49–79 (p. 77) (first published as 'João Cabral: poesia e poética', *O Estado de São Paulo*, 27 August 1966, 3 October, and 17 September 1966).

Introduction

Yet, one could argue that this apparent lack of order is in fact deliberate, and that, in Cabral's earlier output, his stated poetic aim of precision was consistently deconstructed. The acclaimed Brazilian critic José Guilherme Merquior pointed out the contrast between the poet's stated intent and output, noting how his poetry was structured on impulses and tensions that conflicted with Cabral's self-image as a Cartesian poet.[11] Elaborating on his comment, Merquior drew attention to the fact that Cabral's poetry proved to be far more problematic than the author himself would have his readers believe:

> Almost all critical appraisals revolve around the celebrated desire for lucidity of Cabral's poetry. [...] Now, this image was gradually considerably undermined by more careful critical analyses, willing to scrutinize the poet's work and not just his statements. When one looks closely at his exaltation of lucidity [...] one notes that it emerges as dialectical struggle between wakefulness and inspiration, between the wish to be guided by the conscious mind and the desire for a porous, avid receptivity to the world.[12]

The case of *A educação pela pedra*, generally regarded as the finest realization of the poet's poetics of clarity and precision, is perhaps the best point of departure to revise this perspective. Antonio Carlos Secchin, who had considerable access to the poet, recalls how Cabral held this collection to be his most accomplished work, thanks to the painstaking attention devoted to the construction of each individual poem and to the structure of the volume as a whole. The original manuscript of the index page of *A educação pela pedra*, edited by Secchin, features annotations by Cabral himself and gives a fair indication of the degree of attention to detail that went into the composition of the 1966 collection.[13]

For example, Cabral classified each poem according to the kind of relationship that linked its two sections (by way of conjunctions or line repetition etc.). Yet, it is curious that such meticulous grammatical classification appears to have had no bearing on the actual organization

---

[11] 'Nosso poeta exemplar', *Jornal do Brasil, Caderno B*, 9 February 1980, p. 10.
[12] 'Quase todas as leituras críticas giraram e ainda giram em torno da celebrada vontade de lucidez do poema cabralino. [...] Ora, essa imagem de marca veio sendo aos poucos bastante minada pela crítica menos desatenta, disposta a esquadrinhar as realizações do poeta, e não só as suas proclamações. Examinando de perto o louvor à lucidez [...] termina aparecendo como dialética entre vigília e inspiração, entre a vontade de controle consciente e o desejo de uma porosa, ávida receptividade ao mundo' (ibid., p. 10).
[13] 'Um original de João Cabral de Melo Neto', ed. Antonio C. Secchin, *Colóquio/Letras* 157-8 (2000 [2002]), 159.

of the volume.[14] In fact, the rationale behind the poet's creative process seemed to have been to undermine order and precision rather than reproduce it. Similarly, Secchin (1985, p. 224) noted Cabral's employment of a longer line length, of approximately eleven syllables, perhaps in rejection of the Portuguese tradition of lyric poetry in twelve-syllable lines. The deliberate disruption of regular line patterns in such a carefully crafted collection is certainly extremely meaningful, given that, as Benedito Nunes observed: 'It would appear that the poet, aiming at regular patterns, then disrupts them the moment he employs them.'[15]

The disconcerting effect produced in the reader by the introduction of permutational poems such as 'O mar e o canavial' and 'O canavial e o mar', which constitute a stylistic innovation within the poet's output, is also a point worth noting. According to Marta Peixoto's analysis, Cabral's reworking of poems through the reshuffling of lines and only minimal vocabulary changes draws attention to the actual process of construction of the poems, denying poetry the status of something that is born as a complete entity thanks to the poet's moment of inspiration.[16] In fact, by reworking poems in this way, the poet is drawing attention to the act of writing as one in which there is no sense of closure.[17]

Arguably, the reaction of the reader when presented with these permutational poems is not simply one of cerebral engagement with Cabral's process of construction but also an emotional one. Because these compositions do not follow on directly from one another in the collection—in which case the process of construction would have been more obviously exposed—the effect on the readers, confronted with a series of poems that uncannily echo earlier ones, is disconcerting.

Thus the qualities of economy and stability, and by association of clarity and precision, implied in the image of the stone, which is central

---

[14] The forty-eight poems of the volume were organized into four subsections, namely, a/b and A/B: the first two comprising shorter poems of sixteen lines, the last two including poems of twenty-four lines, with the a/A sections dealing with north-eastern themes, and the b/B sections deal with a broader subject range.

[15] 'Dir-se-ia que o poeta, visando sempre a esses padrões regulares, desregula-os no momento de utilizá-los', *João Cabral de Melo Neto*, 2nd edn (Petrópolis: Ed. Vozes, 1971), p. 132.

[16] *Poesia com coisas (Uma leitura de João Cabral de Melo Neto)* (São Paulo: Perspectiva, 1983), p. 178.

[17] Cabral's interview with Secchin is extremely revealing in this respect, since he confirmed having written forty-eight versions of one of the poems of *A educação pela pedra*, although only two were eventually published. See Secchin (1985, p. 305).

to the collection, are subverted in the actual poems, and the image comes to encapsulate a far more complex set of features than would at first appear. In the title poem of the collection, for example, there proves to be a fundamental paradox underlying Cabral's 'education by stone' because, if on the one hand this concrete object reveals its 'resistência fria | ao que flui e a fluir' [cold resistance | to what flows and to flowing] (p. 338), it also eludes being 'maleada' [moulded] (p. 338).[18]

Much could be said about Cabral's subversion of the idea of precise construction and order when considered in relation to the socio-political backdrop against which the collection was written (1962–5), straddling a period defined by Brazil's expansionist policy, of which the earlier founding of a new capital, Brasília, in 1960, had been the most striking materialization, as well as the political instability of the early 1960s and the eventual military coup of 1964.[19] From this perspective, Cabral's writing of the following collection, *Museu de tudo* (compiled between 1966 and 1974) and published in 1975, also seems to respond to the exacerbation of the political crisis in Brazil's recent history, with the deepening hard line adopted by the military and the restriction of civil liberties (the infamous AI5 decree, instituting aggressive state censorship and abolishing political freedom, was passed by the military regime in 1968).

The disintegration of structural and thematic order in *Museu de tudo* in relation to the (seemingly) rigid structure of *A educação pela pedra* amounts to a coherent progression within the poet's output and emerges as less problematic than would at first appear to be the case. In both collections, he can be seen as responding to a critical political climate. Indeed, by deliberately undermining the possibility of having a clearly defined structure (particularly in *Museu de tudo*), Cabral appears to be questioning the limitations of notions of Law and Order, concepts intrinsically associated with the political establishment of the time.

Looking more closely at the relationship between *A educação pela pedra* and *Museu de tudo*, we can see how the image of the stone, central to the former, and the recurring sand images of the latter share a

---

[18] The apparent contradiction underlying this image has been eloquently summarized by Peixoto (1983, p. 191), who contends that, as a metaphor for poetic language, the stone encapsulates the impossibility to control it absolutely.

[19] Justin Read's insightful analysis of *A educação pela pedra* and its dialogue with the modernist architectural model identifies Cabral's critique of the limitations of modern Brazil. See Justin Read, 'Alternative Functions: João Cabral de Melo Neto and the Architectonics of Modernity', *Luso-Brazilian Review* 43.1 (2006), 65–93.

common level of meaning as metaphors of resistance to domination. In *A educação pela pedra*, Cabral had drawn on Swift's *Gulliver's Travels*, in 'The country of Houyhnhnms (outra composição)' (p. 355), to reflect on the language needed to speak on and for the Yahoos (embodiment of the oppressed). He concluded that the ambiguity inherent in irony and satire is the most effective means of addressing questions of social injustice. Here, ambiguity is encapsulated in the image of the stone, but also, significantly, comes to be associated with the image of the knife, another of Cabral's recurring images:

> Para falar dos *Yahoos*, se necessita
> que as palavras funcionem de pedra:
> [...]
> Para falar dos *Yahoos*, se necessita
> que as palavras se rearmem de gume,
> como numa sátira; ou como na ironia,
> se armem ambiguamente de dois gumes. (p. 355)

[To speak of the Yahoos, one needs | words to work like stones: [...]| To speak of the Yahoos, one needs | words to rearm themselves with the blade, | as in satire; or in irony, | arm themselves ambiguously with a double-edged blade.]

The complexity inscribed in the image of the stone (at once a symbol of definition and ambiguity) is also attributed to the image of sand in *Museu de tudo*. Reflecting the inevitable natural process by which hard rock formations are eventually eroded into granular form, the transition from one collection to the next constitutes a coherent progression. In the poem 'Díptico' (p. 376), Cabral indicates that the publication of *Museu de tudo* within his output mirrors the organic cycle of creation and destruction, part of a single creative process because:

> quem tenta
> encontrará ainda cristais,
> formas vivas, na fala frouxa. (p. 376)

[whoever tries | will still find crystals, | living forms, in the loose language.]

Marta de Senna (p. 187) described the publication of *Museu de tudo* as signalling a transitional moment within the poet's work, but the collection did not, in my view, ultimately pave the way for the emergence of an 'anti-Cabral' (Senna, p. 187), as one might have justifiably anticipated, and the work was, in fact, developing tendencies that were already evident in the poet's earlier output. In this way, a division of his work into two distinct phases, before and after *A educação pela pedra*, seems problematic. The fact that this collection should form part of the second volume of his complete works published by Nova Fronteira, entitled *A educação pela pedra e depois* (1997), and, therefore, be included among his later works, seems to corroborate this point.[20]

It might be useful to consider his earlier works more closely. *O engenheiro* is widely regarded as initiating a new phase in Cabral's *œuvre* and representing a shift from the surrealist-like mood of his first collection, *Pedra do sono*. In his overview of Cabral's works up to *Serial* (1961), the critic Luiz Costa Lima points to two opposed poetic threads that come into conflict in *O engenheiro*. The first, which he qualifies as a 'lunar',[21] of surrealist inspiration, contrasts with a kind of poetry defined as 'solar' (p. 208), with the eponymous poem of the collection representing a moment in which dreams are rejected in favour of rational thought (p. 213).

I would contend, however, that rather than rejecting the experience of dreaming, the poem 'O engenheiro' (pp. 69–70) seems to explore a link between the processes of the unconscious and those of the conscious mind. This becomes clear from the fact that the poem first evokes the disjointed images of the dreams of the engineer (surfaces, tennis shoes, a glass of water) (p. 69), and then, in the second stanza, the processes of the conscious mind, with a focus on the tools of his trade and, subsequently, his projects and calculations:

> O lápis, o esquadro, o papel;
> o desenho, o projeto, o número:
> o engenheiro pensa o mundo justo,
> mundo que nenhum véu encobre. (p. 70)

[The pencil, the set square, paper; | the drawing, the project, the number: | the engineer thinks the world just, | a world that no veil covers.]

The conscious and the unconscious mind are not mutually exclusive here, but parts of an organic whole, as is suggested in the closing image of the poem, where the man-made structure sits harmoniously within a natural

---

[20] The first volume is entitled *Serial e antes* (1997). This division of his output meant that the length of the two volumes was conspicuously uneven, with the first comprising 325 pages and the second 385 pages of poetry. Had Cabral included *A educação pela pedra* (forty pages) in the first, there would have been a closer balance between the two, which would have conveyed more effectively the order and mathematical precision with which he has traditionally been associated. Importantly, Paulo Venâncio Filho's comments on the back cover reveal that the author was personally involved in this edition.

[21] 'A traição conseqüente ou a poesia de Cabral', in *Lira e antilira. Mário, Drummond, Cabral*, 2nd edn, rev. Sinval Liparoti (Rio de Janeiro: Topbooks, 1995), pp. 197–331 (p. 208).

setting: 'na natureza o edifício crescendo de suas forças simples' [in the natural world, the building | growing from its simple strengths] (p. 70).[22]

Thus, as Merquior rightly noted, Cabral is not repudiating the world of dreams per se in favour of rationality. In the critic's formulation: 'The poem does not rise against "inspiration", but shows that inspiration is only valid when active, when positively incorporated and consciously transformed.'[23]

In fact, Gledson has successfully argued that the early collection *Pedra do sono* forms 'a coherent part of a development which cannot be accounted for by such simple dichotomies',[24] and whose understanding is crucial in gauging the complexity of Cabral's poetics of construction. According to Gledson's penetrating analysis, the dreamlike and often nightmarish atmosphere of this inaugural collection is deliberate: it is not, as he states, 'the result of an unresolved conflict between an "objective" and a "subjective" Cabral' (p. 44). By his conscious re-creation of the sensations of sleep—that *Pedra do sono* is not a straightforward surrealist collection is demonstrated by the fact that Cabral did not engage in automatic writing—the poet has rejected the clear-cut opposition of the objective and subjective. On this point, Gledson explains: 'For sleep [...] is the perfect case of a state in which the subjective mind becomes its own object, contemplates itself as if it were another being or thing, seeing quite

---

[22] John Gledson has rightly drawn attention to the contrast between the positive rendition of modernist architecture by Cabral in this poem and the bleak configuration of modern living by Drummond in the poem 'Edifício esplendor', published in *José* (1942), with which Cabral would have been familiar. See John Gledson, 'Epílogo', in *Influências e impasses. Drummond e alguns contemporâneos*, trans. Frederico Dentello (São Paulo: Companhia das Letras, 2003), pp. 233–80 (p. 248). Similarly, Cabral's rendition of the theme contrasts with Manuel Bandeira's juxtaposition of the architect with the poet in 'Testamento', from *Lira dos cinqüent'anos* (first published in 1940): 'Fiz-me arquiteto? Não pude! | Sou poeta menor, perdoai!' [Become an architect? Alas, I could not! | I am a minor poet, forgive me!], in *Poesia completa e prosa*, 4th edn (Rio de Janeiro: Nova Aguilar, 1983), pp. 261–2 (p. 262). Cabral's last collection, *Andando Sevilha*, reveals a shift in emphasis on the poet's part, as he openly celebrates the labyrinthine urban network of Seville rather than the modernist architectural model. This shift will be discussed in detail in Chapter 5.

[23] 'O poema não se ergue "contra a inspiração", ele mostra que a inspiração só é válida quando ativa, quando acolhida sem passividade e transformada conscientemente.' See 'Nuvem civil sonhada—ensaio sobre a poética de João Cabral de Melo Neto', in *A astúcia da mímese (Ensaios sobre lírica)*, 2nd edn, rev. Frederico Gomes (Rio de Janeiro: Topbooks, 1997), pp. 84–187 (p. 95).

[24] 'Sleep, Poetry, and João Cabral's "False Book": A Revaluation of *Pedra do sono*', *Bulletin of Hispanic Studies* 55 (1978), 43–58 (p. 43).

clearly things which it cannot control, though they are part of itself' (p. 45).[25]

According to this view, Cabral's first published collection emerges as the starting point of a coherent literary career spanning over five decades, in which ambiguity and instability are not eschewed outright, but are consciously incorporated into his writings in a variety of different ways. Even in *Morte e vida severina,* ambiguity played a major part, given that the poet famously left the denouement of his *auto* open to interpretation, rejecting a definitive solution in relation to the fate of Severino. Indeed, the reader is left guessing whether Severino will ultimately choose life over death or whether he will succumb to his suicidal instincts. The poet justified his resort to ambiguity, defining it as a feature inherent in the work of any successful poet: 'I did not give his drama a conclusion. I believe that finding solutions of this kind is not the responsibility of poets, but the business of politicians or sociologists.'[26]

My interest here lies precisely in probing into Cabral's exploration of ambiguity, particularly his keen attention to liminal images, his blurring and subversion of the boundaries between different phenomena, which I believe were aimed at undermining forms of oppression and domination. The roots of such relativistic perception of reality can be traced to Cabral's early compositions, such as the poems of *Serial,* in which a single phenomenon is observed from different but equally valid angles, as noted by Stephen Reckert:

What is common to Cabral's frequent paradoxes and the metrical, syntactical and semantic oscillation that characterizes so much of his work, is that each represents a way of alternating between different and even opposed points of view, distinct but equally legitimate outlooks on the same phenomenon.[27]

Taking my cue from Reckert's analysis and concentrating on Cabral's fascination with marginal states—such as the state of sleep, which he

[25] How this emerges in the poems is exemplified in the closing lines of 'Os olhos' (p. 43), where the images conjured up are underpinned by a fundamental contradiction: 'Juntos os peitos bateram | e os olhos todos fugiram. | (Os olhos ainda estão muito lúcidos)' [Together the hearts beat | all eyes fled. | (The eyes are still very lucid)] (p. 43). As Gledson argues, the experience evoked in these lines is one of a divided and alienated self because 'the eyes are both absent and present, in frantic flight and entirely lucid' (p. 44).
[26] 'Não dei uma conclusão ao seu drama. Creio que essas soluções não cabem ao poeta e sim ao político ou ao sociólogo', in interview with Gilson Rebello, 'O árduo trabalho do poeta Cabral', *O Estado de São Paulo,* 2 November 1980, p. 41.
[27] 'João Cabral: from *Pedra* to *Pedra*', *Portuguese Studies* 2 (1986), 166–84 (p. 181).

explored in *Pedra do sono*—I address the need for closer critical scrutiny of Cabral's later works and will begin with a study of *A escola das facas*. Echoing the poet's complex treatment of the image of the stone in *A educação pela pedra*, the knife provides a powerful metaphor for the ambiguity that informs Cabral's writing in both form and content in this collection. In an interview with Fábio Freixeiro, Cabral spoke of his avoidance of abstract nouns in preference of concrete words which avoid ambiguity.[28] However, his rendition of the image of the knife in *A escola das facas* offers a productive starting point for this enquiry into how he created the very ambiguity that he purported to eschew.

A precedent can in fact be found in the early work *Uma faca só lâmina* (first published in the collected edition *Duas águas*, of 1956).[29] This poem is constructed on a fundamental paradox because the regular line length (six syllables) and stanza patterns (quatrains) contrast with what Marta Peixoto has identified as the imbalance within the imagery, which is composed of incomplete metaphors and similes (Peixoto, 1983, p. 126). Indeed, the opening section of the poem is made up of eight quatrains including similes in which the second term of comparison is deliberately omitted. In a riddle-like fashion, Cabral successfully conveys the turmoil and frustration that his obsession, as a quest for what is absent, entails. Drawing on Benedito Nunes's (1974, p. 104) assessment that the poem reproduces the always deceptive hunt for images implicit in any literary endeavour, Peixoto (1983, p. 135) points out that dealing with the very elusiveness of language is a stimulating challenge to which Cabral was drawn.

In an attempt to discuss these features of Cabral's work in greater detail, I will aim to provide an appraisal of the poet's achievements in later years, since comprehensive evaluation of the poet's later output has so far not been available.[30] That said, I share the view that there is a need

---

[28] 'João Cabral de Melo Neto—roteiro de auto-interpretação', in *Da razão à emoção II. Ensaios rosianos. Outros ensaios e documentos* (Rio de Janeiro: Tempo Brasileiro, 1971), pp. 179–92 (p. 186).

[29] This volume included his previously published works and the unpublished *Morte e vida severina*, *Paisagens com figuras* and *Uma faca só lâmina*.

[30] For example, Luiz Costa Lima's *Lira e antilira*, first published in 1967 and revised in 1995, deals with works up to *Serial*, Benedito Nunes's *João Cabral de Melo Neto* (1974; first published in 1971) provides a broad overview of the poet's output up to *A educação pela pedra*, as do Lauro Escorel's *A pedra e o rio. Uma interpretação da poesia de João Cabral de Melo Neto* (1973) and João Alexandre Barbosa's *A imitação da forma* (1975). The 1980s saw the publication of four seminal overviews of the poet's work: Marta de Senna's *João Cabral: tempo e memória* (1980), which discusses the theme of

to turn to neglected aspects of the poet's *œuvre* with a growing number of critics. Among those who have engaged in revaluations of Cabral's poetry is Marta Peixoto, who recently observed that it is possible to speak of not one but many poetics when we consider his work.[31] Likewise, Antonio Carlos Secchin recently suggested that only a superficial eye can view Cabral's body of work as a 'monolithic block'; the critic's recent study of *Agrestes* pointed to the 'fissures' in Cabral's work that emerged from his reworking of similar images and themes.[32]

The focus adopted in much of the criticism available appears to have been fostered by the poet himself to some degree, because he was often keen to stress the cerebral formalism of his writing and his unsentimental approach to even the most profound personal concerns.[33] The reason for placing such an emphasis on these features of his writing might be explained by the fact that they ensured his position as a marginal figure within Brazilian poetic tradition. This is a reputation he clearly valued, for it reflected his original contribution to his

time in Cabral's work up to *Museu de tudo*, Danilo Lôbo's *O poema e o quadro: o picturalismo na obra de João Cabral de Melo Neto* (1981), which considers poems up to *A educação pela pedra*, Marta Peixoto's *Poesia com coisas (Uma leitura de João Cabral de Melo Neto)* (1983), including a brief analysis of *A escola das facas*, and Antonio Carlos Secchin's *João Cabral: a poesia do menos* (1985), which also closes with a study of the 1980 collection. More recently, attention has been directed to the poet's later works: Rosa Maria Martelo's *Estrutura e transposição* (1990) comprises readings of poems published up to *Crime na Calle Relator* (1987), Ivo Barbieri's *Geometria da composição: morte e vida da palavra severina* (1997) refers to poems up to *Sevilha andando* and *Andando Sevilha* (1990) and Níobe Abreu Peixoto's *João Cabral e o poema dramático: Auto do frade (Poema para vozes)* (2001) centres its analysis on Cabral's second *auto*. Overall, however, the perspective adopted in these critical enquiries is one from which I attempt to depart, proposing a revisionist approach to Cabral's writing. I will make specific reference to criticism available on the poet when discussing individual poems and collections.

[31] Marta Peixoto, 'Um pomar às avessas': género e configuração da escrita em Jõao Cabral de Melo Neto', *Colóquio/Letras* 157–8 (2000 [2002]), 229–40 (p. 229). Peixoto discusses Cabral's meta-textual poetry from the perspective of gender studies.

[32] Antonio Carlos Secchin, 'João Cabral: outras paisagens', *Colóquio/Letras* 157–8 (2000 [2002]), 105–24 (p. 106). Secchin's emphasis on Cabral's struggle against ambiguity is not in line with the approach taken in this book, although his assessment of the poet's acute sense of the elusiveness of language is a point which will be developed here. As Secchin observes, Cabral's anxiety stems 'da intensa consciência de que as palavras actuam simultaneamente como instrumento de revelação e de encobrimento, e nem sempre se pode desentranhar [...] uma parcela da outra' [from the intense awareness that words act simultaneously as instruments of revelation and cover-up, and it is not always possible to untangle [...] one side from the other] (2000 [2002], p. 110).

[33] This is a point originally made by Gledson when commenting on the oversimplification characterizing much of the criticism on the poet (1978, p. 43).

country's literary output, as his interview with the poet Mário Chamie, given in 1978, reveals: 'I confess that in an essentially lyrical country, which speaks of stars and the eyes of the beloved, I engaged in a style of writing that has nothing in common with this.'[34]

Yet, the poet was also scathing of the reductive nature of many of the readings. In the same interview with Chamie, he was disparaging of the fact that much of the criticism on his work took as its starting point for analysis 'the construction, symmetry, repetition, formal objectivity, essence as opposed to existence'.[35] Commenting on the 'visão esclerosada e repetida da crítica' [sclerotic and repetitive perspective of the critics] (p. 40), Cabral wished for other facets of his writing to be explored.[36]

Over the course of the next five chapters, I will therefore take a revisionist approach and will consider Cabral's last six collections, taking as my cue configurations of the knife in the collection *A escolas das facas*, which followed *Museu de tudo*. Cabral's fascinating renditions of the image of the knife in this collection inflect his revisitation of the past (personal and national) through images of cutting and fragmentation in which an acute sense of instability is conveyed.

Cabral's autobiographical approach in this work was unprecedented and was followed by a further enquiry into the past, in his following work, *Auto do frade*. Cabral's attraction to historical narratives and his obsession with liminal states of being forms the basis of this *auto*, which is analysed in the second chapter. There, I will consider the implications of Cabral's choices for the political significance of this work, as well as for his own developing thoughts on poetry.

I will then move on to a study of *Agrestes*, taking my cue from Silviano Santiago's formulations on the *entre-lugar* (in-between space) as a *locus* of enunciation where forms of cultural colonialism are undermined. My interest lies especially in Cabral's figurations of marginality and hybrid forms, which transpire in the title of the collection itself— taken to allude to the north-eastern region of Brazil between the *zona*

---

[34] 'Confesso que resolvi escrever, num país essencialmente lírico, que fala de estrelas e dos olhos da amada, uma literatura que nada tem a ver com isso', Mário Chamie, 'Desleitura da poesia de João Cabral', in *Casa da época* (São Paulo: Conselho Estadual de Artes e Ciências Humanas, 1978), pp. 39–59 (pp. 53–4).

[35] 'A construção, a simetria, a recorrência, a objetividade formal, a essência contra a existência' (ibid., p. 39).

[36] 'Eu gostaria que minha poesia tivesse uma leitura em que outras coisas fossem vistas' [I would like my poetry to be read so that other things were seen] (ibid., p. 41).

da mata and the *sertão*. The manner in which *Agrestes* as a whole conflates concrete and imaginary landscapes, following the poet's physical journeys as a diplomat as well as his intellectual and emotional ones, even at a very superficial level, is evidence of the blurring of boundaries underpinning this collection.

Cabral's playful appropriation of the detective story genre is what first prompted my strong interest in his following collection, *Crime na Calle Relator*, and I will look at his use of the anecdote and the implications of his treatment of crime narratives in which cases remain, generally, unresolved.

In the final chapter of this book, I will analyse both *Sevilha andando* and *Andando Sevilha*: initially published as one collection in 1990, they maintained a close thematic affinity even after extensive reworking. I will look at representations of Andalusia and more specifically of the *sevilhana* [Sevillian woman], established *topoi* in the poet's output, to tease out the implications for Cabral's continued criticism of forms of oppression and domination and evaluate their significance as far as Cabral's own evolving thoughts on writing were concerned.

1
Life on a knife-edge: *A escola das facas*

1.1 INTRODUCTION

A escola das facas comprises poems written between 1975 and 1980,[1] years that Cabral spent in Dakar and later Quito, as Brazilian Ambassador to Senegal and Ecuador.[2] With this in mind, it is striking that neither the African nor the Ecuadorian landscapes should feature at all in this volume, which is in fact entirely devoted to Pernambuco.[3]

The poet revisited his birthplace from personal memory, foregrounding childhood experiences, characters, and places from his north-eastern background, in addition to surveying Pernambuco's history, dealt with only sporadically in earlier collections.[4] The degree of exposure of the

---

[1] On publishing his collections, Cabral always ensured that the dates of composition were clearly stated. Thanks to this, we can verify that his writing spans almost the entirety of his adult life, from his early collection *Primeiros poemas* (1937–40), published in 1990, to *Sevilha Andando* (1987–93). No new collections were published in the final years of the poet's life, which were plagued by ill-health and depression.

[2] Cabral held the post of Ambassador to Dakar, and cumulatively that of Ambassador to Mauritania, Mali and Guine-Conakry, from 1972 to 1979. During his years in Senegal, Cabral enjoyed a close personal friendship with the writer and then President Léopold Sédar Senghor. According to the biographical account given by José Castello, it was Senghor himself who, wishing Cabral to remain in Senegal beyond the initial stipulated period, petitioned Brazilian President Ernesto Geisel personally in order to have the Ambassador's posting extended. Senghor's intervention was effective, and Cabral was only appointed to his following post, as Ambassador to Ecuador, after the end of the Geisel administration, in 1979, even though he had been quite anxious to move (Castello, 1996, p. 141).

[3] In keeping with this focus on Pernambuco, the title that Cabral originally intended for the collection was *Poemas pernambucanos*. On the eve of publication, and following the advice of the critic Antônio Cândido, the title was changed to *A escola das facas* (ibid., p. 143).

[4] Cabral spoke of his keen interest in history (see Alcino Leite Neto, 'O maior poeta menor', *IstoÉ Senhor*, 31 January 1990, pp. 3–7 [p. 5]). His engagement with historical themes is more apparent in his later works, especially in *A escola das facas* and *Auto do frade*, though his early writings show evidence of his desire to consider social issues from a historical perspective. In *Morte e vida severina*, for example, the protagonist Severino's

Life on a knife-edge: A escola das facas

poetic self in Cabral's treatment of autobiographical themes in this volume signals a departure in his *œuvre* which, as John Gledson observed, usually achieves an insight into subjectivity 'obliquely, through meditation on objects, animals and landscapes' (1978, p. 43). The employment of the first person pronoun and verb forms in eighteen out of forty-eight of the poems, as opposed to, for example, five out of the eighty poems of *Museu de tudo*, his preceding collection, reveals a shift towards a greater lyrical involvement.

The autobiographical slant of this volume has so far been the main focus of critical enquiry. Marta Peixoto signalled the innovation of the collection's memoiristic tone (1983, p. 211), a point also taken up by Fernando Py, who stated: 'In fact, besides the markedly autobiographical poems, the whole book is a means of opening up, speaking about oneself, a feature which had been absent from his poetry up until then.'[5]

Drawing on these earlier readings of the collection, I will account for Cabral's enquiry into personal and indeed national memory but give particular thought to how the poet challenges common perceptions of different phenomena as he throws into question the existence of defined boundaries between them. At the heart of this worldview seems to lie the sense of being haunted by the precarious nature of all that is living, an obsession which defines the poet's configurations of writing as well as his renditions of life and death, which deconstruct the notion that two opposite realities are involved.

Echoing the poet and critic Haroldo de Campos, Peixoto pointed out the tensions and struggle between opposites articulated in Cabral's work

---

allusion to the 'sesmaria' [uncultivated plot of land] from which he sets off in search of a better life subtly inscribes the *retirante*'s [north-eastern migrant] plight within the question of Brazil's historically iniquitous land distribution. Indeed, 'sesmaria' originally designated a plot of land allocated by the Portuguese Crown to high-ranking settlers to Brazil, and therefore establishes a link between the current state of affairs on the land and Brazil's colonial past. Cabral managed to combine his interest in history with his diplomatic career from 1956 to 1958, when he undertook research at the Archivo de las Indias, in Seville, where documents on the colonization of America are held. This resulted in the publication of the book *O arquivo das Índias e o Brasil* (Rio de Janeiro: MRE, 1966), comprising a catalogue of material relating to Brazil.

[5] 'Aliás, pondo de parte os poemas marcadamente autobiográficos, todo o livro é um meio confessar-se, contar de si, faceta até então inexistente em sua poesia' ('Começa a temporada', *Jornal do Brasil*, 10 January 1981, p. 9). The critic João Alexandre Barbosa takes a similar line in 'Balanço de João Cabral', in *As ilusões da modernidade. Notas sobre a historicidade da lírica moderna*, rev. Plinio Martins Filho (São Paulo: Perspectiva, 1986), pp. 107–37 (p. 135) (first publ. in *Brasilianische Literatur* [Frankfurt: Surkhamp, 1984]).

(1983, p. 215).[6] Focusing on the theme of violence, through which such tensions are conveyed to a great extent, Peixoto observed: 'In the majority of collections, themes revolve around the struggle between adversaries, and victory, when there is one, is precarious.'[7]

One could argue that this feature emerges in *A escola das facas* on both a thematic and linguistic level, through Cabral's skilful manipulation of language structures and exploration of polysemy. Central to this is the multifaceted image of the knife, included in the title itself, and around which the collection is constructed. If on the one hand, as Antonio Secchin observed, it is true that the knife represents for the poet 'uma certa forma de *produzir*, de ordenar o real' [a certain way of *producing*, ordering reality] (1985, pp. 125–6), as an image of objectivity and incisiveness, it is equally apparent that configurations of the knife in *A escola das facas* conjure up images that challenge any ordered perception of the world.[8]

Indeed, these two perspectives coexist. In the poem 'As facas pernambucanas' (pp. 436–7), of *A escola das facas*, for example, mathematical and grammatical order are embodied in the fish knives and daggers of Pernambuco:

> Se a peixeira corta e conta,
> o punhal do Pajeú, reto,
> quase mais bala que faca,
> fala em objeto direto. (p. 437)

[If the fish knife cuts and counts, | the dagger from Pajeú, straight, | almost closer to a bullet than to a knife, | speaks of direct objects.]

Notwithstanding these configurations, the knife is endowed with a complexity of signification that we can also identify in one of Cabral's

---

[6] Campos noted in relation to Cabral that: 'sua poesia é dialética não para o conforto de alguma síntese ideal, hipostasiada no absoluto, mas pela guerra permanente que engendra entre os elementos em conflito, à busca de conciliação, e onde o possível se substitui normativamente ao eterno' [his poetry is dialectic not because it aims at the comfort of some ideal synthesis, representing an absolute truth, but because of the permanent war it articulates between elements in conflict, seeking a conciliation, where possibility normally replaces eternal solutions]. See 'O geometra engajado', in *Metalinguagem. Ensaios de teoria e crítica literária*, ed. Rose Marie Muraro (Petrópolis: Vozes, 1967), pp. 67–78 (pp. 72–3).

[7] 'Na maior parte das coletâneas, o nível temático também se organiza como uma luta entre adversários, e a vitória, quando há vitória, é precária' (1983, p. 14).

[8] António José Ferreira Afonso takes a similar line to Secchin, when he contends that knives and other weaponry in *A escola das facas* point to the 'ordem que existe na pedra' [order that exists in the stone]. See *João Cabral de Melo Neto. Uma teoria da luz* (Braga: APPACDM Distrital de Braga, 1995), p. 122.

earlier poems, 'Diálogo' (pp. 162-4), of the collection *Paisagens com figuras*, where we read: 'no fio agudo de facas | o fio frágil da vida' [on the fine edge of knives | the fragile line of life] (p. 163).

Indeterminacy is also a structural feature. It can be no coincidence, for instance, that the poem 'A cana e o século dezoito' (p. 445) is followed by 'Moenda de usina' (pp. 445-6), with its contrasting representation of the sugar cane. In the first of these poems, the plants are viewed as an epitome of decorum, with their 'cabeleiras bem penteadas' [well combed heads of hair] (p. 445). Quite the reverse is true in the following poem, where the violence of the harvest and the death of the living sugar cane mean that it becomes an image of dishevelment:

> ante a moenda (morte) da usina:
> nela, antes esbelta, linear,
> chega despenteada e sem rima. (p. 445)

[faced with the mill (death) at the sugar cane plant: | though tall and linear before, | she reaches it dishevelled and with no rhyme.]

It is worth noting that, in the edition included in his *Obra completa*, of 1994, Cabral added three poems to the original collection of forty-five. In this edition, unique in format in relation to all others, the inclusion of 'Menino de três engenhos', 'A múmia' and 'Porto dos Cavalos' meant that the poem 'Autocrítica' was no longer the closing composition. These substantial amendments to the format of the collection essentially give rise to two different editions, the existence of which points to a structural lack of closure which mirrored the thematic one.[9]

Such lack of closure is, for Silviano Santiago, a distinguishing feature of Cabral's work from *A escola das facas* onwards.[10] Although rejecting his view of two clear-cut phases in the poet's literary production, I would

---

[9] A point of interest in relation to the alterations of 1994 is that the three poems added to the original selection had already been published in *Crime na Calle Relator*, of 1987. The fact that Cabral felt the poems to be suitable for inclusion in both collections suggests a close dialogue between the two. Significantly, it is possible to chart a narrative progression in Cabral's revisitation of the past in these works: from the genesis of the poet's perception of the world as marked by violence and instability in *A escola das facas*, to his enquiry into questions of culpability and criminality in the later collection, in which he suggests that a definition of either is always problematic.

[10] In the critic's view, this volume evinces 'uma visão diferenciada e complexa da realidade' [a differential and complex vision of reality] whereas his earlier works articulated a worldview that was 'simplificada, excludente e autoritária' [simplified, excluding and authoritarian]. Silviano Santiago, 'As incertezas do sim', in *Vale quanto pesa. (Ensaios sobre questões político-culturais)*, rev. Heitor Ferreira da Costa and Heidi Strecker Gomes (São Paulo: Paz e Terra, 1982), pp. 41-5 (p. 45).

concur partly with the assessment that in *A escola das facas*: 'The uncertainty which underlies dealings with reality enters the semantic field of the poems, through words and constructions in which differences do not emerge clearly.'[11]

To understand how such boundaries are blurred, I will consider poems from both the 1980 and 1994 editions, thereby probing into the motives and the implications of the poet's re-working of this collection, with its very personal memories of the north-east and its bleak view on the history of his native land.

1.2 EXPLORING AMBIGUITY: EDUCATION THROUGH THE KNIFE

The epigraph to *A escola das facas*, 'rooted in one dear, perpetual place', is extracted from W. B. Yeats's poem 'A prayer for my daughter', published in the volume *Michael Robartes and the Dancer* (1921). In Yeats's poem, the father's hopes in relation to his offspring's future are projected onto the image of the evergreen laurel tree, a vision of enduring vitality: 'O may she live like some green laurel | Rooted in one dear perpetual place.'[12]

Yeats's line conveyed Cabral's enduring attachment to the north-eastern heritage he shared with his siblings, to whom the collection is dedicated. Some four years prior to the publication of *A escola das facas*, Cabral quoted this same line when speaking to Gilberto Freyre about his emotional ties with his birthplace:

Therefore, please forgive me if I can't quantify my Pernambucan nature. But I believe that I continue being a Pernambucan because despite not having lived in Recife for over half my life [...] I always tend to compare or articulate any experience that I have outside of Pernambuco or even outside of Brazil with things, landscapes, features typical of Pernambuco. Whether the Pernambuco I speak about is authentic or not, is not up to me to judge. In any case: I consider myself always a Pernambucan less for what truth there might be in what I write

---

[11] 'A própria incerteza no trato com a realidade começa a habitar o campo semântico do poema, exprimindo-se em palavras e construções onde ficam pouco nítidas as diferenças' (ibid., p. 43).
[12] *The Oxford Authors. W. B. Yeats*, ed. Edward Larrissy (Oxford: Oxford University Press, 1997), pp. 92–4 (p. 93).

but because I consider myself still, to quote Yeats's line, 'rooted in one dear perpetual place'.[13]

In the epigraph, Cabral is quoting Yeats's line out of context, thus simultaneously foregrounding both life and mortality, as suggested in the image of the roots and the adjective 'perpetual' respectively. The result is a sense of contiguity between the two that is not conveyed by Yeats's original image of the laurel tree and which adumbrates the often mutual inflection of configurations of life and death in Cabral's collection.

Cabral took great pleasure in manipulating his sources of inspiration, and his use of Yeats is no exception. It is equally apparent in the title of the collection as a whole, about which he stated: 'I imitated Molière, who wrote *The School for Wives*, in the same way that Gide and Cocteau imitated him. But my book has nothing to do either with Molière or the others.'[14]

Such intertextuality is echoed in the introductory poem of the collection, 'O que se diz ao editor a propósito de poemas' (p. 417).[15] Cabral himself did not comment on this particular point, but the title's closeness to Arthur Rimbaud's 'Ce qu'on dit au poète à propos de fleurs' is intriguing.[16]

The French poem addresses Théodore de Banville, poet and leader of the Parnassian Movement, in what is an uncompromising indictment of its tenets. The flowers favoured by the Parnassians—such as lilies, violets, and roses—Rimbaud argues, should be replaced by images that are relevant to a reader living in the industrial age.[17] Such meta-textual thread is

---

[13] 'Assim desculpe se não posso quantificar meu pernambucanismo. Mas creio que continuo pernambucano porque apesar de já viver fora do Recife mais da metade da minha vida [...] é com coisas, paisagens, maneiras próprias de Pernambuco que tenho sempre a tendência de comparar, ou elaborar qualquer experiência que me ocorre fora de Pernambuco e mesmo fora do Brasil. Se esse Pernambuco de que falo é autêntico ou não, não é a mim que cabe julgar. Em todo caso: considero-me sempre pernambucano menos pelo que possa haver de verdade pernambucana no que escrevo mas porque me considero ainda, como no verso de Yeats, "rooted in one dear perpetual place".' In Gilberto Freyre and others, 'João Cabral de Melo Neto. "O poeta não vive em órbita. E um ser social"', *Manchete*, 14 August 1976, pp. 110–12 (p. 112).

[14] 'Imitei Molière, que tem *A escola de mulheres*, como o imitaram também Gide e Cocteau. Mas o meu livro não tem nada a ver com o de Molière nem com os dos outros.' In Félix de Athayde, *Idéias fixas de João Cabral de Melo Neto* (Rio de Janeiro: Nova Fronteira, 1998), p. 117.

[15] It should be noted that Cabral's title for the poem in the 1980 edition was 'O que se diz ao editor a propósito de *A escola das facas*'. The subsequent amendment to 'a propósito de poemas' [about poems] suggests that the intent was a reflection on the act of writing itself rather than solely on the collection.

[16] See 'Ce qu'on dit au poète à propos de fleurs' in Arthur Rimbaud, *Œuvres complètes*, ed. Antoine Adam (Paris: Gallimard, 1972), pp. 55–60.

[17] Rimbaud ridicules the floral imagery of the Parnassians for being a 'Tas d'œufs frits dans de vieux chapeaux' [load of fried eggs in old hats] (ibid., p. 57).

shared by Cabral's poem, though the intent here is not to outline a poetic ideal, nor engage in literary polemic, but rather share very personal thoughts on life and the act of writing. Cabral draws on Rimbaud's innovative use of medical and scientific terms, such as 'clystères' [enemas], to demystify the creative process through graphic references to surgical operations, internal organs and corpses.[18]

Marta Peixoto (1983, p. 211) rightly suggested that Cabral here debunks the image of the poet as constructor or surgeon, in a dramatic turnaround in relation to earlier works, of which one example is the poem 'O engenheiro' (pp. 69–70), of the eponymous collection published in 1945. Indeed, as Ivo Barbieri noted, Cabral's configurations of writing in the introductory poem of *A escola das facas* hinge on images of revolt against forms of control, mirroring 'the rebellious unsubmissiveness of life'.[19]

Such struggle to control the creative process is inscribed within a sense of existence as being in a constant state of flux. Though not explicitly mentioned in this poem, the knife, present in the title of the collection, is suggested in the numerous references to instances of cutting and amputation which the process of writing implies.

In the poem's opening lines, the author labels himself an 'incurable Pernambucan', a description which also serves to introduce the theme of finality and the regionalist character of the volume as a whole. Cabral enquires whether his editors intend to publish his collection, so that he can at last put an end to its reworkings and embalm it.[20] The implication is that, once published, the collection is dead—the end result of a process of composition in which poetry is visualized as a living being

---

[18] In Rimbaud, configurations of the human body are often employed in his challenge to poetic conventions and established views on beauty, as with his rendition of the unglamorous 'Venus Anadyomène' emerging from an old bath, with a rather unflattering 'ulcère à l'anus' [anal ulcer] (ibid., p. 22). Cecil Hackett observed that in Rimbaud's verse, the human body became a 'potent dramatising force' (*Rimbaud: A Critical Introduction* [Cambridge: Cambridge University Press, 1981], p. 34). This seems to have been an influence on Cabral's treatment of the theme, as the introductory poem to *A escola das facas* suggests.

[19] 'A insubmissão rebelde da vida.' *Geometria da composição. Morte e vida da palavra severina* (Rio de Janeiro: Sette Letras, 1997), p. 117.

[20] Cabral's association of death with the writing process was echoed in an interview he gave on occasion of the publication of *A escola das facas*: 'Gosto de ver o livro já pronto, com o seu atestado de óbito, consumado mesmo, assim ele fica intocável' [I like to the see the book ready, with its death certificate, finished, that way it is untouchable], in Rebello (p. 41). He did, of course, make changes to the 1994 edition of the collection (by adding a number of poems), suggesting that its 'death' was not 'final', thus mirroring his treatment of the themes of life and mortality in this collection.

subjected to violence, as appears in the second stanza: 'enquanto ele me conviva, vivo, | está sujeito a cortes, enxertos' [while it lives in me, alive, | it is subjected to cuts, grafts] (p. 417).

The perception of writing as a source of anxiety and vitality (as conveyed in the cuts/grafts binary) is reflected in the fluidity with which the reader is led in a to and fro movement between images of life and death, towards the visualization of the poem as a hybrid entity which takes on both human and plant form, suggested respectively in the allusions to its 'stutter', for example, and the grafts quoted above.

On a linguistic level, this tension is also achieved through the evocative manipulation of double meanings. In the first line of the poem, Cabral introduces his latest work by stating: 'Eis mais um livro (fio que o ultimo)' (p. 417) [Here is another book (I believe to be my last)]. His choice of the verb form 'fio' as a synonym of the Portuguese *confio, acredito* [trust, believe] in preference to others is suggestive, since it can also be the Portuguese for knife-edge, as in *fio da navalha*, which is evoked obliquely in the poem's images of mutilation. Similarly, ambiguity is conveyed in the penultimate stanza, where 'as quatro operações' (p. 417) [the four operations] refer to the unstable condition of poems, existing on a knife-edge between life and death. Cabral here plays with the double meaning of the term 'operações', signifying both mathematical and surgical operations, the latter echoed in the references to cuts and amputations discussed earlier. Significantly, references to medical treatments, such as pancreas transplant, fail to point to any full recovery from illness. Moreover, within the pervasiveness of images of cutting and fragmentation, it is noteworthy that the organs mentioned—liver, pancreas, and lungs—are vital in their function of 'breaking down' the body's intake of food and air.

In the final stanza, a parallel is drawn between the poem and cancer, an illness which is paradoxical by its nature, for it uncannily causes death by its very growth. The use of such a simile is extremely revealing of the ambiguity that Cabral saw as inherent to the act of writing, because, as Peixoto commented in connection to his use of the image of cancer in the earlier collection *Museu de tudo*: 'It proposes the process of undoing as inherent to the act of construction, through a metaphor which is new in the work of João Cabral: cancer, malignant and subversive disintegration which underlies the process of constructing.'[21]

---

[21] 'Propõe o desfazer como processo inerente ao ato construtivo, por meio de uma metáfora nova na obra de João Cabral: o câncer, desagregação maligna e subversiva oculta no cerne do construir' (Peixoto, 1983, p. 209).

The association is conveyed through the metaphor of the 'potro solto' [free colt], a creature that resists any form of restraint, be it 'química, cobalto, indivíduo' [chemistry, cobalt, individual] (p. 417).[22] This animal imagery allows Cabral to play with the common expression 'galopante' [galloping] used to refer to full-blown diseases. Echoes of the metaphor Cabral employed in his earlier *Fábula de Anfion* (pp. 87–92), in which poetic composition was visualized as a 'cavalo solto e louco' [free and mad horse] (p. 92), can be detected here, and a key feature of both these renditions is a sense of unpredictability, of the inevitable limitations of human agency.

Yet, while in the 1947 work the creative process was conveyed through images of life and fertility, such as 'semente' [seed] (p. 92) and 'grão de vento' [grain of wind] (p. 92), in the poem of the 1980 collection, the use of ambiguous metaphors emphasizes an acute sense of the transience of existence and, by implication, of writing. Any sense of balance and order is undermined further through the disruption of the linearity of the poem's narrative with an abrupt shift from present to past tense in the penultimate line. In 'O que se diz ao editor a propósito de poemas', therefore, poetry enacts the very processes that define it. Sensitive to the fragility of existence, the writer successfully constructs a vision of reality as fragmented, where ambiguity often remains unresolved.

The origins of such a worldview can be traced in his perception of the human and natural landscape of Pernambuco as fundamentally violent, where the experience of death is overwhelming. This is apparent in compositions such as the eponymous 'A escola das facas' (p. 429), where the themes of cutting and amputation, along with that of education implicit in the title, are developed.

Within a collection in which deferral of meaning is so central to the poet's concerns, it is significant that this piece should not feature as its introductory composition but appear as the fifteenth poem of the volume, thereby duplicating, on a structural level, the deferral that Cabral explored on a thematic one.

The poem is centred on the landscape of the north-east, with violence as its most prominent feature. Even the lush vegetation of the coastal region is, paradoxically, evoked through images associated with death. The leaves of the coconut trees and the sugar cane are visualized as sharp blades through which the south-easterly wind sweeps—a process of

---

[22] 'Cobalto' alludes to 'cobalt 60', used in cancer therapy.

education into violence captured as it progresses through the fertile *zona da mata*: 'cursando as folhas laminadas' [following its course through the blade-like leaves] (p. 429).

According to João Alexandre Barbosa (1986, p. 135), the metaphor of the knife encapsulates Cabral's poetics of contained emotion and economy of vocabulary, thus drawing on an association established in his earlier *Uma faca só lamina*. Yet, one can argue that the knife here embodies the hunger and the violence that define life in the north-east, whose qualities are attributed to living beings and inanimate objects alike. The poem charts the journey of the anthropomorphized *alísio* wind deep into the interior of the north-east, and even in the fertile coastal strip poverty and deprivation are shown to be endemic—'[suas mãos] ganham a fome e o dente da faca' [[its hands] acquire the hunger and teeth of the knife] (p. 429). By the third and final stanza, the *alísio* has reached the arid lands of the *agreste* and *sertão*, and the closing metaphor is one in which the images of the hand and the knife are dramatically conflated. It is in fact as a 'mão cortante e desembainhada' [a hand unsheathed and ready to strike] (p. 429) that the wind blows in those regions, thus conveying the violence between humans and the harshness of the natural landscape.

One can identify in the trajectory of the *alísio* the inverted journey of the thousands of *severinos* who leave the interior of the north-east, where prospects are bleak, in the hope of finding a better life on the fertile and industrialized coastal regions. By retracing their steps in reverse order, Cabral is able to start off by focusing on the violence of the *zona da mata*: 'O coqueiro e a cana lhe ensinam, | sem pedra-mó, mas faca a faca' [The coconut tree and the sugar cane teach it, | without the grindstone, but knife to knife] (p. 429).

The plight of those living in the interior emerges as a consequence of the inequities perpetrated in the more prosperous regions: regardless of the north-east's diverse natural landscapes, deprivation and violence remain its enduring features.

1.3 PERSONAL MEMORY

Cabral's recollections of his early years in Pernambuco revolve around an awakening to the surrounding violence from a very young age. Whether cast in the sombre tone of 'Menino de engenho' (pp. 417–18) or conveyed humorously, as in 'Horácio' (pp. 418–19), his depictions of childhood provide an insight into the poet's obsessive preoccupation with mortality.

The poetic self emerges obliquely, from Cabral's reflections on concrete objects.[23] In the case of 'Menino de engenho', João Alexandre Barbosa comments on how the poet's treatment of memory reveals an 'adequação entre experiência e linguagem' [adjustment between experience and language] (1986, p. 136), given that the restraint with which the expression of subjectivity is articulated stems from the uncompromising reality around him, where lyrical sentimentality was uncalled for (1986, p. 136). However, in spite of the economy with which the self is treated, a complex set of experiences emerges from the contact with the outside world narrated in the first poem of the collection.

The poem's title, 'Menino de engenho', suggests an obvious intertextuality with the homonymous 1932 debut novel by fellow north-eastern writer José Lins do Rego, to whom Cabral paid homage.[24] Yet, his appropriation of Rego's title draws as much attention to the regionalist themes he shared with the novelist as to his different approach to them, therefore playing on the ambiguity underlying his dialogue with his fellow writer. Unlike Rego's occasionally nostalgic descriptions of the disappearing world of the pre-industrial rural estates (*engenhos*), the poet's reminiscence of the past is not idealized.[25] As he focuses on an incident during which, as a boy, he was cut by the blade-like foliage of a sugar cane plant, Cabral's concern is with the human suffering on the

---

[23] Barbosa (1986, p. 135) commented on how Cabral's autobiographical stance emerges obliquely, in line with what he had identified as the defining principle of Cabral's writing process, 'a imitação da forma' [the imitation of form]. According to Barbosa: 'João Cabral [...] foi literalmente *aprendendo* com os objetos uma forma de *imitar* a realidade. Para dizer tudo: a sua é antes uma *imitação da forma* do que de conteúdos dados pelo real' [João Cabral literally learned from concrete objects ways of imitating reality. In other words: his is above all an *imitation of form* rather than of content provided by reality]. See João A. Barbosa, *A imitação da forma* (São Paulo: Duas Cidades, 1975), p. 153.

[24] Cabral dedicated his book *Serial* (published in the collection *Terceira feira*, in 1961) to José Lins do Rego. The writer is also mentioned in the poem 'O circo', of *Crime na Calle Relator*, as one of the most reliable sources of information on life on the plantations (p. 608).

[25] Rego's more forgiving rendition of life on the plantations in relation to Cabral's is exemplified in the following description of the *flagelados*, which is how the rural migrants fleeing the droughts are known: 'O engenho e a casa da farinha repletos de flagelados [...] conversavam sobre os incidentes [...] achando graça até nas peripécias de salvamento' [The sugar cane mill and the manioc flour mill filled with migrants [...] chatting about the accidents [...] even laughing about the drama of their rescue] (*Menino de engenho* [Lisbon: Livros do Brasil, n.d.], p. 33). The harmonious view of life in the *engenho* is also explored by Rego: 'Nas cozinhas das casas-grandes vivem as brancas e as negras, nessa conversas como de igual para igual' [In the kitchens of the masters' houses, white and black women mix, chatting as though they were equals] (p. 95).

plantations and the lasting psychological effects of his encounter with this world.

The opening line of the poem is eerily lapidary and introduces the theme of violence through a metaphor of destruction, while a full stop syntactically cuts off the opening sentence from the rest of the composition: 'A cana cortada é uma foice' [The cut down sugar cane plant is a scythe] (p. 417). Here, the scythe evokes the image of the Grim Reaper, the 'inexorável igualizadora' [inexorable leveller],[26] in an image which turns what is normally an object of violence (the sugar cane) into an instrument of destruction, thanks to a two-way exchange, 'em dar-se mútuo' [in mutual giving] (p. 418). The violent encounter remembered in this poem illustrates one of the recurring principles of the world that emerges from Cabral's poetry, and which Peixoto described as the 'princípio de transferência de qualidades' [principle of transferral of qualities] (1983, p. 212).

For Peixoto, the manner in which the child's interaction with the world is presented reveals a significant shift in authorial perspective in relation to earlier collections. The emphasis is no longer being placed on rationality but rather on pre-rational, childhood experiences of violence, which modulate the narrative voice (1983, p. 215). In this respect, for Peixoto 'Menino de engenho' challenges the established view of a 'rational' Cabral and stresses the emotiveness involved in the experience described: 'What was a process of learning and conscious imitation becomes unintentional infection. Unlike the stone, the sugar cane does not educate an attentive pupil, but cuts him as it strikes.'[27]

Secchin (1985, p. 276) argues that 'Menino de engenho' could be read as a poem of initiation, charting Cabral's journey against lyric conventions, but if so, it is one involving what can be described as a negative epiphany: there is no moment of revelation for a child left with unanswered questions, still striving to make sense of his experience.

Pivotal in this process is once again the image of the knife-edge. As it revisits the moment in which the boy came into contact with the sharp-edged sugar cane plant, the poem plays on the paradoxical idea of the scar received at once being and not being there: 'e uma cicatriz, que não

---

[26] Jean Chevalier and Alain Gheerbant, *Dicionário de símbolos*, 6th edn, trans. Vera da Costa e Silva and others, ed. Carlos Süssekind (Rio de Janeiro: José Olympio, 1992), p. 443.

[27] 'O que era aprendizado e imitação consciente faz-se contágio involuntário. Ao contrário da pedra, a cana não educa um aluno atento, mas o atinge com seu corte' (Peixoto, 1983, p. 213).

guardo, | soube dentro de mim guardar-se' [and a scar, which I no longer have | was able to leave its mark in me] (p. 418).

The use of repetition in these lines duplicates the oscillating movements of the scythe, which also mirrors the act of remembering in its 'bringing back' what is effectively removed in space and time. With its challenge to the dualities of presence/absence (of the object of memory) and disparity/identity (of the sugar cane and the scythe), the poem also questions the very nature of the injury suffered by the boy: was what was inoculated a virus or vaccine? Cabral fails to provide a definitive answer to this point, deliberately foregrounding the fact that the distinction between these categories is not always clear for the reason that both involve contact with a potentially harmful foreign body.

The broader implications of the episode recounted here take us back once again to the legacy of the poet's north-eastern background: Cabral seems bent on allowing his readers to draw their own conclusions as to whether it was thanks to his experience of the north-east that he was able to scrutinize the injustices of its socio-economic structures, or whether it was because of the unique insight he gained into the reality of the north-east that he was forever drawn to it, engaging with the question of mortality almost obsessively. By leaving the question unanswered, Cabral seems to suggest that the answer lies somewhere in between.

A startling shift in mood occurs in the following poem, 'Horácio', with its humorous rendition of one of the most memorable characters in *A escola das facas*. The story of the alcoholic Horácio's squandering on *cachaça* [sugar cane spirit] the money destined to keep the caged birds entrusted to him alive is recounted by way of double meanings (through the alternation of 'alpiste' [bird food] and 'cachaça' [sugar cane spirit]) (pp. 418–19) and colloquial Portuguese.

'Horácio' opens in a fashion similar to the preceding poem, with a laconic and almost lapidary one-line verse, punctuated with a full stop at the end: 'O bêbado cabal.' [The perfect drunk] (p. 418). The lack of any verb conveys a sense of stasis that is associated with those incapacitated by drink, and can also be seen as mirroring the drunk's inability to construct grammatical sentences. Additionally, and on a structural level, this syntactical truncation seems to reflect the theme of finality developed in the poem.

On centre stage is the figure of Horácio, who indulged in *cachaça* instead of providing for the birds that the young poet and other schoolchildren trusted to his care. As in the preceding poem, the experience of childhood is here also associated with illness (*doença*):

Life on a knife-edge: A escola das facas 35

> Quando nós, de meninos,
> vivemos a doença
> de criar passarinhos. (p. 418)

[When as young children, | we used to go mad over | keeping birds.]

As the poem progresses into the second stanza, Cabral draws a parallel between the caged birds and the 'imprisoned' children, treated as animals in the 'rotina de rês' [routine of cattle] (p. 418) that was school. The abrupt curtailment of the children's freedom is captured in the reference to the end of the holidays and emphasized by the insertion of the hyphen in the inevitable 'horrível outra-vez | do colégio' [horrible back-to-school] (p. 418), in which a sense of the imminent resumption of formal education is conveyed.

Instability rather than stability defines the moment focused in the poem; the brevity of the freedom enjoyed by the children is mirrored in the uncertainty surrounding the condition of the birds themselves. We learn how the small change left by the children was aimed at being spent on 'keeping them alive', thereby suggesting an imminent danger of death. Indeed, the sense of foreboding that this implies is confirmed in the following stanza, where we discover that within a couple of days the birds are indeed dead, strikingly visualized in the image of the personified 'silent' cages, the 'gaiolas sem língua' [cages without tongues] (p. 418). Here, the denouement acquires a tragic dimension of greater proportions, since the cages become a haunting metaphor for the devastating reality of the north-east: 'eram tumbas aéreas | de morte nordestina' [they were aerial tombs | of north-eastern death] (p. 418).

In spite of the humorous mood of the poem, a serious social point is being made here: that the excesses of the few inevitably redound in the deprivation for others, at any socio-economic level. Despite his low social standing, implied by his addiction to *cachaça*, Horácio is the 'master' in relation to the caged birds, and their death is the immediate result of his neglect.

This broad social critique accounts for Cabral's use of black humour in what is only superficially a light-hearted anecdote. Indeed, if Secchin (1985, pp. 278–9) has argued that Horácio exemplifies one of Cabral's positive characterizations of the poor inhabitants of the *engenhos*, by attributing to him the ability to break from the dominant order through alcohol, it can equally be said that Horácio emerges as much a marginalized figure in society as an oppressor himself. On this point too, it seems, a deliberate challenge to established dualities (in this case, victim/dominant order) is at play.

Thus, as Barbosa (1986, p. 137) commented, like *Museu de tudo*, *A escola das facas* represents a shift from lucidity towards playfulness, with no prejudice to the former. Indeed, thanks to skilful wordplay, 'Horácio' incorporates humour without losing sight of a clear social purpose. For example, a remarkable shift from the initial sombre mood is achieved through Cabral's humorous employment of the word 'alpiste', with its double meaning of bird food and, in colloquial Brazilian Portuguese, of *cachaça*. Paradoxically, the 'alpiste' [bird food] that Horácio did not buy for the birds becomes the 'alpiste-cachaça' [bird food-spirit] (p. 419) to whose temptation he soon succumbs, and which, in turn, stands as a counterpoint to the free water that he did not care to replenish. The weaving of colloquial expressions that Horácio himself would easily have used, such as 'alpiste', infuses the poem with local colour. Furthermore, thanks to this use of colloquialisms the anecdote emerges as an imaginative and carefully crafted paraphrase of the Brazilian expression according to which *cachaça* is 'água que passarinho não bebe' [water that birds don't drink].

Such playfulness is reinforced by the ambiguous image of the birds in the closing lines of the poem. Here, they are simultaneously dead in their cages and alive in the singing of the drunken Horácio, suggesting the tenuous the line between life and mortality: 'alma do passarinho | que em suas veias cantava' [the soul of the bird | which sang in his veins] (p. 419).

As he draws the readers into his own witty, riddle-like poem, Cabral seeks answers on the unresolved issues of north-eastern reality, for beyond his jocular linguistic manipulation, a desire to challenge complacency and articulate urgent social concerns is revealed.

1.4 NATIONAL MEMORY

In addition to Cabral's excursions into personal memory, *A escola das facas* includes a substantial number of poems on Pernambuco's history of political unrest. Its principal historical theme revolves around the movements of 1817 and 1824, both aimed at the independence of Pernambuco: the first from the Portuguese Crown, the second from the newly proclaimed Empire of Brazil. Poems such as 'Abreu e Lima'

(p. 440)[28] and 'Um poeta pernambucano' (pp. 448–9)[29] exemplify Cabral's fascination with history and his attachment to his native land. It was this attachment that motivated Cabral to research Brazil's revolutionary movements. In his interview with Gilson Rebello, the 'incurable Pernambucan' acknowledged: 'At the moment, I am interested in studying Latin America's struggles for independence, because I've found out that many Pernambucans had direct association with Simón Bolívar, such as Natividade Saldanha, to whom I dedicated a poem.'[30]

[28] The title bears the name of Captain José Inácio de Abreu e Lima, who was the son of Padre Roma, one of the leaders of the 1817 uprising. Padre Roma's arrest for conspiracy coincided with his son's detention in the same prison under the accusation of insubordinate behaviour in the army. Padre Roma was sentenced to death soon after his arrest, and Abreu e Lima witnessed the execution. See Pedro Calmon, *História do Brasil*, 7 vols, 2nd edn (Rio de Janeiro: José Olympio, 1963), IV, 1468–9; and Brasil Bandecchi and others, *Novo dicionário da história do Brasil* (São Paulo: Melhoramentos, 1971), p. 18. Abreu e Lima's own involvement in Latin America's struggle for independence provided the inspiration for Cabral's poem.

[29] Born in Pernambuco in 1796, the poet and republican revolutionary José da Natividade Saldanha took part in the uprising of 1824, which culminated in the proclamation of the short-lived independent republic in the north-east known as the Confederação do Equador. He fought alongside Frei Caneca, protagonist of Cabral's following work, *Auto do frade*. After the rebellion was crushed, Natividade Saldanha escaped the death penalty by fleeing abroad, dying in Colombia in 1830. (*Grande enciclopédia portuguesa e brasileira*, 40 vols, ed. Magnus Bergström and others [Lisbon: Editorial Enciclopédia Ltda, 1936–87], XXVI, n.d., 708). Saldanha wrote poetry of nativist inspiration and he features in Sérgio Buarque de Holanda's *Antologia dos poetas brasileiros da fase colonial* (São Paulo: Perspectiva, 1979), pp. 471–84. He is, however, one of the lesser-known poets, testified by the fact that Alfredo Bosi makes but a cursory reference to his literary output, highlighting his political involvement in the activities instead (*História concisa da literatura brasileira*, 3rd edn [São Paulo: Cultrix, 1990], p. 92). Revealing Cabral's obsession with mortality, the poem recalls the bizarre circumstances surrounding Saldanha's death: while living in exile in Bogotá, he drowned after falling in a gutter during a storm, supposedly while under the influence of alcohol.

[30] 'Atualmente estou muito interessado em estudar os movimentos de independência na América Latina, porque descobri que vários pernambucanos estavam diretamente ligados a Simón Bolívar, como Natividade Saldanha, a quem dediquei um poema', in Rebello (p. 41). Cabral's attitude towards contemporary politics seems to have been defined by the same regionalist bias. Asked about how he voted in the first direct presidential elections since the end of the military dictatorship of 1964–85, Cabral replied provocatively: 'Eu sou pernambucano, então voto em Pernambuco. Se se provasse que Satanás é pernambucano, eu votaria nele. [...] Votei em Lula que é pernambucano também' [I am from Pernambuco, therefore I vote for Pernambucans. If it was proved that Satan was Pernambucan, I would vote for him. [...] I voted for Lula, who is also from Pernambuco] (in Leite Neto, p. 6).

An exception among the historical poems, 'Vicente Yáñez Pinzón' (p. 441) goes back over five hundred years and deals with the controversial circumstances of the discovery of Brazil.[31] In the poem, Cabral dismisses official narratives of the discovery by the Portuguese and focuses on the Spanish landing at the Cabo de Santo Agostinho, an episode which the poet infuses with a sense of absence and loss.

Almost fifty years prior to the publication of *A escola das facas*, the poet Murilo Mendes, whom Cabral considered one of his masters,[32] had also been inspired by the controversial figure of Pinzón and had included a poem on the Spanish discoverer in his collection *História do Brasil*, of 1932. This volume is informed by the playful irreverence typical of the early modernist movement, and particularly that of the *Pau-Brasil* poetry,[33] from which Mendes distanced himself in favour of a more solemn mood in later works.[34]

Mendes's decision to preface his parody of historical narratives with the poem 'Prefácio de Pinzón'[35] supports the Spaniard's situation 'at the

---

[31] Although largely omitted from the official historiography, Pinzón is known to have discovered Brazil on 26 January 1500, therefore three months before Pedro Álvares Cabral landed on the coast of Bahia. According to accounts such as those of Juan Manzano Manzano and Frei Bartolomé de las Casas, the Spanish navigator's first sighting of the American sub-continent was of the coast of Pernambuco and, more specifically, of what is today the Cabo de Santo Agostinho, which he named Cabo Santa Maria de la Consolación. (For further information on Pinzón's travels to Brazil, including to the Amazon river, see Frey Bartolomé de las Casas, *Historia de las Indias*, 3 vols, ed. Agustín Millares Carlo [Mexico: Fondo de Cultura Económica, 1951], I, 58, and Juan Manzano Manzano, *Los Pinzones y el descubrimiento de América*, 3 vols [Madrid: Cultura Hispánica, 1988], I, 201–97).

[32] On the subject of Murilo Mendes's early influence on his career, Cabral stated in his interview with Alceu Amoroso Lima: 'Creio que nenhum poeta brasileiro me ensinou como ele a importância do visual sobre o conceitual, do plástico sobre o musical' [I believe that no other Brazilian poet taught me as much as he did about the importance of the visual over the conceptual, over the musical] (in Freyre and others, p. 112).

[33] Oswald de Andrade's *Pau-Brasil* collection, first published in 1925, also included a group of poems entitled *História do Brasil*. However, the figure of Pinzón did not feature in the collection, which opens with the poem 'Pero Vaz Caminha', name of the scribe who authored the famous *Carta*, the letter to the Portuguese monarch detailing the arrival of the Portuguese in Brazil, and whose account the poem parodies.

[34] Murilo Mendes considered the satirical tone of *História do Brasil* incongruous within his *œuvre* and for this reason did not include the collection in the 1959 edition of his complete works. See the introduction 'Pequena história da *História do Brasil* de Murilo Mendes' in *História do Brasil*, ed. and intro. Luciana Stegagno Picchio (Rio de Janeiro: Nova Fronteira, 1991), p. 5.

[35] Murilo Mendes, *Poesia completa e prosa*, ed and intro. Luciana Stegagno Picchio (Rio de Janeiro: Nova Aguilar, 1994), p. 143.

margins' of official historiography.[36] Differing from Mendes's rendition of the theme, Cabral omits any reference to the official discovery of Brazil by the Portuguese Pedro Álvares Cabral and includes his poem on Pinzón in mid-collection, thus placing this controversial episode at the very heart of his account of the history of his country. In line with this approach, Cabral's sombre mood contrasts with the abrasive humour of Mendes's verse, which we find in the opening lines of his 'Prefácio de Pinzón', with its allusion to Brazil as Portugal's rural outpost: 'Quem descobriu a fazenda, | Por San Tiago, fomos nós' [It was we who discovered the estate, | in the name of St James] (p. 143).

Cabral's poem opens with an uncompromising historical statement, 'dethroning' the official discoverer of Brazil and pointing to Pernambuco (rather than Bahia) as the scene of the discovery: 'Ele o primeiro a vê-lo, e a vir, | (na barra do Suape) ao Brasil' [He who first saw it, and came here, | (to the port of Suape) to Brazil] (p. 441).

The parentheses in the second line literally enclose the 'barra do Suape' and separate it from 'Brazil', as well as from the earlier references to verbs of vision and motion, 'ver' [to see] and 'vir' [to come]. Punctuation, then, becomes a graphic means by which the 'disregard' for the true circumstances surrounding the arrival of the Europeans in Brazil is conveyed. A similar result is achieved by the insertion of the comma in the first line, 'a vê-lo, e a vir', which syntactically 'cuts' between the verbs of 'seeing' and 'coming', thereby connoting the ultimate abandonment by the Spanish discoverer. The outcome of the episode at hand is confirmed in the following line, where Pinzón is described as leaving no traces of his presence: 'não deixou lá quandos nem ondes: | só anos depois confessou-se' [he left no whens nor wheres there: | he only confessed years later] (p. 441).

The use of adverbs of time and place as nouns produces the startling effect of highlighting precisely the lack of concrete time and place references, in reflection of the lack of information available on Pinzón's Brazilian legacy and drawing attention to the fact that the Spanish presence in the country was short-lived.

Yet, the aim here is not simply to debunk official narratives of the discovery, in an attempt to undermine the Portuguese. This is because Pinzón's integrity also comes under scrutiny, thanks to the reference to

---

[36] Mendes followed this introductory poem with three satirical compositions on the Portuguese arrival on Brazilian shores, respectively, '1500', 'O farrista' and 'Carta de Pero Vaz'.

what Cabral suggests as being his 'confession', censuring him for turning his back on the newly discovered land and casting him as a father figure guilty of abandoning an unwanted child.

It is also as a 'confession' that, in the following couplet, Cabral quotes Pinzón's description of the north-east as 'a terra de mais luz da Terra' [the place with the brightest light on earth] (p. 441).[37] Counter to the Edenic vision of the New World outlined in the *Carta* by Pero Vaz de Caminha, the official chronicle of the Portuguese arrival in Brazil, Cabral attributes to Pinzón a sense of foreboding in relation to what ensued. The light of the region is described as a metallic light which prefigured the violence that was to come:

> Ele, talvez, nessa luz tanta
> tenha pressentido a arma-branca
>
> com que em tudo se expressaria
> a gente que lá, algum dia. (p. 441)

[He, perhaps, in the brightness of that light | sensed the presence of the knife | with which in everything the people would express themselves | people who there, one day.][38]

These negative renditions of light within the context of the north-east contrast with positive representations found in Cabral's earlier work, a case in point being the poem 'Paisagem pelo telefone' (pp. 225–7), published in *Quaderna*, in 1960. In this piece, the vision of the seascape evoked by the woman does not suggest violence, but is exhilarating and liberating:

> de jangadas, que são velas
> mais brancas porque salinas,
>
> que, como muros caiados
> possuem luz intestina. (p. 226)

---

[37] Cabral confirmed to Professor Secchin that he had extracted the quotation from Pinzón's own account of his journey to Brazil. I am grateful to Professor Secchin for sharing this information with me. Pinzón's response to the north-east clearly held considerable resonance for the poet, since he incorporated the same quotation ('terra de mais luz da terra') in the earlier poem 'O Cabo de Santo Agostinho' (p. 408), included in *Museu de tudo*. In this composition too, Pinzón's vision is inscribed within negative configurations of Brazil's colonial past—the brightness of the landscape being associated with the natural resources to which the navigators were drawn.

[38] Cabral's spelling of 'arma-branca' [literally, 'white weapon', i.e. knife] with a hyphen (not necessary in Portuguese) seems to establish a closer correlation between nature (implied in the use of 'branca' [white], suggestive of 'luz branca' [white light]) and the culture of violence (encapsulated in the reference to 'arma' [weapon]).

[of sailing rafts, whose sails | are whiter because on the salty sea | and which, like whitewashed walls, | are endowed with internal light].

The poet's imagined unclothing of the female body as he speaks to his lover on the telephone is thus visualized in a landscape filled with light, where nature and cultural constructs appear in harmony, as the irradiant whitewashed walls exemplify. Almost everything in the landscape pictured in this early poem is a source of light, from the sails out at sea to the woman herself: 'a água clara não te acende: | libera a luz que já tinhas' [the clear water does not light you up: | it releases the light already in you] (p. 227).

No such harmony between nature and culture is articulated in 'Vicente Yáñez Pinzón', where the critical perspective adopted in relation to the colonial experience means that the 'meio-dia mineral' [mineral noon] of the earlier poem is re-worked into the more threatening image. The gleam of the metal light that fills the landscape evokes the violence brought about by the greed of explorers and settlers alike, 'dazzled' by the possibility of finding gold on Brazilian soil. It is for this reason, it seems, that Cabral innovatively employs the intransitive verb 'enceguecendo' [to become blind] transitively, rather than using 'cegar' [to blind] thereby emphasizing that the causes of destruction associated with the knife stem precisely from within the New World (its riches) and its visitors (their greed):

> Ele se foi só por que não?
> [...]
> ou porque aquela
> luz metal, que corta e encandeia,
> acabaria enceguecendo
> mesmo o andaluz mais sarraceno? (p. 441)

[Did he leave just because 'why not'? | or because that | metal light, that cuts and dazzles, | would end up blinding | even the most Saracenic of Andalusians?]

From the third stanza onwards (and over the following six out of a total of ten) the composition includes four questions, directed at Pinzón, about the reasons for him not settling in Brazil. The poem asks why Brazil did not manage to make him stay, and the synecdoche employed here, 'não prendeu muito tempo os pés' [did not keep hold of his feet for long] (p. 441), contributes to the general sense of cutting and alienation that the poem conveys. The synecdoche is followed by a series of geographical references that establishes Pinzón's origins:

> homem de Palos de Moguer,
> Moguer, da clara, Andaluzia,
> caiada em Cádiz, em Sevilha. (p. 441)

[man from Palos de Moguer, | Moguer, the bright, Andalusia, | whitewashed in Cadiz, in Seville.]

The repetition of 'Moguer' on two separate lines conveys Pinzón's longing for his native land, also suggested by the separation of the adjective 'clara' from 'Andaluzia' by way of punctuation. Such references to Spanish locations suggest the wish to give a detailed account of Pinzón's roots, which contrasts with the dearth of accurate accounts of Brazil's colonial history.

As Cabral probes into the reasons for Pinzón's departure, he enquires whether it was because of the boundaries stipulated in the Tordesillas Treaty (1494) by the imperial powers of the Iberian Peninsula:

> Ele se foi por que não?
> Por ver-se na demarcação
> de Portugal? (p. 441)

[Did he leave just because 'why not'? | Because he found himself within the boundaries | of Portugal?]

Thanks to the enjambement in these lines, Cabral is deliberately disrupting the 'boundaries' between the couplets in question, subtly but subversively criticizing the political boundaries of colonial rule on which the future of his country hinged.

Another explanation for Pinzón's short-lived stay in Brazil is hazarded in the last two couplets of the poem, where it is suggested that the Spaniard's departure might have been prompted by his realization that violence, above all else, was to define human relationships in the northeast (as encapsulated in the image of the 'arma-branca'). On a metatextual level, Cabral suggests that such violence was instrumental in shaping his own style of writing. Indeed, the image of the 'arma-branca', which defines the way north-easterners communicate and interact, can be read as a metaphor for Cabral's elliptical style—conjuring up the vision of the knife (ellipsis) and of the white page (silence)—whose economy of means resulted in an effective idiom of social critique.

Such interpretation seems to be justified in the closing line of the poem, in which the verb is omitted: 'a gente que lá, algum dia', which can literally be translated as 'the people who there, one day' (p. 441). The absence of a verb in this reference to the people of the north-east (including Cabral himself) which might define their relationship with the region, be it 'viver' [to live] or 'estar' [to be], for example, evocatively incorporates the themes of cutting and amputation (explored earlier in the collection) on a stylistic level. This conveys both the social alienation (invisibility) of the people and their history of migration to other regions. The poet himself left his native land as a young man to improve his career prospects, and it is noteworthy that Cabral's own distance from his native land should mirror the 'absence' of its first discoverer.

Thus, 'Vicente Yáñez Pinzón' exemplifies how Cabral's focus on violence in his treatment of the historical theme in *A escola das facas* is coherent with the other main thematic threads of the collection, and indeed, its overall structure. Moreover, his treatment of the binaries of life and death in this poem illustrates how his writing reflects the paradoxes of Brazilian history, encapsulated in the moment of its discovery, where life and destruction are intimately associated. Therefore, I would concur with Jaime Guinsburg when he noted: 'The logic that presides over Cabral's aesthetic aims is, in a way, similar to the way in which Brazil's history evolved.'[39]

1.5 TWO CLOSING POEMS

The lack of closure that Cabral often explored on a thematic level is reflected on a structural level by the existence of two different formats of *A escola das facas*. In the edition of Cabral's *Obra completa*, of 1994, the collection closed with the poem 'Porto dos Cavalos' (pp. 460–1), while all other editions ended with the shorter poem 'Autocrítica' (p. 456). This decision exposes two differing authorial stances, whose implications deserve to be probed further.

'Autocrítica' articulates the anxieties of a typically self-deprecating poet, whose concerns are also echoed in the preceding composition, 'De volta ao Cabo de Santo Agostinho' (p. 456). There, the poet voiced his scepticism in relation to the efficacy of his poetics of objectivity as an instrument of social and political critique, 'de ter

---

[39] 'A lógica que preside a concepção estética de Cabral é de certo modo análoga a um traço das bases de composição da experiência histórica brasileira.' See 'Morte e origem: notas sobre o dualismo na poesia de João Cabral de Melo Neto', in *João Cabral em perspectiva*, ed. Maria do Carmo Campos (Porto Alegre: Editora da Universidade/ UFRGS, 1995), pp. 37–48 (p. 47).

dado a ver' [to have brought to light] (p. 456), whereas the closing poem focuses on the themes developed through these poetics of the concrete world.

By its very title, 'Autocrítica' denounces the poet's unease at only being able to engage with a limited range of subjects—Pernambuco and Andalusia being the two fundamental sources of inspiration for his work:

> Só duas coisas conseguiram
> (des)feri-lo até a poesia:
> o Pernambuco de onde veio
> e o aonde foi, a Andaluzia.
> Um, o vacinou do falar rico
> e deu-lhe a outra, fêmea e viva,
> desafio demente: em verso
> dar a ver Sertão e Sevilha. (p. 456)

[Only two things managed | to lead him to write: | Pernambuco where he was from | and Andalusia, where he went. | The first, vaccinated him against high-sounding language | and the other, female and alive, | gave him a crazy challenge: | to show, in verse, *Sertão* and Seville.]

Cabral associates the origins of his writing with pain and suffering, as suggested in the play on words in the opening lines. Here, the theme of cutting that Cabral had explored in earlier poems is conveyed in the use of brackets in '(des)feri-lo', which provide the visual representation of separation of the verbs 'desferir' (among whose meanings are 'to throw' or 'to hit') and 'ferir' (to hurt, to wound). Through just such play on words, the image of the knife is evoked, even though it is not developed explicitly. In fact, the playful use of '(des)ferir' suggests that violence underpins the very origins of the creative process, in line with, for example, 'Menino de engenho'. This substantiates Marta Peixoto's observation that 'struggle and violence emerge throughout his work, continually redefined and in new combinations'.[40]

Cabral's perception of Pernambuco and Andalusia as landscapes which have the power to wound (conveyed by the verb 'ferir') means that they are initially subsumed within the sphere of death, although the very categories of life and death are subsequently shown to be unstable. Indeed, although Andalusia is described as 'viva', it is capable of triggering some degree of psychological disorder ('desafio demente', i.e. crazy challenge). And while Pernambuco is juxtaposed with the

---

[40] 'A luta e violência perduram em toda a obra, redefinindo-se e formando novas articulações' (Peixoto, 1983, p. 14).

'female and alive' Andalusia, it is also associated with health, as implied by the reference to vaccination in relation to the poetic language he developed, which rejected the 'falar rico'.

In the light of this, it becomes clear that by choosing this poem to close the collection, Cabral intended it to provide an answer to the question that had remained unsolved in 'Menino de engenho'. In that poem, the question of Pernambuco's legacy in Cabral's poetry remained open, whereas in 'Autocrítica' it is shown to be a 'vacina' rather than a 'vírus', suggesting Cabral's sense of accomplishment at having developed a style and language that were far removed from the 'falar rico'. In this way, 'Menino de engenho' and 'Autocrítica', dealing respectively with the poet's childhood and maturity, frame the collection in a logical sequence, bringing the poet's enquiry into the theme of education within the reality of the north-east to a coherent conclusion.[41]

'Autocrítica' demonstrates that rather than just being two contrasting *topoi*, as Peixoto (1983, p. 214) observed in relation to this poem, the treatment of Pernambuco and Andalusia encapsulates precisely Cabral's debunking of polarizations. On a structural level, the use of a single eight-line stanza conveys the closeness of these seemingly disparate realities.

A similar conflation of binary oppositions occurs in 'Porto dos Cavalos' (pp. 460–1), the closing poem of the 1994 edition. The poem is set along the banks of the river Capibaribe and revisits places the poet knew well as a young boy. Ambiguity underpins Cabral's engagement with his native land, as he describes himself as the 'amigo-inimigo' [friend-enemy] (p. 461) of the Capibaribe river, a metaphor of the poor and oppressed for whom he purported to speak. The reasons behind his dual role as friend/enemy are the fact that Cabral's self-appointed role as champion of the disenfranchised was somewhat at odds with his position as a member of one of the landed families of Pernambuco. Being part of the educated elite, his rendition of the plight of the poor would inevitably be articulated

---

[41] *A escola das facas* is, therefore, a carefully structured volume of poems—more so than the poet, it seems, wished his readers to believe: 'Sim, poemas soltos, como no meu último livro, *Museu de tudo*, lançado em 1975. Os meus livros anteriores tinham um plano. Mas depois que eu fiz 60 anos perdi a paciência de escrever poemas longos, trabalhados. Os livros vão saindo aos poucos, à medida que a gaveta enche. Foi assim que saiu *Museu de tudo* e é assim que apareceu *A escola das facas*' [Yes, poems thrown in together, like in my last book, *Museu de tudo*, published in 1975. My earlier books had an overall plan. But after I turned 60 I lost the stamina to write long, constructed poems. My books are published little by little, as my cupboards fill up. It was like that with *Museu de tudo* and it was how *A escola das facas* came about] (interview with Benício Medeiros, 'João Cabral, nu e cru', *IstoÉ*, 5 November 1980, pp. 52–5 (p. 52)).

'noutro ritmo' [in another rhythm] (p. 461) from that of the marginalized population of the *mangues* of Recife, which the Capibaribe embodies.

Ambiguity is also integral to the representation of the most disadvantaged. The poem makes several allusions to the stories told by the Capibaribe, though the actual content of these narratives is conspicuous by its absence. By playing on what is not openly mentioned, Cabral is effectively duplicating the invisibility of the poor and marginalized, while concurrently pointing to the fact that their silence is pregnant with meaning:

> o Capibaribe, em silêncio
> (pouco ele foi de sobressaltos),
>
> o Capibaribe repete
> o que diz e contei no 'Rio'
> Me diz de viés, não me diz. (p. 461)

[the Capibaribe, silently | (he was never one for causing a stir), | the Capibaribe repeats | what he says and what I recounted in 'O Rio' | He tells me obliquely, doesn't tell me.]

Cabral draws an explicit parallel between the voice of the river, 'sua voz são os cheiros que lembram' [his voice is the smells that remind me of things] (p. 461),[42] and Proust's famous episode with the *madeleine* in *À la recherche du temps perdu*.[43] In both instances of remembrance, the

---

[42] In editions of the poem other than that of 1994, the line reads 'sua voz é o perfume que apresenta' [his voice is the perfume that presents]. The more prosaic noun 'cheiro' [smell] which substituted 'perfume' [perfume] was probably felt to be more appropriate to the landscape of poverty alluded to in this poem. If the visual impact provided by the use of 'apresenta' [presents] was somewhat diminished by Cabral's use of 'lembram' [remind], it was none the less maintained to some degree by the verb 'convoca' [summons] in the closing line. It exemplifies the poet's aim when dealing with the theme of memory: 'Minha poesia é um esforço de "presentificação", de "coisificação" da memória' [My poetry is an attempt by memory to 'make present', to 'make concrete']. See interview with Alfredo Bosi and others, 'Considerações do poeta em vigília', in *João Cabral de Melo Neto. Cadernos de literatura brasileira*, ed. Antonio Fernando de Franceschi (Rio de Janeiro: Instituto Moreira Salles, 1996), pp. 18–31 (p. 31).

[43] Cabral was an avid reader of Proust—see, for example, interview with Luiz Costa Lima and others, 'João Cabral de Melo Neto', *34 Letras*, 3 (1989), 8–45 (p. 38). The poet dedicated a composition to the French writer in *Museu de tudo*. In 'Proust e seu livro' (p. 412), writing and life are intertwined, 'com a vida e a obra emaranhadas' [with life and works bound up together] (p. 412). Conversely, bringing the process of writing to an end is associated with death: 'acabá-la [a obra] | era matar-se em livro, suicidá-lo' [to end it | was to kill oneself in the book | to suicide it] (p. 412). In a subversion of grammatical norm, the verb 'suicidar' is used transitively, thereby alluding simultaneously to the death of the author and of the work of literature. Consistent with the poet's disruption of fixed boundaries, on a linguistic level, definitions of writer and writing, humans and inanimate beings are shown to be indistinct.

past is symbolically brought back to life through memory; like the taste of the *madeleine* in Proust, the smells exuding from the river evoke a world that no longer exists. This allusion to times gone by recalls Cabral's obsession with finality, which informs his rendition of the setting of 'Porto dos Cavalos' as a space in between life and death. The pervasiveness of death is encoded in the landscape familiar to the poet, as is shown in the opening lines of the second stanza: 'Havia oitizeiros (cortados), | as casas de tios passados' [There were *oitizeiro* trees (cut), | the houses of dead uncles] (p. 460). The name of the location seems to encapsulate the elusiveness of reality, as in the third stanza: 'Depois, o Porto dos Cavalos, | de nome gratuito ou perdido' [Then, the Port of Horses, | a name gratuitous or of forgotten origin] (p. 461).

Whether it is gratuitous or whether its origin has been 'lost' in time, either way the name 'Porto dos Cavalos' carries with it a sense of void, since it is ascribed to something that never existed or no longer does.[44] The sense in which the world is perceived in a state of flux results in Cabral drawing attention not only to what is no longer present (such as the trees that have been cut down) but also to what is not immediately obvious to the naked eye. A case in point is found in his reference to the well-disguised gyratory window built into the Hospital da Roda, in which unwanted newborn babies could be left: 'há o muro secreto da Roda, | como a caridade, caiado' [there is the secret wall of the Roda, | whitewashed, like charity] (p. 460).[45]

Therefore, as it articulates Cabral's reflections of writing and memory, this poem too deals with the lessons learnt during his years in Pernambuco, his 'escola das facas', and portrays a world that is fundamentally elusive. Yet, the poet here is less critical and less apologetic about his choice of subject matter than in 'Autocrítica' and, more than in 'Autocrítica', highlights the social engagement of his writing.

---

[44] Such an association with finality will be echoed in the poem 'Lembrança do Porto dos Cavalos' (p. 528), included in the later collection *Agrestes*, where Cabral established a parallel between that same geographical location and poetry, both visualized in borderline images which are deeply revealing of the fear of death that haunted the poet throughout his life: 'cheira na linha da poesia: | entre o defunto e o suor da vida' [its smell takes me to the place of poetry: | between the dead and the sweat of life] (p. 528).
[45] The orphanage of the Roda is the theme of the poem 'A roda dos expostos da Jaqueira' of *Agrestes*, which will be discussed in detail in Chapter 3.

1.6 CONCLUSION

The violence and social injustice pervasive in his native land defined much of Cabral's writing, and the image of the knife emerges as central metaphor to his conceptualizations of poetry and existence. Images of cutting and alienation in *A escola das facas* convey a sense of the precariousness of life. Fragmentation also underpins the structure of the collection itself, in which different themes intertwine, past and present coexist and moods change abruptly. The processing of cutting and grafting are conceived as being integral to the creative process, encapsulating Cabral's style of writing, at once elliptical and incorporating intertextual references, reflecting his perception of life, in which mortality is intimately associated with renewal.

This perspective was also central to his rendition of the history of his native land, defined by violence, evidence of which is his treatment of the controversial discovery of Brazil by Pinzón. Such engagement with historical sources was carried through to his following work, *Auto do frade*, in which his interest in the violent history of Brazil, and of the north-east in particular, was explored further. This had particular resonance in the light of Brazil's recent experience of dictatorial rule, as will be discussed in the following chapter.

2

Speaking from the margins: the haunting voices of *Auto do frade*

2.1 INTRODUCTION

Nearly thirty years after *Morte e vida severina* appeared, Cabral published his second *auto*, or one-act play, a dramatization of the final hours of Frei Joaquim do Amor Divino Caneca (1779–1825), one of Pernambuco's heroes of democracy and independence. *Auto do frade*[1] combines the author's fascination with the history of his native land and his obsession with mortality, developing themes already evident in *A escola das facas*. The poet's obsession with death is evinced in the working title 'O último dia de Frei Caneca (Auto)' that features on the cover of the typeset copy of the play to be found at the Fundação Casa de Rui Barbosa, in Rio de Janeiro.[2] This title, to a greater degree than the definitive one, suggests the importance that the theme of mortality played in Cabral's portrayal of one of Pernambuco's most prominent historical figures. As Alfredo Bosi observed: 'Of Frei Caneca's life spanning fifty years, João Cabral only picks out his passion and death. It is the end, that which is close to death, that attracts him.'[3]

Auto do frade is structured into seven scenes, which chart Frei Caneca's last journey through the streets of Recife. The play follows his

---

[1] The annotation at the end of *Auto do frade*, 'Quito, 1981, and Tegucigalpa, 1983', dates its composition to the years of Cabral's postings in Ecuador and Honduras.

[2] The dedication in this copy reads: 'Ao caro Plínio Doyle, o "Auto do Frade" antes de ser batisado [*sic*]. E com abraço do João Cabral de Melo Neto. Rio, dez. 1983' [To dear Plínio Doyle, the 'The Friar' before it is baptized. With Best Wishes from João Cabral de Melo Neto. Rio, December 1983].

[3] 'João Cabral recorta, dos cinqüenta anos de vida de frei Caneca, só a paixão e a morte. É o desfecho que o atrai, o que está perto da morte.' Alfredo Bosi, 'O auto do frade: as vozes e a geometria', in *Céu, inferno. Ensaios de crítica literária e ideológica*, ed. José Roberto Miney (São Paulo: Ática, 1988), pp. 96–102 (p. 97) (first published in *Folha de São Paulo*, 8 April 1984).

progress from prison to the fort where he will be executed for leading the rebellion against the government of Dom Pedro I. The rebels perceived the government as economically biased in favour of the southern regions of Brazil and resented it for dictating the fate of the north-east from the faraway capital of Rio de Janeiro.

The play opens with the protagonist fast asleep in his cell, while the crowds outside line the street, anxiously waiting to catch a glimpse of the man who dared conspire against the Crown. Before reaching the fort, outside the Church of the Terço, Frei Caneca is first dressed in ecclesiastical vestments and then stripped of his canonicals, in a symbolic ceremony of execration.

The slow pace of the play mirrors that of Frei Caneca's walk towards his death. As the execution is delayed, because nobody is willing to carry it out, tension mounts among the crowds, who hang on to the hope of a timely reprieve. The despair of Caneca's father after his son's execution is compounded by the bleak ending of the play, in which the body of the dead friar is deposited anonymously at the entrance of the Basílica do Carmo, to be buried there in the dead of night.

Apart from concentrating on the hours leading up to the friar's death, the *auto* provides information on his background and politics through the accounts of members of the Establishment as well as people lining the streets, who act as a chorus. Importantly, such accounts of Frei Caneca's life are fragmented and not organized according to a linear chronological order, interspersed as they are among the comments on his actual progress through the streets, his execration and death. It could be argued that such disruption of narrative linearity is one of the strategies of subversion through which, on a structural level, the play undermines the very notion of Order, which the powers of political oppression condemned in the play were determined to maintain.

Cabral's engagement with the story of Frei Caneca and his treatment of the theme are significant on a number of levels. From a social and political perspective, it is certainly revealing that the *auto*, with its indictment of a repressive political regime in nineteenth-century Brazil, should be published as the country was gradually emerging from twenty years of military rule. In fact, the political background against which the *auto* was written must surely be taken into account, even though the poet denied engaging in a critique of contemporary politics. Asked by Níobe Abreu Peixoto whether Frei Caneca's social ideal, which in *Auto do frade* is captured in the metaphor of a 'civil geometria' [civil geometry], was intended to echo Brazilian civil society's aspirations during the years of repression, Cabral replied:

> No. When I wrote *Auto do frade*, I was serving as Ambassador in Honduras. I didn't write it with the military dictatorship in mind. Although I was against the dictatorship, I was serving as Ambassador of a country under military dictatorship. This idea of mine of a civil geometry is the communist ideal [...]. I was not thinking of the dictatorship.[4]

In view of his diplomatic status and of the political persecution he had suffered in the early 1950s because of his support of communism, it is perhaps understandable that the poet should wish to distance himself from any political reading of the play that might jeopardize his position. Yet, there can be little doubt that the poet must have had Brazil's recent history in mind when he articulated his communist ideas through the character of Frei Caneca. By incorporating a number of anachronisms into the narrative, and manipulating historical sources, Cabral ensured that the *auto*'s relevance to the challenges facing contemporary Brazilian society was enhanced, contributing to the production of a highly subversive play. In addition to ambiguous time settings, hovering between past and present, the poet situated his protagonist on the margins between life and death, blurring the boundaries between the two. This also impinged on his treatment of the other characters, particularly of the crowds in the streets, who emerge as ghost-like figures.

Cabral did not create clearly defined characters, for only Frei Caneca's voice is truly distinctive. This feature, in conjunction with the lack of any real interaction between the majority of the characters and the extensive use of repetition, results in a play in which the experience of haunting is re-created. Reiterated references to echoes and screams seem to corroborate such reading, as does the subtitle of the play, 'Poema para vozes' [Poem for Voices].

On this last point, Cabral acknowledged Dylan Thomas's (1914–53) *Under Milk Wood. A Play for Voices* (1954) as being a source of inspiration. In his interview with Abreu Peixoto, he stated: 'I chose the subtitle *Poem for*

---

[4] 'Não. Quando escrevi o *Auto do frade* era embaixador em Honduras. Não escrevi pensando na ditadura militar. Embora eu não aceitasse a ditadura militar, eu fui embaixador da ditadura militar. Essa idéia minha de civil geometria é a idéia do mundo comunista ideal [...]. Não pensei na ditadura.' 'Conversa com João Cabral de Melo Neto', in *João Cabral e o poema dramático. Auto do frade (poema para vozes)* (São Paulo: Annablume, 2001), pp. 135–44 (p. 137).

Voices with Dylan Thomas in mind.'[5] Thomas wrote *Under Milk Wood* as a radio play and masterfully succeeded in exploring the dramatic effects produced by the 'disembodied' voices of the actors. Their accounts of a day in the life of a small Welsh seaside town convey the fluidity with which the play moves between the world of the living and that of the dead. As John Ackerman observed, 'often the life of the play is conveyed through the impassioned nostalgia of the dead'.[6] A similar device was also employed in Cabral's second *auto*, with considerable political implications.

Indeed, the experience of haunting produced by the anonymous characters of the play aimed at debunking the regime of which they were victims. One may ask whether the play was ever intended for the stage or whether Cabral wished its political message to be conveyed to the solitary reader, as she/he responded to the 'disembodied' voices of the various characters. That this was indeed the case seemed to have been hinted at by the author himself, when he acknowledged the practical difficulties any staging of his *auto* would come up against: '*Auto do frade* is difficult to stage.'[7]

In reality, the inclusion of *Auto do frade* in any one genre is problematic, for it combines poetry, drama, and cinema. Written for the most part in narrative verse, but also including some sections in prose, Cabral defined it as a poem in the subtitle. Yet, he also classified it as a play in the title, although stage directions were not included and actual dramatic action is scarce, with the reader having to rely on narration by the various voices in the street. In a further disruption of boundaries of genre, Cabral resorted to cinematic effects in order to convey the bleakness of the play's denouement. The result is the structurally hybrid character of this work, which I will consider here.

In interviews, Cabral revealed that he believed the big screen would provide the perfect medium for the story of Caneca's execution, and it was only due to the Brazilian film industry's failure to show any interest in the project that the *auto* was eventually written (Castello, p. 148).

---

[5] 'Eu botei *Poema para vozes* pensando no Dylan Thomas', in ibid., p. 136. Cabral's admiration for Thomas was recorded in the poem 'As cartas de Dylan Thomas' (p. 380) of *Museu de tudo*: 'a incapacidade de ser, | ao fazer, massa e não fermento: | o incapaz de tocar a massa | sem lhe mudar o fazimento' [unable to be | while making, the dough and not the yeast: | unable to touch the dough | without changing its making] (p. 380).

[6] John Ackerman, *A Dylan Thomas Companion: Life, Poetry and Prose* (Basingstoke: Macmillan, 1991), p. 249.

[7] 'O *Auto do frade* é difícil de levar em teatro' (in Peixoto, 2001, p. 140). According to Peixoto, there are only records of a 1985 staging in São Paulo, which would corroborate this point (2001, p. 48).

Cabral attributed such lack of interest to the ignorance in relation to Frei Caneca's importance for Brazilian history.[8] However, he persisted with his project, in the hope that his daughter Inez would adapt the play to cinema.[9] In so doing, he was conscious of the fact that he was deliberately drawing on historical material with which much of his readership would have been unfamiliar. This must have reinforced his belief that he was a poet at the margins of Brazilian literary tradition.[10]

Although not widely studied, *Auto do frade* has, overall, been well received, with the critic Pedro Lyra ranking it among the masterpieces of Brazilian literature.[11] Yet, one famous negative appraisal came from the poet Carlos Drummond de Andrade, one of Cabral's masters at the outset of his literary career. Drummond's unequivocally dismissive view was that 'João Cabral has taken things so far that he has ended up writing a poem without poetry.'[12]

---

[8] Speaking in 1987, Cabral commented that 'vai ver que eles [os cineastas] não sabem nem quem é frei Caneca. Eu vi muita gente me perguntar: Por que frei Caneca? Eu digo: Por que não frei Caneca?' [it's likely that they (film directors) don't know who Frei Caneca is. I've come across many people who've asked me: Why Frei Caneca? To which I reply: Why not Frei Caneca?] (in Athayde, 1998, p. 48).

[9] As a lover of cinema, Cabral regretted that, due to his failing eyesight, he would not be able to see the film. See posthumously published interview with Norma Couri, 'Poesia precisa de provocar emoção', *Jornal de Letras*, 26 January 2000, pp. 8–10 (p. 9). In my interview with Inez Cabral, on 28 August 2002, in Rio de Janeiro, the poet's daughter confirmed that she still hoped to carry out the project whenever financial backing was found.

[10] Cabral spoke of his status at the margins of Brazil's poetic tradition in his interview with Werneck (p. 86). The poet made explicit reference to his rejection of lyrical writing, which characterizes much of the poetry published in Brazil and named the Portuguese poet Cesário Verde (1855–86) and the American Marianne Moore (1887–1972) as examples of other poets at the margins of their own literary traditions.

[11] 'O crime de Caneca', in *O real no poético II. Textos de jornalismo literário* (Rio de Janeiro: Cátedra; Brasília: Instituto Nacional do Livro, 1986), pp. 169–79 (p. 179) (first publ. in *Jornal do Brasil*, 17 March 1984).

[12] 'João Cabral tanto fez que acabou criando um poema sem poesia' (in Castello, p. 174). By the time *Auto do frade* was published, relations between the two poets had famously cooled, and they no longer shared a mutual appreciation of each other's writing. It is significant that, while Drummond accused Cabral of taking his pursuit of anti-poetry to the extreme, the younger poet was scathing of Drummond's later output for exactly opposite reasons. Speaking in 1988, Cabral stated: 'Gostei dos primeiros livros do Drummond, quando ele era um poeta de língua presa. Gostei, digamos, até *A rosa do povo*. A poesia dele caiu de intensidade e densidade depois que se deixou influenciar pela língua solta de Pablo Neruda' [I liked Drummond's first books, when he was a tongue-tied poet. I liked his works, say, up to *A rosa do povo*. His poetry lost intensity and density after he allowed himself to be influenced by Pablo Neruda's verbosity] (in Athayde, 1998, p. 123).

Readings of the work generally situate the play within Cabral's poetics of precision, with emphasis placed on the constructed and geometrical structure of the work. This is the perspective of the critic Alfredo Bosi (1988, p. 97), who noted how the author divided the play into seven scenes, exactly half of the number of stages of the cross, which the friar's progress along the streets of Recife replicates. In a similar stance, Ivo Barbieri (1997, pp. 38–9) speaks of the symmetrical structure of the various scenes, which reflects the repressive social order that the play introduces. Likewise, João Alexandre Barbosa stressed the uncompromising precision with which Cabral engages with history, particularly when re-creating the voices of the people in the street.[13] Ultimately, what emerges from these readings is the tendency to identify in the text 'the qualities of luminosity, precision, and compression which we have come to associate with João Cabral de Melo Neto's poetry', as we read in John Parker's analysis of the play.[14]

My aim here is to challenge this approach, considering the play's dialogue with a variety of artistic idioms (literary and not) which articulated his revision of the poetic ideal of clarity and precision that had been outlined several decades previously in his *Fábula de Anfion*, of 1947. It seems, in fact, that the play occupies a pivotal place in the development of the author's output as a whole. I would contend that probing into the complex character of Frei Caneca will reveal more than the 'recreation of the thoughts and character of Caneca himself', as Ivan Junqueira stated.[15] Rather, I would argue that much will be gleaned about the poet's own evolving ideas on his writing.

2.2 HISTORICAL BACKGROUND

Frei Caneca was born in the district of 'Fora de Portas', in Recife, in 1779. The son of a local cooper, he took pride in his humble origins and adopted his father's nickname, 'Caneca' [mug/tankard] when, in 1796,

---

[13] 'João Cabral ou a educação pela poesia', in *A biblioteca imaginária*, ed. Plínio Martins Filho (São Paulo: Ateliê Editorial, 1996), pp. 239–47 (p. 246) (first publ. in *Folha de São Paulo, Caderno Mais*, 1995).

[14] 'João Cabral de Melo Neto: "Literalist of the Imagination" ', *World Literature Today*, 66 (1992), 609–16 (p. 615).

[15] 'Recriação do pensamento e da maneira de ser do próprio Caneca.' See 'As vozes de Frei Caneca', in *O encantador de serpentes. Ensaios* (Rio de Janeiro: Alhambra, 1987,), pp. 75–84 (p. 81).

he took religious orders and entered the Convent of Nossa Senhora do Carmo, in Recife. These biographical details are mentioned in the play and explain the wide support he enjoyed among the people:

> —Não quis esconder que seu pai
> um simples operário era,
> nem mentir parecendo vir
> das grandes famílias da terra. (p. 509)

[—He did not want to hide that his father | was a simple workman, | nor did he wish to lie by pretending to come | from one of the great landed families.]

The play also alludes to Frei Caneca's intellectual brilliance, which is confirmed in historical accounts. The historian Brito Lemos recalls how the friar was admired for his classical erudition and how, in 1803, he was appointed as the Convent's reader in rhetoric and geometry.[16] In addition to excelling in his academic career, Frei Caneca rose to prominence for his outspoken criticism of the government of Rio de Janeiro and for his involvement in the north-eastern revolutionary movements of 1817 and 1824. He was jailed in Bahia for four years for the part he played in the uprising of 6 March 1817 and in the short-lived republican government that ensued. In the play, the people recall the harsh conditions of his imprisonment:

> —Em dezessete na Bahia
> de fome e sede ele sofrera.
> —Viveu piolhento, esmolambado,
> guardado quase como fera. (p. 495)

[—In 1817 in Bahia | he experienced hunger and thirst. |—He lived like a pauper, infested with lice, | locked up much like a wild beast].

Two years after his release in 1821, Frei Caneca's uncrushed political drive materialized in the launch of the revolutionary newspaper *Typhis pernambucano*, on which the people comment too:

> —Foi assim frade e jornalista,
> e em vez de bispo, padre-mestre.
> —Viveu bem plantado na vida,
> coisa que a gente nunca esquece. (p. 497)

[—He was a friar and a journalist, | and rather than bishop, he was a teacher. |—He lived rooted in the real world, | something that we, the people, never forget.]

---

[16] Brito Lemos, *A gloriosa sotaina do primeiro império. (Frei Caneca)* (São Paulo: Companhia Editora Nacional, 1937), p. 27.

Historical sources reveal that his journalistic activities fiercely advocated democracy, freedom of press, social as well as racial equality (Lemos, p. 69). He himself was of mixed race, being of Indian and Portuguese descent. As the historian Evaldo Cabral de Mello, brother of João Cabral, recalls, Frei Caneca argued that, had he been of African descent, he would equally have been proud of his roots, because 'the time has come for us to pride ourselves greatly about our African blood'.[17]

The events leading up to his execution on 13 January 1825 revolve around his participation in the revolutionary movement of 1824, against the rule of Emperor D. Pedro I. In the wake of Brazil's independence, in 1822, there had been widespread dissatisfaction in the northeast, caused by the sense that its political and economic interests were still not being safeguarded (Mello, p. 20). This is a point which the play is keen to highlight: '—Veleiro que chega do Rio | pouco traz (mas leva o que for)' [—Sailing ships that arrive from Rio | bring little (but take away whatever they can)] (p. 496).

When Dom Pedro I, in an absolutist intervention in local politics, dissolved the regional constitutional assembly, deposed the president of the province of Pernambuco, Manuel de Carvalho Paes de Andrade, who had been democratically elected, and named Francisco Paes Barreto in his place, the 1824 uprising ensued.[18] As with the earlier movement of 1817, the republican experience of 1824 was short-lived: the Confederação do Equador, which included the states of Paraíba, Rio Grande do Norte, Ceará, Piauí and Pará (Paranhym and França, p.15), was defeated within months by the forces of the emperor and most of those involved in the uprising were executed. Only a handful escaped with their lives, having sought refuge abroad.[19] For his participation in these events, Frei Caneca is vilified by one of the guards in the play:

> Separatista, pretendeu
> dar o Norte à gente do Norte.
> Padre existe é para rezar
> pela alma, mas não contra a fome. (p. 472)

---

[17] 'Já está à porta o tempo de muito nos honrarmos do sangue africano', cited in Evaldo Cabral de Mello (ed.), 'Frei Caneca ou a outra independência', in *Frei Joaquim do Amor Divino Caneca* (São Paulo: Editora 34, 2001), pp. 11–47 (p. 11).

[18] Orlando da Cunha Paranhym and Rubem França, *Frei Caneca em prosa e verso* (Recife: Governo de Pernambuco, Secretaria de Educação e Cultura, 1974), p. 15.

[19] Among those who survived was José da Natividade Saldanha, to whom Cabral devoted the poem 'Um poeta pernambucano', of *A escola das facas* (pp. 448–9).

[As a Separatist he intended | to give the north back to the northerners. | Priests are there to pray | for our souls, but not against hunger.]

To this day, Frei Caneca is all but unknown outside Pernambuco, although he is held in high regard in his native land, as Evaldo Cabral de Mello explains:

> Unlike [Emperor] D. Pedro I or [Statesman] José Bonifácio, Frei Caneca did not become a national figure. The fact that in spite of these limitations he should represent in Pernambuco the other Independence, that is to say, the possible alternative to the way Brazil's emancipation, dictated from Rio de Janeiro, panned out, constitutes a creditable homage to the power of ideas in politics, in a country which has a centuries-old tradition of not believing in them.[20]

As an 'incurável pernambucano', Cabral shared this admiration for the figure of the revolutionary friar and denounced the oblivion into which he had fallen.[21] He dedicated *Auto do frade* to his children, thus symbolically 'passing on' the story of Frei Caneca to the next generation and demonstrating the importance he attached to this historical figure of his region's heritage. In his interview with Níobe Abreu Peixoto (p. 136), he stated: 'I've always admired Frei Caneca. It annoys me that nobody in Brazil acknowledges Frei Caneca. Here in Rio, his name is associated with that of a prison.'[22] In the poem 'Frei Caneca no Rio de Janeiro' (pp. 411–12), included in *Museu de tudo*, the poet deals precisely with the irony of the fact that, having died in the name of freedom, this 'crioulo e enciclopedista' [black encyclopaedist] (p. 412) should have given his name to one of Rio de Janeiro's most infamous prison complexes.[23] In the face of this ironic twist of fate, Cabral strove

---

[20] 'Ao contrário de d. Pedro I ou José Bonifácio, frei Caneca não chegou a ser uma figura nacional. Que a despeito destas limitações, ele represente em Pernambuco a outra Independência, vale dizer, a alternativa imaginável à forma pela qual a emancipação do Brasil, comandada do Rio de Janeiro, veio efetivamente a ocorrer, constitui uma honrosa homenagem ao poder das idéias na política, num país que tem a secular tradição de não acreditar nelas' (p. 15).

[21] The poet stated he had first been motivated to write on Frei Caneca after reading an article by the historian Mário Melo while still residing in Recife, proving that the *auto* had been a long-standing project. See interview with Teresa C. Rodrigues, 'João Cabral e o seu "Auto do frade": um poema evoca o martírio de Frei Caneca', *O Globo*, 6 December 1983.

[22] 'Sempre tive grande admiração por Frei Caneca. Eu fico irritado porque o Brasil inteiro ignora Frei Caneca. Aqui no Rio, ele é nome de cadeia.'

[23] The friar is also celebrated in 'Descrição de Pernambuco como um trampolim', of *A escola das facas* (pp. 424–7), and 'Cenas da vida de Joaquim Cardozo', of the later collection *Crime na Calle Relator* (pp. 620–4), where he embodies Pernambuco's history

2.3 THE 'PASSION' OF FREI CANECA

In the wake of the celebrations held in Pernambuco to mark the two hundred and fiftieth anniversary of the death of Frei Caneca, in 1975, interest in the story of the revolutionary friar increased dramatically, spawning a number of texts and plays on the subject.[24] A brief comparison between one such play, Cláudio Aguiar's *Suplício de Frei Caneca. Oratório dramático* (1977), and *Auto do frade* reveals some significant differences. Aguiar's emphasis on Caneca's religious and political ideas contrasts with Cabral's evident authorial interference in the voice of the protagonist, alongside his stress on Caneca's humanity and anxieties in relation to death. If, on one level, Cabral's play engages in a critique of authoritarian regimes, it also represents a moment of personal and literary reflection. Indeed, the play operates at the interface between the realms of the public and the private, which allowed Cabral to construct a powerful work that touches on his preoccupations with social justice, mortality and the act of writing. In engaging with the first two of these concerns, Cabral drew on and subverted the narrative of Christ's Passion. This is because there is no resurrection for Caneca, while emphasis is placed on depicting his final hours as experienced in a state of limbo.

True enough, many of the elements of the story of the Passion found their way into Cabral's second *auto*. For example, the friar's walk along the streets of Recife towards the fort mirrors Christ's ascent towards Mount Calvary. Moreover, the mockery of Jesus at the hands of the soldiers is re-enacted in the central scene IV of Cabral's *auto*, when Caneca is humiliated outside the church of the Terço and stripped of his

---

of defiance in the face of oppression. Drawing on the story of the apparition of the Virgin on the day of Frei Caneca's execution, an episode also incorporated in the narrative of *Auto do frade*, the subversive poem 'O helicóptero de Nossa Senhora do Carmo', of *Agrestes* (pp. 534–6), accuses the Virgin herself of failing to rescue the Carmelite friar, a sign of the poet's strong anti-religious sentiments and of his admiration for Caneca.

[24] For further information, see Cláudio Aguiar, *Suplício de Frei Caneca. Oratório dramático* (São Paulo: Editora do Escritor, 1977). As mentioned earlier, it is noteworthy that Cabral's interest in the story of Caneca dated to his early years in Recife and had, therefore, been long-standing.

religious orders. The comments by the crowds in the street also suggest similarities between Christ's progress and Caneca's walk towards the fort: '—Na tão estranha procissão | é o santo que anda, e anda aos tombos' [—In this strange procession | it is the saint who is walking, and stumbles as he walks] (p. 473). In a parallel with Christ, the suffering of Caneca exposes flaws in religious as well as political institutions. The Church and the judiciary are shown to collude with an exploitative regime and to be corrupt and self-serving. As a mirror image of Pontius Pilate, the Judge does not take charge of Caneca's trial, preoccupied as he is with surveying his vast sugar cane plantation:

> seu imenso canavial
> [...]
> que para corrê-lo em total,
> se precisa de muitas viagens
> em lombo de escravo ou animal. (p. 469)

[his vast sugar cane plantation [...] | which to explore entirely,| requires many journeys | whether on the back of a slave or of an animal.]

Even the image of the crown of thorns and the Roman soldier's spear of Christ's Passion is suggested in the words of 'A gente no largo' [The people in the square]: '—Para quem está esperando | cada minuto vale um espinho' [—For those who wait | every minute is a thorn] (p. 505). Yet, despite dealing with a man who devoted his life to the Christian faith, the play rejects any religious message and undermines the duality of life and mortality by portraying Frei Caneca as one of the living dead.

This perspective is certainly consistent with Cabral's obsession with liminal states, a feature that John Gledson highlighted in his analysis of Cabral's early work *Pedra do sono*. Having studied the reproduction of the sensations of sleep in the poet's first collection, the critic concluded:

He is fascinated, in fact, by the marginal, quasi-contradictory state of consciousness (or unconsciousness) which we call sleep, by the fact that in it we are both absent and present, alive and dead. One can understand why he so readily associates such figures as condemned or persecuted men with dreams, for they exist in just such a marginal state. (Gledson, 1978, p. 45)

In drawing attention to such configurations of liminal states, Gledson's analysis proves extremely pertinent to the treatment of death in *Auto do frade*. In fact, the very association of sleep and death is established in the opening scene of the play, in the description of the sleeping Frei Caneca by the provincial head of his religious order and his prison guard:

> —Dorme, como em pouco, morto, vai dormir
> [...]
> —Dorme fundo como um morto.
> —Mas está vivo. Vamos ressuscitá-lo. (p. 465)

[—He is sleeping, as soon, dead, he will sleep |[...] |—He sleeps deeply like a dead man. |—But he is alive. Let's resuscitate him.]

Here, Cabral plays with indeterminacy between life and death and also subverts the theme of Christ's resurrection, since Caneca's awakening to his last few hours echoes Christ's rising from the dead. This is carried forward into scene II, where Frei Caneca symbolically 'rises from the dead' as he emerges into the morning light, having left behind his dark prison cell. There the skulls of the hanged were kept, a clear parallel with the biblical Golgotha, literally meaning 'the skull', site of Christ's crucifixion.[25] In this way, Caneca's symbolic return to life (emergence from prison) actually precedes his physical death, which occurs in scene VI.[26] Cabral's materialist perspective and rejection of any metaphysical reality is thereby revealed. A captive of an oppressive regime, Caneca is visualized as a living dead, as in Frei Caneca's opening monologue:

> —Acordo fora de mim
> como há tempos não fazia.
> [...]
> como fora nada eu via,
> ficava dentro de mim
> como vida apodrecida. (p. 468)

[—I wake to the world | as I had not done for ages |[...] | since I could see nothing outside, | I remained closed in myself | like rotting life.]

The irreverence with which the re-enactment of the Christian Passion is treated means that Caneca gains the status of neither martyr nor saint:

---

[25] The link between prison and death must have been inspired by the gruesome details of Caneca's imprisonment. The historian Mário Melo, whom Cabral had read, recorded how Frei Caneca was held in the infamous 'cubículo das cabeças' [cell of the heads], the tiny, dark room where the skulls of those who had been hanged were kept. See 'Frei Caneca', *Revista do instituto archeológico, histórico e geográphico pernambucano*, 147–50 (1933), 7–37 (p. 27).

[26] This interpretation contrasts with Vera Lúcia Follain de Figueiredo's analysis, when the critic states that in the *auto* 'a morte perde o seu caráter irreversível e se deixa permear pela idéia de ressureição' [death looses its irreversible character and is permeated by the idea of resurrection]. See 'Auto do frade—a hora e a vez de Frei Caneca', *2º Congresso da Abralic. Anais*, 3 vols, ed. Eneida Maria de Souza (Belo Horizonte: Abralic, 1991), III, 267–73 (p. 269).

'—Não sou ninguém para ser mártir, | não é distinção que eu mereça.' [—I am not worthy of being made a martyr, | it's not an honour I deserve] (p. 490).[27]

This characterization contrasts with that of the Brazilian revolutionary Tiradentes, as celebrated by Cecília Meireles in her *Romanceiro da inconfidência* (1953), a collection of poems on the failed movement for the independence of the state of Minas Gerais which occurred in 1789. Cabral's second wife, the poet Marly de Oliveira, suggested in her preface to the poet's *Obra completa* (published by Nova Aguilar) that *Auto do frade* was intended as a response to Meireles's work: 'The author seeks recognition for Frei Caneca, head of the separatist revolt of 1824, for his leading role and his heroic status in the fight for the creation of the Republic in Brazil.'[28] Yet, it is essential to note the extent to which the portrayals of these two historical figures differ in their treatment of religion. Unlike Cabral's rendition of Caneca, the *Romanceiro da inconfidência* draws explicit parallels between the Passion of Christ and the suffering of Tiradentes as he walks to the gallows, with no intent to subvert religious imagery: 'Ah, solidão do destino! | Ah, solidão do Calvário.' [Ah, solitude of destiny! | Ah, solitude of Calvary!].[29]

Conversely, Cabral's subversion of the theme of the Passion is evident and informs the closing moments of the play, included under the heading 'Cinema no Pátio' [Cinema in the Church Square], which Cabral intended as film sequence, with its nihilistic portrayal of the friar's dead body:

Quatro calcetas com duas tábuas ao ombro, nas quais se pode distinguir o corpo de um homem deitado, dirigem-se à porta principal da Basílica do Carmo, e deixam cair no chão, grosseiramente, o corpo que traziam. Batem na porta, aos pontapés, e vão embora, sem esperar. (p. 513)

[Four prisoners, bearing two planks on their shoulders, on which one can make out the body of a man lying down, head for the main entrance to the Basilica of the Carmo, and let the body they were carrying fall heavily to the ground. They kick against the door and leave without waiting for anyone to answer.]

---

[27] The poem 'Frei Caneca no Rio de Janeiro' (p. 411), mentioned above, also touches on this point.

[28] 'O autor reivindica para frei Caneca, líder da revolução separatista de 1824, prioridade e o heroísmo na luta pela instalação da República do Brasil.' In Melo Neto, 1994, p. 22.

[29] *Romanceiro da inconfidência*, in *Poesia completa*, 4th edn, ed. Walmyr Ayala (Rio de Janeiro: Nova Aguilar, 1994), p. 588.

No faith in an afterlife is suggested here but rather that a repressive political order has ultimately prevailed.[30] The fact that Caneca's body is carried by four 'calcetas', prisoners condemned to hard labour, emphasizes this point, as does the fact that all the characters in these closing moments of the play remain anonymous, including Frei Caneca and the Carmelite who buried him. Arguably, their anonymity also reflects the oblivion to which Frei Caneca would eventually be relegated.

The visual impact of the images of the 'Cinema no Pátio' is enhanced by the lack of speech, which contrasts with the profusion of voices that immediately precede these closing frames. Cabral himself justified his manipulation of voice and silence to convey the climate of political repression:

I ended the film script with a section in prose because I believe that that scene in which the guy takes the body of Frei Caneca to the church of the Carmo, and then later when his body is lifted onto the planks, would produce an extraordinary effect in a film. Now, I couldn't possibly recreate this effect in a play, in verse, with dialogues without ruining the scene. There was no point in anybody talking at that moment, since Frei Caneca was dead and the prisoners had no reason to talk. Therefore, I ended with prose writing in order to give greater impact to the image.[31]

Cabral outlined his aims with regard to the play's conclusion and drew attention to the hybridity of his composition by referring to the *auto* as a 'filme', a classification he also employed when he discussed the background to his composition:

I believe my work to be very visual, a consequence of my first impression that the last moments of Frei Caneca's life would make a good film, and it is odd, an

---

[30] The play reproduces the atmosphere surrounding the disposal of Frei Caneca's body as documented in historical records. However, according to some sources, including Mário Melo, to which Cabral had access, Caneca's father was actually at the Convent of the Carmo when his son's body was left outside (see Melo, 1933, p. 37). The omission of this detail ensures that the ostracism of which Caneca was victim is more powerfully conveyed.

[31] 'Eu acabei o filme em prosa porque eu acho que aquela cena em que o sujeito leva o corpo de frei Caneca para a igreja do Carmo e, no convento, puxam e levam ele em cima de umas tábuas, aquilo daria uma coisa formidável no cinema. Agora, eu não poderia fazer aquilo em teatro, em verso, com diálogo, para não estragar a cena. Não adiantava ninguém falar ali, Frei Caneca estava morto, óbvio, os calceteiros [*sic*] não tinham nada o que falar. De modo que eu escrevi em prosa para deixar mais forte a imagem' (in Athayde, 1998, p. 118).

The haunting voices of Auto do frade 63

auto is written for the theatre, not for the cinema. The result is *Auto do frade*, imagined as a film, written in verse and structured for the theatre.[32]

Cabral acknowledged on a number of occasions that he did not consider himself a playwright,[33] but the complex structure of *Auto do frade* points to a deliberate manipulation of genres and, thereby, a conscious subversion of literary conventions. While cinematic devices would provide the visual immediacy that the poet himself alluded to, the theatre (or reading performance) of the story of Frei Caneca would allow the author to give a voice to those whom official history had misrepresented. These would be best conveyed in verse form, because, as the *provincial* comments in relation to Caneca: '—Mesmo sem querer fala em verso | quem fala a partir da emoção' [—Though not deliberately, in verse | speak those who speak with emotion] (p. 478).[34]

Taking all three genres into account, it could be said that the unconventional structure of the text was intended to produce the greatest impact.[35] On an additional level, it could be argued that the *auto*'s blurring of genres is also intrinsically political: Cabral's subversion of convention duplicates Frei Caneca's struggle against the Empire, reflecting, on a structural level, his intent to rebel against the dominant order.

The absence of voices in the closing moments of *Auto do frade*, juxtaposed with the visual impact of a film projection in the Pátio do Carmo, emphasizes the correlation between voice and agency that is established throughout the play. In this respect, the organization of the protagonist's speeches is also highly relevant. The fact that he does not speak at all after scene V, when he arrives at the Forte das Cinco Pontas

[32] 'Acho que eu fiz uma coisa muito visual, consequência daquela minha primeira impressão de que os últimos momentos de frei Caneca dariam um bom filme, e é estranho, um auto é feito para o teatro, não para o cinema. O resultado é o *Auto do frade*, imaginado como um filme, escrito em versos e estruturado como para teatro' (in Athayde, 1998, pp. 117–18).

[33] See, for example, interview with José Correia Tavares, 'João Cabral de Melo Neto', *Jornal de Letras e Artes*, 8 June 1966, p. 1 and p. 16: 'Como sabe, não sou homem de teatro' [As you know, I am not a dramatist] (p. 1).

[34] It follows that the matter-of-fact announcements by the Meirinho [Bailiff] and those of the authorities during the ceremony of degradation should be in prose.

[35] Arguably, it also reflects the unconventional treatment to which Frei Caneca was submitted, which the people witnessing the execution recognize as such: '—Será fuzilado na forca, | num suplício híbrido e novo' [—He will be shot on the gallows, | in a hybrid and new form of death] (p. 506).

[Fort of the Five Points], conveys his disempowerment, and, therefore, his symbolic death, which precedes his physical one.[36]

2.4 THE 'VOICES' OF FREI CANECA

In the scene of the Praça do Forte [Fort Square], the drama mounts to a climax, as the guards struggle vainly to find an executioner, even after attempting to recruit one among the convicts held in the jails of Recife. The convicts' support of Caneca evokes Christ's exchange with the sinner on the cross and is juxtaposed with the readiness of some sections of society to turn against the accused, as the people themselves acknowledge: '— Fosse a oferta feita na praça, | teriam carrascos às pencas' [—Were the offer made in the square, | they would have executioners galore] (p. 501).

Such lack of social unity emphasizes the protagonist's isolation. In this play, Frei Caneca, who devoted his life to social causes and is remembered as a great orator, barely communicates with those around him. Although lengthy, his speeches comprise six soliloquies (of forty lines each) but only one brief exchange with another character, namely one of the guards accompanying the cortège, who urges him to keep his silence: '—Um condenado não pode falar. | Condenado à morte, perde a língua' [—Those sentenced to death cannot speak. | Under sentence of death, a man loses his voice] (p. 477). This intervention draws attention to the prisoner's loss of the right to speak openly, a fact that effectively enabled Cabral to highlight the personal thoughts rather than the public views of Frei Caneca—privileging the character's intimate turmoil over his public statements. In fact, Cabral's main concern is not with Caneca as a great political leader, nor as a saintly figure, but as a human being faced with his own mortality.

Among the mass of anonymous voices, that of Frei Caneca is the only one to emerge as truly distinctive; a result which Cabral achieved also by casting his soliloquies into seven-syllable lines, rather than into eight-syllable lines, as in the majority of the remaining verses. In the midst of the factual accounts by the people in the streets, Frei Caneca's reflections gain an ever-increasing degree of abstraction and are marked by

---

[36] Historical accounts of the execution mention that Caneca wished to address the crowds one last time only moments before his death, though he was persuaded to keep his silence by a fellow friar (see Melo, 1933, p. 36). Cabral makes no reference to this episode, preferring to focus on Caneca's silence.

increased authorial intrusion. At the outset, Caneca's anxieties revolve around his own predicament and the shortcomings of the clergy, while the inevitability of death and the nature of what awaits him are the central concerns in his final monologue.

Cabral's aversion to the high-sounding rhetoric often adopted by intellectuals or people in authority is well documented,[37] and was articulated in poems such as the humorously abrasive 'Um piolho de Rui Barbosa' (pp. 561–2), of *Agrestes*. With this in mind, it is perhaps not entirely surprising that he should not have Frei Caneca engage in any public address, even though it does conflict with what is known of the latter's relationship with the people. Indeed, in contrast to the saints, who are perceived as being 'moucos' [deaf], Caneca is acclaimed for his ability to relate to them:

> —Por que será que nesse frade
> mais do que em santos, tenham crença?
> [...]
> —Viveu sempre como eles todos,
> nunca se isolou com sua ciência. (pp. 478–9)

[—Why is it that in this friar | more that in the saints they put their faith? |[...]|
—He always lived like all of them, | he never isolated himself in his erudition.]

In the light of this, it is striking how the play foregrounds the oppression of which the protagonist is a victim and casts him as a man wrapped up in his own thoughts. This is in fact coherent with configurations of the human voice as a metaphor for human agency, a link established in Frei Caneca's very first monologue. Paradoxically, instruments of repression such as the rifles with which he will be executed are here endowed with a power of speech denied to those humans who dare to defy the dominant order:

> esse bosque de espingardas
> mudas, mas logo assassinas
> sempre à espera dessa voz
> que autorize o que é sua sina. (p. 468)

---

[37] 'O poeta João Cabral [...] foi quem primeiro me chamou a atenção para o fato de que, no Brasil, as mais diversas entidades—não só grêmio literários, mas clubes esportivos, associações de classe etc.—incluíam no organograma de sua diretoria (além de presidente, secretário, tesoureiro) o indefectível cargo de orador' [The poet João Cabral was the first to point out to me the fact that, in Brazil, organizations of all kinds—not only literary associations, but sports clubs, class associations etc.—included in their organization chart (besides the post of president, secretary, treasurer) the unavoidable post of speaker] (Francisco Bandeira de Mello, 'Falar/falaz', *Jornal do Comércio*, 11 October 1998, p. 4).

[this forest of rifles | silent, but soon murderous | always waiting for the voice | that will authorize what is their fate.]

That Frei Caneca's reserve encapsulates his condition as a 'living dead' is suggested in his second monologue. Indeed, the friar himself refers to the cortège as a funeral procession 'em que o morto caminharia' [in which the dead would walk] (p. 475). For their part, the clergy are described as revelling in his demise, in a profoundly ironic take, in which the proximity of death is graphically conveyed: 'Irmãos da Misericórdia, | [...] | com passadas de urubu' [Brothers of Mercy, | [...] | with their vulture-like gait] (p. 475).

The manner in which the *auto* plays with readers' expectations and challenges clearly defined boundaries is also evinced during Frei Caneca's conversation with the officer, in scene III. When questioned by the guard about the topic of his second monologue, Caneca's reply is disconcerting, for he states that he is speaking about the brightness of the light of Recife, which, in reality, is the theme of his following speech. In addition, by way of a paradox, Caneca debunks the very duality of voice and silence by announcing: '—Passarei a falar em silêncio. | Assim está salva a disciplina' [—From now on I will speak in silence. | Thus, discipline will be saved] (p. 477). As he hovers between silence and the act of speech (he goes on to speak four more times), Caneca warns us that both should be accounted for.

The ambiguity that underpins the characterization of Frei Caneca is heightened in his subsequent monologues, marked by the anachronistic interference of the authorial voice, in which a revision of the rigorous poetic ideal of precision set out in Cabral's early work is articulated. In the third monologue, Caneca anachronistically compares the bright light of Recife with the negative images of the sun 'que dirá Sofia um dia' [which Sofia will speak about one day] (p. 479), thus referring to the Portuguese poet Sophia de Mello Breyner Andresen (1919–2004), with whom Cabral had a special affinity.[38] Such poetic closeness had

---

[38] Cabral greatly admired the poetry of Sophia de Mello Breyner Andresen. In an interview given in 1985, he recalled: 'Rubem Leitão me deu a ler uma porção de poetas portugueses interessantes, sobretudo Sophia de Mello Breyner, que até hoje é, para mim, o grande poeta da minha geração em Portugal, de quem sou amigo até hoje' [Rubem Leitão [Portuguese writer] gave me several works to read by Portuguese poets, which I found interesting, above all Sophia de Mello Breyner, who is in my view the greatest poet of my generation in Portugal, and with whom I'm friends to this day] (in Athayde, 1998, p. 140).

been acknowledged earlier in his career in the famous poem 'Elogio da usina e de Sofia de Melo Breiner Andresen' (p. 339), of *Educação pela pedra*, where Cabral celebrated Sophia's poetics of the concrete object and consciously laboured approach to writing, seen as very close to his own ideal: 'Sofia faz-refaz, e subindo ao cristal, | em cristais (os dela, de luz marinha)' [Sophia works-reworks, and reaching crystals, | in crystals (hers, those of seaside light)] (p. 339).

Yet, in *Auto do frade*, he takes his cue from Sophia's negative configurations of light, referring to the 'sol inabitável' [inhabitable sun] (p. 479) featured in her work. A possible influence for this image can be found in Sophia de Mello Breyner Andresen's self-reflective exercise in 'Arte poética I' (published in *Geografia*, in 1967).[39] In this first-person narrative, the Portuguese author articulates her thoughts on writing, which are intimately linked with her understanding of her place in the world, in the face of the transient nature of existence. In order to gain this understanding, she first has to depart from a merely rational approach (symbolized by the image of the sun):

In Lagos in August the sun is straight above and there are places where even the paving stones have been whitewashed. The sun is heavy and the light is faint. I walk along the pavements close to the wall but there is not enough shade for me. The shade is a narrow strip. I dip my hand in the shadow as though I were dipping it into the water.[40]

It is in the in-between space characterized by the half-light in a pottery shop that Sophia discovers a place where binary oppositions are overcome. There, she comes across the fluid shapes of an amphora, which as a concrete representation of the union between the natural world and human creativity, and, more significantly, as a symbol of female fertility, encapsulates her condition in the world: 'A ânfora estabelece uma aliança entre mim e o sol' [The amphora establishes an alliance between myself and the sun] (p. 94).

The images found in this opening passage of Sophia's short composition are strikingly close to those of Frei Caneca's third monologue, where a similar progress towards the indeterminacy of darkness is traced:

---

[39] See Sophia de Mello Breyner Andresen, 'Arte poética I', in *Obra poética*, 3 vols, rev. Secção de Revisão da Editorial Caminho (Lisboa: Caminho, 1990–1), III, 93–4.
[40] 'Em Lagos em Agosto o sol cai a direito e há sítios onde até o chão é caiado. O sol é pesado e a luz leve. Caminho no passeio rente ao muro mas não caibo na sombra. A sombra é uma fita estreita. Mergulho a mão na sombra como se a mergulhasse na água' (p. 93).

> vou revivendo os quintais
> que dispensam sesta amiga
> detrás das fachadas magras
> com sombras gordas e líquidas. (p. 479)

[I feel as if I am back in the gardens | that provide friendly respite | behind the thin façades | with their fat and liquid shadows.]

Though shadows may traditionally be associated with death, the epithets 'gordas' [fat] and 'líquidas' [liquid] indicate that, in this instance, they are visualized as a welcome respite from the surrounding barrenness (conveyed by the adjective 'magras' [thin]) and, by association, are endowed with fluid, life-giving properties.

There seems to exist a disjunction between appearance and reality in the landscape Frei Caneca describes, between the thin façades and the fat shadows that are found beyond them. His acceptance that not all is what it seems contrasts with the frustration displayed by the protagonist of Cabral's *Fábula de Anfion*, in which his early poetic ideal was outlined. This shift in stance carries through to the remaining soliloquies, in which the poet is in dialogue with himself, as he revises images from his earlier work.[41]

There, Cabral's reworking of the myth of the construction of the city of Thebes, according to which Amphion caused the stones to move at the sound of his lyre, focused on the mythical figure's pursuit of absolute control over his creative process. This was conveyed through images of circularity:

> Anfion,
> como se preciso círculo
> estivesse riscando. (p. 87)

[Amphion, | as though a precise circle | he were tracing.]

Yet, in Cabral's rendition of the myth Amphion eventually realizes that 'O Acaso' [Chance] has played a part in his creation and that he has failed to build his ideal city:

---

[41] Sophia de Mello Breyner Andresen recognized the complexity of Cabral's poetic ideal in her poem 'Dedicatória da Terceira Edição do *Cristo cigano* a João Cabral de Melo Neto'. In the poem, included in *Ilhas* (1989), Sophia recognizes that his quest for clarity and precision should not be taken at face value: 'Pois há nessa tão exacta | Fidelidade à imanência | Secretas luas ferozes | Quebrando sóis de evidência' [For there are in this exact | Faithfulness to immanence | Secret and fierce moons | Breaking the suns of evidence] (Andresen, 1991, III, 338).

The haunting voices of Auto do frade

> Onde a cidade
> volante, a nuvem
> civil sonhada? (p. 92)

[Where is the city | floating, the cloud | of civil life that I had dreamt about?]

Because of this, he discards the instrument that betrayed him:

> A flauta, eu a joguei
> aos peixes surdos-
> mudos do mar. (p. 92)

[The flute, I threw it | to the deaf- | dumb fish in the sea.]

In *Auto do frade*, the fourth soliloquy outlines Caneca's ethical ideal through images of geometrical precision, including 'mar era redondo' [the sea was round], 'céu também redondo' [the also round sky], 'meio-círculo de Guararapes a Olinda' [half circle between Guararapes and Olinda (localities in the state of Pernambuco)] (p. 481), which are similar to those that defined Amphion's aesthetic ideal. However, like Amphion, Caneca realizes that his ideal (and, by implication, Cabral's poetic ideal) comes up against the limitations of the real world, whose complexity it must incorporate. Yet, he does not share Amphion's despair:

> Sei que o mundo jamais é
> a página pura e passiva
> [...]
> O mundo tem alma autônoma
> é de alma inquieta e explosiva. (p. 481)

[I know that the world is never | a pure and passive sheet of paper | [...] | The world has a soul of its own | it has a restless and explosive soul.]

For this reason, indeterminacy is inscribed into Caneca's vision of social justice, as becomes apparent at the end of his fifth monologue:

> Debaixo dessa luz crua,
> sob um sol que cai de cima
> e é justo até com talvezes
> e até mesmo com todavias,
> quem sabe um dia virá
> uma civil geometria? (p. 492)

[Under this raw light, | under a sun that beats you from above | and that is just even with maybes | and even with howevers, | who knows, one day | a civil geometry may come?]

The unusual subversion of grammatical categories in these lines involves the use of an adverb *talvez* [maybe] as a plural noun (*talvezes*) and a similar treatment is reserved to *todavia* [however]. What is particularly striking about this manipulation is that both these words already imply indeterminacy to a certain degree: the adverb suggesting unspecified possibilities, the conjunction suggesting the potential for difference. That such disregard for grammatical categories should be attributed to Frei Caneca, a scholar in Portuguese and author of a *Gramática da língua portuguesa*,[42] is deeply ironic and surely revealing of a deliberate authorial interference destined to criticize Cabral's own uncompromising early literary ideal.

Caneca's last speech consists of a long reflection on death. Once again, the monologue includes considerable authorial intrusion, because, apparently, it is not Frei Caneca's religious beliefs but rather Cabral's anxieties in relation to mortality that are the focus, as the following lines suggest: 'Temo a morte, embora saiba | que é uma conta devida' [I fear death, though I know | that it is a debt to be paid] (p. 495).

Two different configurations of death emerge in Caneca's final monologue, in which it is possible to chart Cabral's thoughts on his own writing once more. At the beginning of the speech, Caneca asks whether death is a 'brancura negativa' [negative whiteness] (p. 494), 'onde coisa não habita' [where nothing survives] (p. 494), suggestive of the desert that Amphion sought to re-create:

> O sol do deserto
> não choca os velhos
> ovos do mistério. (p. 88)[43]

[The desert sun | doesn't hatch the old | eggs of mystery.]

Later, Caneca enquires whether a different kind of reality awaits him; this second visualization of death features the very same eggs that threatened the order sought by Amphion:

> Ou será que é uma cidade
> [...]
> toda de branco caiada
> como Córdoba e Sevilha,
> como o branco sobre branco

---

[42] Frei Caneca wrote his *Gramática da língua portuguesa* during his first spell in jail in Bahia (1817–21) (see Melo, 1933, p. 9).
[43] The third section of *Fábula de Anfion* carries the subtitle 'Anfion busca em Tebas o deserto perdido' [In Thebes, Amphion searches for the lost desert] (p. 90).

que Malevitch [sic] nos pinta
e com os ovos de Brancusi
dispostos pelas esquinas? (pp. 494–5)

[Or is it a city | [. . .] | entirely whitewashed | like Cordoba and Seville, | like the white on white | that Malevich paints for us | and with Brancusi's eggs | placed on street corners?]

Both the painting of the Russian Kazimir Malevich (1878–1935) and the sculptures of Romanian artist Constantin Brancusi (1876–1957) are underpinned by an economy of means that echoed Cabral's own contained language. Yet, it is as images of subversion against geometrical precision, in this case equated with political domination, that they feature in Caneca's deeply anachronistic final soliloquy.

In fact, Brancusi's egg shapes, through which the Romanian artist explored the simplest forms, with the clear aim to 'give joy',[44] avoiding the sense of conflict and opposition that an intricate play of different surfaces would create, contrast with circular forms featured earlier in the play. A case in point is the scene in which the friar is stripped of his holy orders. Here the military officer determines that the troops form a circle around the prisoner, warning that: 'Quem tentar romper esse círculo | rebelde se confessará' [Whoever attempts to break that circle | will admit to being a rebel] (p. 484). The shift towards more fluid, oval, forms in Frei Caneca's last speech is symbolic of his breaking free from oppression in death. It also signals a softening of the friar's political views, towards an understanding that reality does not fit into rigid categorizations. This is in contrast with his childhood view of a world defined by geometrical precision, where the sea and sky were perfectly round: 'de igual luz e geometria!' [of equal light and geometry!] (p. 481). In view of the intense authorial intrusion in the voice of the friar, the progression towards fluidity also reflects the poet's re-evaluation of some of his early statements of poetic intent, for, unlike in the *Fábula de Anfion*, oval images are endowed with positive connotations.[45]

---

[44] Sidney Geist, *Brancusi: A Study of the Sculpture* (New York: Hacker Art Books, 1983), p. 144.

[45] Amphion's search for the desert is visualized in the image of the perfect circle: 'Anfion, | como se preciso círculo | estivesse riscando' [Amphion, | as though a precise circle | he were tracing] (p. 87). As a metaphor for the poetic ideal of precision, clarity, rationality, the desert is juxtaposed to the unpredictability implied in the image of the egg, as seen above.

Frei Caneca's reference to Malevich is equally significant. In his bi-dimensional Suprematist paintings, the artist achieved a sense of depth and movement through the juxtaposition of colours.[46] His 'White on White' painting, to which Frei Caneca alludes, consists of two square shapes of different shades of white, with the smaller contained within the larger. What is noteworthy, in the context of *Auto do frade*, is that the smaller square is actually tilted, thus conveying the idea of movement by effectively disrupting the geometrical precision of the composition.

The abandonment of colour in favour of solely white squares represented, for Malevich, a particular vision of the world, and one defined by freedom: 'the white square is also an impetus towards the foundation of world construction as 'pure action' [...] the white square is the bearer of the white world (world construction) by imposing the mark of purity on human creative life' (in Zhadova, pp. 286–7).

The colour white conveyed the ultimate liberation from artistic conventions, as Malevich himself suggested: 'I have come out into the white [...]. Swim! The white free abyss, infinity is before you' (in Zhadova, p. 283).

Together with Brancusi's oval sculptures, Malevich's painting conveys Caneca's sense of liberation from his fear of death, since he is finally at peace with what awaits him, 'entro nela com alegria' [I enter it with joy] (p. 495).[47] Much in the same way as Malevich's painting, Brancusi's egg-shaped sculptures exemplify a departure from the rigours of geometrical precision: in Caneca's closing speech, they conjure up a vision of death as a city where natural (unpredictable) elements have not been banished. This encapsulates the poet's shift away from a merely rational approach to reality, associated here with political oppression. On a meta-textual level, the implications are considerable, since Cabral proves to have been in dialogue with himself, as he questioned some of his early thoughts on writing. Such re-evaluation did not imply any reduction in his writing's political significance, as shall be discussed in the next section.

---

[46] Larissa A. Zhadova, *Malevich: Suprematism and the Revolution in Russian Art 1910–1930*, trans. Alexander Lieven (London: Thames & Hudson, 1982), pp. 43–7.

[47] In all editions except that of 1994, Cabral employed the past participle 'largados' [dumped] instead of 'dispostos' [placed], in his visualization of Brancusi's eggs. The sense of unpredictability that the image of the egg conveys is certainly increased by the element of chance that is implied in the past participle 'largados'. The use of these two different wordings is an indication of the poet's ongoing dialogue with himself.

2.5 THE VOICES IN THE STREETS

Cabral's ironic treatment of the high-sounding rhetoric associated with members of the dominant order differs from his endorsement of the voices speaking from the margins. As Flora Süssekind observed in relation to the poet's output: 'Because it is above all voices that have no sound, hoarse, cold, half silent, sometimes appearing distant—like a loudspeaker—or on the limit—like the [flamenco form of the] *cante hondo*—that they feature in Cabral's poetry.'[48] This is equally the case in *Auto do frade*, where the voices of the clergy are undermined and where most of the action is conveyed through the accounts of the voices of the crowds in the streets. Functioning as a chorus, they comment on Caneca's political activities and his final hours.

It can be argued that, in line with Frei Caneca's liminal status between life and death, Cabral sought to reproduce the experience of haunting in his characterization of the people in the street. This is achieved by exploring the anonymity in which the voices are shrouded, the extensive use of repetition, as for example incremental repetition within groups of speeches, in which the various voices actually appear simply to be echoing each other rather than interacting.

This mood is set in the scene of the prison cell, in which the utterances of the provincial and the prison guard echo each other as they attempt to wake Frei Caneca from his sleep. The use of anaphora is central in achieving this effect, as is the fact that both voices remain anonymous and somewhat difficult to distinguish.[49]

References to disembodied sounds, such as echoes and screams, also contribute to the sense that the setting of the play is that of a world hovering between life and death. In one of the speeches by members of the judiciary, even distances seem to be measured in terms of disembodied manifestations: '—A Taborda, como está longe.| —A mais de três

---

[48] 'Porque são sobretudo vozes que não soam, roucas, frias, meio mudas, por vezes parecendo à distância—como um 'alto-falante'—ou no limite—como um *cante hondo*—que se manifestam na poesia cabralina.' Flora Süssekind, 'Com passos de prosa. Voz, figura e movimento na poesia de João Cabral de Melo Neto', *Revista USP*, 16 (1992–3), 93–102 (p. 96) (first publ. as 'Stepping into Prose', trans. Regina Igle, *World Literature Today*, 66 (1992), 648–56).

[49] Historical records do in fact name the *provincial* as being Frei Carlos de São José (see Melo, 1933, p. 31). It is all the more revealing of the effects Cabral wished to achieve that he should maintain the character's anonymity.

gritos deste onde' [—Taborda, how far it is. | —More than three screams from this whereabouts] (p. 467).[50]

The cramped conditions in which Frei Caneca was held while in prison are described by way of an allusion to the absence of echoes: '—Lá não tinha com quem falar, | as paredes nem eco tinham' [—There he had no one to talk to, | the walls had no echo even] (p. 475). In contrast, before he is stripped of his orders, the people comment on the 'dead and deserted' convent, abandoned by people unwilling to witness Caneca's execution: '—Assim todos estarão longe | do condenado e, assim, dos ecos' [—Thus they will all be far away | from the convict and, so, from the echoes] (p. 482). There is also a direct reference to the spirit world when one of the potential executioners refuses to carry out the task: 'não vem por medo | do que lhe dizem os espíritos.' [he's not coming because he is afraid | of what the spirits are telling him] (p. 499).[51] Such allusions to disembodied and reflected sounds are compounded by the numerous repetitions found in the various speeches, where the characters seem to echo each other rather than engage in dialogue.

Adding to this is the use of undifferentiated lines of dialogue to introduce the various speakers, whereby the anonymity of the voices is suggested. The clusters of speeches by the people, for example, are introduced by references as generic as 'A gente nas calçadas' [The People on the Pavements] or 'A gente no Largo' [The People in the Square]. Similarly, in scene VI, for example, a group of four speeches, of two lines each, included under the heading 'A gente no Largo' [The People in the Square], is followed by one long, eight-line speech also uttered by the same group. This produces a certain degree of ambiguity, as it is not clear whether the people speak in unison or whether only one individual

---

[50] 'Taborda' is the locality where Frei Caneca was executed. The author's account of how he first came across this expression reveals that the idea of death was inherent in the image of the scream as a measure of distance: 'O grito como distância, isso não é invenção minha. Isso eu ouvi de uma bailarina andaluza, muito camarada minha [...]. Eu acho um negócio extraordinário: você dá um grito, o grito morre, um sujeito dá outro, e depois outro' [The scream as measure of distance is not my idea. I heard this from an Andalusian dancer, who was a very good friend of mine [...]. I think it's a brilliant idea: a person lets out a scream, the scream dies, another person screams, and then another] (in Lima and others, p. 38).

[51] The apparition of Our Lady of Carmo in Recife reportedly interceding to save the life of Frei Caneca is recorded in historical accounts (Melo, 1933, p. 87). It is telling of Cabral's atheism and of the atmosphere he wished to re-create that the episode should be conveyed as a manifestation of the supernatural and not simply of divine intervention.

takes centre stage.[52] Occasional deviations from linguistic norms are not enough for the readers to distinguish one speaker from the next, and they are constantly reminded of the difficulty of knowing who is speaking.

As with Frei Caneca's soliloquies, anachronisms are also found in speeches by the crowd, uttered from the vantage point of the present: '—Não há musica, é bem verdade, | ainda não se inventou o frevo' [—There is no music, that's true, | *frevo* has not yet been invented] (p. 474).[53] As participants in the action of the play and commentators of it from the present day, the people appear to exist essentially in a temporal limbo between past and present, which adds to the indeterminacy of their condition. Moreover, in maintaining the people's anonymity, Cabral suggests an atmosphere of social tensions, and insinuates the potential threat to the dominant order posed by the congregation of the masses, of which they are well aware: '—Muita gente em ruas e praças | é coisa que a muitos assusta' [—Crowds in the streets and squares | is something that frightens many] (p. 476).

These images of social disquiet are contrasted with references to crowds congregating during Carnival, when they are not perceived as a threat by the authorities: '—Sabem que no Carnaval, toda | a gente, em mil gentes, se parte' [—They know that at Carnival, all | people, in a thousand others, divide themselves] (p. 477). Carnival as a metaphor of social alienation is of considerable political import, given that, in relation to Brazil's recent history, Cabral would have been aware of the military dictatorship's celebration of the festival as a manifestation of

---

[52] From a linguistic point of view, the absence of the main clauses in the first speech by 'A gente nas calçadas' produces a syntactical fragmentation that duplicates the absence of any well-defined individuality: '—Se já está morto. Se não dorme. | Sua cela é escura como um poço' [—If he is already dead. If he is not sleeping. | His cell is as dark as a well] (p. 466). A rare case in which an individual voice might be detected occurs in a later speech by the crowds. Here, an unusual syntactical construction is employed for the purpose of rhyme, resulting in a turn of phrase that sounds foreign to a Portuguese speaker (specifically the use of 'quando mesmo', possibly intended as a literal translation of the French 'quand même' [even so/anyway]) and perhaps suggesting the presence of a francophone voice among the people: '—Uma procissão sem andor | é uma procissão quando mesmo' [—A procession without a float | is a procession anyway] (p. 493). For details of French presence in Recife since the early days of colonization see Gilberto Freyre, 'O Recife e os franceses', in *Guia prático, histórico e sentimental da cidade do Recife*, 4th edn (Rio de Janeiro: José Olympio, 1968), pp. 15–18 (p. 15).

[53] *Frevo* is a Pernambucan popular dance form.

social harmony.[54] It is therefore legitimate to suggest that a response to Brazil's recent dictatorial past is articulated here.

The atmosphere of social disquiet is, arguably, also conveyed by the play's overall structure. Critics such as Barbieri have been keen to point out the symmetrical structure of the play, but, on closer inspection, the organization of the various speeches reveals that the symmetry found at the outset disintegrates as the play moves towards its denouement.[55] Following the brief opening scene in the prison cell, with its total of twenty-four speeches between two characters, the speeches in scene II do indeed follow on from one another in symmetrical order, with Frei Caneca and the Meirinho [Bailiff]—oppressed and oppressor—at the centre.[56] However, this structure is unmatched in any of the other scenes, with their increasing utterances by the people, who dominate scene VI. They are also the only ones to be heard in scene VII, being as it is permeated by a sense of social unease.

It is perhaps through this lack of internal symmetry that Cabral wished to capture such unease, duplicating, on a structural level, the attempts to subvert the Establishment (be it the nineteenth-century monarchy or the recent dictatorial regime), which order comes to represent. One of Cabral's earlier poems, 'O vento no canavial' (pp. 150–1), of *Paisagens com figuras*, seems to prefigure the portrayal of the people in *Auto do frade* and appears to bear this point out:

> Não se vê no canavial
> nenhuma planta com nome,
> nenhuma planta maria,

---

[54] For a discussion on Carnival and on Brazilian writers' responses to such manipulation of the festival see Gonzalez and Treece (pp. 314–15).

[55] Barbieri argues that scene I mirrors the closing scene, VII, where Caneca's father throws the images of the saints into the sea in response to what had been foreseen at the outset of the play, when the saints are accused of being deaf (p. 465). Scenes II and VI both include remarks by the people on the absence of a representative of the dominant order: in the first the judge is absent, in the second the executioner. Scene IV stands alone at the centre of the play, as Frei Caneca, a new Christ, is stripped of his orders and handed to his prosecutors. Finally, Barbieri notes that scenes III and V are the only ones in which the reader actually gets a sense of the movement of the procession and are also the ones in which Caneca's humanity is highlighted in his speeches, outlining his political and social ideals.

[56] The sequence is organized as follows: O meirinho; O clero; A gente nas calçadas; A tropa; A gente nas calçadas; A justiça; Frei Caneca; O meirinho; A justiça; A gente nas calçadas; A tropa; A gente nas calçadas; O clero; O meirinho [The Bailiff; The Clergy; The People on the Streets; The Troops; The People on the Streets; The Judiciary; Friar Caneca; The Bailiff; The Judiciary; The People in the Streets; The Troops; The People in the Streets; The Clergy; The Bailiff].

> planta com nome de homem.
> [...]
> Se venta no canavial
> [...]
> É solta sua simetria:
> como a das ondas na areia
> ou as ondas da multidão
> lutando na praça cheia. (pp. 150–1)

[One can see in the sugar cane plantation | no plant with a name, | no plant called maria, | no plant with a man's name | [...] | If the wind blows in the plantation | [...] | Its symmetry is loose: | like the waves on the sand | or the waves of the people | fighting in the crowded square.]

2.6 CONCLUSION

As we approach *Auto do frade* we are initially confronted with a riddle-like epigraph taken from Gertrude Stein (1874–1946), in which the emotional state of the poetic self can only be defined by that which it is not: 'I salute you and I say I am not displeased I am not pleased, | I am not pleased I am not displeased' (p. 464).

The chiasmic structure of these lines translates the experience of a self that hovers between pleasure and displeasure, in a state of turmoil that remains ultimately unresolved. The first person pronoun, 'I', is repeated six times and the initial self-assertive tone of the poetic self, as suggested by the verbs used, 'I salute you and I say...', is swiftly lost in the chiasmus that follows, which is rendered more effective by the minimal use of any punctuation. In this respect, the quotation enacts what Marjorie Perloff identified as one of the great achievements of Stein's writing: 'the gradually changing present of human consciousness, the instability of emotion and thought'.[57]

The repetition of the first person pronoun in the quotation corresponds in number to the six soliloquies by the protagonist of *Auto do frade*, inviting the reader to draw a parallel between the indeterminate state of being of the poetic self in Stein's lines and that of Frei Caneca. The latter certainly emerges as an ambiguous character, thanks to the deliberate intrusion of the authorial voice; his own evolving thoughts as

---

[57] *The Poetics of Indeterminacy: Rimbaud to Cage* (Princeton: Princeton University Press, 1981), p. 98.

well as those of the author are articulated in his soliloquies. To add to this, ambiguity in the characterization of the protagonist also emerges in his liminal status, as a man in between life and death, thus reflecting the author's obsession with finality and the reality of a world scarred by political oppression, where all individuality is denied and which is inhabited by ghost-like figures.

Cabral's provocative disruption of the boundaries between different genres led to a work that is hybrid in form, intended at once to be a poem, an *auto* and a film. Such structural indeterminacy reflects the condition of Frei Caneca, who is speaking from the margins of existence. In exploring this feature, Cabral was able to express his own fears of mortality and voice his indictment of Brazil's oppressive political regimes. Furthermore, the poet's enquiry into his writing shows him to be conscious of the political dimension of ambiguity and indeterminacy in his work. In short, for the insight it provides into the complexity of Cabral's aesthetic ideals and into profound human concerns, the significance of *Auto do frade* within his *œuvre* should not be underestimated. In fact, the exploration of Frei Caneca's condition at the margins of existence developed into Cabral's exploration of the in-between space in his following work, *Agrestes*, which I will consider in the next chapter.

3
In between wor(l)ds: the image of the 'entre-lugar' in *Agrestes*

3.1 INTRODUCTION

João Cabral's obsession with mortality takes shape in his collection *Agrestes* more powerfully than in any of the works analysed earlier, and its title offers an intriguing starting point for analysis. The critic Félix de Athayde suggests that the title *Agrestes* derives from the adjective *agreste*, signifying *rude* [harsh] and *áspero* [rough].[1] With this in mind, he holds the term to express Cabral's pursuit of the prosaic and to be additional proof of his wish not to be included in what he defined as the 'clube dos líricos' [lyrical poets' society].[2] Taking a similar line, Antonio Carlos Secchin argues that the title also recalls the dry region of the interior of the north-east, between the fertile coastal strip and the aridity of the interior, and as such encapsulates 'o seu [Cabral's] verso "pedregoso" e a sua rala floração adjetiva' [his 'rocky' verse with its sparse adornment of adjectives] (Secchin, 2000 [2002], p. 107).

However, I would contend that it is precisely the interstitial nature of the region of the *agreste* evoked in the title that provides the most productive point of departure for studying the image of the in-between space in the collection, through which Cabral's poetic aims are evinced. Indeed, the a*greste* is the region located between the fertile lands of the *zona da mata* and the arid expanses of the *sertão*, in the interior. It is, in fact, a semi-arid region, an 'in-between' land, through which he seems

---

[1] Félix de Athayde, *A viagem ou itinerário intelectual que fez João Cabral de Melo Neto do racionalismo ao materialismo dialético* (Rio de Janeiro: Nova Fronteira, 2000) p. 102.
[2] Cabral employed the expression in his speech of acceptance of the Neustadt Prize, awarded to him by the University of Oklahoma in 1992. See 'Agradecimento pelo Prêmio Neustadt', in Melo Neto (1994, pp. 797–800 (p. 800)).

to capture the essence of existence in precarious balance between life and death, as a state of limbo.

Cabral spoke about his first-hand understanding of the complex geographical and human landscape of the north-east in his interview with Norma Couri, when he recalled:

> I engage with reality. I am from Pernambuco and cannot escape this fact. Northeasterners are more attached to the earth than people from Rio or São Paulo. My world is different, I was brought up on a sugar cane plantation, my family are plantation owners, belonging to the class of the plantation masters, on the fertile coastal strip, far away from the poverty of the interior, but I know the two sides well. My father bought a house in Carpinha, near Angicos [...] which was located exactly on the border between one area and the other.[3]

The theme of the 'in-between' space which Cabral explores in *Agrestes* operates on three levels. Firstly, in his definition of his own writing, which he saw as standing at the margins of Brazilian literary tradition, in an imaginary space between poetry and prose. Secondly, on a social level, the *agreste* encapsulates a space inhabited by those excluded and marginalized by society, often visualized as surviving on the fringes of existence. In this marginal space, Cabral recognizes and explores the subversive power of the voices of the oppressed, which he presents as a challenge to the dominant order. Thirdly, the *agreste* is an in-between space where he pitches his dialogue with literary tradition as he scrutinizes the experience and aftermath of colonization from a Latin American and African perspective. All these points will be the focus of analysis in this chapter, in order to examine how the image of the in-between space is configured.

Structurally, the six sections into which *Agrestes* is divided follow Cabral's own physical and intellectual journeys during his long career as a diplomat. The first section, totalling nineteen compositions, is entitled 'Do Recife, de Pernambuco' [On Recife, in Pernambuco] and is devoted to a revisitation of his native land. In the study of this section, the focus will be on configurations of liminal states, through which Cabral voiced his critique of Portuguese colonization and its legacy. In this respect,

---

[3] 'Meu engajamento é com a realidade. Sou pernambucano e não posso deixar de ser. O nordestino é mais telúrico que o carioca ou o paulista. Meu mundo é outro, fui criado num engenho, minha família é de senhores de engenho, da classe da Casa Grande, da zona da mata, longe da miséria do sertão, mas conheço bem os dois lados. Meu pai comprou uma casa em Carpinha, nos Angicos [...] que ficava bem na divisão entre uma zona e outra' (in Couri, p. 9).

particular attention will be devoted to his dialogue with Fernando Pessoa (1888–1935) and Manuel Bandeira, as he rejected both the colonial discourse he perceived to be encapsulated in Pessoa's *Mensagem* (1934) and the idealized configurations of Brazil in Bandeira's poem 'Uma evocação do Recife' (published in *Libertinagem*, in 1930).

The second section includes fourteen poems on Spanish themes, grouped under the heading 'Ainda, ou sempre, Sevilha' [Still, or Always, Seville]. In studying representations of the margins in this group of poems, this chapter aims to highlight how Cabral perceived Seville to be the epitome of life, precisely because it is a space where established social boundaries and conventions are deliberately undermined. The third section, 'Linguagens alheias' [Language of Others], comprising twenty-four poems in all, revolves around the poet's reflections on the act of writing and his dialogue with writers and artists, including a poem on the 'art' of Brazilian football. By placing this, the largest group of poems in the entire collection, after the one devoted to Seville, the author is symbolically acknowledging the bearing that his time in Spain had on his finding his own voice as a writer. From the literary and artistic affinities revealed in these poems, Cabral's appreciation for art forms in which established boundaries had been deliberately crossed becomes apparent, an example of which is the poet's celebration of Marianne Moore, which will be discussed in detail.

Postcolonial concerns explored in earlier sections become the main theme of the fourth section of *Agrestes*, 'Do outro lado da rua' [From the Other Side of the Street], comprising ten poems on West Africa, and of the fifth section, 'Viver nos Andes' [Living in the Andes], also of ten poems, where the inequities of the European colonial heritage become inscribed in the Andean landscape. In these sections, the in-between space is where the victims of former colonial rule exist, in a liminal state between life and death. In both these configurations of the postcolonial condition, the stress is on the potential for transgression of the margins rather than actual instances of revolt against domination. This amounts to a bleak outlook in terms of the short-term future of the countries with which he was engaging.

A shift to a more inward-looking stance is perceived in the sixth and final section, 'A "Indesejada das gentes"' [The Undesired One], comprising fourteen poems which betray a degree of personal involvement unparalleled in the poet's earlier output. The social perspective which guided Cabral's treatment of the theme of death in other sections of *Agrestes* and in many of his previous works, such as in *Morte e vida severina*, is eschewed here, and the question of mortality is inscribed within the context of ordinary everyday life, through a series of short poems, whose anecdotal tone anticipates that of Cabral's following collection, *Crime na Calle Relator*. The degree of emotional involvement revealed in these poems can perhaps be explained by the fact that the writing of *Agrestes*, from 1981 to 1985, coincided with a period fraught with personal tragedy, during which Cabral's first wife, Stella, was diagnosed as suffering from cancer, of which she eventually died in 1986. Configurations of suicide as a metaphor for defiance of social conformity are particularly striking in this final section of *Agrestes*, and will be analysed here.

The writing of *Agrestes* partly coincided with that of the earlier *Auto do frade*, written between 1981 and 1983. In the *auto*, as well as in the preceding *A escola das facas*, the focus was specifically on Brazil, making it all the more noteworthy how *Agrestes* incorporated different landscapes, providing a broader reflection on the poet's life spent in three different continents, while still remaining committed to addressing questions of inequality, injustice, poverty and exploitation, as this chapter will discuss.

The six sections of *Agrestes* are framed by an introductory and a closing poem, the former, 'A Augusto de Campos', dedicated to one of the leaders of the Brazilian Concrete Poetry movement of the 1950s, the latter, 'O postigo', dedicated to the poet Theodemiro Tostes (1903–86). The fact that Cabral should open his collection by paying homage to a canonical, yet unconventional, Brazilian poet and close it with a tribute to a minor figure within the modernist movement of the state of Rio Grande do Sul translates his desire to challenge literary conventions overtly. Before embarking on an analysis of the various groups of poems of *Agrestes*, I will consider the opening and closing poems of the collection, given that they both deal with the act of writing through images of liminal states in which a constant negotiation of established literary boundaries is implied.

3.2 THE IMAGE OF THE 'ENTRE-LUGAR' AS A *LOCUS* OF SUBVERSION

In a now classic article written in 1971, the Brazilian critic Silviano Santiago analysed the relation between the discourse of Latin American writers and the cultural production of former colonial powers and the economically dominant countries of the West. Santiago questioned the categories of 'source' and 'influence' and formulated the theory of the *entre-lugar* [in-between space], which he defined in the following terms: 'Between sacrifice and play, between imprisonment and transgression, between submission to the norm and aggression, between obedience and rebellion, between assimilation and expression,—there, in this seemingly empty space, in its time and place of clandestinity, is Latin American literature's anthropophagic ritual performed.'[4]

The relevance of the 'entre-lugar' as a *locus* of subversion to Cabral's writing is apparent in the introductory and closing poems of *Agrestes* and also explains the poet's choice of epigraph for the collection as a whole. The quotation, 'Where there is personal liking we go.| Where the ground is sour...' (p. 516), extracted from the poem 'The Hero' by the modernist American writer Marianne Moore (1887–1972), invites the reader to follow the poet along a journey over inhospitable ground and introduces the image of the *agreste* as a poetic *locus* to which Cabral is drawn. The epigraph echoes Cabral's choice of title for the collection by conjuring up the idea of travel, which we find in the different locations featured in *Agrestes*, and a taste for what are, at first sight, rather unwelcoming lands.

However, Cabral is deliberately quoting Moore out of context in his epigraph. This is because the 'sour' ground featured in Moore's poem is where 'love won't grow',[5] and where the 'Hero' learns to go *in spite of* his personal liking. Moore's hero treads sour ground as part of a process of individuation and of learning social conventions, as we read in the second stanza of her poem:

> We do not like some things, and the hero
> doesn't; deviating headstones
> and uncertainty;
> going where one does not wish
> to go; suffering and not saying so; standing and listening where something
> is hiding. (Moore, p. 8)

---

[4] 'Entre o sacrifício e o jogo, entre a prisão e a transgressão, entre a submissão ao código e a agressão, entre a obediência e a rebelião, entre a assimilação e a expressão, —ali, nesse lugar aparentemente vazio, seu tempo e seu lugar de clandestinidade, ali, se realiza o ritual antropófago da literatura latino-americana.' Silviano Santiago, 'O entre-lugar no discurso latino-americano', in *Uma literatura nos trópicos. Ensaios sobre dependência cultural*, rev. Aníbal Mari (São Paulo: Perspectiva, 1978), pp. 11–28 (p. 28).

[5] Marianne Moore, *The Complete Poems* (London: Faber & Faber, 1967), p. 8.

The hero deviates headstones, causing them to turn, thus attempting to uncover the secrets of the dead. Struggling against his dislike for what is not fully comprehensible, the hero sets out to probe the unknown. By employing the verb 'deviating' transitively, Moore emphasizes the hero's courage to confront the greatest of uncertainties facing Mankind. Cabral seems to endorse the qualities displayed by Moore's hero, but, unlike the traveller of sour lands, he shows no distaste for the inhospitable or the unknown.

This becomes apparent in the opening poem of *Agrestes*, 'A Augusto de Campos' (pp. 517–18). Here, Cabral claims to be writing on 'as mesmas coisas e loisas' [the same things and headstones] (p. 517) and entrusts Campos with the ability to find in *Agrestes* 'coisas não mortas de todo' [things not entirely dead] (p. 517). This last image captures Cabral's fascination with existence at the interface between life and death, which is one of the instances in which the image of the *entre-lugar* is explored.

The image central to the poem is that of the *aceiro* [clearing] and, more precisely, that of the 'aceiros da prosa' [prose clearings], an 'in-between' space in which Cabral visualizes his own writing. As a strip of uncultivated land, kept clear to prevent fire spreading across contiguous crops, the *aceiro* represents the poet's aversion to sentimental expression in favour of emotional containment. It is also, significantly, the boundary, an 'in-between' land at the margins of poetry and prose.

Cabral situates his own poetry within the 'aceiros da prosa', in a visual representation of his subversion of mainstream poetic conventions. On a structural level, this is clear in the second stanza, where he deliberately disrupts a metric pattern of seven-syllable lines by incorporating an eight-syllable line, less favoured in Portuguese tradition, in line seventeen, 'o pouco-verso de oito sílabas' [the lesser verse of eight syllables] (p. 517), described as being '(em linha vizinha à prosa)' [a line close to prose] (p. 517). He also opts for the 'imperfect' assonantal rhyme, 'que apaga o verso e não soa' [which flattens the line and does not resound] (p. 517), challenging expectations of a Portuguese-speaking readership more familiar with and appreciative of consonantal rhyme.[6]

In this way, Cabral defies poetic conventions from within (as for example, through his manipulation of rhyme and metre), whereas

---

[6] In an interview with Arnaldo Saraiva, Cabral spoke of his use of eight-syllable lines and assonantal rhyme as aimed at challenging readers' expectations and creating a less harmonious verse. See 'João Cabral de Melo Neto: o que a vida tem de melhor é, para mim, a literatura', *Jornal de Letras*, 7 September 1987, pp. 6–7.

Augusto de Campos is celebrated for actually challenging the boundaries of conventional poetry, his involvement in the Concrete Poetry Project and rejection of traditional verse form exemplifying his innovative aesthetic intent.[7]

The image of the 'aceiro', introduced in the opening poem of *Agrestes* and key to understanding Cabral's poetic aim, is revisited through the agricultural imagery found in 'O postigo' (pp. 584–5), with which he closes the collection. This time, however, Cabral voices his scepticism about his ability to carry on writing, given that it requires a continual renegotiation of poetic boundaries: 'escrever é sempre estrear-se | e já não serve o antigo ancinho' [writing is always to begin again | and the old rake is of no use] (p. 584). His anxieties proved unfounded, of course, because he went on to write two more collections.

That said, such pessimism is consistent with Cabral's typically self-deprecating stance, perceived in his dialogue with Augusto de Campos. In fact, the opening poem is constructed on a play on oppositions between himself and his fellow writer, whose work is celebrated for its non-conformity, visualizing it in the figure of a woman at the window who relishes her status at the margins, 'rindo de ser sem discípula' [laughing at not having followers] (p. 518).

But it is primarily to Augusto de Campos the literary critic that Cabral dedicates *Agrestes*, emphasized by the reference to Pound, whose *ABC of Reading* (1934) Campos translated into Portuguese.[8] Thus, Campos's defiance of poetic norms and his critical appreciation of other writers lie behind Cabral's tribute.[9] Such qualities are also

---

[7] The exponents of 1950s Concrete Poetry, Augusto de Campos (b. 1931), Haroldo de Campos (1929–2003) and Décio Pignatari (b. 1927) saw Cabral as one of their masters and acknowledged their debt to the older poet in their 'Manifesto da poesia concreta', published in *Noigrandes* in 1958. Cabral provided the Concretists' with models of impersonal, rational poetry, constructed with minimal vocabulary (see Gonzalez and Treece, p. 244). Augusto de Campos also published a study on Cabral in *Poesia antipoesia antropofagia* (1978), which he described on the cover as a collection of essays on poetry that instigates an ethical and artistic debate, Cabral's work being representative of this kind. See Augusto de Campos, 'Da antíode à antilira', in *Poesia antipoesia antropofagia* (São Paulo: Cortez & Moraes, 1978), pp. 49–54 (p. 52) (first publ. in *Correio da manhã*, 11 December 1966).

[8] Translated into Portuguese as *ABC da literatura*, org. Augusto de Campos, trans. Augusto de Campos and José P. Paes (São Paulo: Cultrix, 1970).

[9] Speaking on Cabral's significance for the Concretists during celebrations in honour of Cabral having being awarded the Queen Sofia Prize (1994), Haroldo de Campos recalled how his brother Augusto replied to Cabral's poetic homage with an equally reverential poem. His poem 'a joão cabral agrestes', was originally published *in O anticrítico* (1986) and then again in *Despoesia* (1994). See Haroldo de Campos, 'Os

displayed by the poet himself in the first group of poems of *Agrestes*, as evinced in his dialogue with Fernando Pessoa's *Mensagem* and with Manuel Bandeira's poem 'Evocação do Recife', which will be analysed in the next section.

3.3 THE SPECTRE OF THE OPPRESSED: IMAGES OF THE NORTH-EAST

It is well known that Bandeira's poetry was a huge inspiration to Cabral. The colloquial language and themes drawn from everyday life which Bandeira incorporated into his work were, by his own admission, a revelation and an inspiration to the younger poet.[10] Cabral's attitude towards the older poet in *Agrestes* is, however, far from reverential, as is his stance in relation to Pessoa, which is apparent at the very incipit of the collection.

It is in the opening poem of the first section of *Agrestes*, entitled 'O nada que é' (p. 519), that Cabral engages with Pessoa. Here, he juxtaposes his own bleak view of the heritage of the discoveries, and the 'birth' of Brazil, with what he read as Pessoa's *Mensagem*'s positive images of the mythical birth of Portugal; through his engagement with the Portuguese poet, Cabral assesses his condition as a *nordestino* and his role as a writer of the north-east of Brazil.

Indeed, the title of Cabral's poem suggests a reference to Pessoa's 'Ulysses', of *Mensagem*.[11] For Pessoa, 'O mytho é o nada que é tudo' [Myth is a nothing that is everything], myth being crucial in the formation of Portuguese national identity and in ensuring that reality becomes meaningful. Myth is for Pessoa the only lasting legacy of the past, beyond which there is only oblivion: 'Em baixo, a vida, metade | De nada, morre' [Below, life, half | Of nothing, dies] (Pessoa, p. 6).

Adopting a highly critical stance in relation to the Portuguese poet, Cabral devised the title of his own poem as a paradox formed from a fraction of the first line of Pessoa's composition. Thanks to this device, a juxtaposition is suggested of the plenitude represented by myth, as

---

"poetas concretos" e João Cabral de Melo Neto. Um testemunho', *Colóquio/Letras* 157–8 (2000 [2002]), 27–31.

[10] See, for example, Süssekind (1996, p. 10).

[11] Fernando Pessoa, *Mensagem* in *Obra poética*, 9th edn, ed. Maria Aliete Galhoz (Rio de Janeiro: Nova Aguilar, 1986), p. 6.

propounded by Pessoa, and the nothingness which Cabral saw as expressing the reality of the north-east. Pessoa celebrated the arrival of Ulysses by sea as the image on which Portuguese identity as a nation of seafarers was constructed. Conversely, Cabral centred his poem on the image of the sea viewed as unfathomable and enigmatic:

> Um canavial tem a extensão
> ante a qual todo metro é vão.
>
> Tem o escancarado do mar
> que existe para desafiar
>
> que números e seus afins
> possam prendê-lo nos seus sins. (p. 519)

[A sugar cane plantation is so vast | that any measure is vain. | It has the vastness of the sea | which exists to defy | that any number or the like | can capture it in their affirmations.]

The possible dieresis in the fourth line of the above quotation means that the eight-syllable line pattern could be disrupted by a nine-syllable line, in a structural representation of the difficulty of measuring the expanses of the sea and sugar cane plantations. Both of these refer to Brazil's colonial past: the former having been 'conquered' by the Portuguese navigators, the latter being a legacy of colonial rule. The fact that neither should be perceived as measurable conveys the Brazilian negative perspective on the 'civilizing' mission and experience of colonization. Moreover, the sea from which Brazil was 'born' provides the image of barrenness through which the sugar cane plantations that still occupy much of the fertile lands are visualized, as a nothing pregnant like the sea. The bleak view of the discovery is thereby reinforced, juxtaposed to the image of fertility in Pessoa's poem, through which the power of legend is captured:

> Assim a lenda se escorre
> A entrar na realidade,
> E a fecundal-a decorre. (Pessoa, p. 6)

[Thus legend flows | As it enters reality, | And impregnates it.]

Cabral also seems to be responding to Pessoa's exaltation of Portugal's cultural and historical heritage by drawing attention to the workers exploited on the sugar cane plantation, through his reference to the anonymity that inhabits this space. While Pessoa exalts myth, or more precisely, what is unreal, as the only true reality, Cabral turns his focus on those who 'exist' but who are not seen. Thus, the Recife that Cabral explores in the first section of *Agrestes* is a place, or rather, a limbo, haunted by ghostly figures, whom he nonetheless acknowledges as social entities. Their plight is one they share with the forgotten children of the Recife orphanages, addressed in 'A roda dos expostos da Jaqueira' (pp. 523–4).

In the poem, Cabral remembers the gyratory window in the wall of the hospital of the Jaqueira district of Recife, where, under the cover of darkness, unwanted newborn babies were left. The 'disappearance' of the children is initially ironically compared to magicians' tricks and alchemic transformation and then chillingly equated to a burial, through which the tragedy of the unwanted children is foregrounded: 'ali sepultar uma vida | que ninguém viu, nem a parida' [there bury a life | seen by no one, not even the child-bearer] (p. 523).

Cabral perceives the fate of the children as that of 'living dead', and this is emphasized by the anonymity that surrounds them. In point of fact, by way of careful grammatical and vocabulary preferences (such as use of impersonal verbs or indefinite pronouns) Cabral conveys their condition as hidden rather than visible creatures.

Cabral recalls how he used to hear the coughing of the young tuberculosis sufferers punctuate their singing in the orphanage choir. The reference to tuberculosis ensures that the monotone sound of the Gregorian chant, rather than representing a religious experience, is infused with the children's physical and emotional plight, particularly given the illness's link with social deprivation. In this way, Cabral subverts any religious message and, instead, views the situation of the children of the Jaqueira orphanage from a social standpoint. What this reveals is that the voice of the poor and the excluded, which informed the sound of the *cantochão* (Gregorian chant), impacted on the poet's writing and on society as a whole:

([...] foi o cantar pernambucano
que deformou a melodia
que pudéssemos ter um dia). (p. 524)

[([...] it was the pernambucan chant | that deformed the melody | we might have had one day).]

By enclosing his final reflection in brackets, Cabral provides a graphic representation of the subversive power of the 'unseen'.

Cabral describes the singing of the children by way of personification, as having its feet on the ground ('um de pés no chão') (p. 524), echoing his definition of his own writing in the earlier poem 'A Augusto de Campos'. Therefore, the victims of social exclusion, from the *entre-lugar* in which they exist, shape the reality of the north-east, and by them Cabral's poetry is also informed.

In articulating his own recollections of the north-east, Cabral opposes colonial discourse, which he read in the celebration of Portugal's myths and history in *Mensagem*. However, in so doing he also carefully avoids any nostalgic or idealized representation of Brazilian cultural identity. In the first section of *Agrestes*, this is apparent in 'Uma evocação do Recife' (pp. 524–5), in which Cabral was responding to Bandeira's reminiscence of his early years in his famous composition 'Evocação do Recife'.[12]

Bandeira's poem exudes a sense of nostalgia, as it re-creates the atmosphere of the everyday life of the Recife that the poet had known in childhood. Fragments of memories bring back to life the voices of the children in the street, the cries from the bustling streets of Recife, and the echo of the voices of the north-east, with their distinctive diction: 'Capiberibe | —Capibaribe' (p. 213).[13]

Bandeira was keen to explore the voices of the people as the only legitimate way forward in forming a true Brazilian literary tradition, as he reveals in 'Evocação do Recife':

> A vida não me chegava pelos jornais nem pelos livros
> Vinha da boca do povo na língua errada do povo
> Língua certa do povo
> Porque ele é que fala gostoso o português do Brasil. (p. 213)

[Life did not reach me through newspapers or books | It came from the mouths of the people in the common tongue of the people | The correct language of the people | Because they speak the delicious Portuguese of Brazil.]

As the critic Giovanni Pontiero highlighted, Bandeira was one of the first to recognize the significance of regional linguistic norms for the expression of an authentic national sensibility.[14] Indeed, ordinary people take centre stage and are the only 'heroes' of Bandeira's childhood memories, making 'Evocação do Recife' the best example of the poet's

---

[12] Manuel Bandeira, *Poesia completa e prosa*, 4th edn (Rio de Janeiro: Nova Aguilar, 1983), pp. 212–14.
[13] In *Itinerário de Pasárgada*, Bandeira recalls how, while at school, he was mocked by José Veríssimo, his geography teacher, for using the north-eastern spelling, 'Capibaribe', rather than 'Capiberibe', on referring to the famous river that flows though Recife. Years later, he would seek sweet revenge on his teacher by including both spellings in the poem. See Bandeira, pp. 28–102, (pp. 51–2).
[14] Giovanni Pontiero, *Manuel Bandeira. (Visão geral de sua obra)*, trans. Terezinha Prado Galante (Rio de Janeiro: José Olympio, 1986), p. 125.

ability to elevate the commonplace to the category of the sublime (Pontiero, p. 120).

Conversely, Cabral's 'Uma evocação do Recife' incorporates no such anecdotal material and responds to the 'voices' in Bandeira with 'silence'. The only voice we hear is that of the poet himself, who conjures up a bleak vision of his native city, through memories of Recife—up to the 1940s when he left to pursue his career in Rio de Janeiro—of acute social division and alienation. On the one hand, there is the industrializing and expanding Recife epitomized in the image of the tram (*bonde*) which spreads its 'spider's legs'; on the other, the mudflats (*mangues*), which the tram network is careful to avoid, bypassing them on the tongues of dry land. Through word play, Cabral employs the image of the 'línguas secas' [dry tongues] (p. 525) to allude to the strips of dry land of the *mangue* through which the tram passes, as it eludes any contact with the poverty on the mudflats. But the image also conveys the plight of the *retirantes* who, having fled the drought-ravaged interior, find that any hope of overcoming their predicament in the big city is denied. Moreover, and most importantly, it conveys their inability to 'speak'.

This powerfully visual representation of Cabral's native land seems to enact what Homi Bhabha saw as the fundamental role of memory in reflecting on the postcolonial condition. For Bhabha, remembering: 'is never a quiet act of introspection or retrospection. It is a painful re-membering, a putting together of the dismembered past to make sense of the trauma of the present.'[15] Indeed, Recife is captured through the metonymic images of a hybrid creature, part arachnid (spider), part human, part beast of prey. From these fragmented images, we visualize a grotesque and disjointed creature, in which a sense of social disintegration and exclusion is projected, since it is not the receptivity of an open hand that the 'dedos espalmados' [spread-out fingers] (p. 525) of Recife evoke.

Cabral points to the silence of the *mangue* and its failure to be represented in the written word, yet also alludes to the destabilizing power of the 'unseen'. He speaks of the inescapable, nightmarish visions which perturb the sleep of all inhabitants of Recife, caused by the 'haunting' power of the 'dead' waters and of those who live near them. Such criticism of social neglect through reference to nightmares is extremely poignant, since it captures the mood of the entire poem, which re-creates the experience of disturbed sleep. As Gledson (1978,

---

[15] In Leela Gandhi, *Postcolonial Theory: A Critical Introduction* (Edinburgh: Edinburgh University Press, 1998), p. 9.

p. 45) highlighted in relation to Cabral's first collection, *Pedra do sono*, here Cabral again seems to revisit this marginal state, exploring its association with death, as he reflects on the question of social alienation. Indeed, 'Uma evocação do Recife' re-creates the sensations of sleep to a destabilizing effect, duplicating the reality of the north-east in a liminal existence between life and death.

Cabral's choice of the 'in-between' space also defines his position in relation to his two 'masters', one Portuguese and one Brazilian. A case in point is precisely the first section of *Agrestes*, which displays neither a quest for heroes of the north-east, as a challenge to the Portuguese heroic past exalted by Pessoa, nor a search for a Brazilian 'voice' as explored by Bandeira. In contrast to both, the Brazil re-created in *Agrestes* is constituted by ghostly figures, living between worlds. Cabral's reflection of Brazil's colonial condition stands therefore at a crossroads between an oppositionist challenge to the discourse of the discoveries (Pessoa) and an almost utopian 'rediscovery' of Brazilian identity (Bandeira). In the earlier *Auto do frade*, the demythologized hero of Frei Caneca exemplified Cabral's unconventional take on north-eastern historical themes and, betraying a similar stance, in defiance of conventional parameters of historical analysis, *Agrestes* rejects official historical perspectives and proposes a re-evaluation of marginal, and often anti-heroic, figures from Pernambuco's past.

An apt illustration of this point is provided by the poem 'Por que prenderam o "Cabeleira"' (pp. 529–30), with its reworking of a common theme in north-eastern folklore, centring on the capture of the infamous *cangaceiro* [bandit]. Right from its epigraph, drawn from a popular rhyme, the focus is on the last hours of freedom of one of the eighteenth century's most feared bandits.[16]

The son of a *mameluco*, and therefore of Indian and European descent, Cabeleira, a nickname he acquired thanks to his full head of hair, spread terror in the north-east of Brazil, before eventually being captured in a sugar cane plantation on the outskirts of Recife. Sentenced to death by hanging, in 1776, alongside his father, believed to be the evil influence on his son's otherwise good nature, and the third leader of the group, Teodósio, he went to his death displaying signs of sincere contrition. The belief that Cabeleira had acted under the pernicious

---

[16] The epigraph reads: 'Quando me prendêro | no canaviá | cada pé de cana | era um oficiá' [When they caught me | in the sugar cane field | every sugar cane | was an officer] (p. 529).

influence of his father, and his repentance for the violence he had perpetrated, made a great impression on the imagination of the people, who eventually elevated him to hero status.[17] The popularity of this figure is testified by the fact that the nineteenth-century fictionalization of Cabeleira's life by the novelist Franklin Távora (1842–88) was based primarily on popular sources, as acknowledged by the author himself.[18]

Notably, the lines used in the epigraph to Cabral's poem had already been incorporated by Bandeira in his well-known poem 'Trem de ferro' (pp. 236–7), from *Estrela da manhã* (1936). Yet, the two poets' appropriation of the theme differs strikingly. Indeed, in Bandeira, the insertion of the lines towards the end of the poem conveys the sense of the train's progression deeper into the interior of Brazil, where popular traditions are more deeply rooted. Inscribed in Bandeira's playful use of rhythm and short line pattern, they also contribute to reproduce the train's increasing speed. Cabral's appropriation of this popular material is anchored onto a reflection of the social roots of the *cangaço* [banditry], casting Cabeleira as the epitome of the disenfranchised.[19] Indeed, the juxtaposition of dominant order and marginalized population is encoded in Cabral's visualization of the landscape in which the bandit was captured, with the *canavial*, where Cabeleira was caught, and the native tropical vegetation of the Chã de Capoeira, in which he had sought cover, reflecting the opposite ends of the social pyramid.

Because of his marginal existence, Cabeleira is perceived as living in a world inhabited by ghosts, his hiding place, haunted. His social invisibility means that he too is visualized as a ghost-like figure, and it is

---

[17] Luís da Câmara Cascudo, *Dicionário do folclore brasileiro*, 6th edn (Belo Horizonte: Itatiaia; São Paulo: Edusp, 1988), p. 162.

[18] 'Notas do autor', in Franklin Távora, *O Cabeleira*, ed. Manuel Cavalcanti Proença (Rio de Janeiro: Edições de Ouro, 1966), pp. 209–16 (p. 209). The novel was first published in 1876.

[19] The *cangaceiros* were always from a poor background, and violence was their only means of escape from poverty, as Maria José Londres points out: 'O valente é sertanejo; é pobre; é mestiço; é feio e é brigão' [The brave man is from the *sertão*, he is poor, mixed-race, ugly and ready for a fight]. See 'O sertanejo valente na literatura de cordel', in *Os pobres na literatura brasileira*, ed. Roberto Schwarz (São Paulo: Brasiliense, 1983), pp. 238–43 (p. 240). North-eastern novelist Graciliano Ramos (1892–1953) seemed to share a similar view, as we see from his analysis of the phenomenon: 'O que transformou Lampião em besta-fera foi a necessidade de viver' [What turned Lampião [famous north-eastern bandit of early twentieth century] into a beast was the need to survive]. See 'Lampião', in *Viventes das Alagoas*, 14th edn (São Paulo: Record, 1984), pp. 135–7 (p. 136).

poignant that his death should coincide with his emergence from the shadows, portrayed as a symbol of his marginality. Significantly, the brightness of the light in the plantations is endowed with negative connotations for it implies the total erasure of the identity of the marginalized.[20] The ambiguity suggested by the word 'lucidez' (lucidity), meaning brightness as well as rationality, indicates that the duality of shadows and light also encapsulates that of irrationality and reason. If the prevalence of one over the other results in the demise of those already marginalized, what seems to be implied in this poem is the need to overcome binary oppositions of this kind. The meta-textual implications of this suggestion are considerable, for it appears to echo the thoughts Cabral had expressed in his earlier *Auto do frade*, with its review of his poetics of clarity and precision.

From a political perspective, it translates a critique of social structures that are underpinned by prejudice and exclusion, while concurrently raising important racial issues, for the *cangaço* was essentially a black phenomenon (Cabeleira himself was of mixed race, albeit of Indian descent), reacting against a white, patriarchal feudal system of power and landownership. Indeed, banditry provided a way out from poverty for the lower classes and, as Graciliano Ramos highlighted, in some instances, also for members of the impoverished higher classes, the famous Corisco who served under the orders of the poor, illiterate, mulatto Virgulino Ferreira, commonly known by the name of Lampião.[21]

Cabral does not, therefore, demonize the *cangaceiro*, as is the case in some popular renditions of the theme.[22] Nor does he portray the bandit as the fearsome character whose possible appearance has instilled terror in generations of north-eastern children.[23] Although portraying Cabeleira as enjoying popular support, Cabral does not foreground any heroic endeavour he might have boasted.[24] Rather, his focus is on Cabeleira as

---

[20] Cabral refers to the 'lucidez de soda cáustica' [lucidity of caustic soda] (p. 530).

[21] 'O fator econômico no cangaço', in *Viventes das Alagoas*, 14th edn (São Paulo: Record, 1984), pp. 128–34 (pp. 131–2).

[22] This is exemplified in the opening lines of a popular song on Cabeleira: 'Fecha a porta, gente. | Cabeleira aí vem! | Matando mulheres, | meninos também.' [Close the door, everybody. | Cabeleira is coming! | Killing women, | and children too.] (in Cascudo, 1988, p. 162).

[23] Gilberto Freyre, *Casa-grande & senzala*, 13th edn, 2 vols (Rio de Janeiro: José Olympio, 1966), II, 457–58.

[24] As Ronald Daus explains, the reputation of the bandits of the north-east would have been enhanced by the poets of Brazil's popular literature, who would aim at directing the audience's sympathies towards the *cangaceiros*. See *O ciclo épico dos cangaceiros na poesia*

victim, epitome of those who have not succeeded in escaping poverty, equating him to a naked, hunted animal, in the heat of a chase, whose plight mirrors the deprivation of those working the sugar cane fields: 'que nem vestem quem as amanha' [which fail to clothe those who work them] (p. 530).

In Cabral's representation of the rural interior of Pernambuco, Cabeleira is a ghostly figure, in the sense that he exists in between worlds, at the margins of society. In contrast to configurations of haunting analysed in the earlier 'Uma evocação do Recife', where the impoverished inhabitants of the 'dead' waters of the *mangue* haunt the city dwellers of Recife, his condition as a ghost is not perceived as a manifestation of the agency of the marginalized. Rather, the indeterminacy that defines the bandit's status as a being existing between life and death is, in this instance, primarily a duplication of his oppression. The theme of haunting thus emerges as a powerful indictment of the rigid social structures regulating north-eastern Brazil. Indeed, once Cabeleira transposes the social limits imposed by the dominant order, he necessarily ceases to exist: 'quis descer pelos canaviais, | onde um fantasma é incapaz' [he wished to come down through the sugar cane plantations, | where a ghost is helpless] (p. 530).

It is noteworthy that the only other voice present in the group of poems 'Do Recife, de Pernambuco', apart from Cabral's own, should be not that of a *nordestino*, but of an Englishman. Indeed, the poem 'Conversa em Londres, 1952' (pp. 525–7) reproduces the poet's conversation with an English interlocutor who is curious to learn about Brazil.[25] As an outsider and citizen of a European colonial power, the latter is able to pinpoint the inequities of the internal colonialism that underpins Brazil's political and economic structures, in which the north-east is seen as having been treated as a colony. In this foreign voice, therefore, the duality of colonizer (Great Britain) and colonized

---

popular do nordeste, trans. Rachel Teixeira Valença (Rio de Janeiro: Fundação Casa de Rui Barbosa, 1982), p. 91. An example of such positive portrayal of these bandits is found in the following lines from a popular poem: 'Este governo atual | julga que a oposição | não tem direito ao Brasil, | pertence a outra nação [...]. | Devido a isso é que o rifle | tem governado o sertão!" [The current government | believes the opposition | has no place in Brazil, | that it belongs to another nation [...]. | It's because of this that the rifle | has been ruling the *sertão*]. In Luís da Câmara Cascudo, *Vaqueiros e cantadores* (Belo Horizonte: Itatiaia; São Paulo: Edups, 1984), p. 164.

[25] Cabral served at the Brazilian Consulate in London from 1950 to 1952.

(Brazil) is thrown into question, and the boundaries between these two categories are shown to be fluid.

Thus, Cabral's reflection of Brazil's colonial heritage stands in an *entre-lugar* in relation to what he read as Pessoa's celebration of Portuguese colonialism and Bandeira's idealized vision of his native land. The theme of the in-between is also evident in the images he constructs of the north-east, his exploration of marginal north-eastern figures whose condition is uncertain, as they are visualized in a limbo, struggling for survival and greater visibility at the margins of existence. These bleak configurations of the north-east are juxtaposed with the positive voices that speak out defiantly from Seville, which will be discussed in the following section.

3.4 DEFYING THE BOUNDARIES OF LIFE AND DEATH: SEVILLE

Cabral's depictions of the city of Seville in the second section of *Agrestes*, 'Ainda, ou sempre, Sevilha' provide a formidable contrast to his bleak renditions of the north-east. The sombre mood that pervades the poems on his native land gives way to a celebration of life, which in Cabral's poetics is epitomized by the Andalusian city. It is significant, however, that Cabral should visualize Seville as also existing in an *entre-lugar*, albeit manifested in quite different terms.[26] While the first section of *Agrestes* was inhabited by ghost-like creatures defined by their limited power to speak, in the second group of poems, the voice of the people is reinstated, viewed primarily as a marginal force constituting an openly subversive challenge to established order. These subversive voices are, overwhelmingly, female.

The act of speech as the manifestation of female empowerment is explored in the first poem, 'Conversa de sevilhana' (p. 537). As the *sevilhana* and her companion lie side by side in bed, in their 'trajes' [clothes], more specifically their *trajes de Adão* [literally, 'Adam's clothes', i.e. birthday suit], she light-heartedly mocks the Church's condemnation

---

[26] Seville featured prominently in Cabral's work. In his diplomatic capacity, the poet had served there from 1956 to 1958 and 1962 to 1964, and, of all his diplomatic posts, it was in Seville that he had felt most at home. Cabral often spoke of his obsession with Seville, even stating that as a result of his years in the city he knew more about bullfighting than he did about literature. (See interview with Couri, p. 10.)

of her 'carnal knowledge' and proceeds to point to all those whom she would like to see joining her in hell. She pokes fun at the fact that her soul is beyond redemption, stating she will go 'ahead of Dante', but, like Dante, makes sure all those who did her a bad turn or who abused their power, from taxi drivers to the police, take up their place alongside her. The humorous afterthought with which the poem closes suggests that she does not in fact fear what is in store for her, or indeed seriously believe in the possibility of damnation, stating that the 'formation march' in hell would benefit from a few more sergeants. Thus, her stance is unequivocally materialistic, rejecting the example of Dante's spiritual journey to heaven, and subversive of patriarchal order, which she is quite prepared, literally, to turn on its head by sending it 'head first' to hell.

Therefore, Cabral begins his revisitation of Seville through the voice of one speaking from the margins of society, and thanks to the effectiveness with which voices such as this one challenge an oppressive established order, the Spanish city comes to symbolize a positive alternative equated to vitality. This also transpires in the cultural manifestations of the city, a case in point being bullfighting, which is the theme of the second poem of the section, 'Lembrando Manolete' (p. 538).

In this composition, the legendary bullfighter defies the boundaries between life and death, living his life on a knife-edge. Cabral speaks of bullfighting as 'expor a vida à louca foice' [exposing life to the mad scythe] (p. 538). While the poem's reiterations and enjambements convey a sense of continuity, this is then undermined, on a visual level, by the blank spaces which separate the six couplets. In this way, the overall structure of the poem ensures that the tenuous balance between life and imminent death is reproduced effectively.[27]

The courage with which the bullfighter parades before the bull demonstrates his defiance of death, reiterated through the repetition of the verbs 'expor' and 'expõe' [to expose/exposes]. Such daring was clearly intended to contrast with the plight of the 'Expostos' [literally, the 'Exposed', i.e. the foundlings] of the orphanage in the Jaqueira,

---

[27] Cabral is here employing a device similar to the one highlighted by Flora Süssekind in another poem of *Agrestes*, 'A Antonio Mairena, cantador de flamenco' (p. 543). Süssekind noted his suggestive manipulation of enjambements and blank spaces, through which he re-created the tenuous balance between sound and silence in the voice of the flamenco singer (see Süssekind, 1992–3, p. 96).

featured in the previous section, thus evincing the poet's contrasting perceptions of Seville and Pernambuco.

Yet, a common feature to both these poetic landscapes is the emphasis placed on liminality, which the *agreste* as a poetic space represents, and can in fact be glimpsed in one of Cabral's earlier poems, 'Alguns toureiros' (pp.157–8), included in the collection *Paisagens com figuras*. In this earlier composition, we learn how Manolete was the one who best calculated the boundaries of 'o fluido aceiro da vida' [the fluid clearing of life] (p. 158). If the bullfighter can be seen as the embodiment of Cabral's own poetic ideal of precision and clarity, at the margins of literary tradition, it is also true that Manolete personifies an ethic of defiance of those living a liminal existence.

This falls in line with the themes explored in the poem 'O mito em carne viva' (p. 540), which raises political, religious, as well as gender issues which are important to our understanding of Cabral's rendition of the *entre-lugar* given their implications in the poet's dialogue with Pessoa.[28] In the poem, Cabral focuses on the encounter between Castile and Andalusia, foregrounded from a historical perspective. Castile, stage of political power, with its strong historical links with the Catholic Church, embodied by the rule of the *Reyes Católicos* [Catholic Kings], for example, comes under the gaze of the marginalized and 'Moorish' Andalusia, embodied by an anonymous *sevilhana*. Castile's expansionist endeavours and its control over Spain's conquest of the New World, however, belong to the past. It is, therefore, all the more poignant that the museum which it is described as having become is now symbolically 'invaded' by the *sevilhana*.

The woman's response to established art form, as she is captured staring at a painting depicting the Crucifixion, is subversive in that she more readily empathizes with the suffering of the Mother of Christ than feigns compunction at the sacrifice of the Son of Man. In a further instance of subversion, her exclamation of 'sisterly' compassion, unmotivated by religious faith, is voiced not in official Castilian, but in her own Andalusian vernacular: '*Lo quié no habrá sufr'io e'ta mujé!* [What this woman must have suffered!] (p. 540).

The subversive, marginal position of the *sevilhana* seems to provide Cabral with the vantage point from which to revisit themes central to

---

[28] In the title of this poem, Cabral explores the ambiguity implied in the expression 'carne viva', which means 'open wound', but which, taken literally, implies vitality, as suggested by the adjective 'viva' [alive].

Pessoa's *Mensagem*, appearing to challenge the power of regeneration held by a mythical saviour and subverting the image of the *névoa* [mist] as the veil that would need to be lifted if greater times are to come. Through the image of the myth in raw flesh, Cabral explores the concept that existence lies solely on a material rather than metaphysical plane. Thus, Cabral unambiguously rejects the validity of myth as encoded in the painting of the crucifixion. The *névoa* that shrouds the painting becomes a metaphor for the message of the possibility of spiritual salvation through the passion of Christ. However, this message goes unheeded, as the *sevilhana* fails to be filled with awe by the great mysteries of the faith, preferring to focus on 'marginal', but nonetheless crucial, elements of the scene of the crucifixion.

The image of the *névoa* that Cabral is subverting in response to Pessoa can be found in the poem, 'A última nau' of *Mensagem* (p. 16). At the close of that poem, D. Sebastião, the mythical saviour, appears from behind the mist, heralding the birth of a new Portuguese empire. Seemingly responding to Pessoa's vision, Cabral projected life and regeneration on to the poetic *locus* of Seville, perceived as a space where the marginalized find a voice. The city, as a liminal space, where diversity is celebrated, captures the only true meaning of 'eternal life', as the title of the section indicates: 'Ainda, ou sempre, Sevilha'.

3.5 READING THE OTHER

In between the sections of *Agrestes* in which Cabral revisits the geographical locations of greatest significance to him, we find a group of poems entitled 'Linguagens alheias', devoted to his dialogue with other writers and artists and including one on football. This might at first seem somewhat incongruous, yet one of the poems of this section provides an explanation for his choice. In 'A literatura como turismo' (pp. 557–8), the poet ponders on how some writers are capable of blurring the boundaries between imaginary and concrete locations for their readers. One can argue that this fluidity is translated in the structure of *Agrestes* itself, where the third and sixth sections deal with inner rather than geographical voyages. It also applies to the heterogeneous group of poems 'Linguagens alheias', which brings together Cabral's dialogue with different art forms.

It is true that Cabral's pursuit of the prosaic, his quest for objectivity and economy of means are all traits that are thrown up in the literary and artistic affinities (and equally important differences) surveyed in this section of *Agrestes*. His poem 'O último poema' (p. 560), for example, expresses his wish that his last poem be 'de antilira, feito em antiverso' [of anti-lyre, wrought in anti-verse] (p. 560) and is an obvious critique of Bandeira's composition of the same title, published in *Libertinagem*, of 1930, in which the older poet wishes his poem to be infused with powerful, if difficult to articulate, human emotions: 'A paixão dos suicidas que se matam sem explicação' [The passion of those who kill themselves without reason] (Bandeira, p. 223). Yet, rather than focus on these much-studied features of his poetry, this section will analyse how borderline imagery articulates important artistic and ethical concerns.

The blurring of boundaries between different art forms and cultural manifestations is at the heart of the seemingly bizarre inclusion of the poem 'De um jogador brasileiro a um técnico espanhol' (p. 557), which revolves around an explanation on football techniques given by a Brazilian footballer to a Spanish coach.[29]

The dynamics between the two figures in the poem question the traditional cultural subordination of the south in relation to the north, focusing on an instance in which the normal flow of information is reversed and cultural boundaries abolished. The poem not only challenges cultural hierarchies on a global level, but also points to how the success of Brazilian football itself lies in the unorthodox handling of the ball, disregard for convention and its 'aritméticas de circo' [circus arithmetics] (p. 557).

Brazil's 'beautiful game' is associated with a circus act—a marginal performing art if we bear in mind, for example, the itinerant life of those traditionally involved in this kind of entertainment. Yet, the ball, when handled by Brazilians, is also compared to a telegram, for the precision and infallibility with which it reaches its target. Given the bureaucratic

[29] Cabral's childhood passion for football never died, indeed, when Brazil's national team played he could get very worked up over it (in Saraiva, 1987, p. 7). A number of Cabral's poems include references to Brazil's national sport, often viewed as a metaphor of resistance. Apart from 'De um jogador brasileiro a um técnico espanhol' (*Agrestes*), another poem on football is 'Ademir da Guia' (p. 383), from *Museu de tudo*. It is dedicated to the legendary player from the São Paulo team Palmeiras, who embodies the subversive agency of the oppressed. In describing Guia's game, Cabral speaks of his pace as replicating the slow motion of those walking on the sand 'de água doente de alagados' [of the ailing waters of the swamps] (p. 383), thus juxtaposing the world of the poor and marginalized with the dominant order and turning the footballer's skill into a metaphor of social revolt. In so doing, Cabral also seems to reflect on the well-known fact that football represents the only way out of poverty for many underprivileged Brazilians.

apparatus associated with telegrams, the use of such a metaphor seems to be at odds with the image of the circus mentioned above. However, Cabral's aim is precisely to conflate two apparently disparate realities into the football pitch, showing how this ball game actually blurs the distinction between the Establishment and marginal sections of society.

In the light of the poet's disruption of artistic hierarchies, it is significant that the opening poem of the third section of *Agrestes* should not be devoted to a fellow writer, but to the pictorial language of the modern German-Swiss painter Paul Klee (1879–1940). 'Homenagem a Paul Klee' (p. 549) captures the quality that, in Cabral's view, epitomizes the painter's idiom: the endless re-invention of himself as a desire to defy pre-determined artistic norms of expression. Klee's theoretical framework, what Cabral calls his 'insane project', is reflected in an artistic practice that is consciously transgressive: 'saltava os muros, | saía a novos serenos' [he jumped over walls, | under new night dews] (p. 549).

From this perspective, insanity is perceived in terms of freedom and authentic self-expression, in which conventions and constrictive codes of behaviour have been eschewed. Within this context, Klee's departure from the norm is proof of considerable courage, since it implies opting for the unknown: 'sem medo, lavava as mãos | do que até então vinha sendo' [without fear, he washed his hands | of that which he had been thus far] (p. 549).

It is with this idea in mind, and paradoxically, in a poetic form tightly compacted in two seven-syllable quatrains, that Klee is visualized as engaged in his 'insane project', in an act of rebellion against all forms of restraint, visualizing the actions of a snake as it sheds its skin, an image which involves connotations of both life and death. Indeed, by disrupting pre-established artistic structures, the artist effectively discovers and celebrates the 'other' within, symbolically rising from the ashes of his former self.[30]

The association of life and death implied in Cabral's configurations of liminality in his homage to Paul Klee is also the focus of one of the most outstanding poems in this third section, 'Murilo Mendes e os rios'

---

[30] On this point, Cabral is at one with Pessoa, for both poets perceive insanity as underpinning greatness of spirit. An example of Pessoa's rendition of the theme is the poem 'D. Sebastião, Rei de Portugal' (pp. 9–10), of *Mensagem*, where insanity is the quality that distinguishes those who refuse to live their lives meekly, in expectation of death, as a 'Cadáver addiado que procria' [A walking cadaver that procreates] (p. 10).

(pp. 551–2), which is infused with the sense of trepidation experienced by those who dare venture into the domain of the *entre-lugar*.

As is the case in many of the poems in this section of *Agrestes*, and perhaps in a deliberate attempt to challenge readers' expectations, Cabral's dialogue with his fellow writer transcends the boundaries of meta-textual reflection and deals with broader existential concerns. The composition recalls Murilo Mendes's custom of invoking the Paraibuna, the river that flows through his native city of Juiz de Fora, whenever he crossed over a waterway. Because of the sense of danger implied in the name of the river of Mendes's early years—Paraibuna meaning 'black waters' in Tupi-Guarani—Cabral is exploring the associations of the crossing with a rite of passage, where a symbolic death is always necessarily implied. In this way, the poem draws on the traditional association of the river crossing with the soul's journey to the underworld; an association that is also encouraged by the phonetic closeness of the 'carro', in which Mendes is travelling, and the mythical Charon, ferryman of the dead.

Cabral's anti-religious sentiments transpire in his deliberate visualization of Mendes, who was a devout Catholic, as superstitiously invoking the Paraibuna, rather than placing his faith in God. Indeed, Cabral ironically alludes to the long, 'episcopal' hand with which Mendes takes off his hat in sign of respect each time he crosses a river, drawing attention to the disjuncture between Mendes's religious beliefs and the quirkiness of his personal ritual. Yet, the poem is not simply intended as a tongue-in-cheek take on Mendes's character or as a challenge to Mendes's religiosity. The composition is above all concerned with how a seemingly comical habit is, in fact, infused with profound existential significance. Cabral is aware of the ambiguity implicit in Mendes's actions, from which they draw much of their poignancy:

> Nunca perguntei onde a linha
> entre o de sério e de ironia
> do ritual: eu ria amarelo,
> como se pode rir na missa. (p. 552)

[I never asked where of the line | between the seriousness and irony | of the ritual: I laughed sheepishly, | as one can laugh at Mass.]

The comparison employed in these lines suggests that serious spiritual anxieties are at play here, revolving around death (symbolized in the act of crossing) and, by association, also around Cabral's ambiguous relationship with religion.[31] The awkwardness implied in his possible 'rir amarelo' during Mass suggests that, although he might proclaim himself an atheist, the significance of the Catholic ritual does not elude him entirely.

Ambiguity, therefore, underpins Cabral's own response to the memories evoked in this poem. He describes himself as hovering between laughter and trepidation, and such an emotional state is duplicated in the act of crossing that is being narrated. Greater effect is achieved on a linguistic level, through the use of vocabulary in which ambiguity is implied, such as the reference to Mendes's 'ambiguous smile'. In this way, configurations of liminal states articulate Cabral's obsession with finality, which transpires in his explanation of Mendes's actions, in the closing lines of the poem. Here, his sense that life is always experienced on a knife-edge becomes apparent: 'nos rios, cortejava o Rio, | o que, sem lembrar, temos dentro' [in every river, he courted The River, | which, though we do not remember, lives inside us] (p. 552).

On a meta-textual level, Cabral's obsession with liminal states emerged in his appraisal of other writers; and his engagement with those whom he saw as having challenged literary boundaries is particularly revealing of his own poetic practice. A case in point is found in his dialogue with the American poet Marianne Moore. His appreciation of her work is evinced in the fact that three poems were penned in her honour in *Agrestes*, namely 'Ouvindo em disco Marianne Moore' (p. 552), 'Dúvidas apócrifas de Marianne Moore' (p. 554) and 'Homenagem renovada a Marianne Moore' (p. 558), in addition to using the aforementioned quotation from her poem 'The Hero' as epigraph to the collection.[32]

As Richard Zenith observed, because of her poetics of the concrete object, Marianne Moore, along with Francis Ponge (1899–1988),

---

[31] In his interview with Couri, shortly before his death, Cabral confessed, for instance, that despite declaring himself an atheist, he always wore a medal blessed at the church of Nossa Senhora do Carmo, Patron Saint of Recife (in Couri, p. 10).

[32] Marianne Moore features extensively in Cabral's work. The first reference to the American poet is found in the poem 'O sim contra o sim' (pp. 297–301), included in *Serial*. Cabral subsequently paid homage to Moore in *A escola das facas*, in the poem 'A imaginação do pouco' (pp. 455–6). He also made a point of remembering the American modernist in his speech of thanks on occasion of his being awarded the Neustadt Prize for Literature, in 1992, where his admiration for Moore's unsentimental poetry is made clear, citing Francis Ponge and Elizabeth Bishop as other examples: 'Na verdade, eles foram poetas cuja visão da poesia não tem nada a ver com aquele lirismo confessional, que, hoje em dia, e desde o Romantismo, passou a ser tudo o que é considerado poesia' [In truth, they were poets whose poetic vision has nothing to do with the confessional lyricism which, nowadays, and since Romanticism, has become everything that poetry is seen to be]. See 'Agradecimento pelo prêmio Neustadt', in Melo Neto (1994, pp. 797–800 (p. 799)).

became an important reference for Cabral.[33] In fact, their '*parti pris* on behalf of things' (Zenith, p. 634) and the emotional detachment with which they turned their gaze to the world around them also underpinned Cabral's poetic practice—a feature celebrated in 'Ouvindo em disco Marianne Moore'. Yet, in *Agrestes* Cabral also openly questions the possibility of being fully objective. Indeed, in 'Dúvidas apócrifas de Marianne Moore', Cabral points to the limitations of their poetic aim, asking whether, inevitably, subjectivity is not obliquely laid bare: 'Mas na seleção dessas coisas | não haverá um falar de mim?' [But in the selection of such things | may there not be a speaking of myself?] (p. 554).

Cabral once famously stated that his writing was a reaction to a sense of void: 'The poem is a crutch that I make to complete myself.'[34] In his attempt to make sense of the self obliquely, by searching for answers in the outside world, he felt a strong affinity with the author of 'The Hero', as he states in 'Homenagem renovada a Marianne Moore':

> E então mostrou, sem pregação
> [. . .]
> que quem faz faz para fazer-se
> —muleta para a perna coxa. (p. 558)

[And then she showed, without preaching | [. . .] | that those who make, make to make themselves | —a crutch for the lame leg.]

Thus, Moore's poetry (like Cabral's) is shown to be deceptive in its objectivity, for the poet's subjectivity is invariably, if indirectly, revealed, with boundaries once again blurred, as the distinction between subjectivity and objectivity is questioned.

Moreover, in 'Homenagem renovada a Marianne Moore', Cabral draws on Moore's poem 'The Hero', from which the epigraph of the collection as a whole is extracted, to compare the American poet's process of writing with the act of crossing 'desertos de frio' [deserts of cold] (p. 558). The inhospitable landscape conflates her rejection of lyrical writing and her pursuit of the prosaic, while her deliberate disruption of the boundaries of poetry and prose is suggested in the use of the verb 'crossing'. Moore's explosion of limits is seen as the reason for her poetic achievement, when Cabral states 'chegou ao

---

[33] See Richard Zenith, 'The State of Things in the Poetry of João Cabral de Melo Neto', *World Literature Today*, 66 (1992), 634–8 (p. 634).
[34] In Selden Rodman, 'João Cabral de Melo Neto', in *Tongues of Fallen Angels* (New York: New Directions, 1974), pp. 218–31 (p. 229).

extremo da poesia | quem caminhou, no verso, em prosa' [reaching the extreme of poetry | the one who, in verse, walked in prose] (p. 558).

It is a trait she shares with artists such as Paul Klee, or writers such as Augusto de Campos, and which sets her apart from those who adopt a conformist stance, that is those who do not dare attempt the crossing. In short, Moore's poetry of non-conformity is visualized in a poetic *locus* between poetry and prose, and it also provides a model for Cabral inasmuch as it challenges the boundaries between a subjective and an objective authorial perspective. In this way, the image of the *agreste* as an interstitial space, an *entre-lugar*, is also relevant to Cabral's visualization of Moore's *œuvre*.

A contrast to the aesthetic approach celebrated by Cabral is provided by the subject of the poem 'Caricatura de Henry James' (p. 551). Here, the American's laboured depiction of society life and the 'moral labyrinth' of society etiquette is unambiguously ridiculed; and a similar irony is reserved for Brazilians of some standing, who, in spite of their questionable intellectual ability indulge in high-sounding rhetoric, as he writes in 'Um piolho de Rui Barbosa' (pp. 561–2):

>veio de tais piolhos grotescos
>o único estilo nacional:
>ler como discurso um soneto;
>
>não poder escrever sem fala;
>e falar sem encher o peito. (p. 561)

[the only national style | came from these gross head lice: | to read a sonnet like a speech; | never write without speaking; | and never speak without puffing up one's chest.][35]

These appraisals suggest a link drawn by Cabral between writers' engagement with social injustice and their defiance of literary conventions in form. The failure to speak from the margins, from the *entre-lugar*, as defined by Santiago, entails an alignment with the status quo. These views are explored further in Cabral's reading of African poets, with whom he engaged as he turned his attention to the reality of postcolonial West Africa in the fourth section of *Agrestes*.

---

[35] Rui Barbosa (1849–1923) was a prominent Brazilian writer, politician, and famed orator. He was a defender of the abolition of slavery, which was inscribed in Brazilian law in 1888.

3.6 THE GHOSTS OF AFRICA

In 1980, Cabral's German translator, Curt Meyer-Clason, approached the poet with a proposal for a film on Recife, the interior of Pernambuco and the landscape along the Capibaribe river. The project was to involve an interview with the poet or, better still, a recital of one of his poems from the anthology *Poemas pernambucanos*. Dampening the enthusiasm of Meyer-Clason and his project team, Cabral did not oblige and instead expressed his outright disapproval of the entire venture. In his reply to Meyer-Clason's letter, he explained:

> To begin with, I am not sympathetic toward the idea of filming Recife and blending in portions of my poems. I know the cineastes of today's highly developed Europe, and I know that their interest in our underdeveloped world is limited to maintaining the misery (for which they are responsible) as well as the picturesqueness that we still possess and they have lost, so that Europe's advanced and thoroughly healthy citizens may enjoy all this in the comfort of a modern movie house following a lavish and very modern dinner. Consequently, although you have my permission to publish my work in German, I must tell you that I am fundamentally opposed to the film project.[36]

Cabral was anxious for his work not to be exploited in sensationalist portrayals of the plight of his native north-east, destined for consumption in the developed world.[37] Echoing the theories of economic dependency developed in the early 1960s to explain Brazil's underdevelopment, Cabral was in little doubt that the roots of poverty were to be found in the global structures aimed at maintaining the economic dominance of wealthy countries and was suspicious of the interest shown by European intellectuals in the poverty and destitution of his fellow Brazilians.[38]

---

[36] In Curt Meyer-Clason, 'João Cabral de Melo Neto—Yesterday, Today, Tomorrow', trans. William Riggan, *World Literature Today*, 66:4 (1992), 674–8 (p. 677).

[37] Cabral never ceased to see himself first and foremost as a *pernambucano* and was always vocal in his condemnation of the exploitation of the north-east by the richer and more developed regions of southern Brazil. In his letter to Meyer-Clason, the poet indicated that, as a *nordestino*, he did not feel it was appropriate to take part in the film project: 'As a Pernambucan writer—i.e., as a son of Brazil's poorest district (it would be different if I came from Rio, from Minas, if I were a Paulist or a gaucho)—I decline to aid the gluttony of highly developed Europe's advance. My dear friend, your letter gladdens me, your invitation honors me; but I know what will result, and I therefore see myself compelled to reject it' (p. 677).

[38] As Gledson explains in his introduction to Roberto Schwarz's *Misplaced Ideas*, a group of Brazilian social theorists and economists, among them Celso Furtado and

Coherent with such views, the fourth section of *Agrestes* criticizes Eurocentric perspectives on the African continent and condemns the legacy of colonial rule. The concerns are articulated in Cabral's reflection on the devastation of postcolonial Africa and in his critique of indigenous poets whom he saw fostering Eurocentric views of their own continent. Responding to these concerns, his poetry reveals the hope in positive action for the abolishment of iniquitous structures of power.

The section 'Do outro lado da rua' is made up of ten poems on West Africa, where Cabral lived from 1972 to 1979, serving as Ambassador to Senegal, while concurrently holding the post of Ambassador to the other former French colonies of Mauritania, Mali and Guine-Conacry. Cabral had included seven compositions on African themes in his earlier collection *Museu de tudo*, yet his rendition of the theme in the later collection is political in a way that is unmatched in the earlier one. Though the proximity of death in his configurations of the African landscape can already be perceived in *Museu de tudo*, it operated on a personal level, articulating the poet's obsession with the passing of time. In the poem 'O sol no Senegal' (pp. 387–8), for instance, the vision of the sun setting into the sea in Africa is juxtaposed to that of the sun rising from the sea in Recife, and reflects the poet's own personal anxiety, as Felipe Fortuna explains:

> What it evinces is not simply a concrete and visual description, but also a chronological one, tightly linked to the poet's life journey: as if the cycle of the sun, which sets out energetically in his native land, Recife, should reach its end alongside the poet, who sees the star already 'wilting' and 'in his 90s' when it 'disappears into the sea'.[39]

---

future Brazilian president Fernando Henrique Cardoso, radically reassessed their country's underdevelopment in the years prior to the 1964 military coup: 'Rather than understanding Brazilian society as a rather more backward version of European capitalism [...] they began to see that its backwardness was necessary to the system in which Brazil had a crucial though structurally subordinate role (as a provider of cheap raw materials).' See introduction to Roberto Schwarz, *Misplaced Ideas. Essays on Brazilian Culture*, ed. and introd. John Gledson and trans. John Gledson and others (London: Verso, 1992), pp. ix–xx (p. xii).

[39] 'Se evidencia no sólo una descripción plástica y visual, sino también cronológica, estrechamente vinculada al destino del poeta: como si el ciclo del sol, que tiene su inicio energético en la tierra natal, Recife, cumpliese el período de vida del propio poeta, que ve al astro ya "marchito" y "nonagenario" cuando "se deshace en el mar".' Felipe Fortuna, 'João Cabral de Melo Neto: perfil de su obra', trans. by Yhana Riobueno, in *João Cabral de Melo Neto, Piedra fundamental. Poesía y prosa*, ed. and introd. Felipe Fortuna, trans. Carlos Germán Belli and others (Caracas: Biblioteca Ayacucho, 2002), pp. xi–xlviii (p. xlvi).

Marta de Senna's analysis of *Museu de tudo* highlights the introduction of this new landscape into Cabral's work. The critic points out how, albeit still providing an oblique reflection on his native Pernambuco, this feature resulted in a significant broadening of poetic material (Senna, p. 182). Indeed, Cabral adopted an overtly postcolonial stance in relation to Africa in *Agrestes*. Prompted by his experience of postcolonial West Africa, he articulated an uncompromising indictment of the legacy of colonial rule and the exploitation of the African continent, remaining equally critical of the national and cultural identity that was being shaped after independence.

The title of the section, 'Do outro lado da rua', implies a sense in which Africa is viewed as the 'other', visualized graphically on the opposite side of the street. The sense of proximity that is implicit in this image, however, suggests a correlation between Africa and the other landscapes surveyed in the collection, and can be seen as anticipating the modern idea of the world as a global village, where, increasingly, the boundaries are economic rather than geographical and political.

It is noteworthy that the title of the section on Africa should be the only one not to make explicit reference to the landscape explored. The sections on Pernambuco and Seville, as well as the section on the Andes that follows are all introduced by unambiguous headings; that the pattern should not have been followed in this section is undoubtedly significant of the poet's treatment of the theme. In what can be seen as a deliberately provocative choice, Cabral appears to wish to keep Africa 'anonymous', anticipating his indictment of the exploitation of the continent and its exclusion from the 'history' written by the West.

This concern is voiced in the first poem of the section, 'O baobá no Senegal' (p. 563). The importance of the baobab tree in West African cultures and religions is reflected in the fact that Cabral devoted two poems to the theme. One of the most striking features of the West African landscape, the large baobab tree, native to the region, is famous for its huge proportions and for its longevity, since it is known to live for thousands of years. Widely represented in African mythology, spirits are believed to inhabit its branches.[40] Besides the fact that its bark is used to extract strong fibres, the tree's importance also lies in the fact that it plays an essential role in the local population's subsistence, since its fruit and

---

[40] G. E. Wickens, 'The Baobab – Africa's Upside-Down Tree', *Kew Bulletin* 37 (1982), 172–209 (pp. 190–1).

leaves, for example, are not only used for their medicinal properties but are also an integral part of the West African diet (Wickens, pp. 192–3).

In Cabral's visualization, rather than an image of abundance, the baobab tree, situated within the African landscape, is associated with the deprivation of the people. Indeed, in 'O baobá no Senegal', he writes:

> É a grande árvore maternal,
> de corpulência de matrona,
> de dar sombra embora incapaz
> (pois o ano todo vai sem folhas). (p. 563)

[It is the large maternal tree, | of a full, matronly figure, | though incapable of providing shade | (since it is bare all year round).]

Cabral implies that the fertility that the image of the tree might evoke—such as the 'matriarch's hips' of its trunk—is deceptive, because its branches have no leaves and its trunk is hollow. These contrasting images are conflated in the final lines of the poem:

> vem dela a efusão calorosa
> que vem das criadoras de raça
> e das senzalas sem história. (p. 563)

[from her comes the warm outpouring | that comes from the creators of a race | and from the *senzalas* that have no history.]

In referring to the *senzala*, the outbuildings found beside the traditional Brazilian manor houses (*casas-grandes*) where the slaves lived before the abolition of slavery, Cabral is conveying the fact that, like the people of Africa, its land has been colonized, possessed. For this reason, the 'senzalas' are 'sem história', because the African people have been objectified, their identity denied. The bareness of baobab branches becomes a graphic representation of the plundering of African resources during colonial rule and the trafficking of its people during the horror of the slave trade.

The allusion to the exploitation of the African continent is made more poignant by Cabral's personification of the tree and, specifically, by the metonymic visualization of its 'portinarianas coxas' [Portinari-like thighs] (p. 563), with its reference to the paintings of the Brazilian modernist painter Candido Portinari (1903–62) and his idiosyncratic depictions of corpulent human bodies. Portinari's fascination with strong human forms came to be translated into paintings of the black rural workers on Brazil's coffee plantations. Drawn to the plight of these descendants of slaves, Portinari denounced their exploitation, not forgetting to celebrate their physical and spiritual resilience.[41]

Following through the anti-colonialist vein of the opening poem on Africa, Cabral returns to the image of the baobab tree in the third poem of the section, 'O baobá como cemitério' (p. 564). In it, he alludes to the West African custom of burying its popular poets, known as *griots*, in the hollow of the baobab trees.[42] In his treatment of the theme, Cabral intriguingly seems to attempt to put forward an explanation for a custom which remains puzzling to this day. One theory, as outlined by Hale (p. 194), argues that these poets were viewed differently from the rest of the population; because of their occult power, a burial in the ground would pollute the earth—a sign of the ambiguous esteem in which they were held.

This traditional burial practice—still carried out today and only very gradually dying out—was recalled to convey Cabral's criticism of the African poets' flattery of the dominant order. In the poem, only a symbolic return to their African roots, symbolized by the baobab tree, can restore some legitimacy to the voice of the roaming poets. The 'bad breath' to which the poem refers implies an association with death—as is also the case in the poem 'O defunto amordaçado' (p. 576), of the last section of *Agrestes*. It is also associated with the flattery conveyed in the poetry of *griots*, which suggests that their symbolic return to their roots after death (the baobab tree) has important political implications, given that Cabral emphasizes the need for Africa to look inward, rather than pander to foreign interests, in order to rebuild itself.

If in the opening poem on Africa Cabral criticized colonial rule, here his critique is directed against the native *griots* for their collusion in perpetuating colonial structures of power. Such a negative view of the *griots* agrees

---

[41] See João Candido Portinari (ed.), *Portinari, o menino de Brodósqui*, 2nd edn (São Paulo: Livroarte, 2001).

[42] *Griots* is the French term designating the travelling storytellers, praise-singers, poets of West Africa. In his study of West Africa's oral tradition, Thomas Hale described the wide-ranging roles of the *griots*, and of their female counterparts, the *griottes*. Because of their musical and poetic skills, the *griots* were employed as genealogists, taking on a major role at naming ceremonies, and as oral historians, to recount the feats of heroes in traditional epics. On a political level, the *griots* were, and in many cases still are, leading advisers to local rulers and patrons, acting as spokespersons, diplomats, mediators and, because of their ability to speak a number of languages thanks to their travelling lifestyle, also as interpreters. Hale's study of the *griots* highlights the enormous influence they exerted, as well as the hostility they attracted, due mainly to that same influence and the benefits they enjoyed. See Thomas A. Hale, *Griots and Griottes. Masters of Words and Music* (Bloomington: Indiana University Press, 1998), pp. 1–57.

with their widespread reputation as mercenaries, about which Hale observes: 'Much praise-singing fits into the stereotype of praise-for-pay and contributes to the negative reputation of "griots" as people who will praise anyone at any time if the reward is sufficient' (p. 48).

Cabral draws on this common perception of the *griots* to suggest what he saw as their failure to defend their people's cultural values. This position becomes clearer in a subsequent poem, entitled 'África & poesia' (p. 565). The poem's opening lines express in no ambiguous terms Cabral's reservations in relation to the poetry of the *griots* and by extension that of Léopold Sédar Senghor (1906–2001), co-founder of the *Négritude* movement in the 1940s and first President of Senegal after its independence from France in 1960:

> A voz equivocada da África
> está nos *griots* como em Senghor:
> ambas se vestem de molambos,
> de madapolão ou tussor. (p. 565)

[The misguided voice of Africa | exists in the *griots* as in Senghor: | both are clothed in rags, | in Madapolan or Tussah].

The *griots*, bearers of Africa's oral tradition, and the French-educated poet Senghor are perceived as failing to address the deprivation of their native land and engaging in superficial exoticism. Whether they be dealing with the poverty of their country, as encapsulated in the image of the 'molambos',[43] or in the products they export to richer nations, implied in the references to 'madapolão'[44] and 'tussor',[45] Cabral believes that a distorted and compromised image of Africa is being projected. What needs to be foregrounded by the *griots* and Senghor is, rather, the obliteration of the continent's pre-colonial heritage and the reality of the everyday struggle for survival:

> de uma arqueologia sem restos,
> que a história branca e cabras negras
> apuraram num puro deserto. (p. 565)

---

[43] Molambo has been incorporated into Brazilian Portuguese and derives from the Kimbundu language, spoken by the Mbundu population of Angola. The term signifies an old, torn, and dirty piece of cloth and, figuratively, can also mean a weak and slothful person. See Aurélio Buarque de Holanda Ferreira, *Novo dicionário da língua portuguesa*, 2nd edn (Rio de Janeiro: Nova Fronteira, 1986).

[44] Madapolão, a woollen fabric, takes its name from the Indian town, a renowned centre of the textile industry (ibid.).

[45] Tussor is a coarse natural silk fabric, whose name derives from the Hindu 'tasar' (ibid.).

[of an archaeology with no remains, | that white history and black goats | ground down to a pure desert.]

In stark contrast to the positive connotations of the goat when visualized within the landscape of the north-east, in which it features as a symbol of resilience in the face of adversity,[46] here this domestic animal becomes associated with destruction. From this, it is possible to infer that Cabral is alluding to the problem of desertification facing many sub-Saharan countries, and which, he implies, is conveniently omitted from the poetry of the *griots* and that of Senghor.[47]

Thus, the poets of West Africa do not, in Cabral's view, address the issues surrounding their native lands in their full complexity, indulging instead in a naïve celebration of their continent, which illustrates how colonialism persists, albeit unofficially and under new guises, in Africa: 'Quem viveu dela e a destruiu | foi expulso, mas está na sala' [Those who lived off and destroyed Africa | were expelled, but are in the front room] (p. 565).[48]

The poetry of praises, equated to the act of singing, is dismissed because 'cantar vale celebração' [singing means celebration] (p. 565). Instead, Cabral defends a poetry of dissent that strives to speak for the marginalized and that is no music to the ears of the 'ex-patrão' [ex-master] (p. 565). It would seem here that Cabral is deconstructing the closing words of Senghor's introduction to the *Anthologie de la nouvelle poésie nègre et malgache de langue française*, of 1948, one of the pioneer achievements in the name of *Négritude*.[49] Senghor ends his piece on the triumphal note of 'Et maintenant, chantent les Nègres!' [And now, may the black people sing!] (1985, p. 2), a celebratory stance to which Cabral seems to object. Though purporting to give a platform for the voices of

---

[46] An example of this can be found in the 'Poema(s) da cabra', included in *Quaderna* (pp. 254–9).
[47] One of the factors that exacerbate the problem of desertification is the low-intensity but extensive cattle rearing by people living on the edge of survival in the semi-arid regions (the Sahel, in Africa, being one of them). See the study by the Food and Agriculture Organization of the United Nations, 'Spreading Deserts Threaten Africa', <http://www.fao.org/desertification/default.asp?lang=en> (accessed 9 September 2003).
[48] The bleak assessment of Senghor's work proposed by Cabral echoes Robert Young's analysis when he draws on Tsenay Serequeberhan's appraisal: 'Senghor's cultural politics are frequently criticized as elitist, and his notion of Africanité dismissed as "nothing more than the ontologizing of eurocentric [sic] ideas projected and presented as the African's own self-conception"' (2001, p. 269).
[49] Léopold S. Senghor and others, *Anthologie de la nouvelle poésie nègre e malgache de langue française*, 5th edn, ed. Léopold Sédar Sénghor (Paris: Quadrige; Presse Universitaire de France, 1985).

the black poets of Africa, Senghor's approach was seen as misconceived, and Cabral did not endorse it when writing about his own native land. His self-definition as an 'incurável pernambucano', in the introductory poem to *A escola das facas* discussed earlier, reveals his unwavering attachment to his roots, a feature in common with Senghor, but he remained unimpressed with the African poet's nostalgic take on his motherland. Revealingly, while the French-educated Senghor was keen to acknowledge his debt to French literary tradition, Cabral's relationship with Portugal's literary tradition is not unproblematic, as his dialogue with Pessoa demonstrates.[50]

Senghor freely acknowledged the influence of the French literary canon on his writing, as in the 'Post-face' to *Éthiopiques*, where he stated: 'I have read widely, from the Troubadours to Paul Claudel. And imitated freely.'[51] As the product of cultural miscegenation, he justified his preference for the French language rather than any of the indigenous languages in compiling his *Anthologie* in terms that are startlingly Eurocentric, speaking of its 'universal value' (1956, p.120).[52] In Senghor's mind, there was no incompatibility between his role as a voice of the black experience and his embracing the culture of the former metropolis, as is exemplified in his appropriation of Baudelaire in the post-face to *Éthiopiques*, when he confesses his fascination with what he defines his 'Royaume d'enfance', kingdom of childhood. Referencing Baudelaire, Senghor states that he wished to bring his childhood world in Africa to life for the reader 'à travers des forêts de symboles' [through forests of symbols] (1956, p. 110).

Senghor's re-visitations of his childhood in Africa conjure up images of an idealized world. An example of his nostalgic evocation of the 'Royaume d'enfance' is provided in the poem 'Joal', the poet's birthplace, as the following lines illustrate:

---

[50] This French influence in Senghor's poetry seems to have been one of the reasons behind Cabral's reservations about his writing (Castello, p. 141).

[51] 'J'ai beaucoup lu, des troubadours à Paul Claudel. Et beaucoup imité.' Léopold S. Senghor, 'Post-face. Comme les lamartines vont boire a la source', in *Éthiopiques* (Paris: Éditions du Seuil, 1956), pp. 103–23 (p. 106).

[52] In contrast to Senghor, Cabral's relationship with the heritage of Portuguese colonialism was ambiguous, as his correspondence with his German translator, Curt Meyer-Clason, reveals. Comparing Brazilian authors with their Spanish American counterparts he commented: 'I am a Portuguese-speaking Latin American. Like most Portuguese authors, I have never had the otherwise laughable worry of overlooking the language of Quevedo because of Camões. As you know, the influence of Spanish literature weighs more heavily on me than that of Portuguese literature' (in Meyer-Clason, p. 677).

Joal!
Je me rappelle
Je me rappelle les signares à l'ombre verte des vérandas
Les signares aux yeux surréels comme un clair de lune sur la grève.
[...]
Je me rappelle les festins funèbres fumant du sang des troupeaux égorgés
Du bruit des querelles, des rhapsodies des griots.[53]

[Joal! | I remember | I remember the *signares* in the shade of the verandas | *Signares* with surreal eyes, like moonlight on the strand. | [...] | I remember the funeral banquets smoking with the blood of the flock | slaughtered | The sound of quarrels, the rhapsodies of the griots.]

Written during Senghor's early years in Paris, the poem reveals his belief in *métissage* as a positive legacy of the colonial experience. This is conveyed in the image of racial miscegenation embodied by the leisurely 'senhares', who, Abiola Irele explains, were 'ladies of the local bourgeoisie, in particular the mulatto ladies of Saint Louis, former capital of Senegal' (in Senghor, 1977, b, p. 98). The evocation of slain sheep, in 'Joal', is a reference to the Muslim day of Tabaski,[54] but the violence suggested in these animal sacrifices is superseded by a sense of social harmony, conveyed by the rhapsodies of the *griots*. A positive vision of a colonial society, where traditional African cultural identity has been preserved, thus emerges.

Echoing Gilberto Freyre's theories on the construction of a multiracial Brazilian society, Senghor saw Brazil as an example of successful miscegenation, not only racial but also, and above all, cultural.[55] Cabral's rendition of the figure of Cabeleira, analysed earlier, betrays a bleaker and more critical vision of Brazilian society, and his visualization of the African continent is equally bleak, foregrounding death as the landscape's pervasive

---

[53] Léopold S. Senghor, *Selected Poems of Léopold Sédar Senghor*, ed. Abiola Irele (Cambridge: Cambridge University Press, 1977), p. 43.

[54] At Tabaski, every Muslim household must kill a sheep for a family feast in commemoration of Abraham, commanded by God to sacrifice his son Isaac. Given that this story is also shared with Jews and Christians, focusing on this feast draws attention to an instance of shared heritage, in line with his vision of social harmony. For information on Tabaski, see Michael Palin, *Sahara* (Weidenfeld & Nicolson: London, 2002), p. 110.

[55] 'Ce que j'ai découvert en ce génie brésilien, c'est une triple volonté de fidélité à la Latinité, à l'Africanité—plus précisément: à la Négritude—à l'Indianité" [What I have discovered in the Brazilian spirit is the triple will to be faithful to its Latin roots, its African roots—more precisely to its black identity—and to its Indian heritage]. Léopold S. Senghor, 'Le Brésil dans l'Amérique Latine', in *Liberté III. Négritude et civilisation de l'universel* (Paris: Seuil, 1977), pp. 27–30 (p. 28).

feature. It is telling that three out of his ten poems on the theme should have trees as their central image, but contrary to their traditional association with life, in Cabral's renditions, the African vegetation resonates with suffering and finality. In this way, the African cashew trees in the final poem of the section, 'Os cajueiros da Guiné-Bissau' (p. 567), are juxtaposed with those growing in the north-east of Brazil. When visualized in the New World, they are seen as symbols of defiance against forms of control. Because of the way in which these trees often grow parallel to the ground rather than vertically, they are perceived as being 'anarchists', whereas those transplanted to Africa by Salazar reflect the oppression of his dictatorial regime: 'São plantados em pelotões. | Desfilam para a autoridade' [They are planted in regimental rows. | Parading before the authorities] (p. 567). Cabral poses the question as to whether the time has not come for Africans to break free from the legacy of colonial rule once and for all and emulate the spirit of revolt found in the marginalized regions of Brazil, which is encoded in the contorted branches of the cashew trees that grow there: 'Já podem dar seu mau exemplo?' [Can they now set their bad example?] (p. 567).

Thus, Cabral's African poems are driven by a sense of urgency for positive action. It is significant that the baobab tree, famous for its long life, should in Cabral's poems appear 'without leaves' and as a cemetery—in every way closer to death than to life. An embodiment of Africa, the tree epitomizes a continent sapped of its energy by colonial rule. It exists, in fact, in between life and death.

Central to Cabral's reflection on Africa is his criticism of the work of its poets, through which he raises the crucial question of self-representation and the formation of a national identity of the independent African states. Cabral's concerns seem to be focused on the fact that any attempt to speak for Africa will fail as long as backs are turned on the continent's condition of underdevelopment. In this respect, Cabral echoes the critic Antônio Cândido, who argued that the literature of the developing world which is truly representative of its people and also appeals to a global readership is that which is not afraid to look inwards: 'It corresponds to the conscience torn by underdevelopment and projects a kind of literary naturalism which references an empirical vision of the world.'[56]

---

[56] 'Ela corresponde à consciência dilacerada do subdesenvolvimento e opera uma explosão do tipo de naturalismo que se baseia na referência a uma visão empírica do mundo.' Antônio Cândido, 'Literatura e subdesenvolvimento', in *A educação pela noite e outros ensaios*, ed. Marta de Mello e Souza (São Paulo: Editora Ática, 1987), pp. 140–62 (p. 162) (first publ. in *Cahiers d'Histoire Mondiale*, 4 (1970), trans. Claude Fell).

The image of the 'entre-lugar' in Agrestes

Cabral's endorsement of writers who engage with the day-to-day reality of their country is unambiguous. His critique of the *griots* and Senghor implies that African poets can only speak on behalf of their people with any legitimacy if they speak from the standpoint of the *entre-lugar* as defined by Santiago. For Santiago, Latin American intellectuals must challenge their cultural dependency and their marginal condition within the process of 'Westernizing of the world'.[57] In *Agrestes*, Cabral takes a similar line to that of Santiago, when the latter declared: 'In peripheral cultures, decolonized texts question, in their very construction, both their status and the cultural domination of the colonizer.'[58]

3.7 THE LOST SOULS OF THE ANDES

The fifth section of *Agrestes* comprises Cabral's reflections on Spanish America. The ten poems included in this section are the result of the years he spent as Brazilian Ambassador to Ecuador, from 1979 to 1981. His experience of life in the Andes proved difficult for Cabral. He did not adapt to the high altitude of 3,600 metres and, on health grounds, was subsequently posted to Honduras, where he served until 1982.

Despite these problems, Cabral felt at home in Quito, since it reminded him of his beloved Seville. He loved the way the city had grown outwards, preserving the houses and palaces constructed by the great landowners intact in the old town centre (Castello, p. 144). Seville, we read in Cabral's last collection, *Andando Sevilha*, is the only city that managed to expand without destroying itself, and is therefore seen as an epitome of life. Cabral's decision not explore Quito's similarity to the Andalusian city in *Agrestes* is significant and more so because Cabral did not refer to Quito at all in this section, concentrating instead on his impressions of the bleak Andean landscape, constructed as a metaphor of the legacy of colonialism.

In the first poem, 'No páramo' (p. 569), the landscape is personified and visualized as hovering between life and death. In the highlands of

---

[57] Santiago speaks of the 'ocidentalização do mundo'. Silviano Santiago, 'Apesar de dependente, universal', in *Vale quanto pesa. (Ensaios sobre questões político-culturais)*, rev. Heitor Ferreira da Costa and Heidi Strecker Gomes (Rio de Janeiro: Paz e Terra, 1982), pp. 13–24 (p. 18).
[58] 'Nas culturas periféricas, os textos descolonizados questionam, na própria fatura do produto, o seu estatuto e o estatuto do avanço cultural colonizador' (ibid. p. 24).

the Andes, normal life functions fail: 'a geografia do Chimborazo | entra em coma: está surda e muda' [the geography of the Chimborazo | slips into a coma: it is deaf and dumb] (p. 569). Nature is ailing, the light is pale and 'sleepy', the sun is 'roncolho, quase lua' [one-testicled, almost moonlike] (p. 569), its weakness visualized through images of emasculation. Thus, not only is the Andean landscape perceived on the limits between life and death, but it its liminal condition also applies to the ambiguous sexual configurations employed here.

In keeping with the pervasiveness of death of this section, and recreating the experience of haunting once again, Cabral visualizes the Andes as a place inhabited by 'lost souls'. The imposing skyline of the extinct, and therefore symbolically dead, Chimborazo volcano is repeatedly visualized through the grotesque figure of a decapitated sheep, in which the biblical image of the lost sheep is evoked obliquely.[59]

The association with the biblical narrative, and by extension with that of the 'lost soul', is also suggested obliquely in 'Cemitério na cordilheira' (p. 572):

> Pela Cordilheira, os carneiros
> são carneiros, literalmente,
> se espalham soltos, sem pastor,
> sem geometrias, como a gente. (p. 572)

[On the mountain range, the sheep | are sheep, literally, | scattered freely, with no shepherd, | with no geometries, like people.]

Cabral plays with the double meaning of 'carneiro', which can signify both a sheep (and, specifically, a ram) and a cemetery, and subverts categories of life and death. Against the backdrop of the Catholic Church's heavy involvement in the colonization of Latin America, and the 'redemption' of the pagan, indigenous population, Cabral's visualization of the region conveys a powerful critique of its colonial legacy.

In this context, the overwhelming silence of the Andes mirrors the plight of its inhabitants, people who have no voice in this section of *Agrestes*, in what suggests the perpetuation of colonialist oppression

---

[59] This is suggested in poems like 'O trono da ovelha' (p. 571), where there is also a further example of Cabral's purposeful disruption of notions of masculinity and femininity. Here, the masculine Chimborazo is visualized as a headless 'ovelha' [ewe] rather than a 'carneiro' [ram]: 'Nos altos pés do Chimborazo | vejo a descomunal ovelha | que ele é, imóvel e deitada, | da qual cortaram a cabeça' [High up at the foot of the Chimborazo | I see the huge ewe | it is, lying motionless, | her head cut off] (p. 571).

through modern systems of domination. In 'Um sono sem frestas' (p. 571), Cabral reflects on the general sense of stasis that the landscape evokes:

> Nas províncias do Chimborazo
> é a terra morta: se dormida
> dorme o sono de vez dos mortos
> [...]
> perdeu o discurso de Bolívar.[60] (p. 571)

[In the provinces of the Chimborazo | the earth is dead: if asleep | it sleeps the final sleep of the dead | [...] it has lost the voice of Bolívar.]

It is revealing that Cabral did not engage in dialogue with any of the Ecuadorian writers whose work we know he read during his years in Quito (Castello, p. 144). At least one of these writers, Alfredo Diezcanseco Pareja (1908–93), was valued by Cabral as one who was fully engaged with the plight of his country. In Cabral's mind, Pareja had not betrayed his own country, as he stated in a letter to Meyer-Clason: 'Alfredo Pareja, who lives in his own country and has his gaze turned to it' (in Meyer-Clason, p. 677). On the other hand, canonical writers such as Julio Cortázar (1914–84) and Gabriel García Márquez (b. 1928), successful among the European public, were criticized for being writers 'who sing the praises of their America from the most comfortable quarters of Paris and Barcelona' (in Meyer-Clason, p. 677). Cabral's knowledge of voices of dissent among Ecuadorian writers makes the omission of any reference to them in this section of *Agrestes* all the more indicative of the poet's radical message, born of his bleak views on postcolonial Spanish America.

Since Cabral's own poetry on Brazil was written mostly during his residency in the kind of 'comfortable quarters' he refers to, he obviously felt that he had not betrayed his roots and had never ceased to empathize with the disenfranchised population of the north-east. His comment also illustrates the extent to which his writing of 'Viver nos Andes'

---

[60] Simón Bolívar (1783–1830), leader of the struggle for independence of Spanish America, is mentioned twice in this section of *Agrestes*. In the closing poem, 'O Chimborazo como tribuna' (pp. 572–3), Cabral pins his hopes on a new Bolívar, for the deliverance of the American continent. For further information on Bolívar, see John Lynch, 'The Origins of Spanish American Independence', in *The Cambridge History of Latin America. From Independence to c. 1870*, 11 vols, ed. Leslie Bethell (Cambridge: Cambridge University Press, 1984–95), III (1985), 3–50 (pp. 43–6).

sought to highlight the inaudibility of 'authentic' Latin American voices.

He achieved this by constructing an Andean landscape characterized by desolation and silence. On the slopes of the Chimborazo, only moss, a plant with no real roots, and not grass, can survive ('No páramo', p. 569). This natural setting replicates the plight of the displaced indigenous people of America who, through the horrors of colonial oppression, have been robbed of their own land and roots and live on the margins of existence. Indians are visualized on the run, searching for pockets of air to breathe, in a battle to stay alive in a harsh natural environment, as in 'O índio da cordilheira' (p. 570). Likewise, in 'Afogado nos Andes' (pp. 570–1), death by drowning is compared to existence in the mountain range, where the gestures of its inhabitants mimic those succumbing to sea waters.

It is perhaps fruitful to remember that the Chimborazo is not only one of the world's highest peaks, but also, because of the equatorial bulge, the furthest point from the centre of the earth. We might say that, because of this, it is also 'closer to God', but clearly, Cabral intended to denounce that there is no salvation for those who live in the Andes and the mission to 'civilize' and 'save' them has failed.

3.8 THE ENCOUNTER WITH DEATH

The title of the final section of *Agrestes*, 'A "Indesejada das gentes"', is a quotation from Bandeira's famous poem 'Consoada', from his collection *Opus 10* (1952). In 'Consoada' (Bandeira, p. 307), Cabral's predecessor reflected on mortality, pondering on the obscure nature of death and on the impending arrival of 'a Indesejada' [the Undesired]. The setting for his imminent encounter with death is that of day-to-day life: death, Bandeira suggests, pervades every moment of our mundane existence and at any moment will come to stake its claim over our lives.

In an atmosphere of intense *pathos*, Bandeira indicates that he is ready to confront his fate: 'O meu dia foi bom, pode a noite descer' [My day was good, may night fall] (p. 307). The sense of the finite nature of human existence is intensified not only by the image of the modest legacy that our hard-working life will yield to those who come after us—tilled fields, a clean house—but also by the realization that objects will in a way survive us, everything in its place. In 'Consoada', the sense of the certainty and inevitability of death are overwhelming.[61]

Cabral drew on the theme of death of Bandeira's poem, but his intent was at variance with that of his master. There is humour in Cabral's reflections on mortality, as for instance in 'Conselhos do conselheiro' (pp. 575–6), the opening poem of 'A "Indesejada das gentes"'. Here, the poet offers some tips on how to cope in old age, undermining Bandeira's sentimental stance:

> Temer quedas sobremaneira
> (não as do abismo, da banheira).
>
> Andar como num chão minado,
> que se desmina, passo a passo.
>
> Gestos há muito praticados,
> melhor sejam ressoletrados. (p. 575)

[Fear falls above all | (not into the abyss, but in the bath). | Walk as through a minefield, | that is cleared, step by step. | Well-practised gestures, | best be spelt out again.]

Bandeira's reflection on the inevitability of death is turned on its head in Cabral's poems, thanks to his allusions to suicide as a right to determine one's own destiny. The following lines from the poem 'Direito à morte' (pp. 579–80) exemplify Cabral's response to Bandeira:

> Viver é poder ter consigo
> certo passaporte no bolso
> que dá direito a sair dela. (p. 579)

[Life means being able to carry | a certain passport in our pocket | which gives us the right to leave it.]

In Bandeira's 'Consoada', the image of the 'mesa posta', the table laid ready for a meal, conveys the poet's acceptance of mortality, as he draws comfort from the rituals associated with the Christian faith.[62] Cabral's

---

[61] In the light of Cabral's dialogue with Bandeira and Pessoa in *Agrestes*, it is noteworthy that Bandeira identified in Pessoa, whom he admired, a resigned stance in relation to mortality akin to his own: 'Simpatizo mais com Alberto Caeiro, talvez porque encontre nele muito do Fernando Pessoa. [...] Caeiro faz a gente encontrar alegria no fato de aceitar: "no fato sublimemente científico e difícil de aceitar o natural inevitável"' [I identify more with Alberto Caeiro, perhaps because I see in him much of Fernando Pessoa. [...] Caeiro leads us to find joy in the fact of accepting: "in the sublimely scientific and difficult fact of accepting what is naturally inevitable"' (p. 692).

[62] 'Consoada' refers to a small meal taken on days of fasting as well as specifically to the Christmas meal. As Davi Arrigucci Jr. noted in his study of Bandeira's poem, the term conjures up images of religious or ritualistic practices: 'O termo envolve reminiscências religiosas e festivas, quer dizer, ritualísticas, ligadas ao espaço doméstico e familiar'

poem, on the other hand, subverts this image of conformity, since suicide appears as the positive manifestation of human agency:

> fazer, num dia que foi posto
> na mesa em toalha de linho,
> fazer de seu vivo esse morto,
> de um golpe, ou gole, do mais limpo. (p. 580)

[to turn, on the day he was laid down | on the linen cloth on the table, | to turn this dead man into a living self, | with one neat blow, or the neatest sip.]

By way of a paradox, Cabral contends that the 'living dead', 'esse morto', only comes to life through the empowering act of suicide, in which his own fate is determined.

This challenging of the boundaries of life and death epitomized the struggle against an order in which the 'other' is denied a voice. The parallel is evident in the poem 'O defunto amordaçado' (p. 576), where the corpse is 'gagged' and prevented from revealing what awaits us after death. Cabral sees in the practice of preparing bodies for the wake a metaphor of society's wish to ignore the reality of death and believe in religious explanations of the afterlife. The dead man's knowledge of the afterlife (or of the inexistence of one) is referred to as a 'sermon' and, as such, is presented as a challenge to religious explanations of mortality. It is for this reason that he is prevented from speaking. Indeed, the 'gagged corpse' comes to represent all those who pose a threat to established order and who therefore need to be silenced.

A similar theme is developed in 'Questão de pontuação' (pp. 582–3), where Cabral playfully takes a set of punctuation marks as symbols of different ways of life:

> Todo mundo aceita que ao homem
> cabe pontuar a própria vida:
> que viva em ponto de exclamação
> (dizem: de alma dionisíaca);
>
> viva em ponto de interrogação
> (foi filosofia, ora é poesia);

[The term involves religious and festive remembrances, that is, ritualistic, associated with the domestic and family realms]. See *Humildade, paixão e morte. A poesia de Manuel Bandeira* (São Paulo: Companhia das Letras, 1990), p. 266. Arrigucci rightly highlighted Bandeira's use of unusual words (an example of which is 'consoada' itself) in a poem otherwise characterized by colloquialisms and common expressions. It can be argued that such a contrast duplicates the setting of the poem: a familiar scene charged with a sense of expectation of the unknown.

> viva equilibrando-se entre vírgulas
> e sem pontuação (na política):
>
> o homem só não aceita do homem
> que use a só pontuação fatal:
> que use, na frase que ele vive
> o inevitável ponto final. (pp. 582–3)

[Everybody accepts that it is up to man | to punctuate his own life: | that he may live as an exclamation mark | (they call it: Dionysian spirit); | that he may live as a question mark | (it used to be philosophy, now it's poetry); | that he may spend life balancing between commas | and without punctuation (in politics): | man only fails to accept that man | use the fatal punctuation: | use, in the sentence he lives in | the inevitable final full stop.]

Those indulging in sensual pleasures 'punctuate' their lives with exclamation marks; the philosophical and poetic approaches are associated with the question mark; while politicians are associated with the absence of punctuation or with the use of multiple commas, alluding to their convoluted and inconclusive arguments. If all these modes of behaviour are socially accepted, the use of the 'ponto final', obviously associated with suicide, is condemned. Notably, the poem features neither exclamation nor question marks, nor are there any clauses carefully 'balanced' between commas, since Cabral deliberately chose not to use a second comma at the end of the penultimate line: 'que use, na frase que ele vive'. What the poem does, however, is employ other punctuation marks that do not fall into the three categories referred to above (philosophy, poetry and politics)—namely, colons, brackets, semicolons. Their use subtly implies that Cabral is positioning himself beyond simplistic categorizations.

The full stop is associated with suicide, which is condemned by society. But Cabral's poem draws the reader's attention precisely to its final full stop, its 'ponto final', a stylistic device which enacts the defiance that is implied in the act of suicide and translates his call for the boundaries that define social conventions to be continually renegotiated.

Thus, the image of the in-between space emerges in this final section of *Agrestes* in the poet's obsession with the immediacy and pervasiveness of death, in his images of the living dead, such as the 'defunto amordaçado'. In revisiting these themes, Cabral also re-articulated his defence of human agency, always associated with a disruption and even subversion of limits.

3.9 CONCLUSION

While denouncing the silencing of the margins, Cabral's aim in *Agrestes* is to give a voice precisely to those who have been oppressed, those who are 'dead' to society. In so doing, he himself speaks from the margins of Brazilian poetic tradition, from the *entre-lugar*, the *aceiros da prosa*, challenging commonly held notions of poetry. As a postcolonial writer, he also does so through a reflection on the traumas of the colonial past, which he expresses through his dialogue with Fernando Pessoa. However, on reflecting on the traumas of the present, he also challenges idealized representations of a national identity, of *brasilidade*, which he feels Bandeira promoted. Cabral endorses neither the discourse of the colonizer nor the simplistic exaltation of the colonized. Once again, in fact, he positions himself in the *entre-lugar*, as defined by Silviano Santiago: 'between obedience and rebellion, between assimilation and expression—there, in this seemingly empty space, in its time and place of clandestinity, there Latin American literature's anthropophagic ritual is performed.' It is in this *entre-lugar*, where boundaries are blurred and challenged that Cabral engages in a reflection on his own writing, on pressing political and social concerns and on a more personal level, on his anxiety in relation to his own mortality. As Silviano Santiago says, this *entre-lugar* is only 'seemingly empty', because it is filled with the voices (or silence) of ghosts past and present, like the singing voices of the children of the orphanage of Jaqueira.

Among the different landscapes Cabral revisited in this collection that of Andalusia stands out as the one where voices from the margins of society are positive voices of dissent, rather than haunting voices of the oppressed struggling to be heard. In this way, it stands in juxtaposition with Pernambuco, and it is revealing how such positive voices were visualized so strongly outside his native land. Written at a time of great uncertainty in Brazil as to what the process of democratization, or *abertura* [literally, opening], might yield (the failure of the *diretas já* campaign, of 1984, being one of the causes for concern),[63] *Agrestes* seems to reflect Cabral's own anxieties in relation to Brazil's future, by returning to questions of inequality that still defined his country's social

---

[63] On the failure of the 'diretas já' [direct elections now] campaign, calling for the right of Brazilians to vote for the president, see Francisco Weffort, *Qual democracia?* (São Paulo: Companhia das Letras, 1992), p. 37.

framework and by probing into the legacies of repressive regimes in other corners of the earth (be these of colonial rule in Africa or Spanish America).

In interviews, the poet was reluctant to comment on the process of *abertura*, giving general, non-committal statements that do, however, suggest that he viewed the transition to democracy with some degree of caution: 'The transition to democracy is always somewhat difficult [...]. We need to stay calm, democracy really is a difficult business ... '[64]

In reality, his renditions of Brazil in both *A escola das facas* and *Auto do frade* do not suggest optimism as far as the country's political future was concerned, and the same is also true of *Agrestes*. In his subsequent collection, *Crime na Calle Relator*, he continued to cast his critical eye on his native Brazil, albeit obliquely. His treatment of the theme of crime and of the anecdote in that collection is central to his reflections on his country and will be the focus of analysis in the chapter that follows.

---

[64] 'Essa transição para o regime democrático sempre traz alguma dificuldade. [...] É preciso calma, democracia é mesmo um negócio difícil ... ', interview with Medeiros (p. 55).

4

Victims or villains? Open verdicts in *Crime na Calle Relator*

4.1 INTRODUCTION

Much of the focus of critical studies of João Cabral's collection *Crime na Calle Relator* has concentrated on two features, namely its humorous tone and the narrative verse employed by the poet—the former being particularly striking when contrasted with the sombre mood that informed the preceding collection, *Agrestes*. In addition to the above, a concern underlying many of the readings of *Crime na Calle Relator* has been to highlight a stylistic continuum between this collection and the poet's earlier output. The emphasis has been on Cabral's more evidently self-reflective poems, read as setting out his poetics of the concrete object, of clarity and precision. While it cannot be disputed that the hallmarks of Cabral's writing continue to be evident in *Crime na Calle Relator*, it is the contention here that the collection also lends itself to the analysis of another, not yet studied, but equally important aspect of the poet's work: his exploration of ambiguity, as a means of undermining forms of domination.

Indeed, written at a time when Brazil was emerging from twenty years of military rule, *Crime na Calle Relator* (which includes poems written between 1985 and 1987) provides a significant, if often oblique, reflection on questions of political and social oppression. The point raised here is that Cabral's enquiry into the intricate question of culpability provided just such a means of social critique, in a strategy similar to that adopted in prose fiction by the exponents of the Brazilian crime novel (known as *romance policial* and referred to by some authors also as *romance reportagem*), whose depiction of life in Brazil's violent urban conglomerates attempted to address the iniquitous legacy of the military regime.[1]

---

[1] Speaking of prose fiction published in the years that followed the process of *abertura* of the military rule, Silviano Santiago recalled: 'Houve ainda o romance-reportagem

All but two of the poems included in the first edition of the collection were written during Cabral's years as Consul in Oporto, Portugal (1982–1987). The shortest of Cabral's later collections, it initially comprised only 14 compositions, to which the poet added the two closing poems, 'O "Bicho"' and 'História de mau caráter', which were written after his return to Brazil, in 1987.[2] However, this was not the definitive edition of the collection. Indeed, merely a year later, the volume of his collected verse published by Nova Fronteira and entitled *Museu de tudo e depois* (1988) appeared, featuring a much increased edition of *Crime na Calle Relator*, which comprised nine additional poems, and closing with 'Cenas da vida de Joaquim Cardozo'.[3] The 1988 format was maintained in the 1997 edition of Cabral's complete works, also published by Nova Fronteira, but had been significantly altered in the earlier 1994 edition, by Nova Aguilar, of his *Obra completa*. In the 1994 edition of Cabral's complete works, the poems 'Menino de três engenhos', 'A múmia' and 'Porto dos cavalos' were edited out of *Crime na Calle Relator* and instead incorporated into *A escola das facas* (originally published in 1980), with *Crime na Calle Relator* closing with an entirely new composition, 'A morte de "Gallito"'.[4]

Cabral's extensive re-workings of *Crime na Calle Relator* essentially produced three different collections—that of 1987 (of 16 poems), the identical 1988 and 1997 editions (of 24 poems), and that of 1994 (with a total of 22 poems). More importantly perhaps, overall they contributed to an open-ended feel to the collection, as most of the alterations affected

---

[...], em que se denunciavam os arbítrios da violência militar e policial nos anos duros do AI-5, arbítrios estes que tinham sido escondidos da população em virtude da censura imposta às redações de jornal e aos estúdios de televisão' [Additionally, there was the crime novel [...], in which the arbitrary violence of the military and the police during the darkest years of dictatorship's AI-5 (Institutional Act-5) were denounced. These had been hidden from the public by virtue of the censorship imposed on newspapers and television channels]. See 'Prosa literária atual no Brasil', in *Nas malhas da letra. Ensaios*, rev. by Mário Vilela (São Paulo: Companhia das Letras, 1989), pp. 24–37 (p. 32). For the significance of crime fiction as a means of critique of the dictatorship's 'official' versions of history, see Malcolm Silverman, *Protesto e o novo romance brasileiro*, 2nd edn, trans. Carlos Araújo (Rio de Janeiro: Civilização Brasileira, 2000), p. 38. It is noteworthy that Cabral himself acknowledged the influence of newspaper material on his writing. See Cabral's interview with Bosi and others (p. 29).

[2] See Cabral's interview with Augusto Massi, 'João Cabral: "Escrever me dá muito trabalho físico"', *Jornal de Letras*, 5 January 1988, pp. 14–15 (p. 14).

[3] In this and all subsequent editions, the poem 'A sevilhana que não se sabia' was edited out and incorporated into *Sevilha andando*, of 1990.

[4] Cabral left no clear indication as to why he chose to remove these poems from the 1994 edition, though it is possible to assume that he felt their autobiographical content would fall in line with the revisitation of the past explored in *A escola das facas*.

the final poems, resulting in the existence of three different closing compositions: 'História de mau caráter' (1987), 'Cenas da vida de Joaquim Cardozo' (1988 and 1997), and 'A morte de "Gallito"' (1994).

The degree of re-working undergone by *Crime na Calle Relator* is unparalleled in Cabral's earlier output and is undoubtedly a hallmark of his writing after *Museu de tudo*. It points to a more relaxed authorial stance, and it falls in line with the thematic lack of closure of many of the poems, which Cabral was keen to explore in his reflection on questions of justice and guilt, through a deliberate exploration of ambiguity.

In relation to this, it was precisely the atmosphere of strangeness identified in the collection by critic Carlos Felipe Moisés that seems to have been heightened in the 1994 format.[5] There can be little doubt that the sense of estrangement yielded by the successful closing poem 'A Morte de 'Gallito'' is greater than that created by either 'História de mau caráter' or indeed 'Cenas da vida de Joaquim Cardozo', ensuring that the 1994 edition was more accomplished in this respect.

The collection is dedicated to the north-eastern artist and writer Luís Jardim.[6] Much of the acclaim Jardim enjoyed as a writer stemmed from his children's books and his depictions of childhood: the poem that Manuel Bandeira wrote in his honour, for example, refers to Jardim as the Brazilian Lewis Carroll.[7]

The dedication to Jardim in *Crime na Calle Relator* is all the more significant when we consider the collection's epigraph, with its reference to Mankind's age of innocence: 'In that ago when being was believing' (p. 588). The line taken from W.H. Auden's poem 'History of Truth', from the collection *Homage to Clio* (1960), recalls humanity's primeval belief in the

---

[5] 'Morte na Calle Relator', *Jornal de Letras*, 5 January 1988, pp. 12–15 (p. 12). It should be noted that Moisés's review consistently refers to Cabral's collection as *Morte* (rather than *Crime*) *na Calle Relator*. The reason for this 'slip' is unclear although it is in itself not entirely surprising, as the apparent light-heartedness of the 1987 collection disguises a deep preoccupation with mortality.

[6] Luís Jardim (1901–82) was born in Pernambuco and moved to Rio in 1936. Better-known as an illustrator, Jardim also authored a novel, *O ajudante de mentiroso* (1980), and a number of collections of short stories, one of which, *Maria perigosa* (1938), was famously, and in retrospect controversially, awarded the Humberto de Campos prize in 1938. In fact, a fellow candidate for the prize had been João Guimarães Rosa, who had entered the competition under a pseudonym with the collection of stories that he later published in *Sagarana* (1946). For further information on Jardim see *Maria perigosa*, 6th edn (Rio de Janeiro: José Olympio, 1981). This edition contains a number of critical essays.

[7] Bandeira's poem 'A Luís Jardim', included in *Estrela da tarde* (1960), establishes the parallel with the English writer.

supernatural and in the existence of an ultimate Truth, and thus touches on themes also explored in Jardim's fictionalization of childhood.

However, extracted from the main body of the poem, the reference is deliberately deceptive because Cabral would have been aware that Auden's poem in fact charts the disillusionment of Mankind, from our ancestors' credence in absolute truths to modern humanity's demur.[8] In Monroe Spears' words, Auden 'contrasts the past world of lasting objects modelled on absolute truth to the present world of paper dishes and untruth as an anti-model'.[9] This same questioning of an absolute Truth is duplicated in many of the poems included in *Crime na Calle Relator*, which tend to trigger a sense of unease in the reader.

The elliptical nature of Auden's line and its manipulation of grammatical categories—with its use of the adverb 'ago' as a noun—challenge readers' expectations and receive special reference in John Blair's analysis: 'The effectiveness of this device depends on its ability to startle the reader into greater attentiveness and to direct that attention to the general concept that is not stated directly.'[10] This seems to be Cabral's aim too, because the poems of *Crime na Calle Relator* thrive on, rather than reject, ambiguity, charting a movement towards disbelief, catching the readers off-guard and throwing their expectations into disarray.[11]

---

[8] See W. H. Auden, *Homage to Clio* (London: Faber and Faber, 1960), p. 66. The epigraph constitutes the opening line of Auden's poem, which is divided into three stanzas. The first two deal with the time when imaginary constructs—'bat-winged lion', 'fish-tailed dog' etc.—satisfied humanity's need to believe in eternal truths in the face of mortality. The final stanza focuses on modern man's lack of faith, evoked by Auden's insistent use of negatives: in today's world, Truth is 'a nothing no one need believe is there'.

[9] *The Poetry of W. H. Auden. The Disenchanted Island*, 2nd edn (Oxford: Oxford University Press, 1968), p. 326.

[10] *The Poetic Art of W. H. Auden* (Princeton: Princeton University Press, 1965), p. 85.

[11] Cabral's appreciation for Auden's writing was long-standing, as testified in interviews such as the one conceded to Couri (p. 9). Auden's ability to draw on the prosaic to ponder on deep human concerns was close to Cabral's own ideal. This is reflected in the poems written in honour of Auden, both dealing with the poet's death unsentimentally: see 'W. H. Auden' (p. 382), in *Museu de tudo*, and 'A W. H. Auden' (p. 555), in *Agrestes*. Yet, most significant, for this reading of *Crime na Calle Relator*, is to note that Auden too had engaged with crime fiction, in a poem entitled 'Detective Story', first published in *Letters from Iceland* (1937), with which, it is fair to assume, Cabral must have been familiar. In Auden's poem, human happiness takes the place of the murder victim of the traditional detective story, and Time is the accused. However, Auden questions the clear-cut outcome of the murder trial, implying that maybe mankind itself is guilty of the murder of its own happiness. This unusual rendition of the traditional crime story on Auden's part was perhaps one of the sources of inspiration for Cabral's treatment of the theme.

If this was Cabral's intent on a thematic level, he also sought to surprise his readers with his choice of form. In fact, in *Crime na Calle Relator*, Cabral wrote narrative poetry but consciously avoided using the traditional ballad form normally associated with the genre (Massi, p. 14). He favoured the eight-syllable over the more common seven-syllable line and employed short stanzas, predominantly quatrains and couplets, with varying rhyme patterns.[12] The unmelodic effect Cabral pursued on an auditory level also contributed to increasing the sense of the bizarre which he explored in the stories—heightened further by his insistence on the veracity of the various episodes.[13]

The first poem to be analysed will be the eponymous 'Crime na *Calle* Relator', a close reading of which will focus on Cabral's treatment of the theme of the unsolved mystery and his dialogue with the kind of crime fiction that was becoming increasingly popular in Brazil. The second and third sections of this chapter will focus more closely on Cabral's exploration of anecdotal narratives revolving around the theme of unpunished crimes in the poems 'Aventura sem caça ou pesca' and 'O "Bicho"'. Special consideration will be given to how the anecdotal approach allowed the poet to challenge patriarchal and colonial discourses and debunk the notion of History as a linear progression towards advancement.

This same historical perspective is discussed in the fourth and fifth sections of this chapter, which will analyse the poems 'História de mau-caráter' and 'Brasil 4 x Argentina 0'. In these poems, the relativity of any definition of guilt is explored to address questions of social inequality and racial discrimination. In the sixth and final section, attention will be given to the poem 'Cenas da vida de Joaquim Cardozo', which closed the 1988 and 1997 editions of *Crime na Calle Relator*. The study will discuss how the social and political concerns raised in earlier poems are foregrounded by drawing on episodes in the life of one of Cabral's north-eastern masters. In

---

[12] This decision to reject widespread poetic practice falls within Cabral's drive to act against established literary tradition. Conversely, his wish to operate within the constraints of poetic form (albeit not those his readers in Brazil would have been familiar with), rather than opting for free verse, exemplifies his understanding of the act of writing as an exercise in discipline. Cabral once explained the reason why he repudiated free verse by quoting Robert Frost: 'Toda a minha poesia é metrificada. É o negócio que Frost diz: escrever em verso livre é como jogar tênis sem rede. De modo que eu procuro me criar dificuldades' [All my poetry is metred. It's what Frost refers to: writing free verse is like playing tennis without a net. So I try to create difficulties for myself] (in Lima and others, p. 17).

[13] In his interview with Massi (p. 14), Cabral assured the readers of the authenticity of the stories.

addition to this poem, the closing composition of the 1994 edition, 'A Morte de "Gallito"', will also be analysed, since the bizarre story of the killing of the famous bullfighter by a visually impaired bull disguises a postcolonial reflection on questions of political domination and offers a significant revaluation of Cabral's poetics of precision.

As mentioned above, the narrative verse employed in this collection has been the main focus of attention; Cabral himself highlighted this feature of *Crime na Calle Relator* in his interview with Massi: 'I wanted to write a book in which I could tell stories. [...] I also wanted to tell anecdotes.'[14] Drawing attention to this aspect of the collection, João Alexandre Barbosa argued that the choice of narrative verse enabled Cabral to incorporate new themes into his work, although meta-textual reflection was to remain, in the critic's view, the poet's main preoccupation. Citing the poem 'O ferrageiro de Carmona' as an example, Barbosa observed that: 'It actually entails an obsessive process of poetic learning from different linguistic forms.'[15]

A similar focus is that of Alcides Villaça's study of *Crime*'s eponymous poem and 'O ferrageiro de Carmona', in which he concludes that two groups of poems can be identified in Cabral's output: poems in which the process of construction is revealed more explicitly and those in which this same process is conveyed implicitly by virtue of their engagement with beings and worldly events.[16] Marly de Oliveira's appraisal of the collection notes Cabral's engagement with narrative poetry, and his use of humour warrants special reference, as does the absence of any indication of the difficult period Cabral was experiencing at the time of writing (in Melo Neto, 1994, p. 23).

If *Crime* initially strikes the reader for its apparent light-heartedness, this study will argue that its tone in fact disguises a serious reflection on moments of intense personal uncertainty, as well as on times of dramatic political and social change.[17]

---

[14] 'Queria fazer um livro no qual pudesse contar histórias. [...] Além de histórias também quis contar anedotas' (in Massi, p. 14).

[15] 'É, de fato, a retomada de uma maneira obsessiva de aprendizagem para a poesia a partir de linguagens diversas.' 'A lição de João Cabral', in *João Cabral de Melo Neto. Cadernos de literatura brasileira*, ed. Antonio F. de Franceschi (Rio de Janeiro: Instituto Moreira Salles, 1996), pp. 62–105 (p. 103).

[16] Alcides Villaça, 'Expansão e limite da poesia de João Cabral', in *Leitura de poesia*, org. Alfredo Bosi (São Paulo: Ática, 2000), pp. 143–69 (p. 155).

[17] The inclusion of 'Rubem Braga e o homem do farol' (pp. 607–8), featuring Rubem Braga (1913–1990), one of Brazil's most famous writer of *crônicas* [newspaper and magazine columns on current affairs and social trends written with a personal focus]

4.2 CRIME FICTION

When considering Cabral's engagement with crime fiction, it is noteworthy how the popularity of the genre in Brazil was mirrored by a similar success in both Portugal and Spain in the years that followed the end of the dictatorial regimes in those countries a decade earlier.[18] This point is all the more significant when we recall that Cabral's posting as Consul in Oporto, from 1982 to 1987, during which *Crime na Calle Relator* was written, meant that he would undoubtedly have been aware of the popular appetite for this literary genre in the years that followed the April Revolution, when the detective story proved to be a fruitful means for Portuguese writers to reassess questions of national identity.[19] In particular, by setting their novels in the past and undermining the existence of a single authorial perspective on narrative events, writers were ultimately reacting against authoritarian versions of history. In her assessment of Cardoso Pires's crime novel *Balada da praia dos cães* and José Saramago's treatment of historical themes in *Memorial do convento*, Ellen Sapega observed: 'Both novels avoid or attempt to correct a tendency of the Salazar regime to present only an "official" version of the past.'[20]

One of the principal exponents of this genre in Brazil, José Louzeiro, highlighted the feature that, to his mind, distinguishes Brazilian writing

---

of the twentieth-century, is a measure of the importance Cabral gave to the anecdotal form. In the poem, Rubem Braga seeks to save the lighthouse keeper from his life of isolation, which is compared to one of mystical contemplation. True to his anti-religious stance, Cabral tells us how Braga attempts to bring the keeper back into contact with the real world and therefore, symbolically, back to life.

[18] José Cardoso Pires's successful novel *Balada da praia do cães* (1982), subtitled *Dissertação sobre um crime*, and Clara Pinto Correia's acclaimed novel *Adeus, Princesa* (1985) are examples of this trend.

[19] Cabral's taste for crime fiction dated back to his early years in Recife. See Cabral's interview with Freixeiro (p. 180). Freixeiro's interview provides no specific information on which authors Cabral might have read. However, the poet's familiarity with Edgar Allan Poe's writing is testified by the intertextuality of Cabral's self-reflective collection *Psicologia da composição*, of 1947, and Poe's famous essay on poetry *Philosophy of Composition* (1846). Moreover, Poe's detective story 'The Murders in the Rue Morgue' (1841), which deals with the mysterious murders of a mother and daughter, must have provided some inspiration for Cabral's *Crime na Calle Relator*.

[20] 'Ambos os romances evitam ou tentam corrigir uma tendência salazarista para apresentar exclusivamente um passado "oficial".' Ellen W. Sapega, 'Aspectos do romance pós-revolucionário português: o papel da memória na construção de um novo sujeito nacional', *Luso-Brazilian Review* 1 (1995), 31–40 (p. 37).

from the traditional crime novel.[21] In Louzeiro's view, the Brazilian *romance policial*, or *romance reportagem*, as he prefers to define the genre, emerges from the writers' acute awareness of the reality of social deprivation and injustice that surrounds them.[22]

In an attempt to assess the correlation between Brazilian crime fiction and the social reality from which it emerged, the critic Tânia Pellegrini, in her book *A imagem e a letra. Aspectos da ficção brasileira contemporânea*, offers a detailed analysis of *A grande arte* (1983), one of the better-known novels by Rubem Fonseca, undoubtedly the greatest exponent of the genre in Brazil since the 1960s.[23] In her study, Pellegrini focuses on Fonseca's subversion of the European literary models as a means of reflecting the reality of a Third World country experiencing a speedy process of industrialization and unprecedented economic growth, while concurrently facing the consequences of the exacerbation of social inequality—the increase in violent crimes being one of the most obvious examples.

Pellegrini argues that Fonseca in fact consciously subverts the traditional format of the European detective story as a strategy of political and social condemnation. According to Pellegrini, Fonseca is far more interested in delving into the murky reality of human emotions and motivations than offering a more traditional plot (such as in Agatha Christie's novels), in which crimes are ultimately solved:

The book cannot easily be classified as a detective story; on the contrary, it subverts the genre [...] it points at the complexity of human nature and motivations, including presenting them as the result of a specific economic and social context, that of contemporary Brazil. It rejects the kind of comforting literature of social integration, in which the criminal is always caught, justice is always made, crime does not pay, and the law and bourgeois values triumph. (Pellegrini, p. 104)[24]

---

[21] José Louzeiro (b. 1932, in the state of Maranhão) has authored a number of novels based on real high-profile crimes. He has also been heavily involved in cinema, contributing a number of screenplays. Among them is that of the critically acclaimed film *Pixote: a lei do mais fraco* (1981), an adaptation of one of his own most famous novels, *A infância dos mortos* (first published in 1977).
[22] See interview with Nilton Carapelli, 'Mataram a moça e caçaram o livro', *Folha de São Paulo*, 13 January 1980, <http://www1.folha.uol.com.br/folha/almanaque/leituras_28mar01.shtml> (accessed 5 December 2001).
[23] *A imagem e a letra. Aspectos da ficção brasileira contemporânea* (Campinas: Mercado das Letras; São Paulo: Fapesp, 1999).
[24] 'O livro não aceita simplesmente o rótulo de romance policial; ao contrário, subverte-o [...] aponta para a complexidade da natureza e das motivações humanas, inclusive colocando-as como resultado de um contexto econômico e social particular,

No study has so far been compiled on the influence of crime fiction on Brazilian poetry of the late twentieth century, though it seems Cabral was not alone in responding to the trend. Indeed, it is significant that Ferreira Gullar should publish his own *Crime na flora* a year before Cabral's collection, in 1986.[25] In Gullar's case, the political import of the collection is immediately clear from its subtitle, *ou ordem e progresso* [or order and progress], with its reference to the positivist motto featured on the Brazilian flag—promoted during the military dictatorship.

Gullar's work dramatically undermines those same tenets on a number of levels. Stylistically, its extensive use of neologisms and syntactical subversion compounds the fluidity with which it brings together prose poetry and verse, which makes its inclusion into any one genre problematic.[26] Moreover, such indeterminacy is reflected in the surrealist atmosphere of the text and its lack of a defined plot, which causes the reader to remain in the dark up to the end as to the circumstances surrounding the crime, including who is to blame, or even the true nature of the murder victim (whether it is a male, female or indeed an angel!).

If, by and large, *Crime na Calle Relator* touches on themes Cabral had explored in previous collections, its originality lies in the distinctive treatment afforded to them. Whilst reflecting on death and the inevitable

---

o do Brasil contemporâneo, ele abandona o caráter de literatura reconfortante e socialmente integrante típico do gênero, em que o criminoso é sempre apanhado, a justiça é sempre feita, o crime não compensa e a legalidade e os valores burgueses triunfam' (ibid. p. 104) As an illustration of this trend, one can recall the short story 'Agruras de um jovem escritor', from Fonseca's famous collection *Feliz ano novo* (1975), in which a writer is wrongly accused of murdering his lover, who had in fact taken her own life. His unjust conviction (based on the evidence of a fake suicide note that he himself had forged in a jumbled attempt to avert any possible suspicion of guilt) is coupled with his realization that his lover had not simply typed the stories he dictated to her, but had in fact rewritten his stories and was therefore the true author of the literature published under his name. Indeed, Lígia had constructed far more elaborate narratives than his imagination would ever have been able to yield. This story of mistaken identity and miscarriage of justice exemplifies the subversion to which Pellegrini refers in relation to *A grande arte* and bears resemblance to what appears to be Cabral's own response to Brazilians' taste for crime narratives. See Rubem Fonseca, *Feliz ano novo* (Rio de Janeiro: Artenova, 1975).

[25] *Crime na flora* (Rio de Janeiro: José Olympio, 1986). In the preface, Gullar (p. vi) revealed that the writing of this work pre-dated its publication by thirty years. The timing of its publication, coinciding with the rise in popularity of crime fiction, is surely noteworthy.

[26] In the preface to *Crime na flora*, Gullar (p. vii) himself acknowledged this difficulty: 'Não era um poema, era outra coisa. Seria um conto, uma novela?' [It wasn't a poem, it was something else. Might it be a short story, a novella?].

passing of time,[27] Cabral deals with these concerns humorously, exploring a sense of bewilderment in the face of the absurdity of life. As Carlos Felipe Moisés noted, the poems of *Crime* are immersed 'em clima de estranheza, **nonsense**, quase magia' [an atmosphere of strangeness, nonsense, almost magic] (p. 12).

In his analysis of the strategies of subversion employed by Brazilian writers, of both poetry and prose, after the inception of the dictatorship, Silviano Santiago observed:

The political stance articulated in post-1964 literature is one totally uncommitted to all and any developmentalist policy for the country, to any programme of integration or planning of a national order. [...] Quality literature post 1964 prefers to suggest its position like cracks in a slab of concrete, in a soft and witty voice, an unrhetorical and modest tone.[28]

Drawing on Santiago's formulations, this chapter will discuss how this same 'soft and witty voice' in *Crime na Calle Relator*, through its appropriation of anecdotal narratives, articulates an enquiry into the question of culpability and a stark condemnation of oppression and exploitation.

4.3 INCONCLUSIVE EVIDENCE

In the collection's opening and eponymous poem, '*Crime na Calle Relator*' (pp. 589–90), the reader learns the strange happenings surrounding the supposed 'crime' of a *sevilhana*. Her first-person account of the night in which she gave her ill and elderly grandmother some fire-water to drink is prompted by her desire to understand whether she was at all guilty of bringing about the demise of her own grandmother: 'Achas que matei minha avó?' [Do you believe I killed my grandmother?] (p. 589). Her question remains unanswered and the 'crime' also unsolved, as the author is intent on sustaining the ambiguity that surrounded events in *Calle Relator*. This reflects his own fascination with the dilemma of the *sevilhana*,

---

[27] Cabral's anxiety with the passing of time and inexorability of death is a feature discussed by Marta de Senna (p. 200), who identifies it as permeating the poet's work throghout.
[28] 'A postura política na literatura pós-64 é a do total descompromisso para com todo e qualquer esforço desenvolvimentista para o país, para com todo programa de integração ou de planificação de ordem nacional. [...] A boa literatura pós-64 prefere se insinuar como rachaduras em concreto, com voz baixa e divertida, em tom menor e coloquial.' 'Poder e alegria. A literatura brasileira pós-64—reflexões', in *Nas malhas da letra. Ensaios*, rev. by Mário Vilela (São Paulo: Companhia das Letras, 1989), pp. 11–23 (p. 18) (first publ. in *Revista do Brasil*). The article is dated 1988.

which he revealed in his own account of the origins of the poem: 'The person who told me this story was a flamenco dancer. [...] I thought the story was fabulous because she did and didn't kill her grandmother.'[29]

Cabral played on the *sevilhana*'s doubts surrounding the death of the elderly grandmother by shrouding the episode in an atmosphere of haunting and ghost-like figures. This is achieved by setting the episode at midnight and by the ambiguous use of imagery suggestive of the fluid nature of boundaries between life and death, as in when the sevilhana recalls how the grandmother 'acordou já morta' [woke up already dead] (p. 590).

A sense of unease is provoked in the reader by ensuring that the realism of the story is maintained and by introducing fantastical elements with careful subtlety. Freud observed that a writer was more successful in producing an uncanny effect in literature when claiming to be operating within the realm of fact and not fiction: 'In doing this he is in a sense betraying us to the superstitiousness which we have ostensibly surmounted; he deceives us by promising to give us the sober truth, and then after all overstepping it.'[30] In *Crime na Calle Relator*, Cabral achieves this same result by focusing on the bizarre nature of real events. Furthermore, his subversion of religious imagery and his ironic manipulation of the image of the *aguardente* [fire-water] adds to the strangeness of the entire scene.

Holy Communion, evoked by the adjective 'comungada' [one who has taken communion] (p. 590) and used in relation to the dying grandmother after she has indulged in alcohol, is not associated with spiritual salvation but with a climax of enjoyment of worldly pleasures, an enactment of the *carpe diem* dictum as suggested by the grandmother's admission that she has drunk her fill. However, a link is also made with the ritual of the last rites, because in the penultimate stanza the *sevilhana* ironically refers to the *aguardente* as the 'santos óleos da garrafa' [holy ointments in the bottle] (p. 590). The two religious rituals, associated respectively with life and death (communion being an enactment of spiritual salvation) are, therefore, conflated in the final

---

[29] 'Essa história quem me contou foi uma bailarina de flamenco. [...] Achei a história estupenda porque ela matou e não matou a avò [sic]' (in Massi, p. 14).

[30] Sigmund Freud, 'The Uncanny', in *The Penguin Freud Library*, 15 vols, ed. James Strachey and Albert Dickson, trans. James Strachey (London: Penguin Books, 1990), LIV, 335–76 (p. 374). Cabral was an enthusiastic reader of Freud and would probably have read this article.

moments of the elderly woman, adding to the episode's sense of indeterminacy.

The image that closes the poem seems to corroborate the irreverent appropriation of religious motifs: the dead, and thoroughly 'unholy', grandmother—'de madeira' [wooden] (p. 590), whose smile 'a aguardente lhe acendera' [was lit up by the fire-water] (p. 590)—subverts the images of devotion of Catholic saints (that the reference to wood conjures up) before whom candles are lit as a symbol of eternal life. This association is also suggested by Cabral's use of 'acendera' [lit] (p. 590) rather than of 'abrira' [opened], the verb that the reader would probably expect.

The indeterminacy engendered by these images is intensified by Cabral's alternate use of the Spanish 'aguardiente', the Portuguese 'aguardente' and 'cachaça'. This succeeds in turning the scene of the 'crime', already characterized by the uncanny, into a poetic *locus* where geographical boundaries are blurred. The fourth stanza is particularly significant in this respect, given its conflation of Brazil and Seville through the images of the Brazilian spirit made from sugar cane (*cachaça*) and flamenco dance (*bulerías*):

> Já vi gente ressuscitar
> com simples gole de cachaça
> e *arrancarse por bulerías.* (p. 589)

[I have seen people come back to life | with a simple sip of *cachaça* | and break into a flamenco dance.]

Thus, the inclusion of Spanish words into the narrative in Portuguese gives greater authenticity to the story told by the *sevilhana*, but also contributes to creating a scene that exists 'in between worlds'.

Three questions by the *sevilhana* punctuate the first half of the poem and demonstrate her need to justify the part she played in satisfying her grandmother's final wish. By complying with the elderly woman's request, the young girl is defying the male dominated medical profession, embodied by the doctor to whom she refers. Her acting outside mainstream codes of conduct is emphasized by the negative comparison used to describe her ministering of the fatal potion, 'como não se mede a cachaça' [as one does not measure *cachaça*] (p. 589). All this intensifies the unusual nature of events surrounding the 'crime' and adds to the unease provoked by the narrative's lack of closure.

Adopting a different take, Alcides Villaça's interpretation of the poem sees it as articulating Cabral's poetics of precision:

The sense of measure displayed by the granddaughter when giving her *cachaça* corresponds to the poet's measured use of language: the grandmother's acceptance of 'enough' drink shares the qualities of moderation and balance of his poetic style; the small details and the overall message of the story dramatize, in sum, a lesson on the value of limits to which Cabral's art is very sensitive.'[31]

Yet, one may argue that greater account needs to be given to the ambiguity encoded in the episode, in which liminal images appear to emphasize their fuzziness rather than their definition.

The implications of this are highly subversive. Indeed, attracted by the unsolvable nature of the 'crime' and, by extension, the elusive nature of Truth, Cabral ultimately purports to question the legal system's efficacy. In fact, the figure of the 'Relator', whose authority is evoked in the street name and who is normally in charge of giving an account of the findings of a legal enquiry, is dramatically undermined.

The young girl and the haunting figure of the grandmother provide an example of how Cabral employs marginal figures to challenge the authority of the dominant order. As a ghost-like figure, the grandmother embodies the invisibility of women within patriarchal society (especially the invisibility of older women) and, in raising such gender issues, offers a fresh slant to the theme of haunting which Cabral had explored in previous collections as a means of social critique. Significantly, unlike in the case of Frei Caneca, the last moments of this elderly woman are treated humorously, and she is not shown to be isolated, thanks to the support of female friendship (embodied by the figure of the granddaughter). Such a rendition of women ensures that Seville becomes a space where patriarchal structures of power are successfully challenged, a theme developed further in Cabral's closing collections, *Sevilha andando* and *Andando Sevilha*. Thus, the political import of what appears to be merely a light-hearted anecdote should not be underestimated, for Cabral seems to be appropriating the potential for denunciation that the *romance policial* had to offer.

His exploration of the theme of the unsolved mystery through a voice speaking from the margins (that of a girl of sixteen—an 'in-between' age group experiencing the transition from childhood to adulthood), allows

---

[31] 'O senso de medida da neta na administração da cachaça guarda correspondência com a administração calculada da linguagem do poeta: a aceitação de '*lo bastante*', por parte da avó, é da mesma natureza dos limites de suficiência e equilíbrio de seu estilo; os detalhes miúdos e o sentido geral da narrativa encenam, enfim, uma lição de limites a que é muito sensível a arte cabralina' (p. 168).

him to challenge any rigid conceptualization of Law, Order and Truth. Encapsulated in the motto 'Ordem e Progresso' featured in the Brazilian flag, these were the very concepts that the military regime had promoted to devastating effect.

4.4 CHILDHOOD MISDEMEANOURS

The poem 'Aventura sem caça ou pesca' (pp. 596–8) revolves around the poet's unauthorized childhood escapades along the riverbed of the Parnamirim, one of the small tributaries of the Capibaribe. This anecdotal revisitation of the past, however, is more than simply an account of childhood adventures, for it provides an uncompromising, if disguised, insight into the poverty and social exclusion endemic to the north-east of Brazil.

By grounding his poem firmly in his own personal experience, Cabral is able to juxtapose anecdotal to historical material, thereby questioning official versions of history and engaging with Brazil's postcolonial condition. In portraying himself as the one who 'got away' in his childhood transgressions, he also playfully situates his poetry at the margins of Brazilian poetic tradition—more specifically through his dialogue with the Romantic poet Casimiro de Abreu.

The poem reveals the boy's transgressive behaviour and alludes to the atmosphere of fear in which he was operating: 'sem que o denunciasse ninguém' [without anybody reporting him] (p. 598). As in Cabral's earlier poem *O rio* (1954), the river is anthropomorphized, though here it is not given a voice (a metaphoric empowerment of the marginalized). Rather, an atmosphere of oppression is suggested by casting it as the boy's unwilling accomplice: 'que vê tudo mas que não tem | como falar' [that sees everything but | cannot speak] (p. 598).

The Parnamirim encapsulates the plight of the poor of Recife, whose existence, significantly, is played out within the boundaries of the 'Ponte do Vintém' (pp. 597, 598), which could be translated as 'Bridge of Tuppence'—a symbol of economic constrictions. As a metaphoric boundary that 'encloses' the Parnamirim, the bridge suggests the life of economic deprivation to which the inhabitants of the mudflats are confined. Although the river no longer exists, it does survive in the poet's memories of secret expeditions to catch crabs during low tide. The impact of urban development is evoked in the childhood recollections, as when he compares the mud in the river to tar, 'lama quase pez' [almost tar-like mud] (p. 597), in an uncanny anticipation of the disappearance of the world of his youth and the metaphoric 'erasure' of the poor from mainstream society.

Wading through the river's mudflats allows the boy to engage with those who live along the riverbanks. Cabral had first turned his attention to this theme in his *O cão sem plumas* (pp. 103–16); in the earlier poem, however, the inhabitants of the *mangue* were visualized directly, albeit through metonymic images of human bodies (reflection of their alienation) whose only clothing is the mud of the Capibaribe:

> § Em silêncio se dá:
> em capas de terra negra
> em botinas ou luvas de terra negra
> para o pé ou a mão
> que mergulha. (p. 106)

[It gives itself in silence: | in capes of black earth | boots or gloves of black earth | for the foot or the hand | that plunges in.]

Cabral's later poem visualizes the human figures obliquely yet no less strikingly, through the images of the crustaceans to which the murky waters of the Parnamirim are also home. In stanza six, the common 'aratu' is described as 'ralé' [riff-raff] (p. 597) and thus becomes a metaphor for the lower sections of society. On the other hand, the 'goiamum', visualized in its blue 'steel' carapace, evokes the image of the Brazilian military: though a rare sight among its poorer relatives, the 'goiamum' (p. 597) is nevertheless a threatening one, pictured in a military armoured vehicle.[32]

Thus, a seemingly innocent childhood adventure disguises a stark visualization of oppressed and oppressors, marginalized and dominant order within the reality of the north-east; and the subtle allusion to the military is particularly significant given the historical context in which Cabral was writing, defined by Brazil's gradual emergence from over twenty years of military rule.

It is the child's physical overstepping of the boundaries of accepted behaviour for someone of his own class that allows him to adopt such a

---

[32] Cabral refers to 'o carro de assalto em que vem' [the assault vehicle in which it came] (p. 597). 'Carros de assalto' was the definition used for armoured tanks up to the 1940s, i.e. during Cabral's childhood. The vehicles then became known as 'carros de combate' [combat vehicles], a definition that survives to this day. See William A. Kirk Jr., 'Brazil' <http://mailer.fsu.edu/~akirk/tanks/brazil/brazil.html> (accessed 13 February 2003) (para 3).

critical perspective on Brazilian society. His metaphorical transgression of rigid social conventions allows Cabral into a space that is defined by hybridity: the Parnamirim is 'mais lama que rio' [more mud than river] (p. 596); while the adventure itself—he is unsure whether it entails hunting or fishing—is also defined by indeterminacy, due to the amphibious and therefore also ambivalent nature of the creatures the child pursues.

Thus, the experience focused on in the poem is one defined by hybridity and marginality, in which cultural difference is articulated and forms of domination are unmasked. Homi Bhabha's definition of such in-between spaces within a postcolonial context illustrates Cabral's own configurations of liminality: 'These "in-between" spaces provide the terrain for elaborating strategies of selfhood—singular or communal— that initiate new signs of identity, and innovative sites of collaboration, and contestation, in the act of defining the idea of society itself.'[33]

The poetic self that emerges from the interstitial space represented by the Parnamirim is indeed one defined by social contestation and condemnation of the plight of the socially excluded.

Cabral recreates this space through anecdotal accounts which he favours over official historical material. Thus, while the boy retraces the steps of former colonial adventurers, '(bem onde um desastre holandês)' [(at the very site of a Dutch disaster)] (p. 597), his endeavour, and not theirs, is foregrounded.[34] Cabral encloses the reference to the historical locality in brackets and ensures that the allusion to the Luso-Brazilian revolt (1645– 54) against Dutch rule (which lasted from 1630–54) remains obscure, thereby engaging in a de-hierarchization of official/marginal historical sources, which is in keeping with the child-like perspective explored here.

The devastation that was brought about during the Luso–Brazilian revolt meant that few vestiges of the Dutch presence survive, leaving behind what has been termed a 'historical hiatus',[35] which is duplicated, on a linguistic level, in Cabral's deliberate omission of clear historical

---

[33] Homi Bhabha, *The Location of Culture* (London: Routledge, 1994), pp. 1–2.
[34] The disaster to which Cabral refers is the defeat of the Dutch by the Portuguese at the site of the Bom Jesus Fort in Recife (1633), which had been built by the Governor of Pernambuco, Matias de Albuquerque. Antonio Carlos Secchin clarified this obscure historical reference during one of his meetings with Cabral. I am indebted to Professor Secchin for sharing this information with me during an interview held on 26 August 2002, in Rio de Janeiro.
[35] Stuart B. Schwartz, 'Colonial Brazil c.1580–c.1750: Plantations and Peripheries', in *The Cambridge History of Latin America*, 11 vols, ed. Leslie Bethell (Cambridge: Cambridge University Press, 1984–), II (1984), 423–99 (p. 450).

references. It is surely revealing of Cabral's perception of Brazil's colonial history that he should view the defeat of the Dutch as a disaster rather than as a triumph.[36] And, indeed, in its location, the poem seems to establish a correlation between the defeat of the Dutch and the reality of social deprivation that the boy's adventure brings to the fore—as Joel Fineman stated: 'the anecdotal is the literary form that uniquely *lets history happen*.'[37]

Stephen Greenblatt, one of the exponents of New Historicism, famously stated of his motivation to reassess the import of personal, marginalized texts in evaluating history: 'I began with the desire to speak with the dead.'[38] Significantly, in appropriating anecdotal form, Cabral is revealing moments of conflict and speaking for those who are 'dead' to society—inscribing a history of oppression (Brazil's distant and recent past) within a space inhabited by the 'joão-ninguém' [a Nobody] (p. 598) river, where hierarchies between humans and non-humans are subverted.

This journey towards greater social awareness is coupled by a process of sexual awakening. Indeed, the psychological turmoil experienced by the child compounds strong emotions of attraction and trepidation—the conflicting feelings duplicated in Cabral's use of the binaries 'amor e medo, pedra e mel' [love and fear, stone and honey] (p. 597). Yet, the story of the boy's adventure amounts to more than an exercise in autobiographical form because, in dealing with the murky sensations of the young boy, Cabral is also engaging with a Brazilian poetic

---

[36] Brazilian historians have described the years of Dutch occupation of Recife as a time of urban development and religious tolerance. According to the historian José Antônio Gonçalves de Melo, prior to Dutch occupation, Recife was a sad town, with no life of its own, where even water needed to be brought in from Olinda. See *Tempo dos flamengos. Influência da ocupação holandesa na vida e na cultura do norte do Brasil* (Rio de Janeiro: José Olympio, 1947), p. 35. This assessment is corroborated by Sérgio Buarque de Holanda, for whom the prosperity Recife enjoyed under the Dutch exemplifies their approach to colonization vis à vis the Portuguese: 'Esse progresso urbano era ocorrência nova na vida brasileira, e ocorrência que ajuda a melhor distinguir, um do outro, os processos colonizadores de "flamengos" e portugueses' [This urban progress was a novelty in Brazilian life, and one which helps to distinguish the colonizing processes of the 'Flemish' from the Portuguese]. See *Raízes do Brasil*, 12th edn (Rio de Janeiro: José Olympio, 1978), p. 33. During my interview with Cabral's daughter Inez, on 28 August 2002, in Rio de Janeiro, she confirmed her father's keen interest in the history of the Dutch occupation of Pernambuco.

[37] Joel Fineman, 'The History of the Anecdote: Fiction and Fiction', in *The New Historicism*, ed. and intro. Aram H. Veesser (London: Routledge, 1989), pp. 49–76 (p. 61).

[38] In 'Introduction', in *The New Historicism*, intro. and ed. Aram H. Veesser (London: Routledge, 1989), pp. ix–xvi (p. ix).

tradition which he criticized for being deeply rooted in Romanticism.[39] Indeed, the poem's intertextuality with Casimiro de Abreu's famous poem 'Amor e medo'[40] underpins his debunking of a tradition he considered steeped in sentimentalism.[41]

Cabral deliberately undermines the dichotomy of sin/virtue on which Abreu's poem was constructed and responds by celebrating sensuality— and female sexuality especially—as a legitimate constituent of human experience.[42] As Mário de Andrade noted, the fear of love in Abreu's poem reveals the poet's struggle against the sexual impulse, in order to preserve the woman's virginal purity: 'In his lines, woman becomes *angel, virgin, child, vision*, terms that exclude her from the full experience of womanhood.'[43] Typically, by juxtaposing Abreu's original 'amor e medo' with his own 'pedra e mel', Cabral is operating a shift from abstract to concrete nouns, which he favoured, and also brings together a traditionally 'poetic' noun such as 'honey' and a 'unpoetic' one such as 'stone'—thus positioning himself in clear opposition to the Romantic legacy.

Cabral subverts the idealized portrayal of the woman in Abreu's poem (with her white dress and virginal countenance) by juxtaposing it with the 'unromantic' setting of mud and poverty. Against this setting, Cabral also challenges Abreu's rejection of a sexual encounter that would cause his beloved to fall from the 'purity of an angel' to being an 'anjo enlodado' [a muddy angel]. In Cabral's revisitation of the

[39] 'A maior desgraça que aconteceu para humanidade [sic] talvez tenha sido o romantismo. No Brasil, então, ninguém até hoje se livrou do romantismo' [The greatest tragedy to befall humanity perhaps has been the Romantic movement. As for Brazil, to this day nobody there has freed themselves from Romanticism] (in Lima and others, p. 14).

[40] Abreu's poem was published in the collection *Primaveras* (1859). Quotations refer to the edition *Poesias completas*, intro. by Murillo Araújo (Rio de Janeiro: ed. Spiker, n.d.), pp. 117–19.

[41] Carlos Felipe Moisés also alluded to Cabral's dialogue with Abreu, though he appears to take the view that the poets share an idealized view of their days as eight-year-olds (p. 13). In fact, it could be argued that Cabral is countering precisely the kind of idealization of the past fostered by Abreu.

[42] In Abreu's poem, the anxieties of the male in the face of female seduction are encoded graphically in natural imagery: 'Ai! Se abrasado crepitasse o cedro, | Cedendo ao raio que a tormenta envia, | Diz: – que seria da plantinha humilde, | Que à sombra dele tão feliz crescia?' [Ah! If the burning cedar crackled, | Under the lightening that the storm brings, | Pray: – what would be of the humble plant, | That under it grew so happy?] (p. 118).

[43] 'Nos versos, a mulher vira *anjo, virgem, criança, visão*, denominações que a excluem da sua plenitude femminina.' 'Amor e medo', in *Aspectos de literatura brasileira*, 5th edn (São Paulo: Martins Editora, 1974), pp. 197–229 (p. 201) (first publ. in *O Aleijadinho e Álvares de Azevedo* (Rio de Janeiro: R.A. Editora, 1935).

experience of young love quite the reverse occurs: 'e era o fim mesmo da aventura | esse andar na lama' [and the aim of the adventure | was this wading through the mud] (p. 597). Indeed, the boy eagerly enters the muddy waters of the river in their 'sensual and warm bed', charged with female sexual energy.[44]

References made to the (female) mud's 'lascivious' nature and its 'woman-like ability to embrace' illustrate how Cabral's attempt to challenge traditional representations of sexuality was questionable, because they unmask his inability to distance himself completely from the stereotypical fashioning of woman as temptress.[45] Yet, it can be argued that this ambiguity in Cabral's gender constructions reflects a fundamentally divided poetic persona, torn between the world of the disavowed (whom he strives to support) and the dominant order (to which he belongs by birth). The fact that, instead of retracing his steps through the mud, 'que a maré emprenha outra vez' [which the tide impregnates once more] (p. 598) (associated with images of life and regeneration), he chooses to return via the 'decrepit quay' (an image of the dominant order—albeit one which is doomed) seems to bear this point out.

The casual use of 'Amém' [Amen] (p. 598), at the close of the poem, emphasizes the boy's lack of compunction over his actions. Cabral employs this exclamation playfully, suggesting nonchalance rather than a solemn expression of religious belief. This rejection of religion is central to the poem as a whole because the boy's entering into the river can be interpreted as an anti-baptism: this is due to the fact that, rather than cleansed of 'sin', the boy emerges from the water a more guilty character. However, just as the boy's behaviour eludes any clear-cut definition, so does any attempt at establishing his culpability because, depending on the perspective adopted, his 'crime' was either to enter the muddy river in the first place or turn away from it on his return journey.

---

[44] The intertextuality with Abreu in this poem is revealing of his rejection of the tenets of Romanticism. Yet, it is possible to see a much earlier dialogue with Abreu, in Cabral's writing of *O rio* (1954), which appears to be responding to Abreu's 'A voz do rio' (published in *Brasilianas*, of 1859). Indeed, Cabral's uncompromising account of the reality of the north-east contrasts the idealized Brazilian landscape celebrated by the river Guanabara in Abreu's composition. Cabral never referred to any dialogue with Abreu in relation to *O rio*, but it is most likely that he would have been familiar with the Romantic poem.

[45] My article on representations of women in Cabral's work traces both stereotypical and subversive renditions of the theme. See '(Dis)covering the Other: Images of Women in João Cabral de Melo Neto', *Bulletin of Hispanic Studies* (Liverpool), 81 (2004), 247–58.

4.5 HISTORICAL CRIMES

In 1948, Manuel Bandeira sent Cabral, then the newly appointed Consul in Barcelona, a copy of his poem 'O bicho'.[46] Bandeira's exploration of the anecdote as a means of reflecting on human degradation and abject poverty was applauded by Cabral: 'I doubt many other poets are able to make poetry out of a "fact", as you do. It is something that you convey without any formality, without any special turn of phrase: rather, on the contrary: as though you wish to suppress any effect created by the means of expression.'[47]

Almost forty years after Bandeira's poem, Cabral wrote the homonymous 'O 'Bicho' (pp. 611–12), and there can be little doubt that he had Bandeira's anecdotal approach in mind when he focused on an incident which occurred aboard Columbus's ship to present a postcolonial perspective of the discovery of the New World. The episode described in Cabral's poem is Columbus's (and the Spanish Crown's) failure to award Juan Rodríguez Bermejo (also known as Rodrigo de Triana) the monetary prize that was intended for the first person to sight land: 'ganhou em nome de rua | o que lhe roubaram em dinheiro' [he earned in street name | what they robbed him in money] (p. 612).

It is evident from historical sources that the episode on board the Santa Maria to which Cabral is referring must, right from the outset, have proved controversial. Even Fray Bartolomé de las Casas (1484–1566), who famously championed the rights of indigenous populations of the New World in the face of Spanish exploitation, took great pains to exonerate Columbus of any wrongdoing. He explained the Spanish Monarchs' decision to reward Columbus rather than Bermejo on the grounds that the former had previously seen a glimmer of light coming from where land was eventually discovered. This was taken to be a symbol of the spiritual light he was destined to take to those living in

---

[46] The poem was subsequently published in *Belo belo* (1948).
[47] 'Não sei quantos poetas no mundo são capazes de tirar poesia de um "fato", como você faz. Fato que v. [sic] comunica sem qualquer jogo formal, sem qualquer palavra especial: antes, pelo contrário: como que querendo anular qualquer efeito autônomo dos meios de expressão.' Letter dated 17 February 1948 sent by Cabral to Bandeira, in *Correspondência de Cabral com Bandeira e Drummond*, org. by Flora Süssekind (Rio de Janeiro: Nova Fronteira; Fundação Casa de Rui Barbosa, 2001), p. 60.

spiritual darkness, in 'tan profundas tinieblas' [such deep darkness] (Casas, I, 199).[48]

Cabral takes up the controversy to question the clear-cut verdict of official historical accounts. He casts doubt over the integrity of Columbus's character and makes direct reference to, and challenges, Paul Claudel's (1868–1955) eulogy of the navigator. The latter had portrayed Columbus as a saintly figure, for his missionary exploits in the newly discovered, uncivilized lands.[49] Not only does Cabral foreground the wealth amassed by Columbus, but he also exposes what he considered as the Italian's dishonest pocketing of a prize that should have gone to Bermejo, stating that the navigator was sleeping when land was sighted:

> pois *San Colón* (no então, dormia),
> depois de embolsar mil mil vezes
> os Grandes Prêmios, exigiu
> que o "bicho" também fosse dele. (p. 612)[50]

[because Saint Colón (then sleeping), | after pocketing a thousand and a thousand times | the Great Prizes, demanded | that the 'bonus' be his too.]

In football jargon, 'o bicho' refers to the bonus awarded to players and coach by virtue of having secured good match results. By employing the term in this historical context Cabral undermines the heroes of colonial history; what Columbus loses in missionary zeal in relation to Claudel's play, he gains in infamous commercial acumen: 'além de embolsar a fatura | embolsou também a gorjeta' [after poketing the invoice | he pocketed the tip as well] (p. 612).

---

[48] This version of events is corroborated by Colombus's own son, who refers to the light seen by his father as 'la luce spirituale che da lui in quelle tenebre era introdotta' [the spiritual light that was brought by him to that land of darkness]. Fernando Colombo, *La historia della vita e dei fatti di Cristoforo Colombo*, ed. Rinaldo Caddeo, 2 vols (Milano: Instituto Editoriale Italiano, n.d.), I, 114.

[49] Paul Claudel devoted a play to the life of the Genoese navigator. In the eyes of the French writer, Columbus's name itself was auspicious of the great mission to which he was destined: 'Mon nom est l'Ambassadeur de Dieu, le Porteur de Christ! Mon premier nom est le Porteur de Christ! Et mon second nom est tout ce qui est lumière, tout ce qui est esprit et tout ce qui a des ailes!' [My name means Ambassador of God, bearer of Christ ! My first name is Bearer of Christ ! And my second name is everything that is light, everything that is spirit and that has wings!] (*Le livre de Christophe Colomb*, 15th edn (Paris: Gallimard, 1935), p. 53).

[50] *Colón* (Spanish translation of Columbus) is also the name of the currency of some Latin American countries (namely Costa Rica and El Salvador). It is likely that Cabral would have had this association in mind when opting to use the Spanish word, thereby stressing the materialistic motives behind the colonization of the New World.

It is telling of Cabral's postcolonial perspective that he should challenge Claudel's view of Columbus (the view of a European, therefore) but make no reference to the equally eulogistic treatment of Columbus by fellow Brazilian poet Jorge de Lima. The latter, whose aim was to 'restore Christ's place in poetry',[51] shared Claudel's regard for Columbus as a bastion of Christianity.[52] An indication of this is found in Jorge de Lima's poem 'São Cristóvão Colombo' (pp. 250–1), published in *Poemas* (1927), in which the navigator's spiritual mission is extolled: 'Meu S. Cristóvão é você, São Cristóvão Colombo que passou Jesus no mar. | Meu S. Cristóvão é você, S. Cristóvão Colombo que passou Jesus para cá' [You are my Saint Christopher, Saint Christopher Columbus who took Jesus across the sea. | You are my Saint Christopher, Saint Christopher Columbus who brought Jesus over here].

In stark contrast to Lima's encomium, Cabral's poem incorporates into the narrative of the discovery material that would conventionally be reputed of secondary value, in order to debunk the image of Columbus the Christ-bearer promoted by colonialism:

> O que não se aprende: Rodrigo
> muda de roupa e aventurança:
> veste mouro, despe uma igreja
> de santidades tão tacanhas. (p. 612)[53]

[What one does not learn: Rodrigo | changes clothes and venture: | dresses as a Moor, strips a church | of such mean holinesses.]

Cabral's lines allude to the fact that Rodrigo, disillusioned with the Spanish establishment after being denied what he felt was rightfully his, on his return to Europe is alleged to have emigrated to Morocco and converted to Islam.[54] The irony of Rodrigo's loss of Christian faith—

---

[51] 'Restaurar a poesia em Cristo.' Interview with Homero Sena, 'A poesia em Cristo', in Jorge de Lima, *Poesia completa*, org. Alexei Bueno (Rio de Janeiro: Nova Aguilar, 1997), pp. 45–6 (p. 45) (first published as 'Vida, opiniões e tendências dos escritores', *O Jornal- Revista*, 29 July 1945).

[52] In Jorge de Lima's view, the greatest Brazilian poetry produced was religious, and Claudel is cited as a model. See interview with Joel Silveira 'Compreensão da poesia', in Lima, pp. 37–8 (p. 38) (first publ. as 'Jorge de Lima fala da poesia', *Vamos Ler!*, 1938–9).

[53] It is not clear how Cabral came across these biographical details on Rodrigo de Triana's life. However, the two years (1956–8) he spent engaged in archival research at Seville's Archivo de las Indias, recording documents related to Brazil's colonial history, and his second diplomatic posting to the city (1962–4) would have enabled him to gain information on the forgotten 'hero' of the discovery.

[54] This information is not easily accessed from conventional historical sources, though numerous references to Rodrigo's conversion are available on

directly blamed on Columbus, the bearer of the Gospel to the New World—is certainly a point that Cabral was keen to highlight. He uses the two antonymous verbs 'vestir' [clothe] and 'despir' [strip/unclothe] in close succession, suggesting a tight association between the two actions they describe, which has the effect of blurring the distinction between them. The reference to his dressing as a Moor suggests Rodrigo's conversion to Islam, the consequence of which is his rejection of Catholicism, with its mean-spirited 'Saints' (ie. Columbus). However, the reference to the 'unclothing' of Rodrigo is somewhat ambiguous, because it could also suggest his 'unmasking' of Columbus' dishonesty, and thus symbolically stripping the Catholic Church of one of its figures of worship.

In this engagement with history, Cabral deals with matters of culpability in relation to one of the key figures of Europe's colonial past, debunking official accounts of the Discovery. In the context of the social inequity that the poem exposes, concepts of good and evil are questioned. If 'O "Bicho"' raises the issue of guilt as a way of addressing the ills of the past, the poem 'História de mau caráter', analysed in the following section, shows how iniquitous power structures have been perpetuated throughout Brazil's history, questioning the moral integrity of those in positions of authority.

4.6 DISHONEST LAWYERS

In 'História de mau caráter' (pp. 612–13), two candidates from very different social backgrounds put themselves forward for the same job of Law Lecturer. The class dynamics that the poem exposes reveal that wealth is ultimately the key factor in determining who will be the lucky applicant. While it is the poor student who manages to find the course book essential for those sitting the selection exam, only the rich man has the means to purchase it. Indeed, he indulges in buying not just one book for himself but also the only other copy on the market, thus ensuring that his cash-strapped rival poses no threat to his application:

---

the Internet, a relative new and until recently marginal medium of information. See, for example, Jack Abramowitz, 'Rodrigo de Triana: "The Forgotten Lookout"' <http://216.239.39.100/search?q=cache:IaEdcRA9U2sC:www.eductrak.com/pdf/triana.pdf+rodrigo+de+triana&hl=en&ie=UTF-8> (accessed 13 February 2003).

"'Esgotou ontem. | Vendemos os dois a um só moço'" [It sold out yesterday. | We sold both copies to one young man] (p. 613).

Cabral is certainly not sparing in his critique of the dominant order, conveyed in his disparaging portrayal of Brazil as a 'terra de advogados' [land of lawyers], to use Sérgio Buarque de Holanda's definition.[55] Coming from a member of the dominant oligarchy who never gained a higher education qualification, and thus failed to conform to what was expected of members of his class,[56] the following critique is all the more poignant:

> Então, ser Lente de Direito
> é mais que ser Governador:
> este só governa quatro anos,
> e aquele é sempre e tem Doutor. (p. 613)

[So, being a Law student | is more than being Governor: | he only governs for four years, | and the other is forever and is 'Doctor'.]

Despite his social message, Cabral rejects simplistic dichotomies of rich/poor and good/evil and engages with the complexity of human psychology, by suggesting that the poor candidate is perhaps not above reproach either. This is hinted at (but not confirmed) in Cabral's lines, whose elliptical nature helps to sustain the element of doubt. What is suggested is that the poor student's motives may not be entirely altruistic when he directs his rich counterpart to the bookshop where the course-book is on sale, in the hope, perhaps, that the wealthy undergraduate might feel compelled to buy him a copy: 'o pobre vendo como tê-lo | vê o rico pela rua vindo [the poor one seeing how to get it | sees the rich one coming down the road] (p. 613).

Because of the lack of equal opportunities, the underprivileged member of society attempts to better his lot by seeking a favour from his rich colleague. His plan fails, however, because the wealthy candidate ignores his subtle request for help. Rather, not wanting to share the resources available, he uses his economic advantage to prejudice the

---

[55] Holanda referred to the *canudo* [degree certificate] as the invaluable asset within Brazilian society: 'onde apenas os cidadãos formados em Direito ascendem em regra às mais altas posições e cargos políticos' [where as a rule only those with a Law degree rise to the highest positions and political posts] (1978 b, p. 115).

[56] We know from José Castello's biography, that at the age of 16 Cabral announced to his father that he did not want to pursue either the science or law courses, which were the options generally taken by students at the time. Cabral's ambition to train for a career in journalism was thwarted by his father, who did not deem it a suitable profession for his son (Castello, pp. 43–4).

poor rival. As a result, the class dynamics dramatized in the poem unmask a social structure based on privilege, where favour plays a major part, but rarely to the advantage of those who most need help.[57]

Moreover, the anecdote raises another crucial question in relation to Brazilian society and culture: that of the influence of foreign trends on Brazilian cultural production. This is evinced in the poem's juxtaposition of the success of the 'bíblia do Grande Italiano' [bible of the Great Italian] (p. 613) with the oblivion to which home-grown thinkers are relegated, 'já no sebo os tratados nossos' [our treatises already in second-hand bookshops] (p. 613). In this respect, it is revealing that this poem should come immediately after 'O "Bicho"', emphasizing the anecdote's significance as an illustration of the modern-day legacy of colonization.

On the vexed question of intellectual and cultural dependency, Roberto Schwarz defined the preoccupation of the Brazilian *intelligentsia* in the following terms: 'To summarize, since last century there exists among people educated in Brazil—a social category, rather than a compliment—the feeling of living among institutions and ideas copied from abroad and which do not reflect the reality on the ground.'[58]

Questioning the very notions of copy and model, Schwarz argues that the power structures Brazil inherited from the slave-based society of colonial times and the power relations that ensued caused new ideas, the circulation of which Schwarz sees as inevitable, to be perceived as 'foreign'.[59] The crux of the matter when considering Brazilian society lies elsewhere, according to Schwarz's analysis: 'O ponto decisivo está na segregação dos pobres, excluídos do universo da cultura contemporânea'

---

[57] For detailed studies on the culture of favour in Brazilian society see Holanda (1978 b), Lívia Neves de Holanda Barbosa, 'The Brazilian *Jeitinho*: an Exercise in National Identity', in *The Brazilian Puzzle. Culture on the Borderlines of the Western World*, ed. David J. Hesse and Roberto da Matta (New York: Columbia University Press, 1995), pp. 35–48, and Roberto da Matta, *Carnavais, malandros e heróis. Para uma sociologia do dilema brasileiro*, 4th edn (Rio de Janeiro: Zahar, 1983).

[58] 'Em síntese, desde o século passado existe entre as pessoas educadas do Brasil—o que é uma categoria social, mais do que um elogio—o sentimento de viverem entre instituições e idéias que são copiadas do estrangeiro e não refletem a realidade local' Roberto Schwarz, 'Nacional por subtração', in *Que horas são? Ensaios*, rev. Marizilda Lourenço, Sandra Dolinsky and Carlos Queiroz Rocha (São Paulo: Companhia das Letras, 1987) (first publ. in *Folha de São Paulo*, 7 June 1986), pp. 29–48 (pp. 38–9).

[59] 'A idéia de cópia discutida aqui opõe o nacional ao estrangeiro e o original ao imitado, oposições que são irreais e não permitem ver a parte do estrangeiro no próprio, a parte do imitado no original, e também a parte original no imitado' [The idea of copy discussed here opposes the national with the foreign and the original with the imitation, oppositions which are unreal and do not allow us to see what is foreign in our own, what there is of imitation in the original, as well as the original in the copy] (Schwarz, 1987, p. 48).

[The main point is the segregation of the poor, excluded from the world of contemporary culture] (p. 47).

The question of foreign influences on Brazilian cultural production appeared to be a source of concern for Cabral, but it was undoubtedly the exclusion of the poor from education and employment (as discussed by Schwarz) that most preoccupied the poet in 'História de mau caráter'. This concern is viewed from a historical perspective, because the poem highlights the continuity between the questionable practices employed at the law school of Olinda (the first one to be founded in Brazil (1827), along with that of São Paulo) and at the school of Recife, where the former was relocated and where students were left in no doubt as to their privileged status: 'de uma aura (a toga?) de Pontífice' [of an aura (the toga?) of a Pontif] (p. 613).

In the poem, Cabral offers his readers precise geographical clues with regard to the scene of the 'crime' (i.e. references to Olinda and Recife, as well as to the Ramiro Costa bookshop). Yet, the riddle he presents in relation to the nature of the university post that became vacant is left unsolved:

> Uma vez, na vaga que abrira,
> de um Direito que acaba em *al*,
> o rico que a ela se apresenta
> tem o pobre como rival. (p. 613)

[Once, for the post that opened, | in a branch of Law ending in *al*, | the rich man who presents himself | has the poor man as rival.]

The '*al*' ending could allude to 'criminal law' among others,[60] and therefore suggests that corruption is endemic among the legal profession. This can also be inferred from the fact that Cabral maintains the anonymity of the two main characters—with the poor student addressing his rich counterpart simply as 'Fulano' [Joe Bloggs] (p. 613). In fact, the poet challenges the very foundations of Brazil's justice system, but at the same time refuses to take on the role of 'Relator' wholeheartedly, for he refrains from pointing the finger at any one individual.[61]

---

[60] An alternative might be 'direito constitucional', i.e. constitutional law.
[61] Cabral's view of the failings of Brazil's justice system and of the forces of law and order often found its way into his poetry. In *Crime na Calle Relator* itself, the poem 'O desembargador' (pp. 599–600), for example, includes a light-hearted reference to the 'judge traffickers' who lure the qualified lawyers away from the north-east of Brazil to the more prosperous south. In 'Antonio Silvino no Engenho Poço' (pp. 617–18), it is the integrity of the police that is thrown into question. In the voice of Cabral's grandfather, the fearful *cangaceiro* Antonio Silvino compares favourably with the forces of law and order. It is also

On the one hand, this would appear to compromise Cabral's own position as a champion of the oppressed, but it ensures that the anecdote becomes an illustration of typical class relations. It provides an insight into the daily injustices perpetrated against those who are at the margins of society, living in a fossilized system in which privilege, rather than merit, ultimately determines how power is apportioned. The racial discrimination that underpins such a system is something that Cabral addressed repeatedly in his writings and is, in fact, one of the central themes of the poem 'Brasil 4 x Argentina 0', which will be discussed in the following section.

4.7 'CRIMINALS' ON THE LOOSE

The poem 'Brasil 4 x Argentina 0 *(Guayaquil 1981)*' (pp. 616–17) illustrates the struggle for empowerment of the oppressed by drawing on that most Brazilian of sports. The poem deals with a football match played in Ecuador, when Brazil beat their old rivals Argentina. The match becomes symbolic of rebellion against domination on a number of levels. The importance of the date of the game, 1981, lies in the fact that all of the countries involved were at the time still in the grip of, or emerging from, years of military dictatorship; while the location at which it took place, Guayaquil, an indigenous place name and a key site in the wars of independence, is symbolic of the struggle of the colonized to preserve their cultural identity in the face of centuries of Spanish colonial rule.

In Cabral's poem, the Brazil/Argentina game is equated to the confrontation of Blacks/Whites (players/coaches); the success of the former achieved at the expense of the latter: 'técnicos mudos, mas surpresos, | brancos, no banco, com medo' [coaches dumbfounded, yet surprised | white, on the bench, in fear] (p. 616). The liberties that the players take with the rules of the game, much to the dismay of the coaches on both sides, are a sign of revolt against racially determined oppression: 'quebraram a chave da gaiola | e os quadros-negros da escola' [they broke the keys to the cage | and the school's blackboards] (p. 616). Significantly, the blackboard is employed as metaphor for the curtailment of black rights—its geometrical frame being in itself an

---

noteworthy that Cabral's *Auto do frade* should highlight the fact that the guilty verdict pronounced against the friar failed to convince those encumbered with the task of carrying out his execution.

image of 'containment'. As a black (blank) space on which white chalk is inscribed, it is also the material representation of the oppression and suppression of black identity. The victory of the Brazilian side (embodiment of the black and marginalized population) meets with the consternation of the members of the dominant order, whose grip on not only the political, but also the educational and even spiritual spheres of society is undermined:

> Chegou até cá a subversão?
> Como é possível haver xadrez?
> Sem gramática, bispos, reis? (p. 617)

[Has subversion reached these heights? | How can we have chess? | Without grammar, bishops, kings?]

The double meaning of 'xadrez'—that is, both a game of chess and jail—the latter being a connotation it has acquired in colloquial Brazilian Portuguese, suggests the degree of transgression with which the players' behaviour is charged.

If, as the poem suggests, grammatical rules are a symbol of control by the dominant culture, it is a measure of Cabral's defence of the oppressed that he should deliberately take advantage of the more flexible norms on pronoun position in Brazilian Portuguese (representative of the colonized) as opposed to that of the European variant (the colonizer). In the subordinate clause included in the third couplet of the poem, Cabral employs the reflexive pronoun after the verb 'que tomaram-se', in contravention of the European norm, but as it is occasionally employed by Brazilian Portuguese speakers: 'Nos fugitivos, é a surpresa, | vendo que tomaram-se as rédeas' [Among the fugitives, there is surprise, | realizing that the reins have been taken] (p. 616).

In the light of this, the poem duplicates on a linguistic level the subversion carried out by the black players, who refuse to be mere recipients of norms and regulations, much to the indignation of those sitting on the benches: 'Voltou a ser jogar de pião?' [Has it gone back to being a game of *pião*?] (p. 617). The reference to 'pião' is significant, since it can mean a top (child's toy), but also one of the movements of *capoeira*, originally a martial art disguised as dance developed by black slaves in Brazil.[62] Cabral draws on these meanings, all of which make a

---

[62] Among the meanings of the variant spelling 'peão' is that of low-paid labourer as well as of pawn in a game of chess (ie. the chess piece of lowest value). Given the reference to 'xadrez' earlier in the poem, it is fair to assume that Cabral intended to make this

link with the most vulnerable sections of society, to suggest the process of empowerment that the match played in Guayaquil entailed.

The audacity of the players to challenge established codes of behaviour is witnessed with horror by those in positions of authority. Yet, the poem embraces the cause of the victims of oppression—'criminals' in the eyes of the dominant order—and debunks presuppositions of law and order. Indeed, the seemingly trivial account of a football match provides Cabral with the opportunity to draw on anecdotes in order to raise important questions of racial discrimination and social exclusion within the context of the colonization of the American continent.

4.8 DIFFERENT ENDINGS

The poem with which Cabral closed the 1994 edition of *Crime na Calle Relator*, 'A morte de "Gallito"' (p. 625), was not incorporated in the subsequent edition of his complete works, published by Nova Fronteira in 1997.[63] The reasons for this omission are unclear, but undoubtedly the sense of bewilderment that the collection aims to provoke in the reader is enhanced by this cleverly constructed poem's unusual take on the theme of bullfighting.

The story on which the poem is based is that of the legendary José Gómez Ortega, known as 'Gallito y Joselito', killed during a *corrida* on 16 May 1920.[64] Much to the disbelief of the spectators, Gallito's exceptional skills were of no avail when he was overpowered by a

---

association, although keeping the spelling 'pião'. In fact, he is playing with the phonetic similarity of the words and exploring the multiple meanings of both variants—all of which are associated with the oppressed.

[63] It should be noted that the poem had previously appeared in the anthology *Poemas sevilhanos* (Rio de Janeiro: Nova Fronteira, 1992), pp. 191–2. This collection had been published (by Nova Fronteira, in collaboration with Itamaraty—the Brazilian Foreign Office) on occasion of the celebrations of the 400th anniversary of Columbus's discovery, which were held in Seville and which Cabral attended. Given the postcolonial level of 'A morte de "Gallito"', its inclusion in the collection is extremely significant of the poet's anti-colonialist stance. Bearing in mind Cabral's diplomatic status and the fact that he was representing no less than the Brazilian President at the Seville celebrations, it also strikes one as ironic and subtly 'undiplomatic'.

[64] *Enciclopedia universal ilustrada europeo-americana*, 70 vols, ed. Telesforo de Aranzadi and others (Barcelona: Hijos de J. Espasa, 1925–1930), XXXVI (1925): 'Su muerte produjo honda impresión en toda España, pues se le suponía poco menos que invulnerable' [His death has a great impact on the whole of Spain, because he was believed to be nohing less than invulnerable] (p. 567).

short-sighted bull. Like the celebrated Manolete, a subject of many of Cabral's poems, Gallito too perfected the art of bullfighting to such a degree as to give his performance the precision of an exact science: 'Ele tinha tal sabedoria | que seu toureio era geometria' [He had such knowledge | that his bullfighting was geometry] (p. 625). However, a set of bizarre circumstances—though short-sighted, the bull sees Gallito from a distance and is thus able to overpower him—meant that the *toureiro*'s expertise was ultimately worthless.

The figure of the bullfighter had fascinated Cabral ever since his first visit to Spain, in 1947. His famous poem 'Alguns toureiros' (pp. 157–8), included in the collection *Paisagens com figuras*, was to be the first in a number of compositions devoted to the theme. Critics, such as Marta Peixoto (2000 [2002], p. 230), have often noted how Cabral's poetic ideal of precision and contained emotions was encoded in the skills of his most admired bullfighters, among whom the famous Manolete excelled:

> com mão certa, pouca e extrema:
> sem perfumar sua flor,
> sem poetizar seu poema. (p. 158)

[with a firm hand, minimal and extreme: | without perfuming his flower, | without poeticizing his poem.]

Beside this meta-textual level of meaning, the bullfighter embodies an ethos of defiance to domination. Manolete's defiance of death, described as 'expor a vida à louca foice' [expose life to the mad scythe] (p. 538) in the second line of the poem 'Lembrando Manolete' (p. 538), included in *Agrestes*, exemplifies this point.

Cabral remained fascinated by bullfighting throughout his life, and indeed in his last collection, *Andando Sevilha*, he paid homage to, among others, some of the bullfighters who had featured in his earlier 'Alguns toureiros' (namely Manolo González and Miguel Baez). With this in mind, it is revealing of the distinctiveness of *Crime na Calle Relator* within Cabral's *œuvre* that 'A morte de "Gallito"' should focus precisely on the demise of a bullfighter caught off guard by a partially sighted bull. Considering the meta-textual connotations that bullfighting acquired in Cabral's poetry, it would be difficult not to read 'A morte de "Gallito"' as a revaluation of Cabral's poetics of rationality and precision, a reassessment that the collection as a whole, with its articulation of ambiguity from a number of different perspectives, seems to foreground.

The first six of the ten couplets of the poem reconstruct the to-and-fro movements of the fight between 'Gallito' and the shortsighted bull. Defying the public's and the *toureiro*'s expectations, the bull gets the better of Gallito, which comes as a surprise, particularly taking into account Gallito's presumed knowledge of the art of bullfighting. The commotion caused by Gallito's death is duplicated by the syntactical disruption of the conventional Portuguese word order in the last couplet: '"A José", e há quem não creia | "matou um touro em Talavera" ["José", and there are those who don't believe it | "was killed by a bull in Talavera"] (p. 625). The structure of these lines aims at reproducing ordinary Spanish syntax, and, along with the conspicuous insertion of the Spanish term 'burriciego' (i.e. partially sighted), it lends the story greater authenticity, as though it were told by a Spanish voice with firsthand experience of the event.

Cabral makes a point of setting the episode within the wider historical context of Spain's involvement in armed struggle, and it is likely that the reference to bombs in the penultimate couplet alludes to the guerrilla war that Spain was engaged in against Moroccan groups opposed to its rule in North Africa.[65] In the light of this, it appears that Cabral perceived the death of Gallito as a metaphor for the eventual collapse of Spanish colonial rule, and the precision (or 'geometry') displayed by the bullfighter becomes synonymous with authoritarianism, which is undermined.

Thus, the poem offers a dramatic reworking of one of the stock images of Cabral's poetry. On an ethical level, it is because Gallito is perceived as an embodiment of the dominant order, that his failure, rather than his achievement, is exposed. The image of the 'gallo' [cock], encapsulated in the bullfighter's name, is also significant, as it draws attention to Cabral's innovative configuration of masculinity, through which gender stereotypes are startlingly subverted. Given that the art of bullfighting is traditionally seen as crystallizing qualities generally understood as masculine, it is somewhat paradoxical that those very same qualities should prove ineffectual when it comes to saving 'Gallito' [literally, 'little cock'], whose name projects him as the epitome of masculinity.

---

[65] *Historical Dictionary of Modern Spain 1700–1988*, ed. Robert W. Kern (New York: Greenwood, 1990), p. 341. The Spanish Protectorate in Northern Morocco was negotiated with France in 1904 and ended in 1956.

On a meta-textual level, the inadequate geometry of Gallito's art stands in stark contrast with the mastery of Manolete, which Cabral, as discussed above, had so often celebrated. It would therefore be difficult not to read 'A morte de "Gallito"' as Cabral's reassessment of his poetics of clarity and precision, according to which binary oppositions are disrupted, as are the hierarchies between humans and non-humans. In fact, the bullfighter, named after a bird, fails in his role as the embodiment of rationality (conveyed by the reference to 'sabedoria', i.e. 'knowledge/wisdom'), and is defeated by an animal, that is, by definition, an irrational being.[66]

'A morte de "Gallito"' was edited out of the 1997 edition, but the reasons for this decision are not known. One possible explanation might be that Cabral felt that the dramatic re-working of the theme of bullfighting in this poem contradicted his treatment of the theme in other compositions and, in a sense, was too revealing of a more relaxed authorial stance. In addition, it is more openly subversive of the dominant order than either 'História de mau caráter', which closed the 1987 edition, or 'Cenas da vida de Joaquim Cardozo', the closing poem of the 1988 and 1997 editions. This is because the poem foregrounds the actual metaphorical overthrowing of those in power—in this case colonial rule—in the killing of the bullfighter by an animal, generally considered to be subordinate to humans.

Nonetheless, it should be noted that 'Cenas da vida de Joaquim Cardozo' (pp. 620–4)[67] too engages with issues dealt with in the other closing poems. In line with the approach of the collection as a

---

[66] Such renderings contrast with Cabral's traditional configurations of his poetic ideal through images of masculinity, as analysed by Peixoto (2000 [2002]). Indeed, in 'A morte de "Gallito"' traditional masculine values are undermined.

[67] Joaquim Cardozo was born in Recife in 1897 and died in Olinda in 1978. Cabral considered him a forgotten master of Brazilian twentieth-century poetry, and his early work *O cão sem plumas* is dedicated to Cardozo. He also wrote a number of poems inspired by his fellow poet, apart from 'Cenas da vida de Joaquim Cardozo': 'A Joaquim Cardozo' (*O engenheiro*), 'A luz em Joaquim Cardozo' and 'Pergunta a Joaquim Cardozo' (*Museu de tudo*), 'Joaquim Cardozo na Europa' (*A escola das facas*). As an engineer, Cardozo worked alongside Oscar Niemeyer in the construction of Brasília. His left-wing views made him the target of political persecution in 1939, when he was forced to leave Recife. See Jamille Cabral Pereira Barbosa and others, 'Biografia' <http://www.biblio.ufpe.br/libvirt/joaquim> (accessed 14 February 2003). References to the political persecution Cardozo suffered are not easily accessible in studies on the poet (see, for example, Alexandre Pinheiro Torres, 'Joaquim Cardoso', in *Antologia da poesia brasileira*, 3 vols (Porto: Lello & Irmão, 1984), III, 389–461. Thus, their presence in Cabral's work indicates his wish to rescue forgotten historical facts.

whole, the poem consists of a series of anecdotes on Cardozo's life and character. In these snapshots of his life, Cardozo is celebrated as a man who suffered political persecution due to his left-wing ideals and as an eccentric in his personal life. In fact, these two features of his life go hand-in-hand, because his non-conformity on a personal level reflected his drive to challenge political domination on a public one. An example is given in the opening section of the poem, entitled 'A tragédia grega e o mar do Nordeste', in which we are told of Cardozo's claim that he could make out the dialogues of a Greek tragedy in the sounds of the wind and sea of the north-east and the lament of the chorus in the murmuring of the coconut trees. Cardozo's tendency to hear these 'vozes sem face' [faceless voices] (p. 620) is seen as an illustration of his being in tune with the voices of those who are invisible within society and who are waiting to be heard. As Cabral states towards the end of this section of the poem, rescuing the voice of the oppressed from the silence of history is the only rightful way of re-visiting the past: 'Não é essa a curva das estórias? | Não é esse o trajeto da História?' [Is this not the curve of stories? | Is this not the trajectory of History?] (p. 621).

In essence, Cabral's aim in *Crime na Calle Relator* reflected a similar challenge to official discourses of history in its rescuing the voices of the marginalized. By the reference to the 'curva das estórias' we can understand his own use of short anecdotal narratives to probe the inequities of his country's History. Moreover, the allusion to the 'curves' of History, suggests his rejection of the notion of a historical linear progression as encapsulated in the positivist motto of 'Ordem e Progresso', strongly embraced by the dictatorship, and position is underlined by the startling comparison Cabral makes between Joaquim Cardozo and Frei Caneca, at the end of the poem, which casts both these figures as victims of repressive regimes. By closing his poem (and therefore also his collection of 1988 and 1997) with an allusion to the wrongful conviction of Frei Caneca, Cabral reminds the readers of the flaws of 'justice' explored in other compositions.

4.9 CONCLUSION

Cabral's investigation into the question of culpability in *Crime na Calle Relator* exposes the difficulties implied in any attempt at defining guilt and reveals that no verdict is ever entirely unproblematic.

The poems 'Crime na Calle Relator' and 'A morte de "Gallito"' are underpinned by an acute sense of the elusiveness of truth, and make no attempt at solving the puzzles that they present. In fact, the poet indulges in narratives that elude any closure. The open-ended nature of the narrative thread of the first and last poems means the collection is effectively 'framed' by compositions defined by indeterminacy. Whether the young *sevilhana* ever played a pivotal role in the demise of her own grandmother is a question that remains unanswered. In turn, the enquiry into the death of 'Gallito' shows that any rational explanation will prove inadequate. Yet, it is precisely this lack of closure that Cabral explores as a political tool, be it in relation to gender relations or postcolonial concerns. Indeed, the *sevilhana* manages to undermine the patriarchal structures of power, while the death of 'Gallito' illustrates how, against all the odds, the oppressed succeed in revolting against colonial domination.

Apart from probing into questions of criminality and guilt to address instances of domination of a global nature, Cabral was specifically concerned with his native Brazil. The poem 'Brasil 4 x Argentina 0' shows how he challenged definitions of unlawfulness with the aim of exposing the racial discrimination and erasure of cultural difference that the colonization of the American continent, and of Brazil specifically, entailed. The game of football is presented as a metaphor for the revolt against racial discrimination through the subversion of established rules and regulations. Set in the year 1981, the poem refers to a time in which South America was in the grip of, or slowly emerging from, military rule, making Cabral's enquiry into questions of Law, Order and Truth all the more topical.

Indeed, albeit in a disguised and oblique fashion, *Crime na Calle Relator* emerges as a collection that engages closely with the social and political background against which it was written. Like the crime fiction that was thriving in Brazil at the time, it explores narratives in which dichotomies of guilt and innocence are thrown into question, challenging authoritarian categorizations.

At a conference in Barcelona in 1990, Cabral discussed the imbalance of the cultural dialogue between north–south and drew attention to the economic and political causes that lie at the root of the problem. In doing so, he expressed his doubts as to the power that creative writing had in addressing the problematic transfer of culture from developed to developing countries, and quoted W. H. Auden by stating: 'Poetry makes nothing happen.'[68] However, if such scepticism was articulated in theoretical terms, there is little doubt that, in his own poetry, Cabral had been heavily engaged in addressing questions of social, racial and sexual oppression, and was particularly concerned with Brazil's postcolonial condition. In *Crime na Calle Relator*, for example, he highlighted the injustices perpetrated against its people during colonial rule and showed how the inequities of the past had remained largely unresolved.

In this way, *Crime na Calle Relator* rejects the concept of history as a linear ordered progression towards enlightenment. This is reflected on a structural level, in its inclusion of different anecdotal narratives, the 'curva das estórias', which results in a collection whose structure is fragmented. Such a feature is compounded by the exploration of the themes of the unsolved mystery and relativity of any definition of guilt. The result is that the very notions of Order and Progress are undermined both structurally and thematically. A relativization of this kind has important implications in the light of Brazil's recent experience of dictatorial rule and demonstrates how the light-hearted tone of *Crime na Calle Relator*, its 'soft and witty voice', to draw on Silviano Santiago's formulations (1989, p. 18), does not detract from its political import. This lies primarily in the emphasis given to the fact that any definitive distinction between victims and villains is never far from contention, highlighting the existence of different and often conflicting points of view.

This emphasis on fluid categorizations was developed further in Cabral's subsequent collections, *Sevilha andando* and *Andando Sevilha*. In these works, the Andalusian city represents a space where marginalized social groups, such as the gypsy community, manage to find self-expression by evading the oppressive control of the dominant order. An epitome of such empowerment is the image of the walking *sevilhana*, who is so elusive that she remains an ambiguous figure who can never be fully captured by the male gaze. Cabral's celebration of such features carries important social and political implications, but is also noteworthy for the insight it provides into his evolving thoughts on the process of writing, as will be discussed in the following chapter.

---

[68] 'A poesia não faz nada acontecer.' See 'A diversidade cultural no diálogo Norte-Sul', in Melo Neto (1994, pp. 789–95 (p. 794)).

5
'Tu eras de mentira e ambígua': images of women and the city in *Sevilha andando* and *Andando Sevilha*

5.1 INTRODUCTION

In the poem 'Os turistas' (pp. 657–8), from *Andando Sevilha*, a flamenco dancer comes under the gaze of a group of foreign, male tourists. Their misconception that she is simply an object to be scrutinized, destined to pander to their desire, comes under attack in Cabral's celebration of the flamenco dancer:

> Nos revôos de tua saia
> que te despia e vestia,
> tu te davas e não te davas,
> tu eras de mentira e ambígua.
>
> Com os revôos de tua saia,
> que poucos compreendiam,
> que tu te ofereces, pensava
> toda a estrangeira maioria. (p. 657)

[In the flights of your skirt | which undressed and clothed you, | you gave and did not give yourself, | you were mocking and ambiguous. | With the flights of your skirt, | which only a few comprehended, | you offer yourself, thought | the entire foreign majority.]

The interest that the dancer excites in the poet lies precisely in the fact that she is 'de mentira e ambígua', that she is not what she initially appears to be. Thanks to these qualities, she can be read as the embodiment of the literary text itself, given that it is fiction and so lends itself to multiple readings and interpretations. This meta-textual level of meaning is not far-fetched: bearing in mind the association of the flamenco dancer with the literary text in Cabral's famous earlier poem 'Estudos para uma bailadora andaluza' (pp. 219–25), of *Quaderna*, it is clear that, beyond the anecdotal account of 'Os turistas', an oblique reflection on writing can be identified.

In fact, the ambiguity of the woman in *Andando Sevilha* is shared by her earlier counterpart, in whose dance the struggle between writer, language and readers is enacted:

> parece desafiar
> alguma presença interna
> que no fundo dela própria,
> fluindo, informe e sem regra,
> por sua vez a desafia
> a ver quem é que a modela. (p. 223)

[she seems to defy | some internal presence | which deep inside of her, | flowing, shapeless and unruly, | in turn defies her | to see who might shape it.]

The elusiveness of the flamenco dancer in both these poems is also central to that of the walking *sevilhana*, who dominates *Sevilha andando*, and who will provide the main focus of analysis on the collection. It is my contention that the elusive, ambulating *sevilhana* provides a metaphor not only for social and sexual empowerment, but also for the literary text itself, because the indeterminacy that defines the visions of the *sevilhana*, who refuses to be 'fixed' or categorized by the male gaze, also mirrors Cabral's understanding of writing. As a result, she encapsulates the thoughts of a mature poet, who played with ambiguity in language, in imagery and often also in structure, as the undefined endings of some of his previous collections show (*Crime na Calle Relator* being an example).

In this chapter, *Sevilha andando* and *Andando Sevilha* will be analysed together by virtue of their thematic closeness. The two collections were originally published as the two sections of one single compilation of poems, *Sevilha andando (Poesia)*, first published in 1990. However, when included in his *Obra completa*, in 1994, and in all subsequent editions, the two sections appeared as collections in their own right. *Sevilha andando*, comprising poems written between 1987 and 1993, was augmented from an initial sixteen poems to a total of thirty-one; whereas *Andando Sevilha*, written between 1987 and 1989, maintained its original format of thirty-six compositions.

A greater balance between the two original groups of poems emerged from such extensive reworkings, yet it is curious that Cabral fell short of ensuring a perfect equivalence in their respective number of compositions. Indeed, this numerical disparity seems at odds with the mirror-like effect produced by the chiasmic structure of the titles, and creates a disjunction that makes the overall structure seem somewhat awry. The same can be identified on a stylistic level in the use of assonantal rhyme (with its 'imperfect' repetition of sounds), through which the poet conveyed his images of femininity and of the city of Seville.[1] Arguably, the disjunction that underpins these structural and stylistic features is intended as a reflection of the elusive and often inscrutable nature of the city, which these collections bring to the fore.

The city of Seville is central to both collections; in the first instance, embodied in the figure of the walking *sevilhana*; in the second, emerging in the human and architectural fabric of the city itself. In both collections, however, the female subject in undeniably prominent, and for this reason my analysis will give particular consideration to their representations of women. To date, criticism on these collections has been scarce, and critical studies that have approached Cabral's work from a gender perspective have been more limited still. Yet, with a growing awareness of the need to explore neglected features of his writing, the question of constructions of femininity and configurations of gender is coming under increased critical scrutiny. Marta Peixoto's study (2000 [2002]) of his configurations of writing in which traditionally masculine values were favoured has provided an important re-evaluation of the poet's *œuvre* within the framework of gender studies.

Indeed, with few exceptions, critical readings of Cabral's representations of femininity have concentrated on the poet's traditional renderings of female subjects, particularly in what can be defined as his love poems. A case in point is José Guilherme Merquior's analysis of 'Imitação da água' (*Quaderna*) (p. 260), of which he stated: 'the theme is woman—a rare theme and an unexpected one in the work of a poet of anti-incantatory devotion, of harshness and rigour'.[2] Yet, despite Cabral's sporadic engagement with the theme of love, it is also true that his representations of women were not restricted to this theme. In fact, whether in stereotypical renditions, as in *Os três mal amados,* or in subversive ones, as in 'A mulher e o Beberibe' from the later *A educação pela pedra,* women have featured throughout Cabral's literary output.

---

[1] In 'A sevilhana que não se sabia' (p. 631), he makes explicit reference to assonantal rhyme as the stylistic device he favoured to show the similarities between the city of Seville and the Brazilian *sevilhana*.

[2] 'O tema é a mulher—tema raro e surpreendente na obra desse poeta de devoção antiencantatória, de aspereza e de rigor.' 'Onda mulher, onde a mulher', in *Razão do poema. Ensaios de crítica e de estética* (Rio de Janeiro: Civilização Brasileira, 1965), pp. 96–101 (p. 97).

That said, the prominence of female figures in his last collections, particularly in *Sevilha andando* but also in *Andando Sevilha*, is unparalleled in the poet's work.

The collections' pivotal images—of city and woman—are often conflated, the boundaries between the urban and human blurred. The result is that Seville becomes a metaphor not only for a particular urban experience, but also for womankind and writing. The theme of travel, which Cabral explored extensively throughout his career, is central to his configurations of Seville. It is present in *Sevilha andando*, in the image of the walking *sevilhana*, who is elusive and, therefore, resists being categorized and symbolically dominated. It is also found in *Andando Sevilha*, where itinerant social minorities are synonymous with defiance of social conventions and the triumph of individuality.

The admiration for, and empathy with, the struggle of the marginalized in these last two collections is testified in Cabral's choice of epigraphs. Both are drawn from Andalusian popular culture, an unprecedented choice within the poet's *œuvre*, given that epigraphs to earlier collections had been extracted from the work of writers of canonical status or figures of prominence within Western high culture.[3] In the case of his last collections, Cabral's predilection for popular sayings pays homage to the possibility of subversion by the oppressed sections of society against the dominant order, of which his celebration of gypsy culture is an example.

It is this potential for subversion from the margins that the first of the two epigraphs aims to introduce. The quotation 'En el cielo que pisan las sevillanas...' [In the sky where the Sevillian women tread...] (p. 628), the source of which is given as being a 'Popular sevilhano' [Sevillian popular saying], captures the defiant nature of the woman from Seville. The ambiguity implied by the verb 'pisan', meaning both 'treading' and 'trampling', suggests that the *sevilhanas* are in heaven, but that they are defiant rather than in awe of God's (male) power. There is undoubtedly an extraordinary quality in the world that Cabral describes, something that the lines which introduce the second group of poems conveys by highlighting Seville's unique position even within Spanish culture: 'Quién no vió a Sevilla | no vió maravilha...' [Whoever hasn't seen Seville | hasn't seen its wonder...] (p. 654).

---

[3] Cabral's first collection, *Pedra do sono*, for example, featured an epigraph from Mallarmé, while a quotation by Le Corbusier introduced *O engenheiro*.

Cabral's fascination with Spain, and Andalusia in particular, is unmatched within Brazilian poetic tradition, although it is shared to a certain degree by his fellow poet Murilo Mendes. Spanish culture and landscapes provided the theme for Murilo Mendes's poems *Tempo espanhol* (1959) and his prose diary *Espaço espanhol*, published in 1975. In the latter, a collection of travel notes written between 1966 and 1969, Mendes acknowledged Cabral's unique appropriation of the Spanish theme, especially his introduction into the Portuguese language of the theme of flamenco dance with his 'Estudos para uma bailadora andaluza', of *Quaderna* (Mendes, 1994, p. 1175). In fact, that Andalusia and not Brazil should have provided the sole inspiration for Cabral's two final collections is noteworthy, but as a poetic space associated with the affirmation of life and individuality—an association that the second section of *Agrestes* also demonstrates—Seville provided an ideal metaphor for Cabral to express the new-found happiness in his personal life.

Indeed, *Sevilha andando* and *Andando Sevilha* were dedicated to his second wife, the poet Marly de Oliveira, whom he married in 1986, following the tragic death of his first wife, Stella. That said, Cabral's revisitation of the city transcended the personal sphere and provided an extremely productive medium to develop his thoughts on writing itself, as well as on questions of sexual and social domination, including from a postcolonial standpoint. In order to discuss the ways in which he articulated these concerns, the first half of the chapter will consider Cabral's personification of the city in the image of the *sevilhana*, while the second half will analyse broader renditions of the urban space.

The starting point will be Cabral's representation of Seville as a woman and poetic text, to assess how his conceptualizations of writing were developed through representations of the human body, in which his obsession with the in-between space re-emerged. Following this discussion on the personification of writing, I analyse images of the city as woman, focusing on the poet's innovative representations of women who defy the possessive male gaze. Cabral's configurations of the urban space through images of women are not in themselves innovative, for they find a wealth of antecedents in modern poetic tradition. But, the manner in which he engaged with such tradition in order to debunk not only sexual stereotypes but also colonial discourses is worthy of note. Therefore, his dialogue with canonical European writers, such as Baudelaire and Nerval, will be examined. The third section of the chapter considers how the postcolonial theme of *Sevilha andando* was developed further in images of navigation, which were intended to undermine colonial narratives of the colonization of the New World. Given the import of the postcolonial subtext of the collection, the fourth section will focus specifically on Cabral's subversion of the theme of the celebrations for the fifth centenary of the Spanish discovery of America, which he had attended in person.

My study of *Andando Sevilha*, in the second half this chapter, begins with an analysis of representations of the city's inhabitants and of its gypsy community in particular. Because of their traditional nomadic lifestyle, gypsies mirror the elusiveness of the walking *sevilhana* of the previous collection. Finally, I discuss Cabral's treatment of the theme of mortality and of the image of the 'aceiro da morte' [literally, 'death clearing', i.e. boundary], where cultural manifestations such as bull-fighting are visualized. Such fascination with liminal states is already evident in *Sevilha andando*'s images of the human body as metaphors for the literary text. In them, the complexity of the work of literature is conveyed through a reworking of the image of the in-between space, as the section that follows will discuss.

5.2 SEVILHA ANDANDO

5.2.1 The City as Text

The image of the in-between space, which Cabral had explored in earlier collections, is reworked in *Sevilha andando* in representations of the city as a metaphor of the poetic text. An explicit example of this association is made in the poem 'Cidade de nervos' (p. 638), where the city is visualized in images of the human body. According to these visualizations, Seville combines the 'texture of the flesh' and the 'skeleton' essential to the human body and poetry alike. The two opposites are seen to coexist in the fabric of the city/poem: the 'carne' [flesh] as a metaphor for sensuality and emotion; the 'esqueleto' [skeleton] as a metaphor for structure and rationality.

The first three stanzas of the poem thus signal a significant development in Cabral's meta-poetic reflections, given that the metaphor of the human flesh is reinstated as an integral part of the creative process, alongside the rationality and detachment associated with the image of the human bones. This seems to undermine the traditional view of Cabral as a cerebral 'engineer' of words, something that is challenged further in the closing stanza, where a new and more appropriate metaphor for the city/poem is suggested, one which transcends binary oppositions:

> Mas o esqueleto não pode,
> ele que é rígido e de gesso,
> reacender a brasa que tem dentro:
> Sevilha é mais que tudo, nervo. (p. 638)

[But the skeleton cannot, | for it is rigid and chalk-like, | reignite the embers within: | Seville is above all, nerve.]

The compromise between the rigid bone structure and the amorphous body of flesh, captured in the image of the 'nervo', is identified as the defining metaphor for the city. Communicative impulse and ultimately vitality are evoked in this image, as the reference to the incandescent embers suggests. In other words, the city, as a metaphor for text, encapsulates a space where binary oppositions have been overcome, since the semi-rigid nerves bear qualities that are shared by both flesh and bones. The morbidity implied in references to the body and, by association, to the text, that was found in *A escola das facas* (as in 'O que se diz ao editor a propósito de poemas') here has given way to a vitality which suggests the presence of a much less self-critical authorial voice.

In line with such perceptions of the literary text, Cabral's renditions of the city of Seville privileged images of liminality in which boundaries are deliberately disrupted. This is true of the central figure of *Sevilha andando*, that of the walking *sevilhana*, whose constant motion reflects her elusiveness and her refusal to be 'fixed' by the male gaze, with significant implications not only as far as gender politics is concerned, but also from a postcolonial perspective.

5.2.2 The city as woman

As the recurring vision of the walking *sevilhana* exemplifies, Cabral constructs his collection around images of travel and movement. The theme of travel is not new in his work—the long poem *O rio*, of 1954, recording the journey of the Capibaribe river from its source to the sea, or indeed *Morte e vida severina*, of 1956, are examples of earlier explorations of the theme. What is striking in this collection is how Cabral conflates just such a motif with that of the unsolved mystery, pivotal to the previous collection, *Crime na Calle Relator*, to conjure up visions of travel in which destination or itinerary are unclear.

This theme might, at first sight, appear to be at odds with the image of the self-assertive *sevilhana*, evoked in the epigraph to *Sevilha andando* and central to many of the poems of the collection. Yet, my contention is that the uncertainty of her itinerary does not undermine her self-determination, the eponymous poem 'Sevilha andando (I)' (p. 639) being a case in point.

The numerical reference featured in the title of 'Sevilha andando (I)' suggests that this might have been intended as the first of a sequence of compositions under the same heading. The absence of a sequence of this kind in the published collection is significant, for it means that the reference alludes to something that effectively did not materialize. This structural void can be said to reflect the elusiveness of the female figure, one of the collection's key concerns. From this point of view, it is also significant that, unlike the preceding *Crime na Calle Relator*, the eponymous poem should not be the first but the tenth in the collection, duplicating the theme of displacement that is explored in relation to the female subject.

The woman's motion is central to her association with the vitality of the city of Seville, as is suggested in the poem's opening stanza:

> Só com andar pode trazer
> a atmosfera Sevilha, cítrea
> o formigueiro em festa
> que faz o vivo de Sevilha. (p. 639)

[Just by walking she can bring | the citric, Seville atmosphere | the bustling party | which makes Seville alive.]

The buzzing city is seen as a 'formigueiro em festa', while the orange trees that famously line its streets produce an atmosphere that is defined as 'cítrea'.[4] That the city's vibrancy should be conveyed through Seville's association with the natural world, in images in which boundaries between nature and culture become blurred, is poignant. Although the image of the 'formigueiro' is in fact a dead metaphor and is frequently employed in Portuguese to allude to a large congregation of people, it is possible to infer that its choice was not fortuitous, but that it was meant to echo the natural imagery of the citrus trees, which

---

[4] 'Formigueiro' literally translates as 'anthill', but is metaphorically used to refer to a space with a large number of people.

has considerable implications for Cabral's innovative representation of women in *Sevilha andando*.

In her seminal article entitled 'Is female to male as nature is to culture?', the feminist anthropologist Sherry B. Ortner discusses the way women's subordinate position within patriarchal society has stemmed from perceptions of women as being closer to nature than men: 'even if women are not equated with nature, they are nonetheless seen as representing a lower order of being, as being less transcendental of nature than men are'.[5] For Ortner, woman in patriarchy exists in an in-between space between nature and culture, in what she defines as 'culture's clearing' (p. 85), which accounts for the polarized and often contradictory representations of woman: 'That she often represents both life and death is only the simplest example one could mention' (p. 85).

Ortner's reference to the 'clearing' in which women are visualized is of particular interest to this reading of Cabral's collection, given the poet's obsession with instances of liminality, of which his configurations of the 'aceiro' in *Agrestes* are an example. Yet, the woman's straddling the realms of nature and culture is endowed with positive connotations in Cabral's poem.[6] In 'Sevilha andando (I)', for example, the 'natural woman' of the first stanza becomes a 'woman of culture' in the final stanza, as she is pictured 'mapping' the world around her: 'faz do ao redor | astros de sua astronomia' [turns what surrounds her | into stars of her astronomy] (p. 639).

In addition to the subversion of the categories of nature/culture, the poem challenges traditional stereotypes of the woman as either saint or fallen woman, stereotypes often associated with representations of the urban landscape. In his study of representations of the city in Western thought, William Sharpe reminds us of the equivalence of woman's sexual purity to the spiritual value of the cities the female gender comes to embody. Thus, for example, the fallen city of Babylon is equated in

---

[5] See Sherry B. Ortner, 'Is Female to Male as Nature is to Culture?', in *Woman, Culture and Society*, ed. Michelle Zimbalist Rosaldo and Louise Lamphere (Stanford: Stanford University Press, 1989), pp. 67–87 (p. 73).

[6] Cabral did not always distance himself from stereotypical conceptualizations of femininity, as exemplified by 'As *plazoletas*' (p. 641), a poem where gender relations defined by male domination and female confinement emerge: 'Quem fez Sevilha a fez para o homem, | [...] | Para a mulher: para que aprenda, | fez escolas de espaço, dentros, | [...] | quase do tamanho de um lenço' [Whoever made Seville made her for man, | [...] | For woman: so that she may learn, | schools of space were made, insides, | [...] | almost the size of a handkerchief] (p. 641).

the book of Revelation to a harlot, while the figure of the virgin embodies the city of New Jerusalem that is to come.[7]

In Cabral's poem, the woman is visualized in the image of the sun, traditionally associated with masculinity, to convey the self-assertiveness of the *sevilhana*: 'capaz de na *Calle* Regina | ou até num claustro ser o sol' [able to be the sun whether in the *Calle* Regina | or within cloisters] (p. 639). Here, the woman moves confidently from the *Calle* Regina, famous for its bustling market, and therefore a symbol of worldly pleasures, to the confines of a convent, evoked by the reference to the 'claustro'. The reiterative use of the verb 'andar' [walk] in the first two stanzas gives way to 'ser' [to be] in the final two stanzas, thus reflecting on a linguistic level the woman's progress towards empowerment, as these lines from the closing stanza illustrate:

> Uma mulher que sabe ser-se
> e ser Sevilha, ser sol, desafia
> o ao redor, e faz do ao redor
> astros de sua astronomia. (p. 639)

[A woman who knows how to be | and be Seville, be the sun, defies | what surrounds her, and turns what surrounds her | into stars of her astronomy.]

As one who defies the boundaries of good and evil, the woman resists classification into the categories of angel or harlot: 'Andaria até mesmo o inferno | em mulher da *Panadería*' [She would walk in hell, even | as the woman from *Panadería*] (p. 639). The comparison with an anonymous inhabitant of the district of Panadería inscribes the woman within the realm of the popular—in line with the spirit of defiance implied in the epigraph that introduced the collection.

Such a positive rendition of the female walker stands in juxtaposition with the treatment of the same image by Baudelaire and consequently his configuration of the urban environment, with which Cabral would have been familiar, since his admiration for the French poet is well documented.[8] In Baudelaire, the fleeting encounter with the *passante*

---

[7] William C. Sharpe, *Unreal Cities: Urban Figuration in Wordsworth, Baudelaire, Whitman, Eliot and Williams* (Baltimore, MD: The Johns Hopkins University Press, 1990), p. 9.

[8] Cabral declared to have purchased nine editions of Baudelaire's complete works (in Athayde, 1998, p. 121). He also stated: 'Para mim, o maior poeta que o mundo já deu foi Baudelaire [...]. Em Baudelaire tem tudo. O que veio depois dele já estava nele' [For me, the greatest poet of all time is Baudelaire [...]. You find everything in Baudelaire. What came after was already in him] (interview with Bosi and others, p. 28).

encapsulates human alienation and the disintegration of society within the framework of urban modernity. Baudelaire's use of natural imagery reinforces woman's stereotypical role as temptress and her association with indomitable nature: 'Dans son oeil, ciel livide où germe l'ouragan, | La douceur que fascine et le plaisir qui tue' [In her gaze, the livid sky where the storm is stirring, | The sweetness that fascinates and the pleasure that kills].[9]

Cabral takes a contrasting approach, as he rejects the polarization of nature and culture, thereby allowing the boundaries between traditional masculine and feminine values to become fluid in his positive vision of the urban space. This subversion of social stereotypes is duplicated in what the Brazilian critic Alcides Villaça has defined as the principle of 'traduzibilidade' [translatability], whereby a disregard of grammatical categories articulates Cabral's combination of very disparate realities: 'To define this universe categorically, adjectives embody the material, adjectives and adverbs serve as nouns, in the same way that proper names can qualify common nouns: "severino death and life", "Cardozo existence", "ipanema morning" etc.'[10]

Villaça's insightful analysis seems pertinent to this reading of 'Sevilha andando (I)', where the woman's transgression of social boundaries is duplicated on a linguistic level in the use of an adverb, 'onde' [where], in place of a noun: 'ela caminha qualquer onde | como se andasse por Sevilha' [she walks any where | as though she were walking through Seville] (p. 639).

The defiance displayed by the woman who exudes the spirit of the Andalusian city is, therefore, subversive of patriarchal values. This is also the case in the poem 'Mulher cidade' (pp. 644–5), where the elusiveness of the woman in which Seville is personified is not seen to be disturbing, as is the case with Baudelaire's *flâneur*, but rather to be a reflection of her emancipation.

Cabral's association of women with the urban space finds an antecedent in his earlier configurations of femininity through architectural imagery. João Alexandre Barbosa commented on these representations of women, emphasizing the similarities with the poet's later renditions:

---

[9] Charles Baudelaire, 'À une passante', in *Les fleurs du mal*, ed. Jacques Dupont (Paris: Flammarion, 1991), p. 137.

[10] 'Para servir à definição categórica desse universo, os atributos encarnam o substancial, os adjetivos e os advérbios valem como substantivos, assim como podem os nomes próprios qualificar nomes comuns: "morte e vida severina", "jeito de existir, Cardozo", "manhã ipanema" etc.' (Villaça, pp. 149–50).

'Already in *Quaderna*, or even in *Agrestes*, it was possible to see in what way the poet's language attempted to capture the link between female sensuality and the language of architecture—example of this [...] being the poem "A mulher e a casa" included in the first of these collections.'[11]

Bearing in mind Barbosa's analysis, it seems necessary to emphasize the change that one can identify in the perspective of the male gaze upon the woman. In the earlier poem, the house's internal spaces were the object of male desire, feminine voids waiting to be filled that came under the scrutiny of the male eye: 'a vontade de corrê-la | por dentro, de visitá-la' [the desire to run around | inside her, to visit her] (p. 242).

Such a drive to scrutinize and control ceases to determine the male experience in *Sevilha andando*. A case in point is precisely the poem 'Mulher cidade', whose short five-syllable lines provide a visual recreation of the narrow streets of Seville along which the poetic self wanders. From a stylistic viewpoint, by adopting the verse form known as *redondilha menor*, widely employed in popular poetry, the poet is duplicating the narrowness of the roads to which he makes reference, as well as deliberately drawing on the popular culture which is being celebrated.

Paradoxically, the experience of wandering along these narrow streets is, on an emotional level, defined as 'perfect' in the first stanza, whereas the rational/intellectual knowledge of the urban network remains incomplete. This is because attempts to 'map', categorize and 'name' the streets of Seville prove ineffectual due to their labyrinthine sameness. The result is, therefore, that the experience of Cabral's *flâneur* is only fully satisfying because he refrains from exerting control. If, as Sharpe observed, 'the city as representative woman [...] reveals much about Western male views of the city as a female space to be mastered or seduced by, a space in which actual women are often rigorously controlled' (p. 9), it is clear that Cabral challenged this view and envisioned his city as a woman escaping male authority. In contrast to Eve, secondary creation in relation to Adam, whose authority over her was epitomized in his power to name all existing beings, Seville encapsulates woman's emancipation precisely because she is visualized as a 'street with no name'.

---

[11] 'Já em *Quaderna*, ou mesmo em *Agrestes*, era possível perceber de que modo a linguagem do poeta buscava realizar a interpenetração entre o sentido para a sensualidade feminina e a linguagem da arquitetura—exemplo disso [...] era o poema "A mulher e a casa" daquele primeiro livro' (1996a, p. 103).

Indeterminacy underpins the experience of the male city traveller, for he is faced with the impossibility of coming to a conclusive definition of the urban space:

> nunca saberá
> se vive a cidade
> ou a mulher melhor
> sua mulheridade. (p. 645)

[he will never know | if he lives the city | or if the woman better | her womanness.]

As the traveller enters the feminine world of Seville, where binary oppositions have been dismantled, the boundaries between the woman and the city also become fuzzy. The neologism 'mulheridade' forged by Cabral can be seen as conflating the terms 'mulher' [woman] and 'cidade' [city], as well as 'mulher' [woman] and 'idade' [age], thereby suggesting simultaneously a spatial and temporal dimension to the city's uniqueness.

The absence of fixity is encoded in the urban landscape itself, where the boundaries between nature and cultural constructs are fluid, as the image of the 'erva nos beirais', the grass growing on the side of the city streets, suggests. This last image invites a comparison between the acceptance of the wanderer in relation to the generalized disorder of the urban landscape and the uncompromising rejection of disorder in Cabral's *Fábula de Anfion*. In the earlier reworking of the myth of the founding of Thebes, Amphion fails to construct a town where all remnants of the natural world have been eradicated. His despair articulates Cabral's own realization that complete objectivity and control over the creative process have been thwarted:

> Esta cidade, Tebas,
> não a quisera assim
> de tijolos plantada,
> que a terra e a flora
> procuram reaver. (p. 91)

[This city, Thebes, | I did not want it like this | planted on bricks, | with the earth and the plants | trying to take over once more.]

In Seville, the traveller experiences no such despair, pointing to a shift from the earlier Cabral and his long-standing admiration for the urban visions of Le Corbusier. Indeed, all that Cabral celebrates in Seville stands at the antipodes of Le Corbusier's project, as outlined in his treatise on modern architecture *The City of Tomorrow* (1924): 'The winding road is the result of a happy-go-lucky heedlessness, of looseness, lack of concentration and animality. The straight road is a reaction, an action, a positive deed, the result of self-mastery. It is sane and noble.'[12]

Le Corbusier's vision of urban life is informed by masculine ideals, because, as Deborah Parsons (pp. 12–13) has observed:

The modern city is repeatedly described as being based on 'man's way', on an exactness of space achieved by an adherence to geometrical law. Where are women in Le Corbusier's urban landscape? [...] For Le Corbusier's modern city is based on a need to accommodate traffic that must move at high speed to deposit its passengers into the heart of a city in order to begin the work of the day. Yet despite the rise of women in employment, this experience is predominantly that of the male.

It is well known that Corbusier's urban project inspired Cabral's poetics of rationality, as he acknowledged in an interview in 1972:

As a young man in Recife, my friends, admirers of the great Joaquim Cardozo, gave me all the works by Le Corbusier to read. No poet, critic, philosopher influenced my work as much as Le Corbusier. For many years, he was, in my eyes, synonymous with lucidity, clarity, constructivism. In sum: the dominance of intelligence over instinct.[13]

In the light of Cabral's own acknowledgement, the correlation between configurations of the city in *Sevilha andando* and a poetry in which ambiguity as opposed to precision is privileged has to be accounted for. Indeed, though Eucanãa Ferraz points out how modern architecture provided 'the ideological and formal guiding principles to his poetics',[14] it seems that *Sevilha andando* explicity sets out to question those same principles.

---

[12] In Deborah L. Parsons, *Streetwalking the Metropolis: Women, the City and Modernity* (Oxford: Oxford University Press, 2000), p. 11.

[13] 'Quando ainda rapaz, no Recife, amigos meus, discípulos do imenso Joaquim Cardozo, me deram para ler todas as obras de Le Corbusier. Nenhum poeta, nenhum crítico, nenhum filósofo exerceu sobre mim a influência que teve Le Corbusier. Durante muitos anos, ele significou para mim a lucidez, claridade, construtivismo. Em resumo: o predomínio da inteligência sobre o instinto.' In Danilo Lôbo, *O poema e o quadro. O picturalismo na obra de João Cabral de Melo Neto* (Brasília: Thesaurus, 1981), p. 55. It could be argued, however, that in practice, Cabral's choice of epigraph for *O engenheiro* ('...machine à emouvoir...') [...machine that stirs emotions...], a metaphor through which Le Corbusier famously described the Parthenon in his book *Vers une architecture* (1923), already points to a conflation rather than to a polarization of construction/rationality and emotion, in line with the themes developed in the later works analysed here.

[14] 'Os princípios ideológicos e formais que iriam guiar sua poética.' Eucanãa Ferraz, 'Máquina de comover: a poesia de João Cabral de Melo Neto e suas relações com a

Significantly, the qualities that the woman/city encapsulates here are not restricted to the Andalusian setting. A case in point is the poem 'Na cidade do Porto' (pp. 639–40), in which the poet recalls his encounter with the 'woman with the Sevillian walk' during his time as Brazilian Consul in that Portuguese city and engages in dialogue with the Portuguese poet Cesário Verde, whom he much admired.[15]

Cabral's intertextuality is specifically with Verde's poem 'Num bairro moderno'.[16] Both his and Verde's compositions are reworkings of Baudelaire's 'À une passante' and depict an encounter with an anonymous woman on the streets of a bleak modern city. Yet Verde's narrator is fictional,[17] whereas the poetic *persona* in Cabral's poem is obviously autobiographical, as the reference to the 'consular' street of Oporto suggests, in an example of the poet's increased personal involvement.[18]

In his study of the Portuguese poet, Helder Macedo observed how 'Um bairro moderno' dramatizes a symbolic invasion of the city by the countryside. The basket of fresh fruit and vegetables sold by the young girl provides a metaphor for the vitality of life in the country, juxtaposed with the drudgery in the modern city that the lower classes endure.[19] Macedo (p. 154) points out that the girl's poverty is depicted as a 'desgraça alegre' [joyful misfortune], and indeed Verde romanticizes the predicament of the street vendor as she is weighed down by her struggle against deprivation:

> E, como as grossas pernas dum gigante
> Sem tronco, mas atléticas, inteiras,

---

arquitetura' (unpublished doctoral thesis, Universidade Federal do Rio de Janeiro, Brazil, 2000), p. 158.

[15] Cabral considered Verde the greatest Portuguese poet and identified with what he defined his 'ausência de retórica, uma visão voltada para o mundo exterior' [unrhetorical style, his gaze turned towards the outside world] (in Bosi and others, p. 29).

[16] Cesário Verde, *Obra completa* (Lisboa: Portugália, n.d.), pp. 81–5. Cabral's earliest homage to Cesário Verde can be found in his poem 'O sim contra o sim', of *Serial*, in which we find an allusion to Verde's juxtaposition of town and country in 'Um bairro moderno': 'Assim chegou aos tons opostos | das maçãs que contou: | rubras dentro da cesta | de quem no rosto as tem sem cor' [Thus he achieved the opposite tones | to the apples of which he spoke: | rosy in the basket | of one whose cheeks are pale] (p. 299).

[17] Helder Macedo highlights the fictional character of Verde's narrator, a small middle-class man who is a either a businessman or a civil servant, frustrated and made ill by his routine life in the modern city, of whose social fractures he is very aware. See Helder Macedo, *Nós. Uma leitura de Cesário Verde* (Lisboa: Plátano Editora, 1975), p. 149.

[18] Cabral was head of mission at the Brazilian Consulate General in Oporto from 1982 to 1987.

[19] Macedo speaks of the 'vida orgânica do campo que invadiu a cidade' [the organic life of the country which has invaded the city] (p. 149).

> Carregam sobre a pobre caminhante
> [...]
> Duas frugais abóboras carneiras. (p. 85)

[And like the thick legs of a giant | With no body, but athletic, long, | They carry above the poor walker | [...] | Two frugal pumpkins.]

As with Verde, the natural world provides the imagery for Cabral's visualization of the *passante*, although this does not convey the woman's struggle for mere survival, but rather her defiance of class discrimination and social inequality: 'cabeça que é, soberana, | de quando a espiga mais se espiga' [head which is sovereign, | as when the corn stands tallest] (p. 640). Indeed, Cabral's *passante* attracts attention thanks to the self-assurance with which she walks down the 'commercial, consular and sad street' of Oporto: 'o esbelto pisar decidido | que carrega a cabeça erguida' [the tall decided walk | which carries the head high] (p. 640).

In these lines, the woman's empowerment is described in images of masculine sexual vigour, as suggested in the phallic image of the ear of corn. Thus, and ascribing to the female subject qualities associated with masculinity, the poem evinces what Marta Peixoto has highlighted as one of the features of Cabral's poetry: 'the exclusivist celebration of masculine cultural and biological features, at times present almost subliminally.'[20] Yet, it is possible to view Cabral's exaltation of masculine values in female subjects as a challenge to sexual stereotypes and, in Peixoto's summation, as a 'critique of a hierarchical structure which ascribes to women certain characteristics, as well as intellectual and practical roles which limit and close other options to them'.[21] In this poem, such disruption of sexual hierarchies duplicates the subversion of rigid social ones, because in Seville, working-class women 'passam com porte de duquesas' [walk by with the deportment of Duchesses] (p. 640).

An added significance to Cabral's reworking of Verde's image is how he envisioned instances of defiance beyond the boundaries of his native Brazil. Cesário Verde was still able to find in the rural world of Portugal a possible answer to his country's dependency on the industrialized countries of the North, whereas for Cabral inspiration lay outside his native land, and more significantly beyond the boundaries of the Portuguese-speaking world. He consciously juxtaposed Portugal (represented

---

[20] 'A exaltação exclusivista do masculino cultural e também do biológico, presente por vezes de forma quase subliminar' (Peixoto, 2000 [2002], p. 238).
[21] 'Crítica a uma hierarquia que prende as mulheres a determinado tipo de características, saberes e fazeres limitativos e impeditivos de outras opções' (p. 239).

by Oporto) with Spain (Seville), celebrating the latter at the expense of Brazil's former parent state. This contrast is encoded in the configuration of the two urban settings found in the poem: on the one hand there is the gloomy commercial street of Oporto, on the other there is the *Calle* Feria of Seville, the vibrancy of which is evoked in the strides of the woman— her head held up high—in contrast to the street-vendor of Verde's poem, who bears two meagre pumpkins.

Cabral's postcolonial critique is conveyed subtly in this poem, but it is there. In fact, as a rare example of the poet's engagement with Portugal, the poem's bleak depiction of Oporto is all the more revealing. Writing as a Brazilian living in Portugal at the time, Cabral deliberately undermined the former metropole in favour of its old enemy, Spain. Yet, in doing so he was not celebrating Spain as a former colonial power in its own right as opposed to Portugal, but rather the subversive character of the *sevilhana* as the embodiment of the marginalized.

Ultimately, the identity of this female figure is not defined/inscribed within fixed geographical boundaries (i.e. Andalusia), but is rather a construct of the imagination, in which attitudes of defiance are subsumed. Such is the case of the woman in Oporto 'of the Seville walk' or of the woman featured in the poem 'A Sevilhana que é de Córdoba' (pp. 640–1), to whom Cabral refers as the *sevilhana* 'cujo andaluzismo eu me invento' [whose Andalusian character I make up] (p. 641).[22] As such, she represents a challenge to social and sexual stereotypes that transposes the boundaries of a given geographical setting. Equally, she embodies a critique of colonialism per se, as emerges from Cabral's rendition of the theme of maritime travels, in which European (not just Portuguese) colonialist endeavours are undermined.

5.2.3 Images of navigation

One of the recurring images in which the experience of Seville is translated is that of the sea voyage in which destination and route are uncertain. In the poem 'A barcaça' (p. 635), for example, the images of

[22] Likewise, in 'A sevilhana que não se sabia' (pp. 629–32), Cabral refers to a Brazilian *sevilhana*, an allusion to his second wife, the poet Marly de Oliveira, who was originally from the state of Espírito Santo: 'sevilhana nela toda, | como se naufragada forma | viesse a encalhar por engano | nas praias do Espírito Santo' [Sevillian she is entirely, | as though a shipwrecked shape | had mistakenly become stranded | on the beaches of Espírito Santo] (p. 630).

the woman and of the city are subsumed into that of the barge, which initially appears to draw on stereotypical association of women with domesticity: 'mulher feita barco e casa' [woman who is at once a boat and a home] (p. 635). Despite seemingly unable to distance himself entirely from conventional configurations of femininity, the poet is in fact presenting gender relations in which there is no room for sexual domination, for in no way is the woman's identity or agency denied:

> Mas nunca fez por anular
> o registro da barca antiga:
> na barcaça pernambucana
> na proa se lê "Sevilha".[23] (p. 635)

[But he never attempted to annul | the registration of the old boat: | on the Pernambucan barge | the prow reads "Seville".]

It seems that the relationship described here rests on a fundamental paradox because, although the poet purports to know Seville, he is also in the dark as to where the vessel will take him: 'Tem o registro de Sevilha | e é sem timão, sem timoneiro' [She is registered in Seville | and has no helm, no helmsman] (p. 635).

Cabral was surely familiar with Baudelaire's rendition of the urban experience through maritime imagery, and the French poet's 'gabarre' [barge] in the poem 'Les septs vieillards' (pp. 132–3) was almost certainly the source for his 'barcaça'. However, the Brazilian poet draws on such imagery to contrasting effect, because, in Baudelaire, the experience of the decaying urban environment is a disturbing and disorientating one: 'Et mon âme dansait, dansait, vieille gabarre | Sans mâts, sur une mer monstrueuse et sans bords!' [And my soul danced, danced, that old barge | Without masts, on a monstrous and shoreless sea!] (p. 133).

A similar subversion of his European master is found in the poem 'Sol negro' (p. 642). In this poem, the figure of the *sevilhana* is captured metonymically in the image of her black hair. The sources that provided the inspiration for Cabral's poem can be traced to Nerval's sonnet 'El desdichado' and Baudelaire's poem 'La chevelure' (pp. 75–6).[24] Cabral's admiration for Baudelaire is well documented, and it is fair to assume that he was also familiar with Nerval's work—if only from his readings of

---

[23] Given that the collection was dedicated to Cabral's second wife, the poet Marly de Oliveira, it is possible to read this poem as a specific reflection on his second marriage.

[24] Gérard de Nerval, *Œuvres complètes*, ed. Jean Guillaume and others, 3 vols (Paris: Gallimard, 1993), III, 645.

T. S. Eliot, whose 'The Waste Land' includes a quotation from Nerval's sonnet.[25] From Baudelaire, Cabral drew the images of the black hair and the images of navigation it conjured up, while Nerval provided the metaphor of the black sun, in which the woman's hair is visualized. However, Cabral deliberately sets out to subvert both these male, canonical, European poets' renderings of such images.

In Baudelaire's poem, the female body is visualized through images of exotic lands of plenty. As the object of male desire, the woman is pictured as the 'languid' Asia and 'burning' Africa, discovered and explored by the male seafarer. In fact, she epitomizes the male fantasy of woman as the 'dark continent', her fate being shared by all women who have been subjugated, of whom Hélène Cixous argues: 'Their bodies, which they haven't dared enjoy, have been colonized.'[26]

Cabral's postcolonial perspective, on the other hand, leads him to dispute Baudelaire's Eurocentric view of the discoveries, while concurrently challenging the patriarchal ideology in which it was inscribed. Rejecting such patriarchal perspective, 'Sol negro' subverts the notion of conquest (colonial and sexual), by picturing the poet on a journey with no fixed destination or trajectory.

Rather than embodying an object of male domination, the woman evokes visions of indeterminacy and freedom: as visualized in the image of the compass that does not guide the way and the lighthouse whose 'gypsy' light is perpetually displaced. The sense of transgression evoked in the image he employs is undoubtedly viewed positively, since Cabral claims that his consciousness is guided by this elusive beacon. As such, Cabral inverts the dynamics of objectification and domination articulated in Baudelaire and, by the same token, counters the idealized vision of the discoveries propounded by colonial discourse.[27]

---

[25] Cabral first read Eliot while serving as Consul in London, from 1950 to 1952. See interview with Edla Van Steen, 'João Cabral de Melo Neto', in *Viver & escrever*, 2 vols (Porto Alegre: L&PM, 1981), I, 99–109 (p. 101). He quoted from Eliot's poem in one of his last published interviews: 'Como disse Eliot em "The waste land": "These fragments I have shored against my ruins." Assim, a memória são fragmentos trazidos à praia contra minhas ruínas' [As Eliot said in 'The Waste Land': 'These fragments I have shored against my ruins.' Thus, my memory are fragments washed ashore against my ruins] (see interview with Bosi and others, p. 31).

[26] In Hélène Cixous and Catherine Clément, 'Sorties: Out and Out: Attack/Ways Out/Forays', in *The Newly Born Woman*, trans. B. Wing, intro. Sandra M. Gilbert (Manchester: Manchester University Press, 1986), pp. 63–132 (p. 68).

[27] In this respect, it is significant that the 'farol às avessas' [the anti-lighthouse], in which Cabral visualized the black hair of the woman, should have featured as a metaphor for Brazil in his earlier poem 'O Cabo de Santo Agostinho' (from the collection *Museu de*

If the woman conjures up images of travel in which destination is unknown and trajectory uncertain, she does not, however, evoke visions of failed endeavours. Indeed, what a patriarchal perspective would view as female inconstancy here encapsulates the woman's refusal to be 'fixed' by the male gaze.[28] This is celebrated, because the awakening at the woman's side is more than a simple emergence from the state of sleep: it amounts to a rebirth, a 're-ser' [being again]. In the new order that emerges from the old, images of femininity are promoted to the detriment of those traditionally associated with masculinity. Thus, the poet's point of reference is not the sun as the centre of the universe, epitome of masculinity, but the nomadic sun of the woman (rather than the reflected light of the moon, stereotypically associated with femininity).

Indeed, Cabral subverted the image of the black sun that he borrowed from Nerval. The French poet's rendering of the image drew on a tradition that cast it as a symbol of disorder and death. The image of 'le soleil noir de la mélancolie' [the black sun of melancholy] of 'El desdichado' (Nerval, p. 645) is steeped in a tradition that has seen the black sun as the antithesis of the sun at its zenith and has associated it with death and evil, encapsulating the destructive forces of the universe, society or the person (Chevalier and Gheerbrant, p. 895). In it, Nerval visualized the torments of love suffered at the hands of the woman, thus inscribing the image within stereotypical representations of gender. In dialogue with such negative representations of femininity, Cabral's 'Sol negro' presents the black sun as a symbol of self-assertiveness. The long hair of the woman (*cabeleira* suggests either long hair or abundant hair) is not cast as a symbol of woman's 'indomitable earthliness' and 'monstrous female sexual energies', as Gilbert and Gubar (p. 27) have shown

---

tudo) to produce a bleak and unheroic vision of its discovery. The Cabo de Santo Agostinho, site of the landing of the first Europeans on Brazilian soil, is portrayed as a place where natural riches blind the predatory seafarers ('navegantes encandeados' [blinded navigators]) dazzled by greed. Pictured in the 'farol às avessas', Brazil is visualized as a place the Europeans are drawn to (rather than avoid). In the case of the poem in *Sevilha andando*, however, the metaphor of the 'farol às avessas' is qualified by that of the 'luz cigana' [gypsy light], which is intended to portray the woman's refractory nature, thus juxtaposing her with the earlier image of Brazil as a land that was conquered and exploited.

[28] Sandra Gilbert and Susan Gubar analysed the subversive treatment given to the theme of the inconstancy of Anne Elliot, in Jane Austen: 'Her refusal, that is, to be fixed or "killed" by an author/owner, her stubborn insistence on her own way' (*The Madwoman in the Attic: The Woman Writer and the Nineteenth-Century Literary Imagination*, 2nd edn (New Haven: Yale Nota Bene, 2000), p. 16.

to be the case in patriarchal writing, but rather as a symbol of female empowerment.

5.2.4 Revisiting the discovery

In 1992, Cabral travelled to Seville, representing the President of Brazil at the celebrations for the fifth centenary of the discovery of the American continent. Given the political import of the event, it is significant that it should have warranted only one poem, 'Sevilha revisitada *em 1992*' (pp. 650–1), and that the piece itself should make no specific reference to the reasons for his journey to Spain.

The poem is set in a hotel room, which, because of its intrinsic artificiality, least reminds the poet of the city outside. This is compensated by the fact that the poet's companion embodies Seville itself, and for this reason there is little incentive actually to visit the urban network. In the company of Seville, it becomes unnecessary both to revisit the past and visit the modern city it has become, where the 'formigueiro' is not of pedestrians, as implied in 'Sevilha andando (I)', analysed above, but of motorists: 'os mil automóveis | que formigueiram hoje Sevilha' [the thousands of motor cars | that these days crawl through Seville] (p. 651).[29]

Echoing the earlier composition 'Sevilha andando (I)', Cabral draws on the dead metaphor of the 'formigueiro', thereby emphasizing how the balance between nature and culture in the modern city has not been disrupted.[30] This implies that progress has taken place without prejudice to either of these realms, and Seville emerges as an organic whole, through images that explore the fluidity rather than the fixity of the boundaries between humans, animals and man-made constructs.

Cabral's critique of colonialism is conveyed in his very omission of any reference to the conquest of the New World and the part played by

---

[29] In the 1997 edition of *Sevilha andando*, included in the volume *A educação pela pedra e depois*, Cabral amended the reference to the past 'Sevilha do tempo já ido' [Seville of times gone by] to 'tempo já lido' [time already read] (p. 353), thus referring to his poetry on Seville rather than to the city itself. The shift in emphasis suggests how Cabral perceived the experience of reading and that of real life as interchangeable, the boundaries between the two being fluid.

[30] Instead of using either the verb 'formigar' or 'formiguejar', Cabral decides to deviate from the norm and create a new spelling for the verb, which is also, unconventionally, employed transitively. The outcome is a linguistic reflection of the uniqueness of the Spanish city to which he is alluding.

Seville in the process of colonization, not least for providing the port whence Christopher Columbus's fleet set sail. In other words, the insertion of only an oblique allusion (by way of date in the title) to the celebrations which he attended must be accounted for.

In this respect, the poem 'Presença de Sevilha' (p. 651), added to the collection in the 1994 edition to replace 'Sol negro' as its closing composition, is a piece whose intertextuality is equally revealing of Cabral's treatment of the theme. Here the poet questions his ability to engage with his Andalusian subject:

> Cantei mal teu ser e teu canto
> enquanto te estive, dez anos;
> cantaste em mim e ainda tanto,
> cantas em mim teus dois mil anos.[31] (p. 651)

[I sang your being and your song badly | while in you I lived, ten years; | you sang in me and still you do | singing in me your two thousand years.]

A particularly noteworthy aspect of this rendition of the theme is the repeated use of the verb 'cantar' [sing] and the association of singing with writing. No specific reference to flamenco, the only kind of music Cabral enjoyed, is made in this poem, which makes it all the more startling, given his long-standing pursuit of non-melodic verse.[32] Rather than proclaim his search of the prosaic, in *Sevilha andando* he appears to

---

[31] The opening lines of this short eight-line composition are almost identical to the ones of the earlier poem 'O *aire* de Sevilha' (p. 649), thereby emphasizing the poet's sense of inadequacy: 'Mal cantei teu ser e teu canto | enquanto te estive, dez anos. | Cantaste em mim e ainda tanto, | cantas em mim teus dois mil anos' [I barely sang your being and your song | while in you I lived, ten years. | You sang in me and still you do | singing in me your two thousand years] (p. 649). In his playful reworking of these lines, Cabral explores the change in meaning brought about by the simple inversion of the two opening words: 'Mal cantei' and 'Cantei mal'. In the first instance, what is suggested is that Cabral barely sang the praises of Seville, while the second opening states that Cabral's rendition of Seville was inadequate. Also noteworthy is the fact that Cabral chose to structure the first composition in couplets, opting for a single eight-syllable stanza in the second one. Indeed, the slower rhythm of 'O *aire* de Sevilha' conveys the difficulties in dealing with memories from a distant past. It contrasts with the quick pace of the second composition, which, thanks to its repeated use of the verb 'cantar', translates the vividness with which the woman evokes the city of Seville. The experience described is paradoxical, since Seville is at once absent (Seville itself) and present ('Sevilha caminhando' [Seville walking]).

[32] Cabral acknowledged he had no ear for the melodic and stated about his writing: 'Só há duas melodias que você tocando eu identifico: são o hino nacional e o hino de Pernambuco' [There are just two tunes that if played I can identify: the Brazilian national anthem and the anthem of Pernambuco] (in Lima and others, p. 15).

regret being unable to engage with the intense emotions that can only be conveyed in lyrical writing and in song.

The absence of any irony in his reference to lyrical verse stands in contrast with his earlier dismissal of this same poetic genre, found in *Agrestes*, for example. In that collection, he had criticized the poets of Africa for engaging in sentimental writing: because 'cantar vale celebração' [singing means celebration] (p. 565), they stood accused of having denied their art the political impact it might have had in denouncing the inequities of colonialism.

In response to this perceived failure, Cabral successfully combined lyrical writing with poetry of political concerns. Indeed, it is truly noteworthy that his references to 'canto' should fail to make any explicit allusion to Camões, the 'father' of the Portuguese lyric. In fact, there appears to be a conscious displacement of his Portuguese antecedent, thereby making not only an important meta-textual point but also, as a postcolonial writer, a political statement of considerable significance. It constitutes his only reference, and an oblique one at that, to the Portuguese Renaissance poet, who extolled the endeavours of the Portuguese explorers in his epic poetry and sang the pleasures and sorrows of love in his lyrical verse.

In his famous 'Canção 6', Camões emphasized the role of love in his writing when he wrote: 'Manda-me Amor que cante docemente | O que ele já em minha alma tem impresso' [Love commands me to sing sweetly | That which in my soul he has engraved.][33]

Conversely, in 'Presença de Sevilha' Cabral regrets his failure as a lyrical poet, but makes no explicit reference to Camões. Such disregard on the part of the Brazilian poet can be perceived as a deliberate disruption of literary hierarchies and, by association, a veiled challenge to Portugal's colonial legacy.

In the light of the overall political import of *Sevilha andando*, its subtle but nevertheless implied dialogue with the tradition of the Portuguese lyric is noteworthy, for it illustrates the north-eastern poet's uncompromising postcolonial stance. From his displacement of Camões, it is possible to ascertain the political concerns of this collection, which proves more than an incursion into love poetry. A similar point can be made in relation to *Andando Sevilha*, whose celebration of marginalized social groups, in particular of the city's gypsy community,

---

[33] Luís de Camões, *Obra completa* (Rio de Janeiro: Nova Aguilar, 1963), p. 314.

resonates well beyond the Andalusian setting in which it is inscribed, as will be studied in the second part of this chapter.

5.3 ANDANDO SEVILHA

5.3.1 The *Sevilhanos*' strategies of subversion

In 'Cidade viva' (p. 647), of *Sevilha andando*, the vision of the walking *sevilhana* and of the city appear indistinguishable: 'vi que Sevilha andava | ou fazia andar quem a andasse' [I saw that Seville was walking | or set in motion whoever was there] (p. 647).

Cabral here explores the double meaning of the verb 'andar', which can mean 'to function' as well as 'to walk', in order to convey how the vitality of one expresses the vibrancy of the other and vice versa. It is therefore apt that, having devoted his attention to the walking *sevilhana*, he should embark on his own personal journey through the city, in *Andando Sevilha*.

The wide-ranging thematic material incorporated in this collection testifies to the poet's familiarity with the Andalusian urban landscape and culture, with its bullfighters and flamenco singers, the city's religious festivals and tourist landmarks. Cabral once stated he knew Seville in such detail that he even remembers the colour of the houses (in Saraiva, 1987, p. 6). The poet's exploration of Seville may appear clichéd, though in fact it 'seeks out the most stereotypical, the most ordinary, the most obvious. And transforms it', as Richard Zenith (1992, p. 634) observed.

Indeed, Cabral's poetic revisitation of Seville produced images of the city as a marginal space, thanks to his focus on the subversive agency of its gypsy community. His obsession with liminal imagery in which boundaries are disrupted would attract the poet to a community living on the margins of society and forced to devise strategies of self-preservation based on dissimulation. In 'Na Cava, em Triana' (pp. 666–7), it is possible to see why the gypsies' ambiguous position within city life had such an impact on the poet, for he viewed it as a constant process of renegotiation of opposites:

> Alma nua sob mil disfarces,
> pois ser cigano força a abrigar-se
> fora da lei, da identidade,
> mesmo se habita uma cidade;

> ser cigano é viver sob tendas
> até se debaixo de telhas,
> um viver que a polícia não acha
> mesmo se da rua e a casa saiba. (p. 666)

[A naked soul under a thousand guises, | because to be a gypsy means having to find cover | outside of the law, of identity, | even when one lives in the city; | being a gypsy is to live under tents | even when under a roof, | a life that the police cannot find | even if they know the road and number.]

The gypsies' condition of being simultaneously within society and outside it echoes the elusiveness that underpinned the configurations of the *sevilhana* in the previous group of poems, captured, for example, in the nomadic light of the 'luz cigana' of 'Sol negro'. Clearly, the appeal that the Spanish city holds for Cabral rests on the successful strategies of resistance perceived there, as transpires in the poem 'Cidade de alvenaria' (pp. 660–1), in which the living, hybrid, animal-like 'carnal' materials in which the poorer buildings of the city are constructed is juxtaposed with the lifeless 'imported and official masonry' used in the building of churches. Eventually, materials of supposedly superior quality, employed in structures associated with the Establishment, acquire the features of the surrounding more modest buildings: 'ganham essa qualidade | que a alvenaria tem com a carne' [they take on this likeness | that bricks share with flesh] (p. 660). Thus, Seville is visualized as an interstitial space, a symbol of vitality precisely for providing a fertile terrain for the dynamic encounter between opposites such as these.

The poet's shift in focus from the female figure to the broader urban fabric in *Andando Sevilha* is exemplified in the poem entitled 'Calle Sierpes' (pp. 659–60), which is in clear dialogue with the poem 'Mulher cidade', of the preceding collection. Both compositions evoke the experience of walking along the winding street of Seville's city centre, but, in this poem, the emphasis has moved from questions of women's struggle for empowerment to postcolonial concerns involving Seville's role in the conquest and domination of the New World. To this end, images of navigation subvert the exaltation of the conquest and of Seville's subsequent trade monopoly with the American colonies.

At its inception, the poem refers to the sense of freedom associated with the urban experience: it is with a spirit of adventure that the walker engages with the city, aimlessly embarking on a haphazard journey that is without destination. The ambulation through Seville amounts to a process of self-discovery, a journey within the self ('é o mesmo que andar-se') (p. 659), yielding physical and spiritual fulfilment above moral dictates, 'vão soltas a alma e a carne' [body and soul go free] (p. 659).

The voyages of discovery are evoked in the experience of the *flâneur*, compared to that of navigation. This evocation is echoed in the reference to the Calle Sierpes, defined as the only compulsory route for any visitor to the city, like the commercial routes of times gone by. The parallel is reinforced in the configuration of the Calle Sierpes as the modern-day equivalent of the trade routes of the past, 'apinhada de leste a oeste' [full from East to West] (p. 660). Yet, Cabral deliberately demythologizes colonial navigation, for the Calle Sierpes is in fact framed by two bars, 'serpenteia entre dois bares' [it winds between two bars] (p. 660), the winding street design mirroring the unsteady progress of inebriated customers, rather than any purposeful trajectory of commercial traders.

Not only is the Calle Sierpes a compulsory destination for any tourist in Seville, but it expects its visitors to learn a new, particular approach to the urban environment. This is because, unlike elsewhere in the city, here visitors cannot stroll in absolute freedom, with no definitive trajectory, 'de leme solto e às cegas' [blindly, with a loose helm] (p. 660), due to the fact that 'navegar é em linhas curvas' [navigation is along curved routes] (p. 660). In this way, the urban setting is defined by heterogeneity, given that the city is characterized by total freedom, 'navegando à vela' [sailing] (p. 659), as well as by its own order—in the Calle Sierpes 'não se pode o andar à vela' [one cannot sail] (p. 660). In the light of this configuration of the urban space, the association between the snake and the street after which it is named is also meaningful. Indeed, the motion of the snake becomes a metaphor for the negotiation of boundaries, since it captures the movement of the travellers as they negotiate their way across the chaos of the crowded street. Thus, the snake represents order, albeit one defined by fluidity rather than by structures that are fixed. As a creature often portrayed as a hermaphrodite, it embodies the hybrid nature of the in-between state that the Calle Sierpes encapsulates.[34]

Engaging with the Spanish city in this way, Cabral drew on García Lorca's renditions of Seville through images of navigation, but his

---

[34] The myths surrounding the hermaphrodite nature of the snake have been recorded by Chevalier and Gheerbrant (p. 815).

postcolonial perspective meant that these were informed by a critical perspective on the narrative of the discovery. Cabral's familiarity with Lorca's work is testified by the fact that he was responsible for the Portuguese translation of *La zapatera prodigiosa* in 1951 (still unpublished). The Spanish poet's influence was considerable, as he acknowledged in an interview in 1968: 'Yes, I'll say that Spanish literature is crucial. You have the generation of 27 [...] led by Federico García Lorca and Manuel Alberti. They are very important to me.'[35]

From his reading of Lorca, Cabral must have been familiar with the poem 'Baladilla de los tres ríos' of *Poema del cante jondo* (1931), and its positive rendition of Seville through maritime imagery.[36] Lorca juxtaposes the cities of Seville and Granada by comparing the rivers that flow through them:

> Para los barcos de vela
> Sevilla tiene un camino;
> por el agua de Granada
> sólo reman los suspiros. (p. 142)

[For the sailing boats | Seville has a route; | along the waters of Granada | only sighs row.]

Lorca's representation of Seville as an epitome of life, here captured through the juxtaposition of the breeze (implied in the image of the sailing ships) with the sighs coming from Granada, would find echo in Cabral's treatment of the theme five decades later. Yet, Cabral's stance as a postcolonial writer meant that, in referring to the trade routes of colonial times, he would deliberately subvert such imagery, as discussed above.

The positive connotations ascribed to the image of the snake of the Calle Sierpes also have implications for Cabral's dialogue with Lorca. It was as a symbol of death that Lorca employed the image in the poem 'Baile', included in the section 'Tres ciudades' of his *Poema del cante jondo* (p. 198). Lorca pictures Seville through the figure of Carmen, visualized

---

[35] 'Sí que le diré que la literatura española es fundamental. Ahora tienen ustedes la generación del 27 [...] encabezados por Frederico [sic] García Lorca y Manuel Alberti. Para mí son muy importantes' (in Zila Mamede, *Civil geometria. Bibliografia crítica, analítica e anotada de João Cabral de Melo Neto, 1942–1982*, (São Paulo: Nobel, 1982), p. 139). In an interview originally published in the *Diário de Lisboa* in 1966, Cabral also confirmed that: 'Lorca para mim é um poeta genial a partir do *Romancero gitano* e do *Cante jondo*' [Lorca is for me a poetic genius from *Romancero gitano* and *Cante jondo*] (in Süssekind, 2001, p. 37).

[36] Federico García Lorca, *Poema del cante jondo. Romancero gitano*, ed. Allen Josephs and Juan Cabellero, 19th edn (Madrid: Cátedra, 1998) p. 142.

as an old woman, dreaming of the days of her youth. In her hair, the headdress shaped in the form of a yellow snake entwined with her hair is a symbol of death, conveying the insidious passing of time.

Lorca's association of Carmen with mortality is subverted in Cabral's appropriation of this iconic female figure in 'A fábrica de tabacos' (pp. 662–3). Here, though he could be criticized for drawing on stereotypical renderings of untamed female sexuality, his choice to engage with this female representative of the gypsy community was intended to be provocative, with the lively, highly sexed woman becoming a paradigm of the struggle for empowerment.[37]

The poem begins by focusing on the disjunction between the convent-like appearance of the factory building and its actual use. This fissure provides the starting point for Cabral's articulation of the subversion of both religious and political orders by the female factory workers, as he suggests the inhumane working conditions endured by the employees in the factory, which is in turn visualized as a hotbed of subversion:

> Lá trabalharam as cigarreiras,
> quase nuas pelo calor,
> discutindo, freiras despidas,
> teologias de um certo amor. (p. 662)

[There the cigar-makers worked, | almost naked in the heat, | discussing, as naked nuns, | theologies of a certain love.]

The factory workers are depicted discussing topics omitted from rhetoric compendiums, and their marginality in relation to the dominant culture is thus brought to the fore. Yet, these women are not stifled, for, as the image of the 'naked nuns' suggests, they are rebelling against the confinement that the implied image of the veil symbolizes, thereby also refusing to be typecast as idealized virgins. In line with this, the women's lively 'jaculatórias' [short, lively speeches] are intended to counterpoint the 'impotent' angel carved out of the stonework above the factory's entrance. The phallic image of the cigars that the 'almost naked' workers roll up is juxtaposed with the angel's equally phallic but redundant, silent trumpet.

---

[37] Thus, Cabral distances himself from clichéd representations of Seville, a point that had been noted by Spanish critics Ángel Crespo and Pilar Gómez Bedate in their seminal article, published in 1964, on the Brazilian poet's appropriation of Spanish motifs. See 'Poemas sobre España de João Cabral de Melo Neto', *Cuadernos hispanoamericanos* 59 (1964), 320–2 (p. 320).

The poem articulates its anti-religious discourse by debunking the myth of the veiled virgin, while concurrently criticizing the male-dominated political establishment by undermining the figure of King Ferdinand VI (1712–59), founder of the tobacco factory. When he refers to the monarch's pivotal role in the factory's establishment, Cabral omits Fernando Sexto's royal title, thus duplicating on a linguistic level the women's disruption of patriarchal order:

> Fernando Sexto edificou
> o que mais parece um convento
> que fosse sem Regras e Prior.[38] (p. 662)

[Ferdinand the Sixth built | what seems more like a convent | without Rules and Prior.]

The shift to modern times in the final stanza suggests that social equality and sexual liberation in contemporary society are being achieved, albeit against a backdrop of male conservatism. The embodiment of this is the angel above the entrance, who pitifully continues to threaten to play his trumpet were a 'damsel' to pass through the gates. Therefore, as the modern-day young women cross the threshold into what once was a factory and is today a university, they are metaphorically reaffirming their challenge to prohibitive boundaries of social and moral behaviour: 'tudo mudou, exceto o anjo | que mudo ameaça ainda, debalde' [everything silent, except the angel | who, dumbfounded, still threatens, in vain] (p. 663).

This successful opposition to conventions is echoed in the *sevilhanos*' cultural manifestations of defiance towards the ultimate boundary which humanity has to face, that between life and death. The centrality of the theme of death in manifestations of Sevillian popular culture—be it in Flamenco or bullfighting—was something that fascinated Cabral, and his reflections on this theme will be the focus of the following section.

5.3.2 Seville: 'viver-se no aceiro da morte'

Cabral revisited the theme of mortality in his last collection and, in so doing, re-engaged in dialogue with his fellow Brazilian poet Murilo

---

[38] The contrast between the factory's convent-like appearance and actual purpose is emphasized with a view to ridiculing its founder, perhaps as a tongue-in-cheek reminder of the monarch's mental problems. For further information on King Ferdinand VI, see Pedro Voltes, *Fernando VI* (Barcelona: Ed. Planeta, 1996).

Mendes. Cabral's ambiguous religious beliefs—he claimed not to believe in God, but never to have lost the fear of Hell instilled in him as a child—influenced his treatment of the spiritual dimension of Andalusia and led him to take issue with the fervent Catholicism of his fellow poet, who had also been drawn to Spanish themes.[39]

Mendes's poetry compilation *Tempo espanhol* (1959) and the posthumous collection of prose writing *Espaço espanhol* (1975) demonstrate the passion for Spanish culture he shared with Cabral. Yet, both poets were acutely aware of their different engagement with Spain, at the heart of which lay their contrasting views on religion. Murilo alluded to this in his poem 'Murilograma a João Cabral de Melo Neto', composed in 1964, included in *Convergência* (1970):

> Comigo e contigo o Brasil.
> Comigo e contigo a Espanha.
> [...]
> Entre mim e ti o barroco,
> A cruz, Antonio Gaudí.[40]

[With me and with you, Brazil. | With me and with you, Spain. | [...] | Between me and you, the baroque, | The cross, Antonio Gaudí.]

For his part, Cabral too noted the difference in approach in relation to Mendes soon after embarking on his Spanish writing.[41] In a letter written in 1959, he observed how Mendes was able to capture both what Cabral defined 'black Spain', or Catholic Spain, and the materialist Spain, or 'white Spain', in contrast to his own strictly materialist perspective:

I am only able to find inspiration in realist Spain, materialist Spain, the Spain of objects. And when a manifestation of what we might call the 'spiritual' side of Spain that you capture so well interests me, you will see that I end up undermining it. Example: the bullfights, something inadmissible to a 'white Spain'

---

[39] Cabral stated on a number of occasions that he did not believe in God, but that, paradoxically, he feared the prospect of hell (see, for example, interview with Lima and others, p. 45).

[40] Murilo Mendes, *Poesia completa e prosa*, ed. Luciana Stegagno Picchio, (Rio de Janeiro: Nova Aguilar, 1994), p. 691. Murilo Mendes is here referring both to Cabral's loss of faith and his dislike for the work of the Catalan architect, of whom Cabral had stated: 'Gaudí é a antiarquitetura! [...] Gaudí não tinha planos! [...] Ele fazia a arquitetura como o poeta romântico escreve' [Gaudí is anti-architecture! [...] He followed no plans! [...] His architecture was like the writings of a Romantic poet] (interview with Lima and others, pp. 12–13).

[41] Cabral's first poems on Spain were included in *Paisagens com figuras* (1956).

such as myself: I reduce them to the dimension of a lesson in aesthetics; the same applies to flamenco, etc. etc. I mean: your intellectual position is much broader and takes into account both white and black Spain.[42]

In the light of this statement, *Andando Sevilha*, written roughly forty years later, points to a shift in emphasis on the poet's part, given that both 'black Spain' and 'white Spain', to use Cabral's definitions, find their way into this group of poems. This is apparent in his impressions of the famous Hospital de La Caridad, which was already the theme of the poem 'Morte situada na Espanha. (La Caridad–Sevilha)' of Mendes's *Tempo espanhol*.[43] Mendes's poem (published in 1959) begins by evoking the religious message of repentance proposed by the founder of La Caridad. The vision of his tomb is a graphic reminder of mortality: 'Distingo perto as ruínas de Don Juan, | Advertência didática de morte' [I can see the ruins of Don Juan close by, | Didactic warning of death] (Mendes, 1994, p. 619).

The poem goes on to capture Spanish fascination with death, as manifested in cultural practices such as bullfighting and focuses on the Spaniards' defiance in the face of political oppression, of which death becomes a metaphor, in an oblique allusion to the Franco regime: 'Operário e estudante espanhóis, | Mortos que sois na flor da greve!' [Spanish workers and students, | Dead as you are, in the prime of the strike!] (Mendes, 1994, p. 619).

As it is seen by Mendes, La Caridad evokes cultural and political Spanish values as well as religious ones. Cabral too engages with questions of spirituality in his renditions of the theme, though his anti-religious sentiments mean that he rejects the Catholic message encoded

---

[42] 'Só sou capaz de me interessar pela Espanha realista, a Espanha materialista, a Espanha das coisas. E quando uma manifestação, digamos assim, desse lado 'espiritual' da Espanha que V. capta tão bem me interessa, repare que sempre a trato amesquinhando. Exemplo: as corridas de touro, coisa inadmissível a um Espanha-branca como eu: eu as diminuo às dimensões de uma lição de estética; o cante flamenco, idem. Etc. Etc. Quero dizer: sua posição intelectual é muito mais ampla e abarca as Espanhas branca e negra.' Letter to Murilo Mendes dated 22 Jan. 1959, in Laís Correa de Araújo, *Murilo Mendes*, 2nd edn (Petrópolis: Editora Vozes, 1972), pp. 191–4 (193–4).
[43] The Hospital de la Caridad was built in 1663 by Miguel de Mañara, a nobleman who entered the religious order of the Hermandad de la Caridad after turning his back on a life of debauchery. It was built as a hospice for the poor and the elderly and is still used for this purpose today. Mañara commissioned paintings intended to reinforce the Catholic message of the importance of good deeds over faith in the hour of Final Judgement. As home to one of the most important Spanish baroque art collections, the hospital is today also one of Seville's main tourist attractions (see José Gestoso Perez, *Sevilla monumental y artística*, 3 vols, 2nd edn (Sevilla: Guadalquivir, 1984), III, 320–40).

in the building, a view which he believes is in part shared by many *sevilhanos*.

Indeed, in his poem 'Hospital de *La Caridad*' (pp. 661–2), the building appears as a bastion of Catholicism, embodiment of the dominant order opposed to the ethos of the man in the street. Its founder, whom Cabral names 'Juan de Mañara' instead of 'Miguel de Mañara', because he was widely believed to be the legendary Don Juan, is defined as the 'Great Torturer' for turning the final hours of the residents of the hospice into an agonizing expectation of death. The stasis within the waiting room of death that the hospice is likened to contrasts with the buzzing city outside; the anguish of the elderly being contrasted with the carefree attitude of the people lounging about in public gardens. The hospice, in fact, becomes the material representation of the moral entrapment brought about by religion, conveyed through the juxtaposition of the categories of containment/freedom in the form of the 'waiting room' (the Hospital) and the 'glorietas' [public gardens] of the city respectively.[44]

Cabral's critique of Catholicism in this poem seems to be determined by the fact that he saw this religion as defending humanity's subdued resignation in the face of mortality. He contrasts this with an attitude of defiance, which he detects in the people's apparent disregard for any concern of a metaphysical nature as they indulge in their leisurely breaks. This does not mean that the sense of finality is not crucial to his understanding the culture of the *sevilhanos*. On the contrary, it is pivotal to their cultural manifestations, such as flamenco or bullfighting, both of which he was drawn to because of the way in which notions of life and death are intimately linked into them.

Indeed, the lament of flamenco song captures the sense of pain and finality that has grown out of the gypsy community's long experience of marginality and discrimination. The manner in which the theme of mortality is incorporated into the song translates this community's fight for survival. If, as Parvati Nair observed, 'flamenco has long provided the western imaginary with a location for passion',[45] its inclusion in Cabral's poetry reveals that he saw it, above all, as a demonstration of

---

[44] By contrasting the hospital with the city's public gardens, known as 'glorietas', Cabral is also subtly contrasting the 'glory' of material pleasures in Seville with the spiritual 'glory' that the elderly await, but whose existence he doubts.

[45] Parvati Nair,'Elusive Song: Flamenco as Field and Passage for the Gitanos in Córdoba Prison', in *Constructing Identity in Contemporary Spain: Theoretical Debates and Cultural Practice*, ed. Jo Labanyi (Oxford: Oxford University Press, 2002), pp. 41–54 (p. 52).

Women and the city in Sevilha andando and Andando Sevilha

defiance. As such, flamenco is the expression of a positive kind of marginality, in accordance with the definition provided by Nair: 'The song eludes containment. In its ongoing struggle for social survival, it mirrors the subaltern crossings of cultural terrains' (pp. 52–3).

Rosa Maria Martelo (1990, p. 101) noted that defiance is a constant feature of Cabral's Andalusia. This certainly applies to the poet's renditions of Seville in this collection, but it is noteworthy how such defiance is ascribed primarily to marginal groups, as exemplified in the poem 'Carmen Amaya, de Triana'(pp. 674–5). Here, Cabral gives voice to the famous gypsy *bailadora*, whose dance captures existence at the limits between life and death:

> Supersticiosa, sou cigana,
> vivo muito bem com a tal dama:
>
> Ela faz mais denso o meu gesto
> e só virá em meu dia certo. (p. 675)

[Superstitious, I am a gypsy, | I live well in the company of that woman: | She makes my gestures more dense | and will only come on the day set for me.]

Carmen Amaya's defiance of death appears to translate the gypsy resistance to social oppression, represented by artistic conventions, as suggested by the fact that, in order to maintain her identity as a gypsy *bailadora*, she necessarily has to reject mainstream dance routines: "Nunca pensei em ser dama, não: | pois toquei fogo na lição." ["I never considered being a lady, no: | because I set fire to the lesson"] (p. 674). Such 'lição' is linked with mortality, as the association with 'gesso' suggests: 'Fugir do que ela faz de gesso, | dançá-la, mas sempre do avesso' [Fleeing from what it turns into chalk, | dance it, but always inside out] (p. 675). Thus, her movement is 'dense', because it expresses the resilience of the gypsy community, as summarized in the words of the gypsy singer and guitarist Pedro Peña: 'You know how to express the song when you're carrying the pain of centuries with you.'[46]

Similar images of liminality of life and death are also to be found in the poem 'Manolo González' (p. 671), where the bullfighter is visualized as existing at the 'extreme of his being'. The poem opens with a series of questions put to the bullfighter himself as to the reasons why he should thrive on danger rather than pursuing a safer mode of bullfighting.

---

[46] In Bernard Leblon, *Gypsies and Flamenco*, trans. Sinead ni Shuinear (Hatfield: University of Hertfordshire Press, 1995), p. 72.

However, as the poem goes on to convey, an explanation from him is not forthcoming:

> Se calava, quase menino,
> de cabelo louro de gringo,
>
> menino vestindo ouro e prata,
> cores da morte celebrada. (p. 671)

[He went quiet almost childlike, | his blond, foreign-looking hair, | a child dressed in gold and silver, | colours of celebrated death.]

Manolo refuses to explain his attitude towards death, which makes any attempt to define him fully all the more difficult, with such indeterminacy being encoded in his physical appearance. His blond hair, described as being 'de gringo', suggests that he does not conform to the stereotypical image of the *sevilhano*. By picturing Manolo as a child-like figure who refuses to justify his actions, the notion of the bullfighter as a metaphor of defiance of conventions is reinforced.[47] As such, he is also a metaphor for Cabral's own poetic intent, as expounded when commenting on his most famous work: 'I want to show things, but do not draw conclusions. See, for example, that in *Morte e vida severina* you do not find out whether Severino commits suicide or not.'[48]

The ambiguity proposed by Cabral runs through this last collection and is also echoed in the image of 'aceiro da morte' central to the poem 'A imaginação perigosa' (p. 679), its penultimate composition. It is noteworthy how the ageing Cabral here intended to foreground the experience of death over life by referring to 'death's clearing' rather than to the 'fluid clearing of life', where he had visualized the famous bullfighter Manolete three decades earlier.[49] This is not to say, however, that the mood of the poem should be in any way more sombre than in

---

[47] Cabral's passion for bullfighting is reflected in *Andando Sevilha*'s three poems on the theme: 'Manolo Gonzalez' (p. 671), 'Miguel Baez "Litri"' (pp. 671–2) and 'Juan Belmonte' (pp. 673–4). Flora Süssekind informs us that Cabral owned a copy of the anthology *Los toros en la poesía* (Madrid: Espasa-Calpe, 1944), organized by José María de Cossío, entirely devoted to the theme of bullfighting (see Süssekind, 2001, p. 37). In a letter to Manuel Bandeira, from 1947, Cabral spoke of his projects for the press he set up in Barcelona, which included an anthology of modern Spanish poetry centred on the theme of bullfighting. Cabral felt he had the necessary understanding of Spanish cultural manifestations to be able to provide an edition with explanatory notes on any vocabulary that Brazilian readers might have found obscure (in Süssekind, 2001, p. 33).

[48] 'Eu quero dar a ver, mas não tiro conclusões. Veja, por exemplo, que em *Morte e vida severina* não se sabe se Severino se suicida ou não' (in Saraiva, 1987, p. 6).

[49] 'Alguns toureiros' of *Paisagens com figuras* (1959), p. 158.

the earlier composition, because 'Imaginação perigosa' exemplifies how the act of continually renegotiating these boundaries amounts to a progress towards empowerment. The opening lines of the poem probe into the reasons for the *sevilhanos*' cultural fascination with death: 'Porque é que todo sevilhano | quer viver-se no aceiro da morte?' [Why does every Sevilllian | wish to live on death's clearing?] (p. 679). In their head-on confrontation with death, beyond a religious perspective, the *sevilhanos* express their defiance in the face of the human condition, and the reflexive use of 'viver-se' suggests that, in so doing, a sense of fulfilment is achieved.

Cabral juxtaposes this stance adopted by the *sevilhano* with that of the gambler, who entrusts himself to fate and luck. According to Walter Benjamin, the figure of the gambler in Baudelaire epitomizes the unheroic nature of modern times: 'This starting all over again is the regulative idea of the game, as it is of work for wages.'[50] Unlike the Baudelairian modern man, who has been 'cheated out of his experience' (Benjamin, p. 176), the *sevilhano* visualized by Cabral does not put his trust in the 'lower god of luck'. For this reason, it is not with the gambler but the acrobat, who relies solely on his skills to defy death, that the *sevilhano* is ultimately associated.

Cabral's obsession with borderline imagery is manifested in the figure of the acrobat who endeavours to maintain his balance as he hovers between life and death on the tightrope: 'viver sobre um fio | tenso, por em cima da morte' [living on a rope | tightly held above death] (p. 679). Beyond an existential interpretation, this poem lends itself to a meta-textual reading, given that the contrasting figures of the gambler and the acrobat can be taken to represent the two approaches to the act of writing which were repeatedly juxtaposed in Cabral's poetry: on the one hand, the gambler, embodiment of the 'inspired' poet, on the other, the acrobat, in whom the cerebral writer is visualized. The second approach to the act of writing, which the poet endorses, is captured paradoxically through instances in which the unpredictability of the outcome is not excluded: the acrobat might be in control of his movements, but there inevitably is some degree of uncertainty as to whether his endeavour will succeed. In line with this, the metal imagery that Cabral employs to visualize the path trodden by the *sevilhanos* is highly meaningful. In fact, the 'fio agudo de cobre' [fine line of copper] is evocative of the knife-edge, itself a powerful borderline image,

---

[50] Walter Benjamin, 'On Some Motifs in Baudelaire', in *Illuminations*, ed. and intro. by Hannah Arendt, trans. Harry Zorn (London: Pimlico, 1999), pp. 152–96 (p. 175).

associated with ambiguity, as discussed earlier in relation to *A escola das facas*.[51]

The figure of the acrobat seen walking along the perilous line between life and death resonates with the connotations of that earlier image, since he is a displaced figure, one who is constantly on the move as part of an itinerant circus community. His refusal to conform to a rigid social structure reflects the uncertainty implied in the stunt he is performing, where one can also see mirrored the very elusiveness of language.

As the metal widely thought to have been the first used by humans, the 'fio agudo de cobre' also epitomizes humanity's progress towards greater empowerment. The reddish hue of copper, which suggests an association with blood, symbolizes the day-to-day struggle of the people.[52] In Cabral's words: 'I believe that man is bettering himself and that progress is necessary. It's just that I am not a naive optimist, believing that such and such a party or person will sort things out. Progress is made through struggle and pain, in the same way as one comes into the world.'[53]

It comes as no surprise, therefore, that the closing poem in his last collection, 'Sevilha e o progresso' (pp. 679–80), should bring together these thematic threads, by reworking the themes of movement, liminality, life and finality in a final positive rendition of the city:

> Sevilha é a única cidade
> que soube crescer sem matar-se.
>
> Cresceu do outro lado do rio,
> cresceu ao redor, como os circos. (p. 679)

[Seville is the only city | which knew how to grow without killling itself. | It grew on the other side of the river, | it grew on the outskirts, like circuses.]

---

[51] As Chevalier and Gheerbrant (p. 432) note, the image of the knife-edge is associated with the experience of transit, rites of passage and the need to transcend opposites in order to reach a higher level of understanding.

[52] Lorca's association of metal and death clearly influenced Cabral's exploration of the motif. Ramon Xirau observed how death and metal are linked throughout Lorca's œuvre. See 'La relación metal–muerte en los poemas de García Lorca', *Revista de filología hispánica*, 7 (1953), 364–71 (p. 364). Lorca himself stated: 'lo más importante de todo tiene un último valor metálico de muerte' [what holds the most importance ultimately has a metallic value of death]. 'Teoria y juego del duende', in *Obras completas*, 3 vols, 22nd edn, org. Arturo del Hoyo (Madrid: Aguilar, 1986), III, 306–18, p. 313).

[53] 'Eu acho que o homem está melhorando e que o progresso é uma coisa necessária. Só não sou optimista beato, acreditando que o partido tal ou fulano de tal é que vai resolver. O progresso se faz com luta e com dor, tal como o nascimento' (in Saraiva, 1987, p. 6).

Seville's urban network has expanded beyond the limits of the river Guadalquivir, meaning that its old quarters have remained unspoilt by modern expansion. The association made earlier between the city's vitality and its gypsy heritage is reiterated in this poem, as the reference to circus life demonstrates. Given that the circus is, by definition, an epitome of life on the move, its reference implies that the boundaries of the heterogeneous modern city (its old centre remaining intact) are continually being renegotiated, since they are not established according to a pre-determined development plan. This is not seen as an easy solution, but rather as one that requires courage: something that is conveyed by the image of the river crossing, for, as in the earlier 'Murilo Mendes e os rios', of *Agrestes*, in it a symbolic death and rebirth are simultaneously implied.

5.4 CONCLUSION

The outstanding feature that may be seen as defining the *sevilhana* in *Sevilha andando* is her emancipation. She is a figure repeatedly pictured on the move, who becomes a metaphor for empowerment, for she refuses to be 'fixed' and, therefore, also metaphorically dominated. Cabral does not adopt a reductively voyeuristic perspective in relation to the female subject, and she emerges as much more than the mere object of male desire. His dialogue with European and Brazilian poetic tradition reveals the extent to which his configurations of the *sevilhana* were largely shaped by political concerns: because she manages to elude the scrutinizing male gaze, she comes to embody both sexual emancipation and postcolonial resistance.

His fascination with the gypsy community of Seville, in *Andando Sevilha*, is coherent with the innovative configurations of femininity found in *Sevilha andando*, since these encapsulate defiance of forms of social domination and oppression, and the poet's reworking of the figure of Carmen exemplifies his treatment of Andalusia in these collections. Cabral debunks sexual stereotypes normally associated with this character, as her irreverence to social conventions epitomizes the emancipation of the young women of today.

The geography of Seville itself, with its winding streets that contrast with the geometrical precision of modern urban planning, such as that of Brasília, becomes a metaphor for an ethos of defiance of rigid social norms. In this way, the poet shows that he has come to reassess his early admiration for Le Corbusier, whose urban and architectural design based on geometrical order stands at the antipodes of the intricate Sevillian urban network over which he enthuses in his last collections. Seville represents a space where rigid boundaries have been brought down, something apparent not only in his renditions of the actual geography of the city but also in the representation of its inhabitants, given that they are visualized in the 'aceiro da morte'.

It is noteworthy how in the earlier collection *A escola das facas*, the fluid boundaries of life and mortality translated a north-eastern reality marked by oppression and exploitation. When this same fluidity was reworked in relation to Seville it was in order to underscore the people's resistance to social discrimination. This contrast certainly is revealing as far as Cabral's bleak outlook in relation to the north-east is concerned. Indeed, it is of considerable import that a positive outcome should only be visualized well beyond the boundaries of his native Brazil.

Conclusion

Cabral's perception of the world as filled with tensions, unstable, teetering on the edge, is one of the central themes of *A escola das facas*, the first of the collections analysed in this book. In this revisitation of the northeast, the image of the knife encapsulates just such a vision of his native land, in which life becomes paradoxically linked with destruction, and death is intimately associated with life and renewal.

The sense of life on a knife-edge conveyed Cabral's understanding of the living world, and what emerges from his writings is an obsession with liminal imagery, in which boundaries are not clearly definable. This not only articulated the poet's anxieties in relation to death, but was also intensely political, since it expressed his concerns regarding his native Brazil, seen as a country of unresolved tensions. Indeed, images of his country in which life and mortality were conflated and where the boundaries between them remained undefined captured both Brazil's violent history and the challenges it still faced. Hence, in *Auto do frade*, he was drawn to Frei Caneca as a man hovering between life and death and created a play filled with anonymous ghost-like characters. The indictment of the nineteenth-century government of Dom Pedro I, articulated through the voices of these characters, is all the more resonant to the modern reader mindful of Brazil's recent experience of dictatorship.

Such obsession with liminal states lies at the heart of the poet's focus on the in-between space in *Agrestes*, where the north-eastern region of the *agreste*, lying between the *zona da mata* and the *sertão*, became a metaphor for a world view according to which nothing can ever be considered in isolation, but always as part of a complex system of shifting relations. This led to a journey through different landscapes—both geographical and metaphorical—in which the boundaries between the physical world and the creations of the human mind have been broken down: 'se lê ou se habita Alberti? | se habita ou soletra Cádiz?' [does one read or inhabit Alberti? | does one inhabit or spell

Cádiz?].[1] The chiasmic structure of these lines conveys the disruption of boundaries that occurs when a work of literature successfully evokes a given geographical location. The fact that the two questions put here remain unanswered articulates the difficulties of distinguishing between imaginary and physical experiences and is symptomatic of the poet's approach throughout his *œuvre*. In it, his clinical eye scrutinizes the concrete world and attempts to draw out the essence of things, but does not presume to give definitive answers.

The manner in which Cabral incorporated Andalusia into his work, with Spanish and Brazilian landscapes often mutually inflected, is further evidence of his breaking down of boundaries. This particular feature of his work stemmed from his own experience as a northeasterner who had lived away from his native land for most of his adult life. Carlos Mendes de Sousa recalls how Cabral lamented the consequences of his itinerant life, stating that 'being a diplomat means living permanently in a foreign language'.[2] While Cabral described life on the move in terms of the experience of marginalization, and therefore negatively, Sousa (2003, p. 161) argues that it was fundamental in defining the poet's own idiom, as he looked at his own country from a fresh perspective and sought a distinctive, original voice with which to convey it. For Sousa (2003, p. 162), what this personal experience ultimately reinforced was the need to overcome any kind of boundary.

It is in line with this resistance to rigid categorizations, that *Crime na Calle Relator*'s treatment of the theme of crime can be understood, with its enquiry into the injustices of the present and of the past and its challenge of the definitions of innocence and guilt. Understood as a response to Brazil's recent history of authoritarian regimes, such a challenge gains in political import, although the poet's treatment of the theme of crime had also important postcolonial implications. Indeed, in his revisitation of the grand narrative of the Discovery, previously featured in *A escola das facas*, the myth of the civilizing mission of Europe vis-à-vis the New World was debunked.

In fact, Cabral's position as a writer critical of the experience of colonialism and its legacy is central to his work. His configurations of the *sevilhana* in *Sevilha andando*, for instance, can be read in this light, given that the elusive woman seen walking through the streets of the Andalusian

---

[1] 'A literatura como turismo' (*Agrestes*), p. 558.
[2] 'Ser diplomata significa viver permanentemente numa língua estrangeira.' In 'João Cabral ou o poema como epitáfio', *Inimigo rumor*, 14 (2003), 156–69 (p. 160).

city is a multifaceted image, encapsulating not only sexual emancipation and the elusiveness of language itself, but also anti-colonial resistance, since she refuses to be 'discovered' and 'colonized'. His celebration of gypsies in *Andando Sevilha* is a development of these themes inasmuch as it foregrounds their resistance to rigid social structures.

Although the main focus here has been on Cabral's later works, his use of ambiguity and fascination with borderline imagery are evident throughout his *œuvre*. In this respect, the poet's early appraisal of the art of Catalan painter Joan Miró, published in 1950, is extremely revealing and provides a valuable insight into the origins of his poetic intent.[3] Cabral's admiration for Miró's paintings stemmed from the artist's deliberate subversion of the sense of harmony that had been achieved in Western art with the introduction of the third dimension. Importantly, Cabral drew attention to how the sense of perspective is obtained by the subordination of all elements to one focal point: 'in its illusion, it expects the viewers to fix their gaze on an ideal point, from which, and only from which, the illusion is provided'.[4] In Cabral's analysis, Miró's refusal to re-create the sense of perspective emerged not simply as an aesthetic choice, but also as an ethical one, given that it encapsulated an act of rebellion against any kind of convention, understood as intrinsically restrictive: 'Miró does not approach the traditional rules of composition in order to reject them. Miró does not attempt to construct opposite rules, a new parallel set to that of Renaissance artists. What Miró seems to aspire to is to do away with rules, precisely because they are rules.'[5]

In this appraisal of Miró, there are echoes of Cabral's own creative process, with its disruption of categorizations, exploration of ambiguity in themes, hybridity in imagery and subversion of genres. As Sérgio Buarque de Holanda first noted, the study's greatest merit lies in the fact that it provides an important insight into Cabral's own poetic aims.[6]

---

[3] *Joan Miró* in Melo Neto (1994, pp. 689–720).
[4] 'Em sua ilusão, exige a fixação do espectador num ponto ideal a partir do qual, e somente a partir do qual, essa ilusão é fornecida' (p. 692).
[5] 'Miró não aborda as leis da composição tradicional para combatê-las. Miró não busca construir leis contrárias, uma nova preceptiva paralela à dos pintores renascentistas. O que Miró parece desejar é desfazer-se delas, precisamente porque são leis' (p. 700).
[6] 'Branco sobre branco', in *Cobra de vidro*, 2nd edn (São Paulo: Perspectiva, 1978), pp. 167–80 (first publ. in *Diário carioca*, 10 August 1952, section 2, p. 3, and in *Folha da manhã*, 14 August 1952).

It is evident that, as Gledson (2003, p. 258) pointed out, Cabral valued Miró for being an artist who encouraged the public to shed all their presuppositions. Indeed, in Cabral's analysis, the painter's merit lay in bringing about an experience of art that was challenging and liberating for artists and consumers alike:

Does the discovery of this free space, where life is unstable and difficult, where the right to remain one minute must be fought for, and the assurance to then remain longer continually negotiated, not have a psychological value in itself, regardless of what it can achieve in terms of artistic production?[7]

This imaginary space, 'where life is unstable and difficult', where Cabral visualized Miró's artistic intent, has much in common with the interstitial space that the poet himself so often created in his writing, thanks to his rejection of sterile binary oppositions and his attraction for what lies in between. This emerges in the image of the *entre-lugar* where he pitched his voice as a postcolonial writer; it is also evident in his innovative negotiation of the boundaries of poetry and prose, writing as he did from the *aceiro da prosa*, and in his obsessive revisitation of the *aceiro da morte*, where the binaries of life and death are shown to be fluid.

In terms of structure, it is reflected in his ambiguous relationship with literary norms by which he subtly subverted poetic conventions (such as metre) but never rejected verse form outright. This feature is also evident in the overall structure of the collections: the poet's use of different endings and his successive reworkings, resulting in the editing out of certain poems as well as the shifting of compositions between collections, meant that the structure of his later collections was not rigid.

The original style Cabral developed throughout his long literary career was much more than the result of a pursuit of clarity and precision, for it deliberately incorporated ambiguity, fluid categorizations and indeterminate endings which reflected his idiosyncratic view of reality and increased, rather than diminished, the political impact of his work.

Cabral never ceased to engage with the social issues of his time, both in relation to Brazil and on a global level. Yet, at heart he remained an 'incurable Pernambucan' and never forgot his roots in one of Brazil's poorest regions. His commitment to the cause of its disenfranchised

---

[7] 'A descoberta desse território livre, onde a vida é instável e difícil, onde o direito de permanecer um minuto tem de ser duramente conseguido e essa permanência continuadamente assegurada, não tem uma importância psicológica em si, independente do que no campo da arte ela pudesse ter produzido?' (p. 718).

population was unfailing, which meant that he also rejected the idea of a unitary Brazilian identity:

> I am Brazilian inasmuch as I am a north-easterner, and I am a north-easterner inasmuch as I am Pernambucan. There is no such thing as a 'Brazilian' in general terms. I've never been to the Amazon state, I've been to Porto Alegre once, I've never set foot in Mato Grosso. How can I consider myself 'Brazilian'?[8]

This questioning of a uniform Brazilian identity is coherent with his problematic configurations of Brazil, from its discovery through to modern times. In this respect, his debunking of binary oppositions of life and death proved extremely productive and point to a political intent, as Jaime Guinsburg has observed: 'We can think of João Cabral de Melo Neto's insistence on representing opposites as a way of breaking with the idea of a totalizing representation, distancing himself from the creation of a mythical unity, a great national accord, so as to point to the existence of contradictions and tensions in the process of Brazil's formation.'[9]

Echoing Guinsburg's interpretation of the life/death imagery, when considering Cabral's later collections, it is possible to see a correlation between the fluidity in structure, themes and imagery that these works evince and the state of flux in which his country found itself at the time of writing, as it gradually came to terms with, and strove to emerge from, twenty years of military rule.

On a more personal level, Cabral's keen eye for the concrete world enabled him to capture the very impossibility of reaching precise, definitive truths.[10] At the heart of this poetic project is the paradoxical nature of his world, as summarized by Rosa Maria Martelo: 'João

---

[8] 'Eu sou brasileiro na medida em que sou nordestino, e sou nordestino na medida em que sou pernambucano. Você não pode ser brasileiro "em geral". Eu não conheço o Amazonas, estive em Porto Alegre uma vez, nunca fui ao Mato Grosso. Como é que posso me dizer brasileiro "em geral"?' (in Athayde, 1998, pp. 67–8).

[9] 'Podemos pensar a insistência de João Cabral de Melo Neto em representar dualidades como uma forma de romper com a idéia de representação totalizante, afastando-se da elaboração de uma mítica unidade, de um grande acordo nacional, e apontar para a presença de contradições e antagonismos tensos na formação do Brasil' (pp. 46–7).

[10] This is a point also made by Maria Andresen de Sousa Tavares, who observed: 'Se a maior concreção se desenha enquanto constructo verbal, esta não é uma palavra que vise ser "de revelação", é antes uma palavra que racionalmente e, por tentativas, recusa sê-lo; e esta é a sua maneira de ser "poesia de coisas", poesia da matéria.' [If a greater concrete quality is identifiable in his language, this is not a language that purports to 'reveal'. Rather, his language, rationally and step-by-step refuses to do just that. And this is its way of being a 'poetry of objects', poetry of concrete matter.] Maria Andresen de Sousa Tavares, 'João Cabral de Melo Neto: *da fome das coisas que nas facas se sente* ou *serventia de*

Cabral [...] strives to reach the heart of "the object", in its invariability, in order to identify it even when it appears different or in order to distinguish fundamental differences in what is identical.'[11]

Beyond Cabral's fascination for the concrete world lay the search for answers to fundamental human concerns. These remain tantalizingly elusive, conveyed in a poetry that is in a constant state of tension. And in this, perhaps, lies the poet's most fascinating and enduring legacy.

---

ideias fixas', in *Poesia e pensamento. Wallace Stevens, Francis Ponge, João Cabral de Melo Neto* (Lisboa: Caminho, 2001), pp. 227–343 (pp. 227–8).

[11] 'João Cabral [...] preocupa-se em atingir a "coisa" no ponto da sua invariância para poder reconhecê-la ainda a mesma quando diferente em aparência ou para distinguir no que é idêntico a diferença em que reside a irredutibilidade.' *Estrutura e transposição. Invenção poética e reflexão metapoética na obra de João Cabral de Melo Neto* (Porto: Fundação Eng. António de Almeida, 1990), p. 121.

Bibliography

REFERENCES

Abramowitz, Jack, 'Rodrigo de Triana: "The Forgotten Lookout"', <http://216.239.39.100/search?q=cache:IaEdcRA9U2sC:www.eductrak.com/pdf/triana.pdf+rodrigo+de+triana&hl=en&ie=UTF-8> [accessed 13 February 2003].

Abreu, Casimiro de, *Poesias completas*, introd. Murillo Araújo (Rio de Janeiro: Spiker, n.d.).

Ackerman, John, *A Dylan Thomas Companion: Life, Poetry and Prose* (Basingstoke: Macmillan, 1991).

Afonso, António J. Ferreira, *João Cabral de Melo Neto. Uma teoria da luz* (Braga: APPACDM Distrital de Braga, 1995).

Aguiar, Cláudio, *Suplício de Frei Caneca. Oratório dramático* (São Paulo: Editora do Escritor, 1977).

Andrade, Mário de, 'Amor e medo', *Aspectos de literatura brasileira*, 5th edn (São Paulo: Martins Editora, 1974), pp. 197–229 (first publ. in *O Aleijadinho e Álvares de Azevedo* (Rio de Janeiro: R. A. Editora, 1935).

Andrade, Oswald de, *Pau-Brasil*, ed. Haroldo de Campos (São Paulo: Globo, 1990).

Andresen, Sophia de Mello Breyner, *O Cristo cigano*, 2nd edn (Lisbon: Moraes, 1978).

Andresen, Sophia de Mello Breyner, *Livro sexto* (Lisboa: Salamandra, 1985).

Andresen, Sophia de Mello Breyner, *Obra poética*, 3 vols, rev. Secção de Revisão da Editorial Caminho (Lisboa: Caminho, 1990–1991), III.

Aranzadi, Telesforo de, and others, *Enciclopedia universal ilustrada europeo-americana*, 70 vols (Barcelona: Hijos de J. Espasa, 1925–1930), XXXVI (1925).

Araújo, Laís Correa de, *Murilo Mendes*, 2nd edn (Petrópolis: Editora Vozes, 1972).

Arrigucci Jr., Davi, *Humildade, paixão e morte. A poesia de Manuel Bandeira* (São Paulo: Companhia das Letras, 1990).

Athayde, Félix de, *Idéias fixas de João Cabral de Melo Neto*, (Rio de Janeiro: Nova Fronteira: Fundação Biblioteca Nacional; Mogi das Cruzes, SP: Universidade de Mogi das Cruzes, 1998).

Athayde, Félix de, *A viagem ou itinerário intelectual que fez João Cabral de Melo Neto do racionalismo ao materialismo dialético* (Rio de Janeiro: Nova Fronteira, 2000).

Auden, Wystan H., *Homage to Clio* (London: Faber and Faber, 1960).

Auden, Wystan, H., *Collected Shorter Poems 1927–1957* (London: Faber and Faber, 1966).

Bandecchi, Brasil, and others, *Novo dicionário da história do Brasil* (São Paulo: Melhoramentos, 1971).
Bandeira, Manuel, *Poesia completa e prosa*, 4th edn (Rio de Janeiro: Nova Aguilar, 1983).
Barbieri, Ivo, *Geometria da composição. Morte e vida da palavra severina* (Rio de Janeiro: Sette Letras, 1997).
Barbosa, Jamille Cabral Pereira, and others, 'Biografia', <http://www.biblio.ufpe.br/libvirt/joaquim> [accessed 14 February 2003].
Barbosa, João A., *A imitação da forma* (São Paulo: Duas Cidades, 1975).
Barbosa, João A., 'Balanço de João Cabral', in *As ilusões da modernidade. Notas sobre a historicidade da lírica moderna*, rev. Plínio Martins Filho (São Paulo: Perspectiva, 1986), pp. 107–37 (first publ. in *Brasilianische Literatur* (Frankfurt: Surkhamp, 1984).
Barbosa, João A., 'A lição de João Cabral', in *João Cabral de Melo Neto. Cadernos de literatura brasileira*, ed. Antonio F. de Franceschi (Rio de Janeiro: Instituto Moreira Salles, 1996), pp. 62–105.
Barbosa, João A., 'João Cabral ou a educação pela poesia', in *A biblioteca imaginária*, ed. Plínio Martins Filho (São Paulo: Ateliê Editorial, 1996), pp. 239–47 (first publ. in *Folha de São Paulo, Caderno Mais*, 1995).
Barbosa, Lívia Neves de Holanda, 'The Brazilian *Jeitinho*: an Exercise in National Identity', in *The Brazilian Puzzle: Culture on the Borderlines of the Western World*, ed. David J. Hesse and Roberto da Matta (New York: Columbia University Press, 1995), pp. 35–48.
Baudelaire, Charles, *Les fleurs du mal*, ed. Jacques Dupont (Paris: Flammarion, 1991).
Benjamin, Walter, 'On some Motifs in Baudelaire', in *Illuminations*, ed. and introd. Hannah Arendt, trans. Harry Zorn (London: Pimlico, 1999), pp. 152–96.
Bergström, Magnus, and others (eds), *Grande enciclopédia portuguesa e brasileira*, 40 vols (Lisbon: Editorial Enciclopédia, 1936–1987), xxvi (n.d.).
Bhabha, Homi, *The Location of Culture* (London: Routledge, 1994).
Bishop, Elizabeth, and Emanuel Brasil (eds), *An Anthology of Twentieth-Century Brazilian Poetry* (Middletown, CT: Wesleyan University Press, 1972).
Blair, John, *The Poetic Art of W. H. Auden* (Princeton: Princeton University Press, 1965).
Bosi, Alfredo, 'O auto do frade: as vozes e a geometria', in *Céu, inferno. Ensaios de crítica literária e ideológica*, ed. José Roberto Miney (São Paulo: Ática, 1988), pp. 96–102 (first publ. in *Folha de São Paulo*, 8 April 1984).
Bosi, Alfredo, *História concisa da literatura brasileira*, 3rd edn (São Paulo: Cultrix, 1990).
Bosi, Alfredo, and others, 'Considerações do poeta em vigília', *João Cabral de Melo Neto. Cadernos de literatura brasileira*, ed. Antonio F. de Franceschi (Rio de Janeiro: Instituto Moreira Salles, 1996), pp. 18–31.
Brandellero, Sara, 'In-Between Wor(l)ds: The Image of the "entre-lugar" in João Cabral de Melo Neto's *Agrestes*', *Portuguese Studies*, 18 (2002), 215–29.
Brandellero, Sara, '(Dis)covering the Other: Images of Women in João Cabral de Melo Neto', *Bulletin of Hispanic Studies* (Liverpool), 81 (2004), 247–58.

Brandellero, Sara, 'A revisão da história oficial em *Crime na Calle Relator*, de João Cabral de Melo Neto', *Revista USP*, 67 (set./out./nov. 2005), 317–20.

Calmon, Pedro, *História do Brasil*, 7 vols, 2nd edn (Rio de Janeiro: José Olympio, 1963), IV.

Caminha, Pero Vaz de, *A carta*, ed. Jaime Cortesão (Rio de Janeiro: Livros de Portugal, 1943).

Camões, Luís de, *Obra completa* (Rio de Janeiro: Nova Aguilar, 1963).

Campos, Augusto de, 'Da antiode à antilira', in *Poesia antiopoesia antropofagia* (São Paulo: Cortez & Moraes, 1978), pp. 49–54 (first publ. in *Correio da manhã*, 11 December 1966).

Campos, Haroldo de, 'O geometra engajado', in *Metalinguagem. Ensaios de teoria e crítica literária*, ed. Rose Marie Muraro (Petrópolis: Vozes, 1967), pp. 67–78.

Campos, Haroldo de, 'Os "poetas concretos" e João Cabral de Melo Neto. Um testemunho', *Colóquio/Letras*, 157–8 (2000 [2002]), 27–31.

Campos, Maria do Carmo (ed.), *João Cabral em perspectiva* (Porto Alegre: Editora da Universidade/UFRGS, 1995).

Cândido, Antônio, 'Literatura e subdesevolvimento', in *A educação pela noite e outros ensaios*, ed. Marta de Mello e Souza (São Paulo: Editora Ática, 1987), pp. 140–62 (first publ. in *Cahiers d'Histoire Mondiale*, 4 (1970), trans. Claude Fell).

Carapelli, Nilton, 'Mataram a moça e caçaram o livro', *Folha de São Paulo*, 13 January 1980, < http://www1.folha.uol.com.br/folha/almanaque/leituras_28mar01.shtml> [accessed 5 December 2001].

Casas, Fray Bartolomé de, *Historia de las Indias*, ed. Agustín Millares Carlo, 3 vols (Mexico; Buenos Aires: Fondo de Cultura Económica, 1951), I.

Cascudo, Luís da Câmara, *Vaqueiros e cantadores* (Belo Horizonte: Itatiaia; São Paulo: Edups, 1984).

Cascudo, Luís da Câmara, *Dicionário do folclore brasileiro*, 6th edn (Belo Horizonte: Itatiaia; São Paulo: Edusp 1988).

Castello, José, *João Cabral de Melo Neto. O homem sem alma* (Rio de Janeiro: Rocco, 1996).

Chamie, Mário, 'Desleitura da poesia de João Cabral', in *Casa da época* (São Paulo: Conselho Estadual de Artes e Ciências Humanas, 1978), pp. 39–59.

Chevalier, Jean, and Alain Gheerbant, *Dicionário de símbolos*, 6th edn, trans. Vera da Costa e Silva and others, ed. Carlos Sussekind (Rio de Janeiro: José Olympio, 1992).

Cixous, Hélène, and Catherine Clément, 'Sorties: Out and Out: Attack/Ways Out/ Forays', in *The Newly Born Woman*, trans. B. Wing, introd. Sandra M. Gilbert (Manchester: Manchester University Press, 1986), pp. 63–132.

Claudel, Paul, *Le livre de Christophe Colomb*, 15th edn (Paris: Gallimard, 1935).

Colombo, Fernando, *La historia della vita e dei fatti di Cristoforo Colombo*, ed. Rinaldo Caddeo, 2 vols (Milano: Instituto Editoriale Italiano, n.d.), I.

Correia, Clara Pinto, *Adeus, Princesa*, 4th edn (Lisbon: Relógio d'Água, 1989).

Cossío, José María de, *Los toros en la poesía* (Madrid: Espasa-Calpe, 1944).
Couri, Norma 'Poesia precisa de provocar emoção', *Jornal de Letras*, 26 January 2000, pp. 8–10.
Crespo, Angel, and Pilar Gómez Bedate, 'Poemas sobre España de João Cabral de Melo Neto', *Cuadernos hispanoamericanos*, 59 (1964), 320–32.
Da Matta, Roberto, *Carnavais, malandros e heróis. Para uma sociologia do dilema brasileiro*, 4th edn (Rio de Janeiro: Zahar, 1983).
Daus, Ronald, *O ciclo épico dos cangaceiros na poesia popular do nordeste*, trans. Rachel Teixeira Valença (Rio de Janeiro: Fundação Casa de Rui Barbosa, 1982).
Escorel, Lauro, *A pedra e o rio. Uma interpretação da poesia de João Cabral de Melo Neto* (São Paulo: Duas Cidades, 1973).
Ferraz, Eucanaã, 'Máquina de comover: a poesia de João Cabral de Melo Neto e suas relações com a arquitetura' (unpublished doctoral thesis, Universidade Federal do Rio de Janeiro, Brazil, 2000).
Ferreira, Aurélio Buarque de Holanda, *Novo dicionário da língua portuguesa*, 2nd edn (Rio de Janeiro: Nova Fronteira, 1986).
Figueiredo, Vera L. F. de, 'Auto do frade – a hora e a vez de Frei Caneca', in *2o Congresso da Abralic. Anais*, 3 vols, ed. Eneida Maria de Souza (Belo Horizonte: Abralic, 1991), III, 267–73.
Fineman, Joel, 'The History of the Anecdote: Fiction and Fiction', in *The New Historicism*, ed. and introd. Aram H. Veeser (London: Routledge, 1989), pp. 49–76.
Fonseca, Rubem, *Feliz ano novo* (Rio de Janeiro: Artenova, 1975).
Fonseca, Rubem, *A grande arte* (Rio de Janeiro: Francisco Alves, 1983).
Food and Agriculture Organization of the United Nations, 'Spreading Deserts Threaten Africa', <http://www.fao.org/desertification/default.asp?lang=en> [accessed 9 September 2003].
Franceschi, Antonio F. de (ed.), *João Cabral de Melo Neto. Cadernos de literatura brasileira* (Rio de Janeiro: Instituto Moreira Salles, 1996).
Freixeiro, Fábio, 'João Cabral de Melo Neto – roteiro de auto-interpretação', in *Da razão à emoção II. Ensaios rosianos. Outros ensaios e documentos* (Rio de Janeiro: Tempo Brasileiro, 1971), pp. 179–92.
Freud, Sigmund, 'The Uncanny', in *The Penguin Freud Library*, 15 vols, ed. James Strachey and Albert Dickson, trans. James Strachey (London: Penguin Books, 1990), LIV, 335–76.
Freyre, Gilberto, *Casa-grande & senzala*, 13th edn, 2 vols (Rio de Janeiro: José Olympio, 1966).
Freyre, Gilberto, 'O Recife e os franceses', in *Guia prático, histórico e sentimental da cidade do Recife*, 4th edn (Rio de Janeiro: José Olympio, 1968), pp. 15–18.
Freyre, Gilberto and others, 'João Cabral de Melo Neto. "O poeta não vive em órbita. É um ser social"', *Manchete*, 14 August 1976, pp. 110–12.
Gandhi, Leela, *Postcolonial Theory: A Critical Introduction* (Edinburgh: Edinburgh University Press, 1998).

Geist, Sidney, *Brancusi. A Study of the Sculpture* (New York: Hacker Art Books, 1983).
Gilbert, Sandra M., and Susan Gubar, *The Madwoman in the Attic: The Woman Writer and the Nineteenth-Century Literary Imagination*, 2nd edn (New Haven: Yale Nota Bene, 2000).
Gledson, John, 'Sleep, poetry and João Cabral's 'False Book': A Revaluation of *Pedra do sono*', *Bulletin of Hispanic Studies*, 55 (1978), 43–58.
Gledson, John, 'Epílogo', in *Influências e impasses. Drummond e alguns contemporâneos*, trans. Frederico Dentello (São Paulo: Companhia das Letras, 2003), pp. 233–80.
Gonzalez, Mike, and David Treece, *The Gathering of Voices: The Twentieth-Century Poetry of Latin America* (London: Verso, 1992).
Guinsburg, Jaime, 'Morte e origem: notas sobre o dualismo na poesia de João Cabral de Melo Neto', in *João Cabral em perspectiva*, ed. Maria do Carmo Campos (Porto Alegre: Editora da Universidade/UFRGS, 1995), pp. 37–48.
Gullar, Ferreira, *Crime na flora* (Rio de Janeiro: José Olympio, 1986).
Hackett, Cecil A., *Rimbaud. A Critical Introduction* (Cambridge: Cambridge University Press, 1981).
Hale, Thomas A., *Griots and Griottes. Masters of Words and Music* (Bloomington: Indiana University Press, 1998).
Holanda, Sérgio Buarque de, 'Branco sobre branco', in *Cobra de vidro*, 2nd edn (São Paulo: Perspectiva, 1978), pp. 167–80 (first publ. in *Diário carioca*, 10 August 1952, section 2, p. 3, and in *Folha da manhã*, 14 August 1952).
Holanda, Sérgio Buarque de, *Raízes do Brasil*, 12th edn (Rio de Janeiro: José Olympio, 1978).
Holanda, Sérgio Buarque de, *Antologia dos poetas brasileiros da fase colonial* (São Paulo: Perspectiva, 1979).
Jardim, Luís, *O ajudante de mentiroso* (Rio de Janeiro: José Olympio, 1980).
Jardim, Luís, *Maria perigosa*, 6th edn (Rio de Janeiro: José Olympio, 1981).
Junqueira, Ivan, 'As vozes de Frei Caneca', in *O encantador de serpentes. Ensaios* (Rio de Janeiro: Alhambra, 1987), pp. 75–84.
Kern, Robert W. (ed.), *Historical Dictionary of Modern Spain 1700–1988* (New York: Greenwood, 1990).
Kirk Jr., William A., 'Brazil', <http://mailer.fsu.edu/~akirk/tanks/brazil/brazil.html> [accessed 13 February 2003].
Le Corbusier, *Vers une architecture* (Paris: Vincent, n.d.).
Leblon, Bernard, *Gypsies and Flamenco*, trans. Sinead ni Shuinear (Hatfield: University of Hertfordshire Press, 1995).
Leite Neto, Alcino, 'O maior poeta menor', *IstoÉ Senhor*, 31 January 1990, pp. 3–7.
Lemos, Brito, *A gloriosa sotaina do primeiro império. (Frei Caneca)* (São Paulo: Companhia Editora Nacional, 1937).
Lima, Jorge de, *Poesia completa*, ed. Alexei Bueno (Rio de Janeiro: Nova Aguilar, 1997).

Lima, Luiz Costa, 'A traição conseqüente ou a poesia de Cabral', in *Lira e antilira. Mário, Drummond, Cabral*, 2nd edn, rev. Sinval Liparoti (Rio de Janeiro: Topbooks, 1995), pp. 197-331.

Lima, Luiz Costa, and others, 'João Cabral de Melo Neto', *34 Letras*, 3 (1989), 8-45.

Lôbo, Danilo, *O poema e o quadro. O picturalismo na obra de João Cabral de Melo Neto* (Brasília: Thesaurus, 1981).

Londres, Maria José, 'O sertanejo valente na literatura de cordel', in *Os pobres na literatura brasileira*, ed. Roberto Schwarz (São Paulo: Brasiliense, 1983), pp. 238-43.

Lorca, Federico García, 'Teoria y juego del duende', in *Obras completas*, 3 vols, 22nd edn, ed. Arturo del Hoyo (Madrid: Aguilar, 1986), III, 306-18.

Lorca, Federico García, *Poema del cante jondo. Romancero gitano*, ed. Allen Josephs and Juan Cabellero, 19th edn (Madrid: Cátedra, 1998).

Louzeiro, José, *A infância dos mortos* (São Paulo: Abril Cultural, 1984).

Lynch, John, 'The Origins of Spanish American Independence', in *The Cambridge History of Latin America: From Independence to c. 1870*, 11 vols, ed. Leslie Bethell (Cambridge: Cambridge University Press, 1984-95), III (1985), 3-50.

Lyra, Pedro, 'O crime de Caneca', in *O real no poético II. Textos de jornalismo literário* (Rio de Janeiro: Cátedra; Brasília: Instituto Nacional do Livro, 1986), pp. 169-79 (first publ. in *Jornal do Brasil*, 17 March 1984).

Macedo, Helder, *Nós. Uma leitura de Cesário Verde* (Lisboa: Plátano Editora, 1975).

Mamede, Zila, *Civil geometria. Bibliografia crítica, analítica e anotada de João Cabral de Melo Neto, 1942-1982* (São Paulo: Nobel, 1982).

Manzano, Juan Manzano, *Los Pinzones y el descubrimiento de América*, 3 vols (Madrid: Cultura Hispánica, 1988), I.

Martelo, Rosa M., *Estrutura e transposição. Invenção poética e reflexão metapoética na obra de João Cabral de Melo Neto* (Porto: Fundação Eng. António de Almeida, 1990).

Massi, Augusto, 'João Cabral: "Escrever me dá muito trabalho físico"', *Jornal de Letras*, 5 January 1988, pp. 14-15.

Medeiros, Benício, 'João Cabral, nu e cru', *IstoÉ*, 5 November 1980, pp. 52-5.

Meireles, Cecília, *Romanceiro da inconfidência*, in *Poesia completa*, 4th edn, ed. Walmyr Ayala (Rio de Janeiro: Nova Aguilar, 1994).

Mello, Evaldo Cabral de (ed.), *Frei Joaquim do Amor Divino Caneca* (São Paulo: Editora 34, 2001).

Mello, Francisco Bandeira de, 'Falar/falaz', *Jornal do Comércio*, 11 October 1998, p. 4.

Melo, José Antônio Gonçalves de, *Tempo dos flamengos. Influência da ocupação holandesa na vida e na cultura do norte do Brasil* (Rio de Janeiro: José Olympio, 1947).

Melo, Mário, 'Frei Caneca', *Revista do instituto archeológico, histórico e geográphico pernambucano*, 147-150 (1933), 7-37.

Melo Neto, João Cabral de, *O arquivo das Índias e o Brasil* (Rio de Janeiro: MRE, 1966).

Melo Neto, João Cabral de, *A escola das facas* (Rio de Janeiro: José Olympio, 1980).
Melo Neto, João Cabral de, *A knife all Blade: or Usefulness of Fixed Ideas*, trans. Kerry S. Keys (Pennsylvania: Pine Press, 1980).
Melo Neto, João Cabral de, *Poesia crítica. Antologia* (Rio de Janeiro: José Olympio, 1982).
Melo Neto, João Cabral de, *Auto do frade* (Rio de Janeiro: José Olympio, 1984).
Melo Neto, Joao Cabral de, *Agrestes* (Rio de Janeiro: Nova Fronteira, 1985).
Melo Neto, João Cabral de, *Crime na Calle Relator* (Rio de Janeiro: Nova Fronteira, 1987).
Melo Neto, João Cabral de, *Museu de tudo e depois* (Rio de Janeiro: Nova Fronteira, 1988).
Melo Neto, João Cabral de, *Sevilha andando* (Rio de Janeiro: Nova Fronteira, 1990).
Melo Neto, João Cabral de, *Poemas sevilhanos* (Rio de Janeiro: Nova Fronteira, 1992).
Melo Neto, João Cabral de, *Obra completa*, ed. Marly de Oliveira and João Cabral de Melo Neto, introd. Marly de Oliveira (Rio de Janeiro: Nova Aguilar, 1994).
Melo Neto, João Cabral de, *Selected Poetry 1937–1990*, ed. Djelal Kadir, trans. Elizabeth Bishop and others (Hanover, NH: Wesleyan Press, 1994).
Melo Neto, João Cabral de, *A educação pela pedra e depois* (Rio de Janeiro: Nova Fronteira, 1997).
Melo Neto, João Cabral de, *Serial e antes* (Rio de Janeiro: Nova Fronteira, 1997).
Melo Neto, João Cabral de, *Prosa* (Rio de Janeiro: Nova Fronteira, 1998).
Melo Neto, João Cabral de, *Poemas pernambucanos*, 2nd edn (Rio de Janeiro: Nova Fronteira, 1999).
Melo Neto, João Cabral de, *Piedra fundamental. Poesía y prosa*, introd. and ed. Felipe Fortuna, trans. Carlos Germán Belli, and others (Caracas: Biblioteca Ayacucho, 2002).
Melo Neto, João Cabral de, *Death and Life of Severino*, trans. John Milton (São Paulo: Pleiade, 2003).
Melo Neto, João Cabral de, *Education by Stone: Selected Poems*, trans. Richard Zenith (New York: Archipelago Books, 2005).
Mendes, Murilo, *História do Brasil*, ed. and introd. Luciana Stegagno Picchio (Rio de Janeiro: Nova Fronteira, 1991).
Mendes, Murilo, *Poesia completa e prosa*, ed. Luciana Stegagno Picchio (Rio de Janeiro: Nova Aguilar, 1994).
Merquior, José G., 'Onda mulher, onde a mulher', in *Razão do poema. Ensaios de crítica e de estética* (Rio de Janeiro: Civilização Brasileira, 1965), pp. 96–101.
Merquior, José G., 'Nosso poeta exemplar', *Jornal do Brasil, Caderno B*, 9 February 1980, p. 10.
Merquior, José G., 'Nuvem civil sonhada—ensaio sobre a poética de João Cabral de Melo Neto', in *A astúcia da mímese. (Ensaios sobre lírica)*, 2nd edn, rev. Frederico Gomes (Rio de Janeiro: Topbooks, 1997), pp. 84–187.
Meyer-Clason, Curt, 'João Cabral de Melo Neto—Yesterday, Today, Tomorrow', trans. William Riggan, *World Literature Today*, 66:4 (1992), 674–8.

Moisés, Carlos F., 'João Cabral de Melo Neto', in *Poesia e realidade. Ensaios acerca da poesia brasileira e portuguesa* (São Paulo: Cultrix, 1977), pp. 49–79 (first published as 'João Cabral: poesia e poética', *O Estado de São Paulo*, 27 August 1966 and 3 October and 17 September 1966).

Moisés, Carlos F., 'Morte na Calle Relator', *Jornal de Letras*, 5 January 1988, pp. 12–15.

Moore, Marianne, *The Complete Poems* (London: Faber & Faber, 1967).

Nair, Parvati, 'Elusive song: Flamenco as Field and Passage for the Gitanos in Córdoba Prison', in *Constructing Identity in Contemporary Spain. Theoretical Debates and Cultural Practice*, ed. Jo Labanyi (Oxford: Oxford University Press, 2002), pp. 41–54.

Nerval, Gérard de, *Œuvres complètes*, 3 vols, ed. Jean Guillaume and others (Paris: Gallimard, 1993), III.

Nunes, Benedito, *João Cabral de Melo Neto*, 2nd edn (Petrópolis: Vozes, 1974).

Ortner, Sherry B., 'Is Female to Male as Nature is to Culture?', in *Woman, Culture and Society*, ed. Michelle Zimbalist Rosaldo and Louise Lamphere (Stanford: Stanford University Press, 1989), pp. 67–87.

Palin, Michael, *Sahara* (Weidenfeld & Nicolson: London, 2002).

Paranhym, Orlando da Cunha, and Rubem França, *Frei Caneca em prosa e verso* (Recife: Governo de Pernambuco, Secretaria de Educação e Cultura, 1974).

Parker, John, 'João Cabral de Melo Neto: "'Literalist of the Imagination'"', *World Literature Today*, 66 (1992), 609–16.

Parsons, Deborah L., *Streetwalking the Metropolis. Women, the City and Modernity* (Oxford: Oxford University Press, 2000).

Peixoto, Marta, *Poesia com coisas. (Uma leitura de João Cabral de Melo Neto)* (São Paulo: Perspectiva, 1983).

Peixoto, Marta, 'Um pomar às avessas': género e configuração da escrita em Jõao Cabral de Melo Neto', *Colóquio/Letras*, 15–8 (2000 [2002]), 229–40.

Peixoto, Níobe Abreu, *João Cabral e o poema dramático. Auto do frade (poema para vozes)* (São Paulo: Annablume, 2001).

Pellegrini, Tânia, *A imagem e a letra. Aspectos da ficção brasileira contemporânea* (Campinas: Mercado das Letras; São Paulo: Fapesp, 1999).

Perez, José Gestoso, *Sevilla monumental y artística*, 3 vols, 2nd edn (Sevilla: Guadalquivir, 1984), III.

Perloff, Marjorie, *The Poetics of Indeterminacy: Rimbaud to Cage* (Princeton: Princeton University Press, 1981).

Pessoa, Fernando, *Mensagem*, in *Obra poética*, 9th edn, ed. Maria Aliete Galhoz (Rio de Janeiro: Nova Aguilar, 1986).

Pires, José Cardoso, *Balada da praia do cães*, 3rd edn (Lisbon: O Jornal, 1982).

Poe, Edgar A., *The Fall of the House of Usher and Other Writings* (London: Penguin, 1986).

Pontiero, Giovanni, *Manuel Bandeira. (Visão geral de sua obra)*, trans. Terezinha Prado Galante (Rio de Janeiro: José Olympio, 1986).

Portinari, João Candido (ed.), *Portinari, o menino de Brodósqui*, 2nd edn (São Paulo: Livroarte, 2001).

Pound, Ezra, *ABC da literatura*, org. Augusto de Campos, trans. Augusto de Campos and José P. Paes (São Paulo: Cultrix, 1970).
Py, Fernando, 'Começa a temporada', *Jornal do Brasil*, 10 January 1981, p. 9.
Ramos, Graciliano, 'Lampião', in *Viventes das Alagoas*, 14th edn (São Paulo: Record, 1984), pp. 135–7.
Ramos, Graciliano, 'O fator econômico no cangaco', in *Viventes das Alagoas*, 14th edn (São Paulo: Record, 1984), pp. 128–34.
Read, Justin, 'Alternative Functions: João Cabral de Melo Neto and the Architectonics of Modernity', *Luso-Brazilian Review*, 43.1 (2006), 65–93.
Rebello, Gilson, 'O árduo trabalho do poeta Cabral', *O Estado de São Paulo*, 2 November 1980, p. 41.
Reckert, Stephen, 'João Cabral: from *Pedra* to *Pedra*', *Portuguese Studies*, 2 (1986), 166–84.
Rego, José Lins de, *Menino de engenho* (Lisbon: Livros do Brasil, n.d.).
Rimbaud, Arthur, *Œuvres complètes*, ed. Antoine Adam (Paris: Gallimard, 1972).
Rodman, Selden, 'João Cabral de Melo Neto', in *Tongues of Fallen Angels* (New York: New Directions, 1974), pp. 218–31.
Rodrigues, Teresa C., 'João Cabral e o seu "Auto do frade": um poema evoca o martírio de Frei Caneca', *O Globo*, 6 December 1983.
Santiago, Silviano, 'O entre-lugar no discurso latino-americano', in *Uma literatura nos trópicos. Ensaios sobre dependência cultural*, rev. Aníbal Mari (São Paulo: Perspectiva, 1978), pp. 11–28.
Santiago, Silviano, 'Apesar de dependente, universal', in *Vale quanto pesa. (Ensaios sobre questões político-culturais)*, rev. Heitor Ferreira da Costa and Heidi Strecker Gomes (Rio de Janeiro: Paz e Terra, 1982), pp. 13–24.
Santiago, Silviano, 'As incertezas do sim', in *Vale quanto pesa. (Ensaios sobre questões político-culturais)*, rev. Heitor Ferreira da Costa and Heidi Strecker Gomes (São Paulo: Paz e Terra, 1982), pp. 41–5.
Santiago, Silviano, 'Poder e alegria. A literatura brasileira pós-64 – reflexões', in *Nas malhas da letra. Ensaios*, rev. Mário Vilela (São Paulo: Companhia das Letras, 1989), pp. 11–23 (first publ. in *Revista do Brasil*).
Santiago, Silviano, 'Prosa literária atual no Brasil', in *Nas malhas da letra. Ensaios*, rev. Mário Vilela (São Paulo: Companhia das Letras, 1989), pp. 24–37.
Sapega, Ellen W., 'Aspectos do romance pós-revolucionário português: o papel da memória na construção de um novo sujeito nacional', *Luso-Brazilian Review*, 1 (1995), 31–40.
Saraiva, Arnaldo, 'João Cabral de Melo Neto: o que a vida tem de melhor é, para mim, a literatura', *Jornal de Letras*, 7 September 1987, pp. 6–7.
Schwartz, Stuart B., 'Colonial Brazil c.1580–c.1750: Plantations and Peripheries', in *The Cambridge History of Latin America*, 11 vols, ed. Leslie Bethell (Cambridge: Cambridge University Press, 1984–), II (1984), 423–99.
Schwarz, Roberto, 'Nacional por subtração', in *Que horas são? Ensaios*, rev. Marizilda Lourenço, Sandra Dolinsky, and Carlos Queiroz Rocha (São Paulo: Companhia das Letras, 1987), pp. 29–48 (first publ. in *Folha de São Paulo*, 7 June 1986).

Schwarz, Roberto, *Misplaced Ideas. Essays on Brazilian Culture*, ed. and introd. John Gledson, trans. John Gledson and others (London: Verso, 1992).

Secchin, Antonio C., *João Cabral: a poesia do menos* (São Paulo: Duas Cidades, 1985).

Secchin, Antonio C., 'João Cabral: outras paisagens', *Colóquio/Letras*, 157–8 (2000 [2002]), 105–24.

Secchin, Antonio C., ed. 'Um original de João Cabral de Melo Neto', *Colóquio/Letras*, 157–58 (2000 [2002]), 159.

Senghor, Léopold S., *Éthiopiques* (Paris: Éditions du Seuil, 1956).

Senghor, Léopold S., 'Le Brésil dans l'Amérique Latine', in *Liberté III. Négritude et civilisation de l'universel* (Paris: Seuil, 1977), pp. 27–30.

Senghor, Léopold S., *Selected Poems of Léopold Sédar Senghor*, ed. Abiola Irele, (Cambridge: Cambridge University Press, 1977).

Senghor, Léopold S., and others, *Anthologie de la nouvelle poésie nègre e malgache de langue française* 5th edn, ed. Léopold Sédar Sénghor (Paris: Quadrige; Press Universitaire de France, 1985).

Senna, Marta de, *João Cabral: tempo e memória* (Rio de Janeiro: Antares, 1980).

Sharpe, William C., *Unreal Cities: Urban Figuration in Wordsworth, Baudelaire, Whitman, Eliot and Williams* (Baltimore, MD: The Johns Hopkins University Press, 1990).

Silverman, Malcolm, *Protesto e o novo romance brasileiro*, 2nd edn, trans. Carlos Araújo (Rio de Janeiro: Civilização Brasileira, 2000).

Sousa, Carlos Mendes de, 'João Cabral ou o poema como epitáfio', *Inimigo rumor*, 14 (2003), 156–69.

Spears, Monroe, *The Poetry of W. H. Auden. The Disenchanted Island*, 2nd edn (Oxford: Oxford University Press, 1968).

Spock, Richard, *Brazilian Painting and Poetry* (Rio de Janeiro: Spala, 1979).

Steen, Edla Van, 'João Cabral de Melo Neto', in *Viver & escrever*, 2 vols (Porto Alegre: L&PM, 1981), I, 99–109.

Süssekind, Flora, 'Com passos de prosa. Voz, figura e movimento na poesia de João Cabral de Melo Neto', *Revista USP*, 16 (1992–1993), 93–102 (first publ. as 'Stepping into Prose', trans. Regina Igle, *World Literature Today*, 66 (1992), 648–56).

Süssekind, Flora, *Cabral, Bandeira, Drummond. Alguma correspondência* (Rio de Janeiro: Fundação Casa de Rui Barbosa; Ministério da Cultura, 1996).

Süssekind, Flora (ed.), *Correspondência de Cabral com Bandeira e Drummond* (Rio de Janeiro: Nova Fronteira; Fundação Casa de Rui Barbosa, 2001).

Tavares, José Correia, 'João Cabral de Melo Neto', *Jornal de Letras e Artes*, 8 June 1966, pp. 1 and 16.

Tavares, Maria Andresen de Sousa, 'João Cabral de Melo Neto: "da fome das coisas que nas facas se sente" ou "serventia das ideias fixas"', in *Poesia e pensamento. Wallace Stevens, Francis Ponge, João Cabral de Melo Neto* (Lisbon: Caminho, 2001), pp. 227–343.

Távora, Franklin, *O Cabeleira*, ed. Manuel Cavalcanti Proença (Rio de Janeiro: Edições de Ouro, 1966).

Thomas, Dylan, *Under Milk Wood: A Play for Voices* (London: Dent & Sons, 1954).

Torres, Alexandre Pinheiro, *Antologia da poesia brasileira*, 3 vols (Porto: Lello & Irmão, 1984), III.

Veesser, Aram H. (ed.), 'Introduction', in *The New Historicism* (London: Routledge, 1989), pp. ix–xvi.

Verde, Cesário, *Obra completa* (Lisboa: Portugália, n.d.).

Villaça, Alcides, 'Expansão e limite da poesia de João Cabral', in *Leitura de poesia*, ed. Alfredo Bosi (São Paulo: Ática, 2000), pp. 143–69.

Voltes, Pedro, *Fernando VI* (Barcelona: Ed. Planeta, 1996).

Weffort, Francisco, *Qual democracia?* (São Paulo: Companhia das Letras, 1992).

Werneck, Humberto, 'Sou um poeta à margem', *IstoÉ*, 20 November 1985, pp. 84–6.

Wickens, G. E., 'The Baobab – Africa's Upside-Down Tree', *Kew Bulletin*, 37 (1982), 172–209.

Xirau, Ramon, 'La relación metal–muerte en los poemas de García Lorca', *Revista de filologia hispánica*, 7 (1953), 364–71.

Yeats, William B., *The Oxford Authors. W. B. Yeats*, ed. Edward Larrissy (Oxford: Oxford University Press, 1997).

Young, Robert, *Postcolonialism. An Historical Introduction* (Oxford: Blackwells, 2001).

Zenith, Richard, 'The State of Things in the Poetry of João Cabral de Melo Neto', *World Literature Today*, 66 (1992), 634–8.

Zhadova, Larissa A., *Malevich: Suprematism and the Revolution in Russian Art 1910–1930*, trans. Alexander Lieven (London: Thames & Hudson, 1982).

FURTHER READING

Almino, João, '"O domandor de sonhos" e outras imagens da pedra. A construção da poética de João Cabral de Melo Neto de "Pedra do sono" a "A educação pela pedra"', *Colóquio/Letras*, 157–8 (2000 [2002]), 127–58.

Alves da Silva, Wanderlan, 'A linguagem literária do poeta engenheiro: um estudo de *Sevilha Andando*, de João Cabral de Melo Neto', *Espéculo. Revista de estudios literarios*. Facultad de Ciencias de la Información. Universidad Complutense de Madrid 36 (2007), http://www.ucm.es/info/especulo/numero36/index.html [accessed 25 September 2008].

Angélica, Joana 'Promessas desfeitas, o poeta em férias prepara novo livro', *O Globo*, 14 June 1981, p. 10.

Araújo, Homero J. V., *O poema no sistema. A peculiaridade do antilírico João Cabral na poesia brasileira* (Porto Alegre: UFRGS, 1999).

Ashcroft, Bill, Gareth Griffiths, and Helen Tiffin, *The Empire Writes Back* (London: Routledge, 1989).
Baptista, Abel B., 'Ortopedia do símile', *Colóquio/Letras*, 157–8 (2000 [2002]), 273–80
Barbosa, João A., 'Linguagem & metalinguagem em João Cabral', in *A metáfora crítica*, rev. Plínio Martins Filho (São Paulo: Perspectiva, 1974).
Barbosa, João A., 'La poesía crítica de João Cabral', *Cuadernos hispanoamericanos*, 598 (2000), 77–82.
Barbosa, João A., 'João Cabral: "Museu de tudo" e depois', *Colóquio/Letras*, 157–8 (2000 [2002], 159–81.
Bowers, Jane Palatini, *Gertrude Stein* (Basingstoke: Macmillan, 1993).
Brasil, Assis, *Manuel e João* (Rio de Janeiro: Imago, 1990).
Campos, Maria do Carmo, 'Nem esplendor nem sepultura: Drummond e Cabral na poesia brasileira no século XX', in *Actas do 5o Congresso da Associação Internacional de Lusitanistas*, 3 vols, ed. Thomas F. Earle (Coimbra: Associação Internacional de Lusitanistas, 1998), I, 505–17.
Cândido, Antônio, 'Um velho artigo', *Colóquio/Letras*, 157–8 (2000 [2002]), 13–19.
Carone, Modesto, *A poética do silêncio: João Cabral de Melo Neto e Paul Célan* (São Paulo: Perspectiva, 1979).
Carone, Modesto, 'Severinos e Comendadores', in *Os pobres na literatura brasileira*, ed. Roberto Schwarz (São Paulo: Brasiliense, 1983), pp. 16–9.
Chamie, Mário, 'Depoimento e confidência', in *Casa da época* (São Paulo: Conselho Estadual de Artes e Ciências Humanas, 1978), pp. 9–32.
Costello, Bonnie, *Marianne Moore, Imaginary Possessions* (Cambridge, MA: Harvard University Press, 1981).
Coutinho, Edilberto, 'João Cabral in Recife and in Memory', *World Literature Today*, 66 (1992), 668–73.
Crespo, Ángel and Pilar Gómez Bedate, 'Realidad y forma en la poesía de João Cabral de Melo Neto', *Revista de cultura brasileña*, 8 (1964), 5–69.
Culler, Jonathan, *On Deconstruction. Theory and Criticism after Structuralism* (London: Routledge, 1994).
Dixon, Paul B., 'Labor Elaborated: Committed Formalism in João Cabral de Melo Neto's "Other People's Cane"', *World Literature Today*, 66 (1992), 665–667.
Eliade, Mircea, 'Brancusi and Mythology', *Ordeal by labyrinth*, trans. David Coltman (Chicago: The University of Chicago Press, 1982).
Fernández-Medina, Nicolás, Tradição e ruptura: João Cabral de Melo Neto, 1947–50, *Luso-Brazilian Review*, 42.2 (2005), 89–109.
Ferraz, Eucanãa, 'Anfion, arquitecto', *Colóquio/Letras*, 157–8 (2000 [2002]), 81–98.
Fonseca, Maria A., *Oswald de Andrade* (São Paulo: Brasiliense, 1983).
Fortuna, Felipe, 'A paisagem corporal: de como se dá o erotismo na poesia de João Cabral de Melo Neto', in *A escola da sedução. Ensaios sobre poesia brasileira*, ed. Sérgio Boek Lüdtke and Luís Fernando Araújo (Porto Alegre: Arte e Ofícios, 1991), pp. 62–72 (first publ. in *O Estado de São Paulo*, 19 August 1989).

Frias, Joana Matos, '"Um olhar nítido como um girassol." João Cabral e Murilo Mendes', *Colóquio/Letras*, 157-8 (2000 [2002]), 63-77.

Garcia, Othon M., 'A página branca e o deserto', in *Esfinge clara e outros enigmas. Ensaios estilísticos*, 2nd edn (Rio de Janeiro: Topbooks, 1996), pp. 177-265 (first publ. as 'A página branca e o deserto. A luta pela expressão em João Cabral de Melo Neto', Separata da *Revista do livro*, 7,8,9,10 [1958-59]).

Gesteira, Sérgio M., 'O nordeste na poética de João Cabral', *Colóquio/Letras*, 157-8 (2000 [2002]), 201-14.

Gomes, Dias *O pagador de promessas*, 29th edn (Rio de Janeiro: Civilização Brasileira, 1986).

Gombrich, Ernst H., *The Story of Art*, 15th edn, rev. (London: Phaidon, 1995).

Gonçalves, Aguinaldo, *Transição & permanência. Miró/João Cabral: da tela ao texto* (São Paulo: Iluminuras, 1989).

Gonçalves, Aguinaldo, 'João Cabral de Melo Neto and Modernity', *World Literature Today*, 66 (1992), 639-43.

Gordon, Avery, *Ghostly Matters: Haunting and the Sociological Imagination* (Minneapolis, London: University of Minneapolis Press, 1997).

Gullar, Ferreira, *Vanguarda e subdesenvolvimento. Ensaios sobre arte* (Rio de Janeiro: Civilização Brasileira, 1969).

Gullar, Ferreira, 'Gullar & João Cabral', *O Globo*, 27 September, 1987, pp. 6-7.

Hadas, Pamela W., *Marianne Moore: Poet of Affection* (Syracuse: Syracuse University Press, 1977).

Hetzler, Florence M. (ed.), *Brancusi, Art and Philosophy: The Courage of Love* (New York: Peter Lang, 1991).

Holanda, Chico Buarque de, and Rui Guerra, *Calabar. O elogio da traição*, 14 edn (Rio de Janeiro: Civilização Brasileira, 1983).

Holy Bible (Bungary: The Chaucer Press, 1978).

Houaiss, Antônio, *Drummond mais seis poetas e um problema* (Rio de Janeiro: Imago, 1976).

Igle, Regina, 'The Sugarcane Plantation in the Poetry of João Cabral de Melo Neto', *World Literature Today*, 66 (1992), 661-4.

Irele, Abiola, and others, *Critical Perspectives on Léopold Sédar Senghor*, ed. Janice Spleth (Colorado Springs: Three Continents Press, 1993).

Janson, H. W. and Anthony F. Janson, *History of Art*, 5th edn rev. (London: Thames & Hudson, 1997).

Johnson, John, *The Epic of Son-Jara: A West African Tradition* (Bloomington: Indiana University Press, 1986).

Leite, Sebastião Uchoa, 'Máquina sem mistério: a poesia de João Cabral de Melo Neto', in *Crítica clandestina* (Rio de Janeiro: Taurus, 1986), pp. 108-48 (first publ. in *Tempo brasileiro* 89 (1982)).

Lima, Luiz Costa, 'Pernambuco e o mapa-mundi', in *Dispersa demanda* (Rio de Janeiro: Francisco Alves, 1981), pp. 176-88.

Lima, Luiz Costa, 'Sobre Bandeira e Cabral', in *Intervenções*, rev. Rafael Varela (São Paulo: Edusp, 2002), pp. 57–69 (first publ. in *Revista USP*, 50 (2001), 39–45).

Lima, Luiz Costa, 'João Cabral: poeta crítico', in *Intervenções*, rev. Rafael Varela (São Paulo: Edusp, 2002), pp. 111–34 (slightly revised version of article first published in *Colóquio/Letras*, 157–8 (2000 [2002]), 45–60.

Loomba, Ania, *Colonialism/Postcolonialism* (London: Routledge, 1998).

Lopes, Óscar, 'Melo Neto', *Ler e depois. Crítica e interpretação*, 2nd edn (Porto: Editorial Inova, 1969), pp. 366–87 (three subsections first publ. in *O Comércio do Porto*, 10 December 1963; *Plano 4* (1966); *O Comércio do Porto*, 10 December 1963).

Magaldi, Sábato, 'Onde está o teatro', *Revista USP*, 14 (1992), 8–10.

Martelo, Rosa M., 'Amostras de mundo. Uma leitura goodmaniana da poesia de João Cabral de Melo Neto', *Colóquio/Letras*, 157–8 (2000 [2002]), 241–55.

Martin, Taffy, *Marianne Moore: Subversive Modernist* (Austin: University of Texas Press, 1986).

Martins, Fernando J., 'O suplício de Frei Caneca', *Revista do instituto archeológico, histórico e geográphico pernambucano*, 41 (1891), 217–38.

Melo Neto, João Cabral de, *Novas seletas*, coord. Laura Sandroni, ed. Luiz Raul Machado (Rio de Janeiro: Nova Fronteira, 2002).

Mendes, Nancy M., 'Ironia, sátira, paródia e humor na poesia de João Cabral de Melo Neto' (unpublished master's thesis, Universidade Federal de Minas Gerais, Brazil, 1980).

Merquior, José G., 'Serial', in *Razão do poema. Ensaios de crítica e de estética* (Rio de Janeiro: Civilização Brasileira, 1965), pp. 89–95.

Milner, John, *Kazimir Malevich and the Art of Geometry* (New Haven & London: Yale University Press, 1996).

Mongia, Padmini (ed.), *Contemporary Postcolonial Theory: A Reader* (London: Arnold, 1996).

Moore, Marianne, *The Complete Prose*, ed. Patricia C. Willis (London: Faber & Faber, 1987).

Natividade, Tânia Maria Afonso, 'O caráter didático brechtiano da obra dramática de João Cabral de Melo Neto' (unpublished Master's dissertation, Universidade de Brasília, Brazil, 1987).

Nunes, Benedito, 'A máquina do poema', in *O dorso do tigre*, 2nd edn (São Paulo: Perspectiva, 1976), pp. 265–75.

Nunes, Benedito, 'João Cabral: filosofia e poesia', *Colóquio/Letras*, 157–8 (2000 [2002]), 37–44.

Oliveira, Marly de, 'A poesia de João Cabral. Um depoimento', *Colóquio/Letras*, 157–8 (2000 [2002]), 33–4.

Parker, John, 'João Cabral: "um sistema para abordar a realidade"', *Colóquio/Letras*, 32 (1976), 31–9.

Perrone, Charles A., *Seven Faces: Brazilian Poetry since Modernism* (Durham: Duke University Press, 1996).

Pontes, Mário, *Doce como o diabo* (Rio de Janeiro: Codecri, 1979).
Portella, Eduardo, 'João Cabral de Melo Neto: poesia e estilo', in *Dimensões I. Crítica literária*, 4th edn (Rio de Janeiro: Tempo Brasileiro, 1978), pp. 110–17.
Ramos, Maria L., *Fenomenologia da obra literária* (Rio de Janeiro: Forense, 1969).
Romero, Sílvio, *Folclore brasileiro. Cantos populares do Brasil* (Belo Horizonte: Itatiaia; São Paulo: Edusp, 1985).
Sampaio, Maria L.P., *Processos retóricos na obra de João Cabral de Melo Neto* (São Paulo: HUCITEC, 1980).
Sant'Anna, Affonso Romano de, *Música popular e moderna poesia brasileira*, 3rd edn (Petrópolis: Vozes, 1976).
Saraiva, Arnaldo, 'João Cabral de Melo Neto', in *Conversas com escritores brasileiros* (Oporto: Congresso Portugal-Brasil, 2000), pp. 39–52.
Secchin, Antonio C., 'Introdução aos *Primeiros poemas*', in *Poesia e desordem. Escritos sobre poesia e alguma prosa*, rev. Ivna Holanda (Rio de Janeiro: Topbooks, 1996), pp. 61–4 (first publ. in Melo Neto, João Cabral de, *Primeiros poemas* (Rio de Janeiro: UFRJ, 1990), pp. v–viii).
Secchin, Antonio C., 'João Cabral: marcas', in *Poesia e desordem. Escritos sobre poesia e alguma prosa*, rev. Ivna Holanda (Rio de Janeiro: Topbooks, 1996), pp. 73–90 (first publ. in Range rede, 0 (1995), 5–17.
Secchin, Antonio C., 'Morte e vida cabralina', in *Poesia e desordem. Escritos sobre poesia & alguma prosa*, rev. Ivna Holanda (Rio de Janeiro: Topbooks, 1996), pp. 65–72 (first publ. in Jornal do Brasil, 22 March 1992).
Sena, Homero, 'A poesia em Cristo', in Jorge de Lima, *Poesia completa*, ed. Alexei Bueno (Rio de Janeiro: Nova Aguilar, 1997), pp. 45–6 (p. 45) (first published as 'Vida, opiniões e tendências dos escritores', *O Jornal- Revista*, 29 July 1945).
Senghor, Léopold S., 'De la Liberté de L'Ame ou Éloge du Métissage', in *Liberté I. Négritude et humanisme* (Paris: Seuil, 1964), pp. 98–103.
Silveira, Joel, 'Compreensão da poesia', in Jorge de Lima, *Poesia completa*, ed. Alexei Bueno (Rio de Janeiro: Nova Aguilar, 1997), pp. 37–8 (p. 38) (first publ. as 'Jorge de Lima fala da poesia', *Vamos ler!*, 1938–1939).
Simões, João G., 'Murilo Mendes. *Tempo espanhol*. João Cabral de Melo Neto. *Quaderna* e *Duas águas*', in *Crítica II. (Poetas contemporâneos) 1946–1961*, 2 vols, (Lisboa: Delfos, n.d.), II, 339–46.
Simões, João G., 'A "xácara" e a "razão matemática" na voz de João Cabral de Melo Neto e Mário Saa', in *Literatura, literatura, literatura. De Sá de Miranda ao concretismo brasileiro* (n.p.: Portugália, n.d.), pp. 341–5.
Simões, Manuel G., '"Morte e vida severina." Da tradição popular à invenção poética', *Colóquio/Letras*, 157–8 (2000 [2002]), 99–103.
Sodi, Manlio, Achille M. Triacca, and Gabriella Foti, (eds), *Pontificale Romanum. Editio Princeps (1595–1596)*, (Città del Vaticano: Libreria Editrice Vaticana, 1997).
Sousa, Carlos Mendes de (ed.), 'Cartas de João Cabral de Melo Neto para Clarice Lispector', *Colóquio/Letras*, 157–8 (2000 [2002]), 283–300.

Souza, Helton Gonçalves de, *A poesia crítica de João Cabral de Melo Neto* (São Paulo: Annablume, 1999).

Stein, Gertrude, 'Portraits and Repetition', in *Look at Me Now and Here I Am: Writings and Lectures 1909–1945*, ed. Patricia Meyerwitz (Harmondsworth: Penguin Books, 1971).

Süssekind, Flora, 'Predomínio do negro', in *A voz e a série* (Rio de Janeiro: Sette Letras; Belo Horizonte: Ed. UFMG, 1998), pp. 215–220 (first publ. in *Caderno Mais, Folha de São Paulo*, in May 1994).

Tapia, Nicolás E., 'João Cabral: de Brasil a España. Notas para un trayecto poético', *Colóquio/Letras*, 157–8 (2000 [2002]), 215–25.

Tavares, Maria de Sousa, 'João Cabral e a tradição literária', *Romànica* (1997), 85–104.

Tavares, Maria Andresen de Sousa, 'João Cabral de Melo Neto. Razão e "serventia das idéias fixas"', *Colóquio/Letras*, 157–8 (2000 [2002]), 257–71.

Tenório, Waldecy, *A bailadora andaluza: a explosão do sagrado na poesia de João Cabral de Melo Neto* (São Paulo: Ateliê, 1996).

Torres, Alexandre Pinheiro, 'Introdução ao estudo da poesia de João Cabral de Melo Neto', in *Ensaios escolhidos II. Estudos sobre as literaturas de língua portuguesa* (Lisboa: Caminho, 1990), pp. 209–28.

Vecchi, Roberto, 'Recife como restos', *Colóquio/Letras*, 157–8 (2000 [2002]), 187–200.

Vernieri, Susana, *O Capibaribe de João Cabral em o cão sem plumas e o rio: duas àguas?* (São Paulo: Annablume, 1999).

Vieira, Else, R. P., 'Postcolonialisms and the Latin Americas', *Interventions*, 2 (1999), 273–81.

Willis, Patricia (ed.), *The Complete Prose of Marianne Moore* (London: Faber & Faber, 1987).

Young, Robert, *White Mythologies: Writing History and the West* (London: Routledge, 1990).

FILMOGRAPHY

Abrantes, Bebeto. Dir. *Recife/Sevilha. João Cabral de Melo Neto*. 2003.
Avancini, Walter. Dir. *Morte e vida severina*. 1981.
Babenco, Hector. Dir. *Pixote: a lei do mais fraco*. 1981.

General Index

A educação pela pedra (1966) 8–9, 10, 11–14, 15 n. 20, 18, 67
'A mulher e o Beberibe' 161
'Elogio da usina e de Sofia de Melo Breiner Andresen' 67
'O canavial e o mar' 12
'O mar e o canavial' 12
stone imagery 12–14, 18, 24 n. 8, 33
'The country of Houyhnhnms (outra composição)' 14
A educação pela pedra e depois (1997) 15, 179 n. 29
A escola das facas (1980) vi, 9, 18, 20, 22–48, 82, 102 n. 32, 112, 123, 125, 165, 194, 196, 197, 198
'A cana e o século dezoito' 25
'A escola das facas' 30
'A múmia' 25, 125
'Abreu e Lima' 36
'As facas pernambucanas' 24
'Autocrítica' 25, 43, 44, 45, 47
cutting imagery 20, 28, 29, 30, 43, 44, 48
'De volta ao Cabo de Santo Agostinho' 43
'Descrição de Pernambuco como um trampolim' 57 n. 23
fragmentation imagery 20, 29, 48
historical themes in 36–43
'Horácio' 31, 34–5, 36
'Joaquim Cardozo na Europa' 155 n. 67
'Menino de engenho' 31, 32, 33, 44, 45
'Menino de três engenhos' 25, 125
'Moenda de usina' 25
mutilation imagery 29
'O que se diz ao editor a propósito de poemas' 27, 30, 165
'Porto dos Cavalos' 25, 43, 45, 47, 125
regionalist character of 28, 30, 32
scars 33–4
theme of finality in 28, 34
'Um poeta pernambucano' 37, 56 n. 19

'Vicente Yáñez Pinzón' 38, 39, 41–3
Abraham 113 n. 54
Abreu, C. de 137
'A voz do rio' 142 n. 44
'Amor e medo' 141, 142 n. 44
Primaveras (1859) 141 n. 40
Abreu e Lima, Captain J. I. de 37 n. 28
aceiro (clearing) 84, 85, 97, 122, 167, 200
Ackerman, J. 52
Adam 170
afterlife 62, 120
Africa 80, 177
colonial rule (colonialism) 106–8, 109, 111, 114, 123
Eurocentric perspective 106, 112
ghosts of 105–15
mythology 107
as 'other' 107
postcolonial 106, 107
sub-Saharan 111
vegetation 114
see also West Africa
agency, human 30, 63, 65, 120, 121
Aguiar, C.:
Suplício de Frei Caneca. Oratório dramático (1977) 58
agreste 7, 31, 79–80, 83, 97, 197
Agrestes (1985) vi, 9, 19, 20, 21, 47 nn. 44 and 45, 57 n. 23, 65, 78, 79–123, 124, 153, 163, 167, 170, 181, 195
'A Antonio Mairena, cantador de flamenco' 96 n.
'A Augusto de Campos' 82, 84, 88
'A "Indesejada das gentes"' 81, 118, 119
'A literatura como turismo' 98, 198 n. 1
'A roda dos expostos da Jaqueira' 47 n. 45, 88
'A W. H. Auden' 127 n. 11
'Afogado nos Andes' 118
'África & poesia' 110
'Ainda, ou sempre, Sevilha' 81, 95, 98

Agrestes (1985) (*cont.*)
  'Caricatura de Henry James' 104
  'Conselhos do conselheiro' 119
  'Conversa de sevilhana' 95
  'Conversa em Londres, 1952' 94
  'De um jogador brasileiro a um técnico espanhol' 99
  'Direito à morte' 119
  'Do outro lado da rua' 81, 106, 107
  'Do Recife, de Pernambuco' 80, 94
  'Dúvidas apócrifas de Marianne Moore' 102, 103
  'Homenagem a Paul Klee' 100
  'Homenagem renovada a Marianne Moore' 102, 103
  'entre-lugar' (in-between) in 79–123, 197
  'Lembrança do Porto dos Cavalos' 47 n. 44
  'Lembrando Manolete' 96, 153
  'Linguagens alheias' 81, 98–104
  'Murilo Mendes e os rios' 100–2, 195
  névoa image 98
  'No páramo' 115, 118
  'O baobá como cemitério' 109
  'O baobá no Senegal' 107, 108
  'O Chimborazo como tribuna' 117 n.
  'O defunto amordaçado' 109, 120
  'O helicóptero de Nossa Senhora do Carmo' 57 n. 23
  'O índio da cordilheira' 118
  'O mito em carne viva' 97
  'O nada que é' 86
  'O postigo' 82, 85
  'O trono da ovelha' 116 n.
  'O último poema' 99
  'Os cajueiros da Guiné-Bissau' 114
  'Ouvindo em disco Marianne Moore' 102, 103
  'Por que prenderam o "Cabeleira"' 91–4
  postcolonial concerns in 81, 106
  'Questão de pontuação' 120
  reading the other 98–104
  tree imagery 107–8, 109, 114
  'Um piolho de Rui Barbosa' 65, 104
  'Um sono sem frestas' 117
  'Uma evocação do Recife' 89, 90, 91, 94
  'Viver nos Andes' 81, 117
aguardente 134–5

Alberti, M. 185, 197
Albuquerque, M. de 139 n. 34
alcohol 35, 37 n. 29; see also *aguardente*, *cachaça* (sugar cane spirit)
Alencar, J. de 2
alísio wind 31
Álvares Cabral, P. 38 n. 31, 39
Amazon river 38 n. 31
Amazon state (Brazil) 201
ambiguity vi, 14, 17, 18, 19 n. 32, 26–31, 36, 45, 46, 66, 74, 77, 78, 93, 101, 102, 124, 159–96, 172, 182, 194, 199; see also *Crime na Calle Relator*, 'ambiguity in'
America:
  5th centenary of Spanish discovery celebrations 164, 179–82
  colonization of 22 n. 4, 80, 118, 151, 152, 157, 164, 180
  indigenous people of 118, 143
  Spanish 115–18, 123
  see also Latin America
Amphion 68–9, 70, 71 n. 45, 171
amputation 28, 29, 30, 43
anaphora 73
Andalusia (Spain) 21, 41, 42, 44–5, 97, 122, 163, 175, 188, 191, 195, 198
  'Moorish' 97
  popular culture 162
Andando Sevilha (1990) vi, 9, 16 n. 22, 18 n. 30, 21, 115, 136, 153, 158, 181–95, 199
  'A fábrica de tabacos' 186–7
  'A imaginação perigosa' 192–3
  aceiro da morte image in 164
  acrobat figure in 193–4
  'Calle Sierpes' 183–5
  'Carmen Amaya, de Triana' 191
  'Cidade de alvenaria' 183
  'Hospital de *La Caridad*' 190
  images of women and the city in 159–96
  'Juan Belmonte' 192 n. 47
  'Manolo González' 191–2
  'Miguel Baez "Litri"' 192 n. 47
  'Na Cava, em Triana' 182
  navigation imagery 183–5
  'Os turistas' 159–60
  'Sevilha e o progresso' 194
  the *Sevilhanos'* strategies of subversion 182–7
  snake metaphor 184, 185

travel and movement in 9, 183–4, 194, 195
  see also *Sevilha andando* (1990)
Andes 107
  European colonial heritage 81
  indigenous people 5
  landscape 81, 115–16, 118
  lost souls of 115–18
Andrade, M. de 2, 3, 141
  Clã do Jaboti (1927) 3
  'O poeta come amendoim' 3
Andrade, O. de 2, 3, 38 n. 33
  Manifesto antropófago (1928) 3
  Pau-Brasil (1925) 3, 38
  'Pero Vaz Caminha' 38 n. 33
  'poetry for export' theory 3
Andresen, S. de Mello Breyner 66–7, 68 n.
  'Arte poética I' 67
  'Dedicatória da Terceira Edição do *Cristo cigano* a João Cabral 68 n.
  Geografia (1967) 67
  Ilhas (1989) 68 n.
  poetics of the concrete object 67
Andresen de Sousa Tavares, M. 201 n. 10
anecdote 21, 123, 128, 129, 133, 136, 137, 139, 140, 143, 148, 150, 152, 158, 160
Angicos (Brazil) 80
anonymity 62, 64, 73, 74, 75, 87, 88, 97, 107, 149, 168, 173, 197
anthropophagy 3, 83, 122
architecture 172, 195–6
  imagery 169–70
  modernist 13 n. 19, 16 n. 22
  see also city; Le Corbusier; urban space
Archivo de las Indias (Seville) 22 n. 4, 145 n. 53
Argentina 150; see also *Crime na Calle Relator* (1987), 'Brasil 4 x Argentina 0 *(Guayaquil 1981)*'
Arriguci, D. Jr 119 n. 62
art 71–2, 199, 200
Asia 177
Athayde, F. de 79
Auden, W. H. 126–7, 157–8
  'Detective Story' 127 n.11
  'History of Truth' 126–7
  Homage to Clio (1960) 126
  Letters from Iceland (1937) 127 n. 11
Austen, J. 178 n. 28

authoritarianism 58, 130, 154, 157, 198
Auto do frade (1984) vi, 9, 20, 22 n. 4, 37 n. 29, 48, 49–78, 82, 91, 93, 123, 149 n. 61, 197
  Basílica do Carmo 50, 61, 62
  Church of the Terço 50, 58
  and cinema 52–3, 61–3, 78, 105
  civil geometry metaphor 50, 51, 69
  death 59, 73; *see also* Caneca, Frei J.
  do Amor Divino, 'death (execution) of'
  Dom Pedro I; 50, 197
  echoes and screams 51, 73, 74
  fort 50, 59
  Forte das Cinco Pontas 63
  historical background 54–8
  individuality in 75 n. 52, 78
  Meirinho (Bailiff) 76
  Pátio do Carmo 63
  political oppression 50, 57 n. 23, 62, 63, 71, 72, 78
  Praça do Forte 64
  prison 50, 60, 73, 74, 76
  use of repetition 51, 73, 74
  voices in the streets 73–7
automatic writing 16
autos (one-act plays) 8, 17, 49, 78;
  see also *Auto do frade* (1984)
avant-garde, European 3

Babylon (city) 167–8
Baez, M. 153
Bahia (Brazil) 38 n. 31, 39, 55
bailadora, gypsy 191
ballad form 128
ballads, medieval Spanish 6
Bandeira, M. 3, 4, 6, 16 n. 22, 81, 86, 91, 95, 118–19, 122, 126, 143, 192 n. 47
  'A Luís Jardim' 126 n. 7
  Belo belo (1948) 143 n. 46
  'Consoada' 118–19
  Estrela da manhã (1936) 92
  Estrela da tarde (1960) 126 n. 7
  'Evocação do Recife' 81, 86, 89–90
  Libertinagem (1930) 81, 99
  Lira dos cinqüent'anos (1940) 16 n. 22
  'O bicho' 143
  'O último poema' 99
  Opus 10 (1952) 118

Bandeira, M. (*cont.*)
  'Testamento' 16 n. 22
  'Trem de ferro' 92
Bandeira de Mello, F. 65 n.
Banville, T. de 27
Barbieri, I. 18 n. 30, 28, 54, 76
Barbosa, J. A. 18 n. 30, 23 n. 5, 31, 32, 36, 54, 129, 169–70
Barbosa, R. 104 n.
Barbosa de Oliveira, S. M. 5, 9, 82, 163
Barcelona (Spain) 5, 6, 7 n. 6, 117, 157, 192 n. 47
Baudelaire, C. 112, 163, 168–9, 176–7, 193
  'À une passante' 169, 173
  'La chevelure' 176
  'Les septs vieillards' 176
beauty 28 n. 18
Benjamin, W. 193
Bhabha, H. 90, 139
Bilac, O. 2
Bishop, E. 1, 102
Blair, J. 127
blank spaces 96
blindness 9, 41
body 28 n. 18, 29, 108, 163, 164
  female 41, 177
Bogotá (Colombia) 37
Bolívar, S. 37, 117
Bom Jesus Fort (Recife):
  Portuguese defeat of the Dutch (1633) 139 n. 34, 140
bonde (tram) 90
Bonifácio, J. 57
Book of Revelation 168
borderline imagery 10, 21, 26, 47 n. 44, 81, 99–104, 166, 182, 191, 193, 197–8, 199
Bosi, A. 37 n. 29, 46 n. 42, 49, 54
Braga, R. 10, 129 n. 17
Brancusi, C. 71, 72
Brasil, E. 1
Brasília (Brazil) 13, 155 n. 67, 195
brasilidade 122
Brazil vi, viii, 1, 2, 6, 7, 8, 22 n. 4, 26, 39, 41, 50, 53 n. 10, 57, 65 n., 82, 89, 92, 94, 95, 114, 117, 123, 128, 131, 135, 147, 149, 157, 163, 174, 175, 177 n. 27, 196, 198, 200–1
  AI5 decree (1968) 13, 124 n.
  abertura, process of 122, 123, 124 n.
  'birth' of 86, 87
  black population 5, 108, 151
  colonial past 22 n. 4, 40 n. 37, 42, 87, 91, 95, 139–40, 145 n. 53, 146, 148, 158, 198
  and crime fiction 124, 130–2
  culture of favour in 148 n. 57
  diretas já campaign (1984) 122
  discovery 38–43, 48
  Dutch rule (1630–54) 139
  expansionist policy 13
  history 36–43, 48, 53, 75; *see also* Brazil, 'colonial past'
  independence (1822) 56, 57
  justice system 149
  literary history 8
  military coup (1964) 13, 105 n. 38
  military dictatorship (1964–85) 37 n. 30, 48, 50–1, 75–6, 78, 124, 132, 133, 137, 138, 150, 156, 158, 197, 198, 201
  monarchy 76
  national anthem 180 n. 32
  nineteenth-century 50
  north-east 4, 6, 7, 9, 20, 22, 26, 31, 35, 36, 40, 42–3, 48, 50, 56, 79, 80, 86–95, 105, 111, 114, 117, 128, 137, 138, 142 n. 44, 149 n. 61, 156, 196, 197
  Portuguese discovery and colonization 38–40, 80, 87
  postcolonial condition 137, 158
  revolutionary movements 37
  urban development 124, 137, 140 n. 36
  see also identity, 'Brazilian'; society, 'Brazilian'
Brazilian Academy of Letters 1
Brazilian Book Chamber 8–9
Brazilian Communist Party 7
Brazilian Concrete Poetry movement 82
Brazilian Diplomatic Service 7
  Cultural Department 7 n. 6
Brazilian film industry 52
Brazilian flag motto 132, 137
Brazilian Indian 2
Brazilian *intelligentsia* 148
Brazilian military 138
Brazilian Portuguese (language) 36, 110 n. 43, 151
Brazilian studies vi, 8
Brossa, J. 6
Buarque, C. 8
Buarque de Holanda, S. 37 n. 29, 140 n. 36, 147, 199

General Index

bullfighting 95 n., 96, 97, 129, 152–5, 164, 182, 187, 188, 189, 190, 191–2
burial 88, 109

Cabeleira 91–4, 113
Cabo de Santo Agostinho (Brazil) 38, 177 n. 27
Cabo Santa María de la Consolación 38 n. 31
Cabral, I. 53, 140 n. 36
cachaça (sugar cane spirit) 34, 35, 36, 135, 136
Cádiz (Spain) 42
Caeiro, Á. 119 n. 61
Café Lafayette (Recife) 4
Calderón de la Barca, P. 6
Camões, L. de 112 n. 52, 181
 'Canção 6' 181
 and love 181
Campos, A. de 85, 104
 'a joão cabral agrestes' 85 n. 9
 Despoesia (1994) 85 n. 9
 O anticrítico (1986) 85 n. 9
 Poesia antipoesia antropofagia (1978) 85
Campos, H. de 23, 24 n. 6, 85 nn. 7 and 9
canavial 92
cancer 29, 30 n., 82
Cândido, A. 22 n. 3, 114
Caneca, Frei J. do Amor Divino 37 n. 29, 49–53, 54–63, 73–7, 78, 91, 136, 156, 197
 death (execution) of 50, 52, 56, 57 n. 23, 58, 60, 61–2, 63 n. 35, 64 n., 65, 66, 70, 72, 74, 149 n. 61
 Gramática da língua portuguesa 70
 'passion' of 58–64
 'voices' of 64–72
cangaceiros (bandits) 91, 93, 94, 149 n. 61
cangaço (banditry) 92, 93
Cannibal Indian 3
Capibaribe river 7, 8, 45, 46, 89, 105, 137, 138, 165
capitalism 8, 105 n. 38
capoeira (martial art/ dance) 151
Cardoso, F. H. 105 n. 38
Cardoso Pires, J. 130
 Balada da praia dos cães (1982) 130
Cardozo, J. 155 n. 67, 156, 172

Carnival 75, 76 n. 54
Carpinha (Brazil) 80
Carvalho Paes de Andrade, M. de 56
Casas, Frei B. de las 38 n. 31, 143–4
casas-grandes (manor houses) 108
Castello, J. 2 n., 22 n. 2, 52, 115, 147 n. 56
Castile (Spain) 97
Catholic Church 59, 95, 97, 146; *see also* Catholicism
Catholicism 101, 146, 188, 189, 190
Ceará (Brazil) 56
Chã de Capoeira 92
Chamie, M. 20
Charon 101
Chevalier, J. 33 n. 26, 178, 194 n. 51
chiasmus 77, 160, 198
childhood 22, 31, 33, 34–5, 45, 71, 89, 112, 126–7, 136–9
 misdemeanours 137–42
children 88, 89, 93; *see also* orphans (orphanage)
Chimborazo volcano (Andes) 116, 117, 118
Christ 59, 64, 76 n. 55, 97, 145
 crucifixion 60, 97, 98
 Passion 58, 59, 60, 61, 98
 resurrection 60
Christianity 145; *see also* Catholicism
Christians 113 n. 54; *see also* faith, 'Christian'
Christie, A. 131
cinema 52–3, 78, 105, 131 n. 21
city 176
 industrialized 8
 modern 172, 173, 179, 195
 in Western thought 167, 170
 and women 159–96
 see also *Andando Sevilha*; *Sevilha andando*; Seville; urban space
Cixous, H. 177
class 146–8, 150, 173, 174
Claudel, P. 112, 144–5
closure, lack of 25, 43, 126, 157
'clube dos líricos' (lyrical poets' society) 79
coconut trees 30, 31, 156
Cocteau, J. 27
Colégio Marista (Recife) 2
colloquialisms 36
Colombia 37 n. 29
Colombo, F. 144 n. 48
colón (currency) 144 n. 50

General Index

colonialism 3, 5–6, 20, 41, 81, 82, 87, 89, 91, 94, 95, 112 n. 52, 115, 128, 143–5, 150, 151, 157, 163, 175, 177, 179, 181, 198, 199; *see also* Africa, 'colonial rule (colonialism)'; Brazil, 'colonial past'; postcolonialism
Columbus, C. 143–6, 152 n. 63, 180
Communism 7, 51
comparative literature vi
Concrete Poetry Project 85
Confederação do Equador 37 n. 29, 56
conservatism, aesthetic 2
contestation, social 139
Convent of Nossa Senhora do Carmo (Recife) 55, 62 n. 30, 102 n. 31
conventions:
  artistic 191, 199
  literary 63, 82, 104
  poetic 33, 84, 200
  social 81, 162, 195
Córdoba (Spain) 70, 71
Corisco 93
Correia Tavares, J. 63 n. 33
corrida 152
corruption 149
Cortázar, J. 117
Cossio, J. M. de:
  Los toros en la poesía 192 n. 47
Costa Lima, L. 15, 18 n. 30, 46 n. 43
Costa Rica 144 n. 50
Couri, N. 53 n. 9, 80, 102 n. 31, 127 n. 11
Crespo, A. 186 n.
Crime na Calle Relator (1987) vi, 9, 18 n. 30, 21, 25 n. 9, 32 n. 24, 57 n. 23, 82, 123, 166, 198
  'A morte de "Gallito"' 125, 126, 129, 152–6, 157
  ambiguity in 124, 126, 127, 133, 136, 146
  'Antonio Silvino no Engenho Poço' 149 n. 61
  'Aventura sem caça ou pesca' 128, 137–42
  'Brasil 4 x Argentina 0 *(Guayaquil 1981)*' 128, 150–2, 157
  'Cenas da vida de Joaquim Cardozo' 57 n. 23, 125, 126, 128, 155
  'Crime na *Calle Relator*' 128, 133, 157
  different endings 152–6, 160, 200
  and dishonest lawyers 146–50
  guilt 126, 128, 142, 156, 157, 198; *see also* culpability
  'História de mau caráter' 125, 126, 128, 146–50, 155
  humour 124, 129, 133, 136
  and inconclusive evidence 133–7
  justice 126, 156
  narrative verse in 124, 128, 129
  'O "Bicho"' 125, 128, 143–6, 148
  'O circo' 32 n. 24
  'O desembargador' 149 n. 61
  'O ferrageiro de Carmona' 129
  open verdicts 124–58
  'Ponte do Vintém' 137–8
  'Rubem Braga e o homem do farol' 129 n. 17
  social and political critique 124, 128, 133, 147–8, 157, 158
  unsolved mystery theme 128, 136, 157, 158, 165
  use of anecdote 21, 123, 128, 129, 133, 136, 137, 139, 143, 148, 150, 152, 158
crime narrative (fiction) 21, 127 n. 11, 128, 130–3
  and Brazilian poetry 132
crimes 123, 198
  historical 143–6
  unpunished 128
  violent 131
criminality 25 n. 9, 157
crônicas 129 n. 17
culpability 25 n. 9, 124, 133, 142, 146, 156
culture:
  Andalusian popular 162
  Brazilian 2, 3, 148, 149
  gypsy 162, 195
  and nature 166, 167, 169, 171
  popular 170
  of Seville 182, 187
  Spanish 6, 162, 188
  Western high 162

Dante 96
Daus, R. 93 n. 24
death 23, 25, 27, 28 n. 20, 29, 30, 31, 34, 35, 36, 44, 46 n. 43, 47, 48, 49, 50, 58, 64, 68, 70, 72, 91, 93, 94, 100 n., 101, 106, 109, 113, 118, 127 n. 8, 132, 153, 154, 167, 178, 185, 186, 187, 189, 190, 193, 197

encounter with 118–21
see also Melo Neto, J. Cabral de, 'life and death (mortality) in the work of'; suicide
democracy 49, 56, 122, 123
desert 70, 71 n. 45, 111
desertification (problem) 111
desire, male 159, 170, 177, 195; *see also* gaze, male; masculinity; sexuality
detective story genre 21, 130, 131; *see also* crime narrative (fiction)
developed world 105, 157
developing world 6, 105, 114, 131, 157
Diezcanseco Pareja, A. 117
disease, *see* illness
divine intervention 74 n. 51
Dois parlamentos (1960) 10 n. 8
domination 14, 17, 21, 65, 80, 117, 124, 139, 150, 153
  colonial 157
  cultural 6
  economic 6, 105
  political 6, 71, 129, 156
  sexual 163, 176, 177, 195
  social 163, 195
Don Juan 189, 190
Doyle, P. 49 n. 2
drama 52, 63
dreams 15–16
drought 7, 32 n. 25
Drummond de Andrade, C. 4, 7 n. 6, 16 n. 22, 53
  'Edifício esplendor' 16 n. 22
  José (1942) 16 n. 22
  A rosa do povo 53 n. 12
Duas águas (1956) 18

Ecuador 5, 22, 49 n. 1, 115, 117, 150, 152
education 30, 33, 35, 45, 149
El Salvador 144 n. 50
Eliot, T. S.:
  'The Waste Land' 177
Emperor D. Pedro I; 56, 57
Empire of Brazil 36, 63
employment 149, 172
engenhos (rural estates) 32, 35
enjambements 42, 96
epiphany 33
Escorel, L. 18 n. 30
estudos cabralinos 9
Europe 105, 145, 146, 198

Eve 170
execration (ceremony) 50
existence 28, 30, 48, 67, 80, 98, 118; *see also* Melo Neto, J. Cabral de, 'life and death (mortality) in the work of'
exploitation 82, 87, 107, 108–9, 133, 143, 196

Fábula de Anfion (1947) 30, 54, 68, 70 n. 43, 71, 171
circularity imagery 68–9
faith:
  Christian 59, 97, 98, 101, 119, 145
  lack of 127 n. 8
  loss of 188 n. 40
femininity 116 n., 141 n. 42, 161, 167 n. 6, 169, 176, 178, 195; *see also* women
feminist criticism vi
Ferdinand VI, King 187
Ferraz, E. 172
Ferreira, V. 93
Ferreira Afonso, A. J. 24 n. 8
fertility, female 67
Filho, P. V. 15 n. 20
Final Judgement 189 n. 43
Fineman, J. 140
flagelados 32 n. 25
flamenco 6, 96 n., 134, 180, 182, 187, 189, 190–1
  cante hondo 73
  dance (*bulerías*) 135, 159–60, 163, 191
flâneur 169, 170, 184; *see also* Baudelaire, C.
Follain de Figueiredo, V. L. 60 n. 25
Fonseca, R.:
  A grande arte (1983) 131
  'Agruras de um jovem escritor' 131 n. 24
  Feliz ano novo (1975) 131 n. 24
football 3, 81, 98, 99–100, 144, 150–2, 157
Fora de Portas (Recife) 54
Fortuna, F. 106
France 5, 110, 154 n.
freedom 35, 57, 72, 100, 177, 183, 190
  of the press 56
Freixeiro, F. 18, 130 n. 19
French language 112
Freud, S. 134

frevo (Pernambucan dance) 75
Freyre, G. 4, 26, 113
Frost, R. 128 n. 12
Fundação Casa de Rui Barbosa (Rio de Janeiro) 49
Furtado, C. 105 n. 38

García Lorca, F. 6, 184–5, 194 n. 52
 'Baile' 185
 'Baladilla de los tres ríos' 185
 figure of Carmen 185–6, 195
 La zapatera prodigiosa 185
 Poema del cante jondo (1931) 185
 Romancero gitano 185 n. 35
García Márquez, G. 117
Gaudí, A. 188
gaze, male 158, 159, 160, 163, 165, 170, 178, 195; *see also* desire, male
Geisel, E. 22 n. 2
gender 97, 136, 142, 161, 165, 167 n. 6, 176, 178; *see also* femininity; masculinity; sexual stereotypes; sexuality; women
gender studies vi, 19 n. 31, 161
generation of 27 (Spain) 185
Gheerbant, A. 33 n. 26, 178, 194 n. 51
ghosts 51, 78, 88, 91, 92, 94, 95, 122, 136, 197
 of Africa 105–15
Gide, A. 27
Gilbert, S. 178 n. 28
Gledson, J. 16, 17 n. 25, 19 n. 33, 23, 59, 90–1, 105 n. 38, 200
God 101, 113 n. 54, 118, 162, 188
Golgotha 60
Gómez Bedate, P. 186 n.
Gómez Ortega, J. ('Gallito y Joselito') 152–6, 157
Gonçalvez de Melo, A. 140 n. 36
González, Manolo 153, 191–2
Gonzalez, M. 3, 8, 76 n. 54
Gospels 146
Granada (Spain) 185
Great Britain 94
Greenblatt, S. 140
Gregorian chant 88
Greek tragedy 156
Grim Reaper 33
griots (popular poets) 109–11, 113, 115
griottes (female popular poets) 109 n. 42
Guadalquivir river (Seville) 195
Guanabara river 142 n. 44

Guararapes (Pernambuco) 69
Guayaquil (Ecuador) 150, 152
Gubar, S. 178 n. 28
Guimarães Rosa, J. 1, 126 n. 6
 Sagarana (1946) 126 n. 6
Guine-Conakry 22 n. 2, 106
Guinsburg, J. 43, 201
Gullar, F.:
 Crime na flora 132
gypsies:
 culture 162, 195
 of Seville 5, 158, 164, 181, 182–3, 186, 190, 191, 195

Hackett, C. 28 n. 18
Hale, T. 109, 110
haunting 2, 49–78, 88, 90, 92, 94, 116, 136; *see also* ghosts
hell 96, 188
Hermandad de la Caridad 189 n. 43
historiography 38 n. 31, 39, 63
history 130, 137, 139–40, 156; *see also* Brazil, 'history', 'colonial past'; Melo Neto, J. Cabral de, 'and history'; Pernambuco (Brazil), 'history'
Honduras 5, 49 n. 1, 51, 115
Hospital da Roda 47
Hospital de La Caridad (Spain) 189
hunger 31
hybrid forms 20, 52, 62–3, 78
hybridity 139, 199

Iberian Peninsula 42
identity 139, 175, 176, 191
 African 113, 114
 black 113 n. 55, 151
 Brazilian 2, 89, 91, 122, 201
 cultural 150
 Portuguese 86, 87, 130
illness 29–30, 34, 88
imperialism 5; *see also* colonialism
in-between space (*entre-lugar*) 20, 78, 139, 163, 164, 167, 184, 200
 in *Agrestes* 79–123, 197
 as a locus of subversion 82–6
 see also marginality
indeterminacy 25, 69, 70, 78, 94, 132, 135, 139, 157, 171, 177, 192, 200
India 7
Indian descent (heritage) 56, 91, 93, 113

individuality 162, 163
industrial age 27
industrialization 131
inequality, social 82, 122, 128, 131, 146–7, 174
insanity 100
instability 17, 20, 25 n. 9, 35, 77
intertextuality vi, 27, 32, 48, 130 n. 19, 141, 142 n. 44, 173, 180
Irele, A. 113
irony 14
Isaac 113 n. 54
Islam 145, 146
Itamaraty (Brazilian Foreign Office) 152 n. 63

Jardim, L. 126–7
  Humberto de Campos prize (1938) 126 n. 6
  Maria perigosa (1938) 126 n. 6
  O ajudante de mentiroso (1980) 126 n. 6
Jesus 58, 145; see also Christ
Jews 113 n. 54
Juiz de Fora (Brazil) 101
Junqueira, I. 54

Kimbundu language (Angola) 110 n. 43
Klee, P. 100, 104
knife-edge 14, 18, 20, 22–48, 96, 102, 194 n. 51, 197

Lagos 67
Lampião (bandit) 92 n. 19
land distribution 22 n. 4
land ownership, feudal system 7, 93; see also plantations
Latin America 80, 117
  colonization 116
  military dictatorships 150, 157; see also Brazil, 'military dictatorship (1964–85)'
  struggle for independence 37
  writers and intellectuals 82, 115, 117
  see also America
law 149
Law, notion of 13, 137, 152, 157
Le Corbusier 162 n., 171–2, 196
  The City of Tomorrow (1924) 171–2
  Vers une architecture (1923) 172 n. 13

Leitão, R. 66 n.
Lemos, B. 55
Lewis Carroll 126
life 163
  absurdity of 133
  imagery 30, 36, 142
  precariousness of 48
  urban 172, 182
  see also existence; Melo Neto, J. Cabral de, 'life and death (mortality) in the work of'
Lima, A. A. 38 n. 32
Lima, J. de 4, 145
  Poemas (1927) 145
  'São Cristóvão Colombo' 145
liminal states, see marginal states
liminality, see marginality
línguas secas 90
Lispector, C. 1
literatura de cordel 8
literature 6
  Brazilian 1, 2, 4, 9, 53, 80, 89, 93 n. 24, 112 n. 52, 133
  Ecuadorian 117
  European 131
  French 112
  Latin American 83, 122; see also Latin America, 'writers and intellectuals'
  Portuguese 112
  Spanish 185
  Spanish American 112 n. 52
  see also poetry
Lôbo, D. 18 n. 30
London (UK) 94 n. 25
Londres, M. J. 92 n. 19
Louzeiro, J. 130–1
  A infância dos mortos (1977) 131 n. 21
  Pixote: a lei do mais fraco (1981) 131 n. 21
Lowell, A. 6
Lula da Silva, L. I. 37 n. 30
Luso-Brazilian revolt (1645–54) 139
Lusophone world 1
Lyra, P. 53

Macedo, H. 173
Madapolão 110
Malevich, K. 71, 72
  Suprematist paintings 72
  'White on White' painting 72

Mali 22 n. 2, 106
Mallarmé, S. 162 n.
mameluco 91
Mañara, J. de 190
Mañara, M. de 189 n. 43, 190
'Manifesto da poesia concreta' 85 n. 7
Manolete (bullfighter) 97, 153, 155, 192
Manzano Manzano, J. 38 n. 31
marginal states 17, 20, 59, 78, 80, 81, 82, 91, 102, 116, 164
marginality 17, 20, 49–78, 80, 81, 92, 93, 94, 95, 96, 97, 98, 99 n., 100, 104, 111, 114, 118, 122, 136, 137, 138, 139, 150, 156, 158, 162, 165, 167, 175, 181, 182, 191, 194, 197, 198
Martelo, R. M. 18 n. 30, 191, 201–2
masculinity 116 n., 141 n. 42, 154, 161, 162, 168, 169, 174, 178
Mass 101, 102
Massi, A. 125 n. 2, 128, 129, 134 n. 29
Mato Grosso (Brazil) 201
Mauritania 22 n. 2, 106
Mbundu population (Angola) 110 n. 43
meaning, deferral of 30
meanings, double 29, 36, 116
medical and scientific terms 28
medical treatments 29
Meireles, C.:
    Romanceiro da inconfidência 61
Mello, E. Cabral de 56, 57
Melo, M. 57 n. 21, 60 n. 25, 62 n. 30, 64 n., 73 n. 49, 74 n. 51
Melo Neto, J. Cabral de:
    'Agradecimento pelo Prêmio Neustadt' 79 n. 2, 102 n. 32
    atheism 57 n. 23, 74 n. 51, 101, 102; *see also* Melo Neto, J. Cabral de, 'and religion'
    autobiographical elements in the work of 22, 23, 32 n. 23, 125 n. 4, 140, 173
    Camões Prize for Literature (1990) 1, 9
    and communism 7, 51; *see also* Melo Neto, J. Cabral de, 'and politics'
    and consciousness/unconsciousness 4, 15–16, 59; *see also* sleep
    'Considerações sobre o poeta dormindo' 4
    and crime fiction 130–3; *see also Crime na Calle Relator* (1987)
    on his critics 20
    debunking of dualisms 34, 36, 45, 59, 66, 93, 94–5, 103, 104, 155, 165, 169, 171, 172 n. 13, 200, 201
    diplomatic service 5–6, 7 n. 6, 9, 22, 49 n. 1, 51, 80, 81, 95 n., 106, 115, 125, 130, 143, 145 n. 53, 153, 173, 177 n. 25
    earlier/ later works distinction 10–11, 14–15, 25
    early career 4–6
    family background and childhood 2, 3, 99 n., 137, 138 n., 140, 188
    and history 22 n. 4, 37, 49, 54, 57, 91, 128, 137, 139–40, 143–6, 154, 156, 158
    and humour 35, 36, 96, 119, 124, 129, 133, 136
    Jabuti Prize (1967/1993) 1, 8
    late years 9
    later writings 9–21
    life and death (mortality) in the work of 23, 27, 28 n. 20, 29, 31, 34, 35, 36, 37 n. 29, 43, 44, 47, 48, 49, 51, 58, 59–60, 64, 70, 73, 78, 79, 80, 81–2, 84, 91, 95–8, 100, 101, 106, 109, 113, 114, 115, 116, 118–21, 122, 132, 134, 164, 187–95, 197, 200, 201
    and love 161
    lucidity and precision in the work of 4, 10, 11, 36, 54, 71, 93, 97, 124, 129, 135–6, 153, 154, 155, 200
    marriage to Marly de Oliveira (1986) 9, 163, 176 n. 23
    marriage to Stella Maria Barbosa de Oliveira (1946) 5
    Neustadt International Prize for Literature (1992) 1, 79 n. 2
    and the north-east of Brazil (Pernambuco) 5, 6, 12 n. 14, 20, 22, 26, 30, 31, 34, 35, 36, 37, 39, 44–5, 48, 50, 79, 80, 86–95, 105, 107, 111, 114, 117, 137, 142 n. 44, 149 n. 61, 156, 196, 197, 200–1
    playfulness in the work of 36, 44
    poetics of the concrete object 124, 201 n. 10

poetics of construction 16
poetry of 9, 11–12, 45, 73, 89, 106, 117, 158, 174, 190, 193
and politics 7, 13, 20, 37 n. 30, 50–1, 52, 58, 72, 75, 122, 124, 129, 157, 158, 181, 195, 197, 200
and postcolonialism 5, 106–7, 122, 129, 143–5, 152 n. 63, 163, 165, 175, 177, 179, 181, 185, 195, 198, 200
posting in Barcelona (Spain) 5, 6, 7 n. 6, 143
posting in Dakar (Senegal) 22, 106
posting as Delegate to the United Nations (Geneva) 9
posting in Honduras 49 n. 1, 51, 115
posting in London (UK) 177 n. 25
posting in Portugal 9, 125, 130, 173
posting in Quito (Ecuador) 22, 49 n. 1, 115
posting in Seville (Spain) 9, 95 n., 145 n. 53
posting in Spain 5–6, 7 n. 6, 81, 153
postings in Latin America 9
postings in West Africa 9
Prize for Best Living Writer at the Theatre Festival in Nancy (1966) 8
Queen Sofia Prize for Ibero-American Literature (1994) 1, 85 n. 9
and religion 57 n. 23, 88, 97, 101, 102, 142, 186, 187, 188, 189, 190
'second phase' of writing career 10
social engagement 5, 6, 7, 8, 10, 36, 47, 58, 122, 157, 158, 200
and Spain 6, 163, 188–9
on writing 20, 42, 47, 48, 54, 72, 78, 80, 81, 88, 122, 158, 160, 163
memory 47, 89, 90, 102
national 23, 36–43
personal 22, 23, 26, 31–6
Mendes, M. 4, 38–9, 101–2, 163, 187–8
'Carta de Pero Vaz' 39 n.
Convergência (1970) 188
Espaço espanhol (1975) 163, 188
História do Brasil (1932) 38
'Morte situada na Espanha. (La Caridad-Sevilha)' 189
'Murilograma a João Cabral de Melo Neto' 188
'O farrista' 39 n.
'1500'; 39 n.

'Prefácio de Pinzón' 38, 39
Tempo espanhol (1959) 163, 188
Mendes de Sousa, C. 198
Merquior, J. G. 11, 16, 161
meta-textuality 5, 19 n. 31, 27, 72, 93, 101, 102, 129, 153, 155, 159, 181
metaphors 18, 29, 30
metonymy 90, 108, 138, 176
metre 84, 128 n. 12, 200
Meyer-Clason, C. 105, 112 n. 52, 117
migration 43
Minas Gerais (Brazil) 4, 105 n. 37
independence movement (1789) 61
Miró, J. 199–200
miscegenation:
cultural 112, 113
racial 113
modernism, Brazilian vi, 1, 2–3, 4, 38
modernity 2, 169
molambos 110
Molière:
The School for Wives 27
Moisés, C. F. 10 n. 10, 126, 133, 141 n. 41
Moore, M. 53 n. 10, 81, 102–4
'The Hero' 83–4, 102, 103
poetics of the concrete object 102
Morocco 145, 154
Morte e vida severina (1956) 7–8, 9, 17, 18 n. 29, 22 n. 4, 49, 81, 165, 192
Severino 8, 17, 22 n. 4, 31, 169, 192
Mount Calvary 58
Municipal Theatre (São Paulo):
Week of Modern Art (1922) 3
Museu de tudo (1975) 9, 10, 13, 14, 18 n. 30, 20, 23, 29, 36, 40 n. 37, 45 n., 46 n. 43, 57, 106–7, 126
'A luz em Joaquim Cardozo' 155 n. 67
'Ademir da Guia' 99 n.
'Díptico' 14
'Frei Caneca no Rio de Janeiro' 57, 61 n. 27
'O Cabo de Santo Agostinho' 40 n. 37, 177 n. 27
'O sol no Senegal' 106
'Pregunta a Joaquim Cardozo' 155 n. 67
sand imagery 13–14
'W. H. Auden' 127 n. 11
Museu de tudo e depois (1988) 125
myth 86–7, 98

Nair, P. 190–1
Natividade Saldanha, J. da 37, 56 n. 19
nativity story 8
naturalism, literary 114
Négritude movement 110, 111
neologisms 132
Neruda, P. 53 n. 12
Nerval, G. de 163, 176–7, 178
 'El desdichado' 176, 177, 178
New Historicism 140
New Jerusalem (city) 168
New World 41, 114, 146, 164
 discovery 143–6, 152 n. 63, 198
 Edenic vision 40
 Spanish conquest 97, 144 n. 50, 179, 183
Niemeyer, O. 155 n. 67
nightmares 90; *see also* dreams; sleep
Nobel Prize for Literature 1
nordestino 80 n., 86, 94, 105 n. 37
Nova Fronteira (publisher) 15, 125, 152
Nunes, B. 12, 18

O arquivo das Índias e o Brasil 22 n. 4
O cão sem plumas (1950) 6–7, 138, 155 n. 67
O engenheiro (1945) 4, 15, 162 n., 172 n. 13
 'A Joaquim Cardozo' 155 n. 67
 'O engenheiro' 15, 28
 'Pequena ode mineral' 4
O Livro Inconsútil 5
O observador econômico e financeiro 7
O rio (1954) 6, 7, 137, 142 n. 44, 165
objectivity 16, 24, 43, 103, 104; *see also* subjectivity
Obra completa (1994) 25, 43, 61, 125, 160
oligarchy 147
Olinda (Pernambuco) 69, 140 n. 36, 155 n. 67
 Law school 149
Oliveira, Marly de x, 9, 61, 129, 163, 176 n. 23
Oporto (Portugal) 125, 130, 173, 174, 175
oppression 17, 21, 35, 50, 54, 57 n. 23, 62, 71, 72, 78, 86–95, 96, 99 n., 116, 118, 122, 124, 133, 138, 140, 150–2, 156, 158, 162, 191, 195, 196; *see also* domination; poverty; social injustice
'Ordem e Progresso' (motto on Brazilian flag) 132, 137, 156
Order, notion of 13, 50, 70, 137, 152, 157, 158
orphans (orphanage) 47, 88, 96, 122
Ortner, S. B. 167
Os três mal amados (1943) 4, 161
Our Lady of Carmo 74 n. 51

Paes Barreto, F. 56
Paisagens com figuras (1956) 6, 18 n. 29, 25, 76, 97, 153, 188 n. 41
 'Alguns toureiros' 97, 153, 192 n. 49
 'Diálogo' 25
 'O vento no canavial' 76
Palmeiras (football team) 99 n.
Palos de Moguer 42
Pará (Brazil) 56
Paraguay 5
Paraíba (Brazil) 56
Paraibuna river 101
Paris (France) 113, 117
Parker, J. 54
Parnamirim river 137, 138, 139
Parnassian Movement 2, 27
Parsons, D. 172
Parthenon 172 n. 13
patriarchal order 96, 128, 157, 169, 177, 178, 179; *see also* society, 'patriarchal'
Pedra do sono (1942) 4, 15, 16, 18, 59, 91, 162 n.
 'Os olhos' 17 n. 25
Peixoto, M. 12, 13 n. 18, 18, 19, 23–4, 28, 29, 33, 44, 45, 153, 155 n. 66, 161, 174
 principle of transferral of qualities 33
Peixoto, N. A. 18 n. 30, 50–2, 57
Pellegrini, T.:
 A imagem e a letra. Aspectos da ficção brasileira contemporânea 131
Peña, P. 191
perception of reality 17, 23, 24, 25 n. 9, 197
Perloff, M. 77
Pernambuco (Brazil) 2, 6, 7–8, 22, 26, 30, 31, 37 nn. 29 and 30, 38 n. 31, 39, 44–5, 47, 49, 56, 57, 58, 80, 94, 97, 105, 107, 122, 126 n. 6, 139 n. 34

General Index

1817 uprising 36, 37 n. 28, 55, 56
1824 uprising 36, 37 n. 29, 56, 61
history 22, 26, 36, 57 n. 23, 91
independence movements 36, 49
national anthem 6, 180 n. 32
Pero Vaz de Caminha:
  Carta 40
Pessoa, F. 81, 91, 95, 97, 100 n., 112, 119 n. 61, 122
  'A última nau' 98
  'D. Sebastião, Rei de Portugal' 100 n.
  Mensagem (1934) 81, 86, 89, 98, 100 n.
  and myth 86–7, 98
  'Ulysses' 86–7
philosophy 121
pião (game) 151
Piauí (Brazil) 56
Pignatari, D. 85 n. 7
Pinto Correia, C.:
  Adeus, Princesa (1985) 130 n. 18
plantations 32 n. 25, 33, 93
  coffee 108
  sugar cane 7, 59, 77, 80, 87, 94
Poemas pernambucanos 105
Poemas sevilhanos (1992) 152 n. 63
Poe, E. A. 130 n. 19
  Philosophy of Composition (1846) 130 n. 19
  'The Murders in the Rue Morgue' (1841) 130 n. 19
poetry 2, 6, 28, 30, 47 n. 44, 52, 53, 78, 80, 84, 85, 102 n. 32, 103, 121, 122, 132, 170, 195
  African 104, 109–12, 181
  Brazilian 1, 3, 19, 53 n. 10, 122, 132, 133, 137, 140–1, 155 n. 67, 163, 195
  epic 181
  free verse 3, 128 n. 12
  and inspiration 12, 16
  love 181
  lyrical 11, 181
  modern American 6
  modern Spanish 192 n. 47
  narrative 52, 63
  Parnassian 2, 27
  Portuguese 11, 66 n., 84, 181
  postcolonial 6
  and prose 80, 84, 103, 104, 200
  see also Romanticism

politics 17, 121; *see also* Brazil, 'military dictatorship (1964–85)'; Communism; Melo Neto, J. Cabral de, 'and politics'
polysemy 24
Ponge, F. 102
Pontiero, G. 89
Pontius Pilate 59
Portinari, C. 108–9
Porto Alegre (Brazil) 201
Portugal 3, 5, 9, 38, 39, 42, 66 n., 87, 130, 174–5
  April Revolution 130
  mythical birth of 86, 98
  Salazar regime 114, 130
  see also identity, 'Portuguese'
Portuguese Crown 22 n. 4, 36
Portuguese language 1, 29, 34, 75 n. 52, 84, 85, 112 n. 52, 135, 151, 154, 163, 166, 174
Portuguese Renaissance poetry 181
Portuguese studies vi
postcolonial criticism vi
postcolonial studies vi
postcolonialism 3, 90, 104, 129, 137, 139, 163, 165, 195; *see also* colonialism; Melo Neto, J. Cabral de, 'and postcolonialism'
Pound, E.:
  ABC of Reading (1934) 85
poverty vi, 5, 6, 7, 8, 31, 35, 45–6, 80, 82, 88, 90, 92 n. 19, 93, 99 n., 105, 110, 137, 138, 143, 149, 173, 189 n. 43, 200
Primeiros poemas x, 22 n. 1
prison 37 n. 28, 50, 57, 60
  and death 60 n. 25
Progress, notion of 158, 194
prose 52, 80, 84, 103; *see also* poetry, 'and prose'
Proust, M. 46, 47
  À la recherche du temps perdu 46, 47
Psicologia da composição com a Fábula de Anfion e Antíode (1947) 5, 130 n. 19
punctuation marks 120–1
Py, F. 23

Quaderna 10 n. 8, 40, 170
  'A mulher e a casa' 170
  'Estudos para uma bailadora andaluza' 159, 163

Quaderna (cont.)
'Imitação da água' 161
'Paisagem pelo telefone' 40–1
'Poema(s) da cabra' 111 n. 46
Quevedo, F. de 112 n. 52
Quito (Ecuador) 22, 115, 117

race 56, 93, 108, 111–12, 157, 158
   discrimination 128, 150, 152
   equality 56
Ramiro Costa bookshop 149
Ramos, G. 92 n. 19, 93
rationality 15–16, 33, 71 n. 45, 72, 93, 153, 155, 164, 170, 172
Read, J. 13 n. 19
Rebello, G. 17 n. 26, 37
Recife (Pernambuco) 2, 4, 5, 7, 8, 26, 49, 54, 57 n. 21, 58, 64, 66, 74 n. 51, 87–90, 91, 105, 106, 130 n. 19, 149, 155 n. 67, 172
   Dutch occupation 140 n. 36
   French presence 75 n. 52
   Jaqueira district 88, 96, 122
   mangues 46, 90, 94, 138
   Poetry Conference (1941) 4
poverty 7, 45–6, 80, 90, 137, 138; *see also* poverty
Reckert, S. 17
redondilha menor 170
Rego, J. Lins do 32
   Menino de engenho 32 n. 25
Rego Monteiro, V. do 4
religion 101, 102, 119 n. 62, 120, 134–5, 140 n. 36, 142, 145, 186, 187, 188; *see also* Catholicism; Christianity; faith; God; Melo Neto, J. Cabral de, 'and religion'
repetition, use of 51, 73, 74, 96, 161
Republic of Brazil 61
retirante 22 n. 4, 90
Reyes Católicos (Catholic Kings) 97
rhyme 25, 75 n. 52, 91, 128
   assonantal 84, 161
   consonantal 84
rhythm 92
Rimbaud, A. 27, 28
Rio Grande do Norte (Brazil) 56
Rio Grande do Sul (Brazil) 82
Rio de Janeiro (Brazil) 4, 50, 53 n. 9, 55, 56, 57, 80, 90, 105 n. 37, 126 n. 6, 140 n. 36

Rodríguez Bermejo, J. (Rodrigo de Triana) 143, 144, 145–6
Roma, Padre 37 n. 28
romance policial (*romance reportagem*) 124, 131, 136
Romanticism 2, 102 n. 32, 141, 142 n. 44, 188 n. 40

Sahel (Africa) 111 n. 47
Saint Louis (Senegal) 113
saints, Catholic 135
Santa Cruz Futebol Club 3
Santa Maria (Columbus' ship) 143
Santiago, S. 20, 25, 82–3, 104, 115, 122, 124 n., 133, 158
São José, Frei C. de 73 n. 49
São Paulo (Brazil) 2, 3, 52 n. 7, 80, 105 n. 37, 149
Sapega, E. 130
Saraiva, A. 84 n. 6
Saramago, J.:
   Memorial do convento 130
satire 14
Schwarz, R. 148–9
   Misplaced Ideas 105 n. 38
scythe 33, 34, 96, 153
sea 40–1, 69, 71, 87, 106, 118, 156
Secchin, A. C. 7, 10, 11–12, 18 n. 30, 19, 24, 33, 35, 40 n. 37, 79, 139 n. 34
self, poetic 23, 32, 77, 139, 170
Senegal 5, 22, 106, 113
Senghor, L. 6, 22 n. 2, 110–12, 115
   Anthologie de la nouvelle poésie nègre et malgache (...) 111
   Éthiopiques 112
   'Joal' 112–13
senhares 113
Senna, M. de 14, 18 n. 30, 107, 133 n. 27
sentimentality 2, 4, 19, 32, 141, 181
senzalas 108
Serequeberhan, T. 111 n. 48
Serial (1961) 10 n. 8, 15, 17, 18 n. 30, 32 n. 24, 102 n. 32, 173 n. 16
'O sim contra o sim' 102 n. 32, 173 n. 16
Serial e antes (1997) 15 n. 20
sertão 7, 21, 31, 44, 79, 92 n. 19, 197
sesmaria (uncultivated plot of land) 22 n. 4

General Index

Sevilha andando (1990) vi, 9, 18 n. 30, 21, 22 n. 1, 125 n. 3, 136, 158, 159–96, 198
  'A barcaça' 175
  'A sevilhana que é de Córdoba' 175
  'A sevilhana que não se sabia' 125 n. 3, 161 n. 1
  'As *plazoletas*' 167 n. 6
  barges 176
  'Cidade de nervos' 164
  'Cidade viva' 182
  displacement 166
  human body 164–5
  images of women and the city 159–96
  'Mulher cidade' 169, 170, 183
  'Na cidade do Porto' 173
  navigation imagery 164, 175–9
  'O *aire* de Sevilha' 180 n. 31
  passante 174
  postcolonial theme 163–4
  'Presença de Sevilha' 180, 181
  'Sevilha revisitada *em 1992*' 179
  'Sevilhana andando (I)' 166, 167, 169, 179
  'Sol negro' 176, 177, 178, 180, 183
  travel and movement 9, 162, 165–6, 171, 178
  see also *Andando Sevilha* (1990)
Sevilha andando (Poesia) 160
sevilhana (woman from Seville) 21, 95, 97–8, 133–5, 157, 158, 159–96, 198
  as metaphor for the literary text 159–60, 163
  walking 158, 160, 161, 162, 164, 165, 168, 169, 173, 175, 182, 195, 198
sevilhanos 187, 190, 192, 193
Seville (Spain) 9, 16 n. 22, 42, 44, 70, 71, 95–8, 107, 115, 135, 136, 145 n. 53, 152 n. 63, 158, 159–96, 198
  as the epitome of life (vitality) 81, 95, 96, 115, 166, 183, 185, 195
  as text 164–5
  'viver-se no aceiro da morte' 187–95
  as woman 165–75
sexual stereotypes 163, 174, 175, 195
sexuality 116, 140–2, 174
Sharpe, W. 167, 170
Silvino, A. 149 n. 61
similes 18
sin 142

slavery 104 n., 108, 109, 148
sleep 16, 17, 59, 73, 90, 91, 178
  and death 59–60
  see also dreams
social alienation 43, 48, 75, 90, 91
social deprivation 88, 131, 140
social injustice 6, 14, 34, 48, 58, 82, 104, 131, 158, 198
society 35, 94, 96, 120, 121, 122, 139, 162, 169
  Brazilian 51, 100, 105 n. 38, 113, 138, 139, 140, 147 n. 55, 148, 151, 152
  patriarchal 136, 167; see also patriarchal order
  Seville 182, 183
sociologists 17
soul 96, 101, 115–18
Spain 5, 6, 38, 130, 152 n. 64, 154, 175, 179, 188–9, 198
  'black' and 'white' 188–9
  conquest of the New World 97, 143, 144 n. 50, 164, 179–82, 183
  Franco regime 189
  rule in North Africa 154
  see also Andalusia (Spain); Barcelona (Spain); culture; Seville (Spain)
Spanish Crown 143
Spanish language 1, 135, 144 n. 50, 154
Spanish Protectorate in Northern Morocco (1904–56) 154 n.
Spears, M. 127
spirituality 189
Stein, G. 77
subjectivity 16, 23, 32, 103, 104; see also objectivity
suffering, human 32, 44, 97, 114
sugar cane 25, 30, 32–3, 34, 135
  plantations 7, 59, 77, 80, 87, 94
suicide 46 n. 43, 82, 99, 119, 120, 121, 131 n. 24, 192
supernatural, the 74 n. 51
surgical operations 28
surrealism 15, 16, 132
Süssekind, F. 73, 96 n., 192 n. 47
Swift, J.:
  Gulliver's Travels 14
Switzerland 5
synecdoche 41

Tabaski (Muslim day) 113
Taborda 73, 74 n. 50

Távora, F. 92
telegrams 99–100
Thebes (city) 68–9, 70 n. 43, 171
Thomas, D.:
 Under Milkwood. A Play for Voices (1954) 51–2
time 18 n. 30, 106, 127 n. 11, 133
Tiradentes (Brazilian revolutionary) 61
Tordesillas Treaty (1494) 42
Tostes, T. 82
Treece, D. 3, 8, 76 n. 54
Troubadours 112
Truth, notion of 126–7, 136, 137, 157
tuberculosis 88
TUCA (São Paulo Catholic University Theatre Company) 8
Tupi-Guarani 101
tussor 110
Typhis pernambucano (newspaper) 55

Ulysses 87
Uma faca só lâmina (1956) 18, 31
uncanny 134, 135
uncertainty 26, 35, 129, 166, 175, 178, 193, 194
underdevelopment 105, 114
underworld 101
urban space 163, 167, 168, 169, 170, 171, 172, 176, 182, 184, 196; *see also* city
usina 25, 67

Verde, C. 53 n. 10, 173–4
 'Num bairro moderno' 173, 175
Veríssimo, J. 89 n. 13
verse, *see* poetry
Villaça, A. 129, 135
 principle of translatability 169
violence 25 n. 9, 29, 30, 31, 33, 40, 42, 43, 44, 48, 92 n. 19, 124
Virgin Mary 57 n. 23, 97
voices 51–2, 54, 62, 63, 64–72, 90, 94, 95, 111, 117, 118, 120, 122, 133, 136, 137, 197, 198, 200
 female 95, 96
 of the oppressed 80, 98, 122, 156
 in the streets 73–7

Werneck, H. 10 n. 8, 53 n. 10
West, the 83, 107
West Africa 81, 104, 105–15
 baobab tree 107–8, 109, 114
 landscape 107, 108, 113
 oral tradition 109 n. 42, 110
 postcolonial 106, 107
 see also Africa
Williams, W. C. 6
women 32 n. 25, 40, 85, 93 n. 22, 95, 97, 136, 159–96
 and domesticity 176
 empowerment 95, 168, 174, 178, 183, 186
 and sexuality 141–2, 167, 178, 186, 199
 see also gender; *sevilhana* (woman from Seville)
writing act 28–9, 30, 32 n. 23, 44, 48, 58, 82, 103, 128 n. 11, 162, 193
 and death 28 n. 20, 46 n. 43
 and life 46 n. 43

Xirau, R. 194 n. 52

Yahoos 14
Yáñez Pinzón, V. 38–42, 48
Yeats, W. B. 26, 27
 'A prayer for my daughter' 26
 Michael Robartes and the Dancer (1921) 26
Young, R. 5, 111 n. 48

Zenith, R. 102–3, 182
zona da mata 7, 20–1, 31, 79, 197